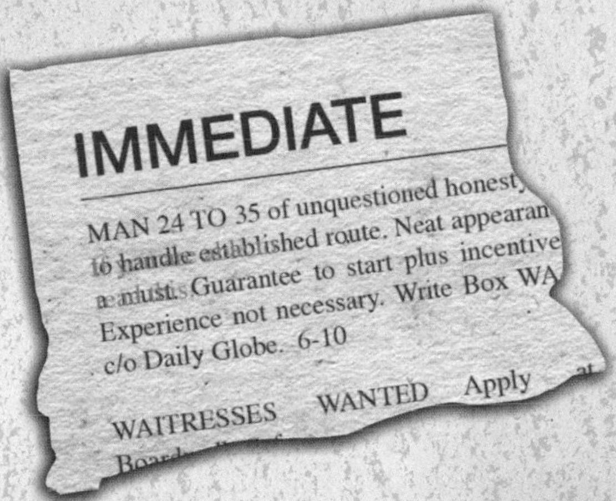
IMMEDIATE

MAN 24 TO 35 of unquestioned honest
to handle established route. Neat appearan
a must. Guarantee to start plus incentive
Experience not necessary. Write Box WA
c/o Daily Globe. 6-10

WAITRESSES WANTED Apply

CLASSIFIED

WOMAN 24 TO 35 with impeccable references wanted for imrcross-country excursion. Benefits and all expenses paid. Please inquire re: $. PO Box 41173

FIELD HANDS WANTED Apply for honest surveillance work. Competitive wages paid. Must h

POSITIONS AVAILABLE

DRIVERS NEEDED for tours of the city. Transportation provided as well as fuel costs.

BUILDERS in need of young inexperienced workers with sketchy architectural knowledge for a low-profile hi-rise construction project. Inquire @ City Center for

MIND
MGMT

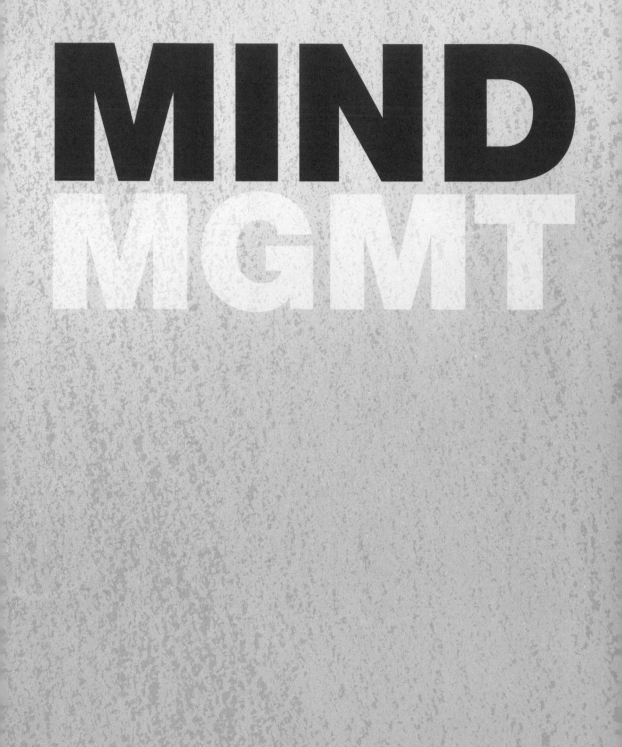

MIND MGMT

VOLUME FIVE: THE ERASER

CREATED, WRITTEN,
AND ILLUSTRATED BY

MATT KINDT

FOREWORD BY
DARWYN COOKE

DARK HORSE BOOKS

PRESIDENT AND PUBLISHER
MIKE RICHARDSON

DIGITAL PRODUCTION
JASON RICKERD
with **CLAY JANES**

DESIGN
RICK DeLUCCO
with **MATT KINDT**

ASSISTANT EDITOR
IAN TUCKER

EDITOR
BRENDAN WRIGHT

Special thanks to Sharlene, Ella, Brendan, Ian, Brian, Marie, David, Karl, Charlie, Charles, and Court.

MIND MGMT VOLUME 5: THE ERASER

This volume collects issues #25–#30 of the Dark Horse comic book series *MIND MGMT*.

Published by Dark Horse Books
A division of Dark Horse Comics, Inc.
10956 SE Main Street
Milwaukie, OR 97222

DarkHorse.com

To find a comics shop in your area, call the Comic Shop Locator Service toll-free at (888) 266-4226.

International Licensing: (503) 905-2377

First edition: July 2015

Library of Congress Cataloging-in-Publication Data

Kindt, Matt.
 MGMT. Volume 5, The eraser / created, written, and illustrated by Matt Kindt ; foreword by Darwyn
Cooke. -- First edition.
     pages cm
 ISBN 978-1-61655-696-9 (hardback)
1. Graphic novels. I. Title. II. Title: Eraser.

 PN6727.K54M6 2015
 741.5'973--dc23

                        2015013348

10 9 8 7 6 5 4 3 2 1

Printed in China

Neil Hankerson, Executive Vice President | Tom Weddle, Chief Financial Officer | Randy Stradley, Vice
President of Publishing | Michael Martens, Vice President of Book Trade Sales | Scott Allie, Editor
in Chief | Matt Parkinson, Vice President of Marketing | David Scroggy, Vice President of Product
Development | Dale LaFountain, Vice President of Information Technology | Darlene Vogel, Senior
Director of Print, Design, and Production | Ken Lizzi, General Counsel | Davey Estrada, Editorial Director
Chris Warner, Senior Books Editor | Cary Grazzini, Director of Print and Development | Lia Ribacchi, Art
Director | Cara Niece, Director of Scheduling | Mark Bernardi, Director of Digital Publishing

FOREWORD

The cat that runs my local comic shop is a good friend named Cal Johnson, and every now and then he pulls books for me that he thinks I may enjoy or need to see. This is how I was introduced to the work of Matt Kindt. The book was *Revolver*, and I loved it. This is how Cal works. He gives you a taste and the next week you're back for more. I picked up *Red Handed: The Fine Art of Strange Crimes*, and by the time I'd torn through it, I had one of those moments that a jaded comics reader values more than any other: the discovery of a singular talent whose point of view appeals to something deeper within you.

We're here today to talk about Matt's most ambitious work, *MIND MGMT*. I worry over these types of introductions, trying to find some way to explain why the work you have in your hands is unique and therefore worth your attention.

There are several conspiracy theory/secret cabal stories out there, but that aspect of the story is usually only window dressing for violent action or character studies. What sets *MIND MGMT* apart is that the stage it plays out upon is epic in scale, but It has been built for you to zoom in on the slightest story detail. "Epic in scale" seems a little underwhelming a descriptor. In trying to nail down the storytelling style, the word that comes to mind is *participatory*. Is that even a word? I'll assume it is and plunge forward. Reading *MIND MGMT* is like having an enormous table covered in cryptic research and notes; as you pour over the myriad pieces in an effort to sort through them, the larger picture begins to emerge.

While the main storyline never loses track of Meru or her strange journey, the road is peppered with context, history, and annotations that create the sense that Mind Management couldn't be anything but a real organization. Flashbacks, ancient texts, Mind Memos, and even *Nancy Drew* novels are used to create a wildly layered, convincing, and credible living history of this clandestine cabal. In classic Kindt fashion, you realize within the first few pages of reading that you can't afford to simply follow the narrative. Every page, damn near every panel, is offering you clues, false clues, symbols, and hidden information that only a careful (or paranoid) reader will notice. This is what makes *MIND MGMT* unique. It is a reading experience that only comics can give you, and only a great storyteller like Matt can pull it off.

A word or two about the artwork and execution. If you read comics on a regular basis, you probably know how rare it is for a cartoonist to write, draw, and letter a monthly book. Not only is Matt doing this, but he's painting each page with watercolor. Take it from a guy who knows: this is an immense amount of work that requires singular and exhaustive commitment. Matt's style suits me (and his material) just right. The work is intuitive, straight ahead, and composed with great thought and imagination. It is something of a schooling in how to visualize complex things in the simplest ways. Eight unconnected lines form a skyline that nails the environment. One bold and confident stroke sets a character's mouth in a way that leaves no doubt of how they feel. A quick switch-up of tools or tint, and Matt brings a clarity to disparate story elements, making his complex narrative graphically easier to take in. Just look at the myriad techniques Matt has marshaled for the covers alone. It's all complete creative expression, where any approach that works, goes.

I'm going deeper into the weeds about craft, and that is usually a sign to wrap this type of thing up. Ahead of you is the kind of read that is so rare these days. Dense and sweeping, relentlessly experimental, and yet always, ultimately, human. So, enough from me. It's time to sit down at that big table of notes and research and story and start digging through its riches.

Darwyn Cooke
2015

Darwyn Cooke is a Canadian comic book writer, artist, cartoonist, and animator, known for his work on the comic books Catwoman, DC: The New Frontier, The Spirit, *and* Richard Stark's Parker.

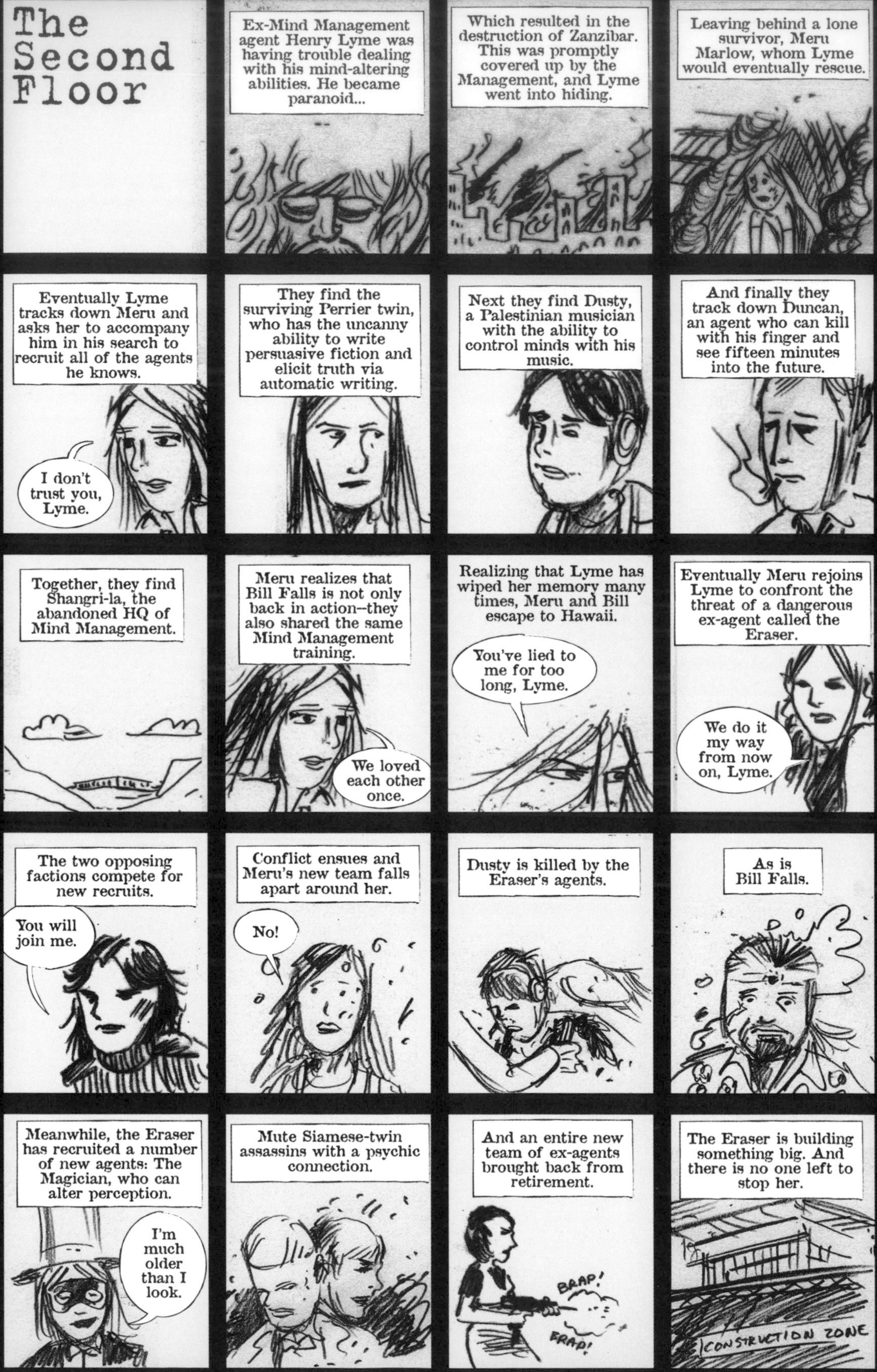

The Second Floor
Ex-Mind Management agent Henry Lyme was having trouble dealing with his mind-altering abilities. He became paranoid...
Which resulted in the destruction of Zanzibar. This was promptly covered up by the Management, and Lyme went into hiding.
Leaving behind a lone survivor, Meru Marlow, whom Lyme would eventually rescue.
Eventually Lyme tracks down Meru and asks her to accompany him in his search to recruit all of the agents he knows.
I don't trust you, Lyme.
They find the surviving Perrier twin, who has the uncanny ability to write persuasive fiction and elicit truth via automatic writing.
Next they find Dusty, a Palestinian musician with the ability to control minds with his music.
And finally they track down Duncan, an agent who can kill with his finger and see fifteen minutes into the future.
Together, they find Shangri-la, the abandoned HQ of Mind Management.
Meru realizes that Bill Falls is not only back in action--they also shared the same Mind Management training.
We loved each other once.
Realizing that Lyme has wiped her memory many times, Meru and Bill escape to Hawaii.
You've lied to me for too long, Lyme.
Eventually Meru rejoins Lyme to confront the threat of a dangerous ex-agent called the Eraser.
We do it my way from now on, Lyme.
The two opposing factions compete for new recruits.
You will join me.
Conflict ensues and Meru's new team falls apart around her.
No!
Dusty is killed by the Eraser's agents.
As is Bill Falls.
Meanwhile, the Eraser has recruited a number of new agents: The Magician, who can alter perception.
I'm much older than I look.
Mute Siamese-twin assassins with a psychic connection.
And an entire new team of ex-agents brought back from retirement.
BRAP!
BRAP!
The Eraser is building something big. And there is no one left to stop her.
CONSTRUCTION ZONE

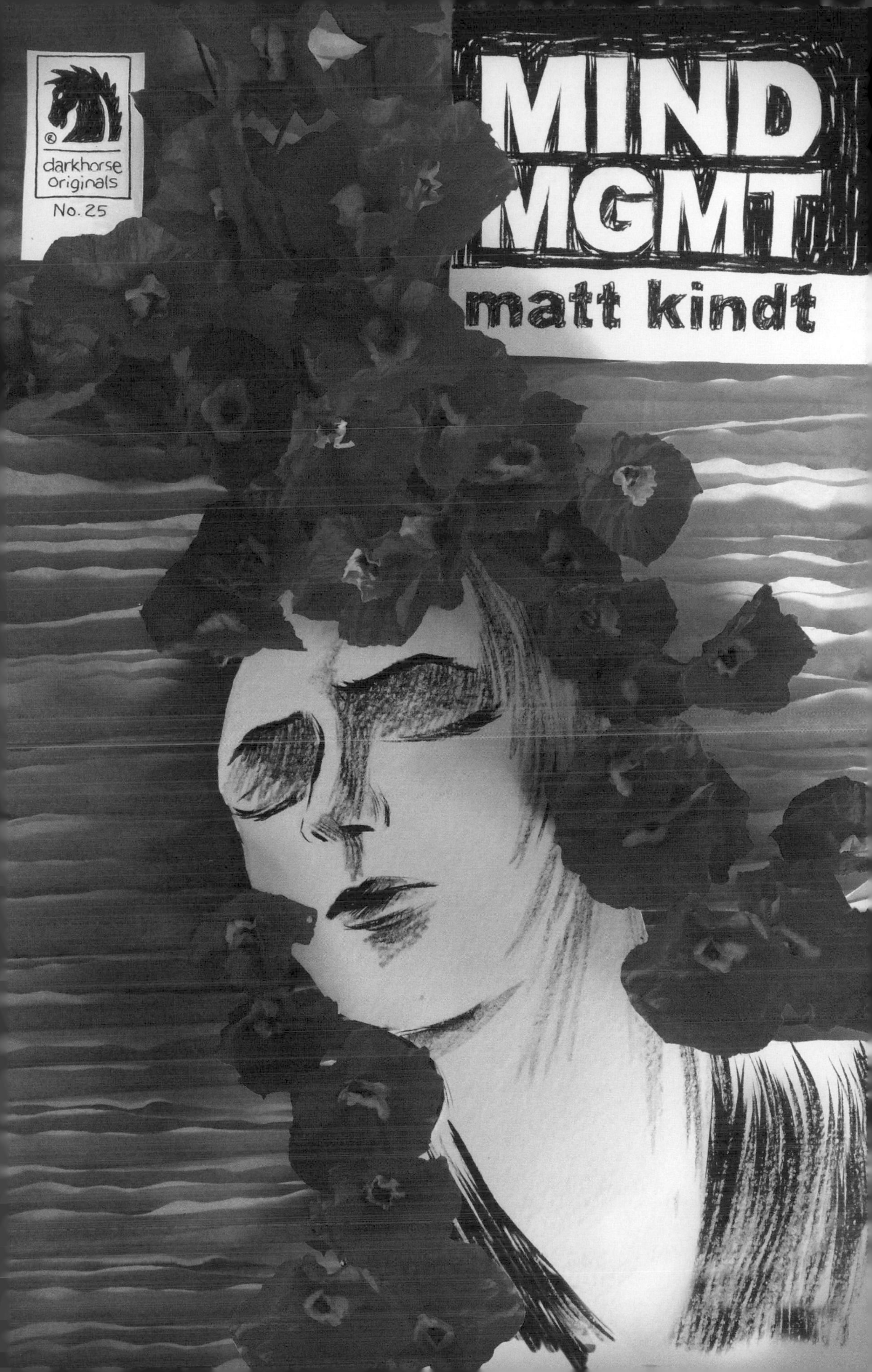

darkhorse originals
No. 25
MIND MGMT
matt kindt

25

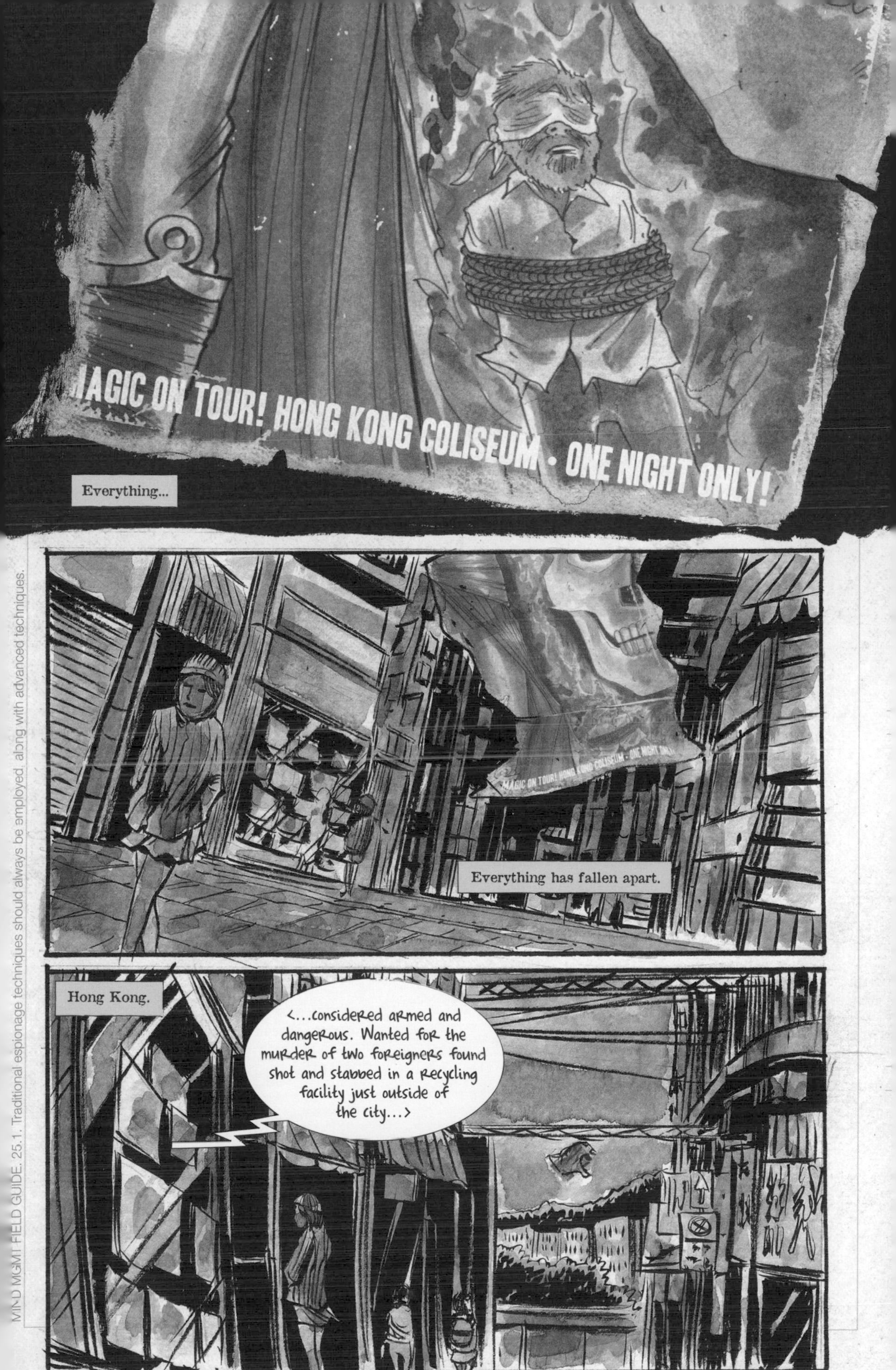

MAGIC ON TOUR! HONG KONG COLISEUM · ONE NIGHT ONLY!
Everything...
Everything has fallen apart.
Hong Kong.
<...considered armed and dangerous. Wanted for the murder of two foreigners found shot and stabbed in a recycling facility just outside of the city...>

MIND MGMT FIELD GUIDE. 25.1. Traditional espionage techniques should always be employed, along with advanced techniques.

WHEN FILING REPORT ALL ESSENTIAL DETAILS MUST FALL WITHIN THIS SOLID "LIVE AREA" BOX. THIS IS THE BORDER FOR A STANDARD, NON-BLEED FIELD REPORT

MIND MGMT FIELD GUIDE. 25.2. Adopting local clothing and concealment of signature physical attributes is essential.

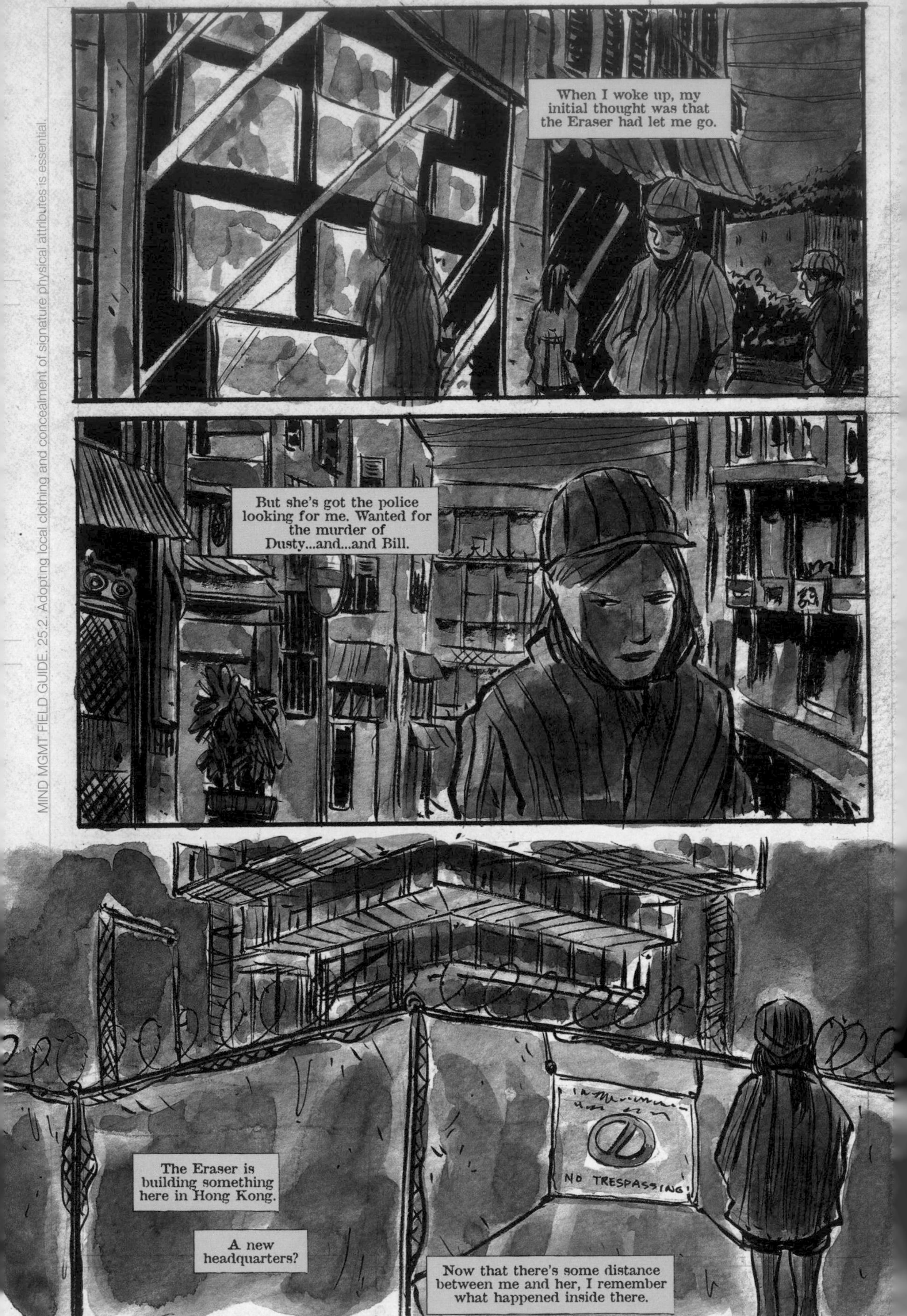
When I woke up, my initial thought was that the Eraser had let me go.
But she's got the police looking for me. Wanted for the murder of Dusty...and...and Bill.
The Eraser is building something here in Hong Kong.
A new headquarters?
NO TRESPASSING!
Now that there's some distance between me and her, I remember what happened inside there.

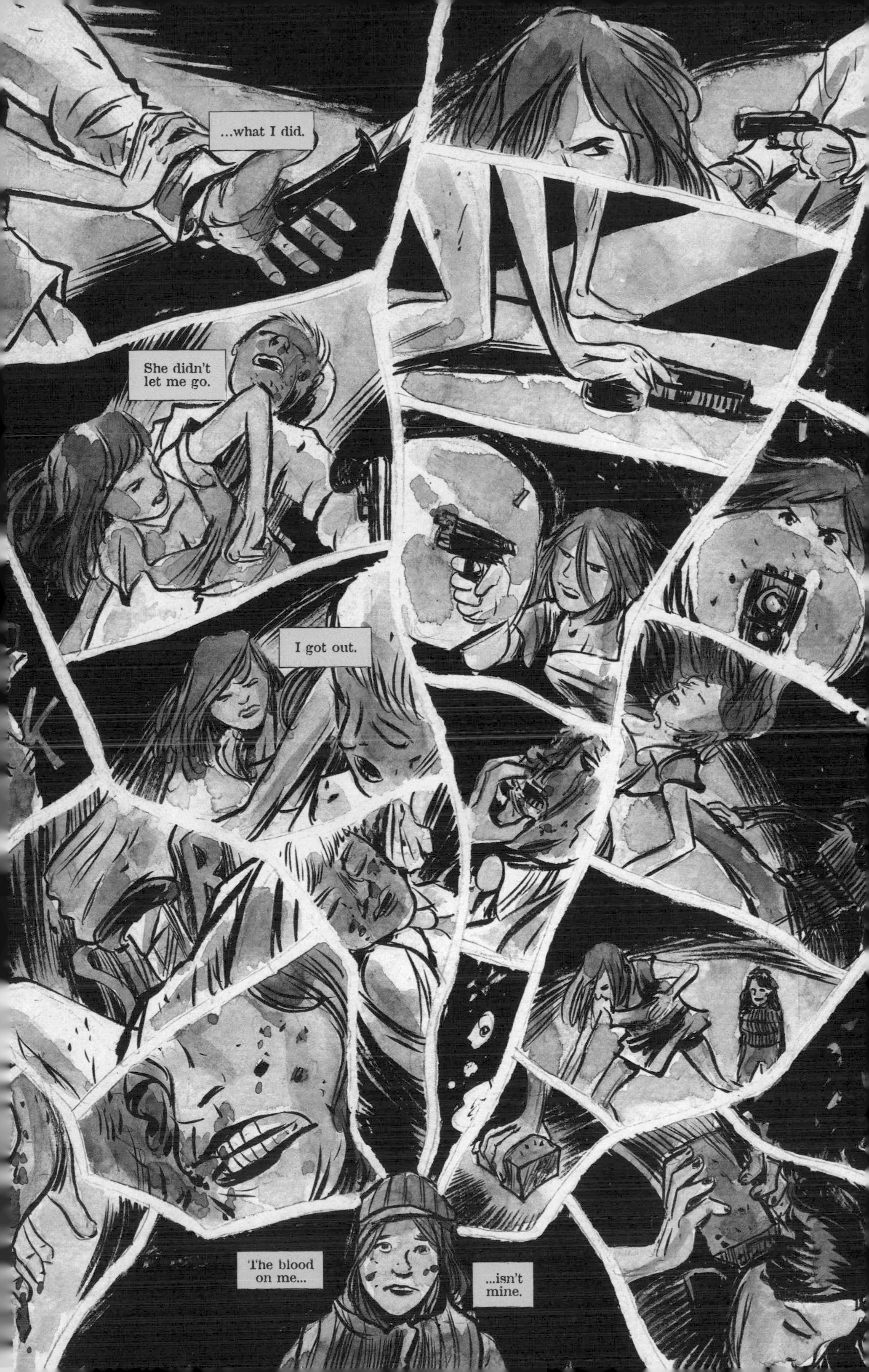

...what I did.
She didn't let me go.
I got out.
The blood on me...
...isn't mine.

MIND MGMT FIELD GUIDE: 25.4. When choosing a non-flux safe house, a room on the top floor is preferable, near neighboring buildings of a similar height, in case a rooftop extraction is required.

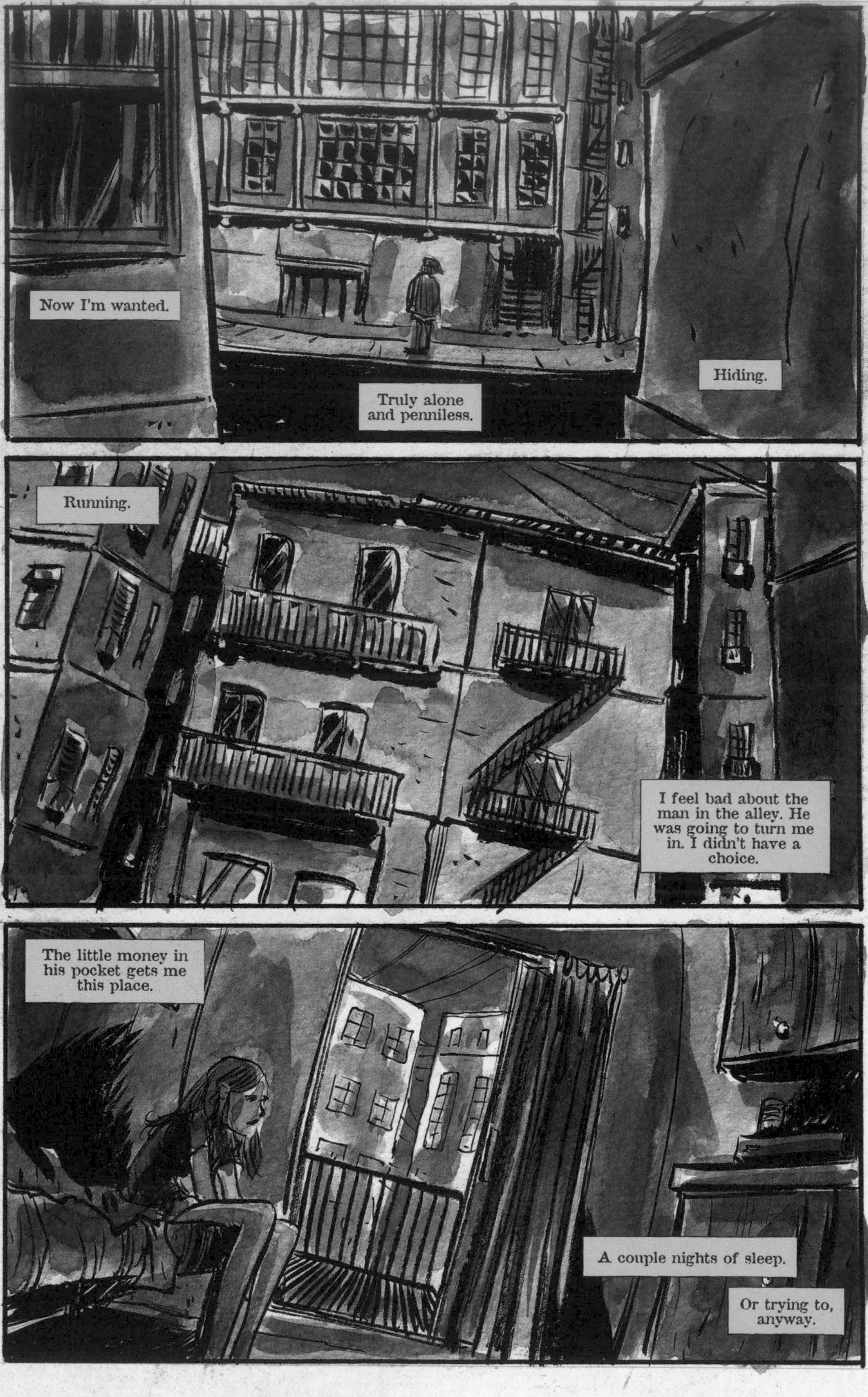
Now I'm wanted.
Truly alone and penniless.
Hiding.
Running.
I feel bad about the man in the alley. He was going to turn me in. I didn't have a choice.
The little money in his pocket gets me this place.
A couple nights of sleep.
Or trying to, anyway.

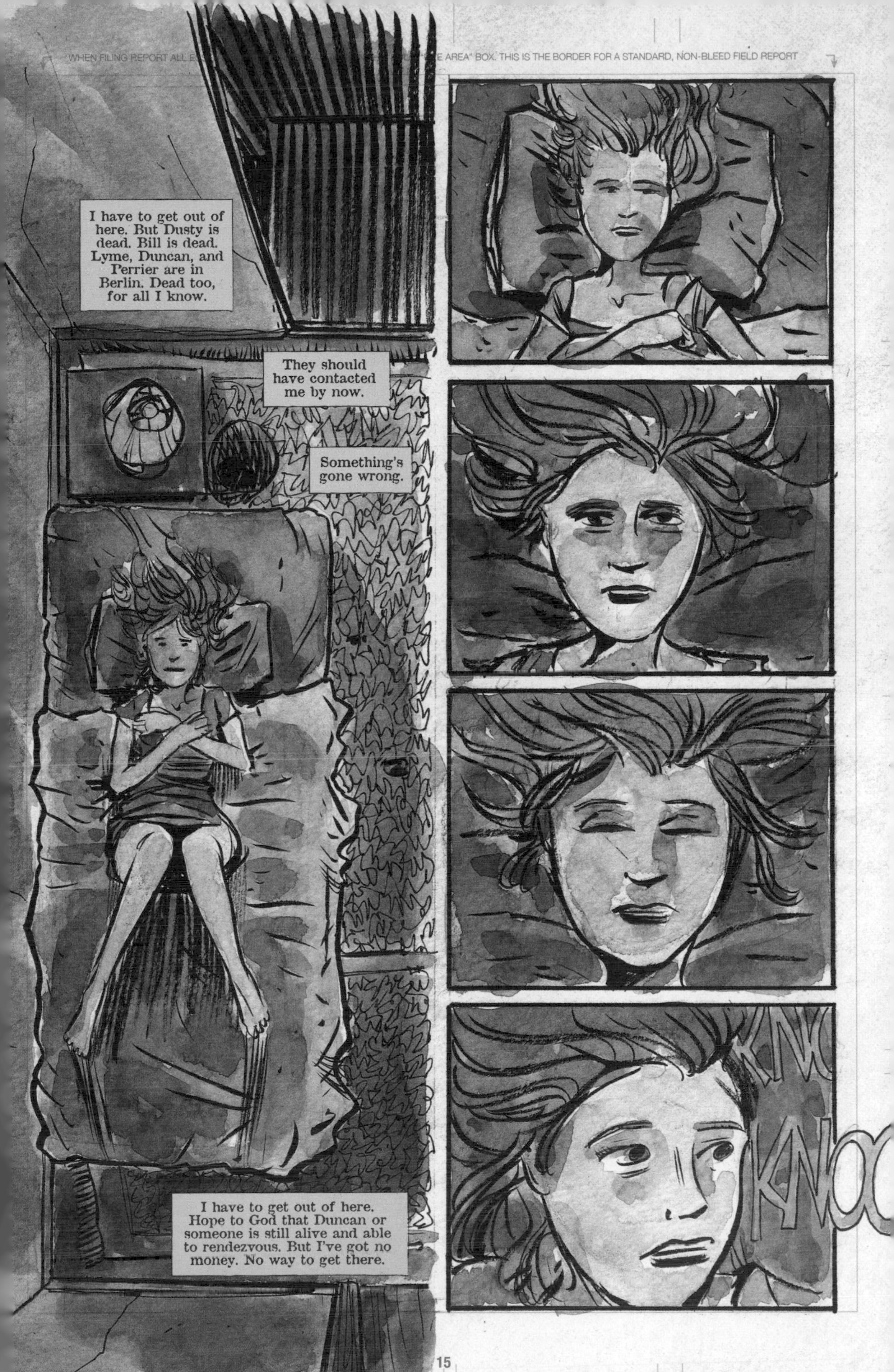
WHEN FILING REPORT ALL E
E AREA" BOX. THIS IS THE BORDER FOR A STANDARD, NON-BLEED FIELD REPORT
I have to get out of here. But Dusty is dead. Bill is dead. Lyme, Duncan, and Perrier are in Berlin. Dead too, for all I know.
They should have contacted me by now.
Something's gone wrong.
I have to get out of here. Hope to God that Duncan or someone is still alive and able to rendezvous. But I've got no money. No way to get there.
KNO
KNOC

MIND MGMT FIELD GUIDE. 25.6. Many new agents will experience moments of déja vu when traveling for extended periods of time. If sleep is not possible, advanced meditation techniques should be employed.

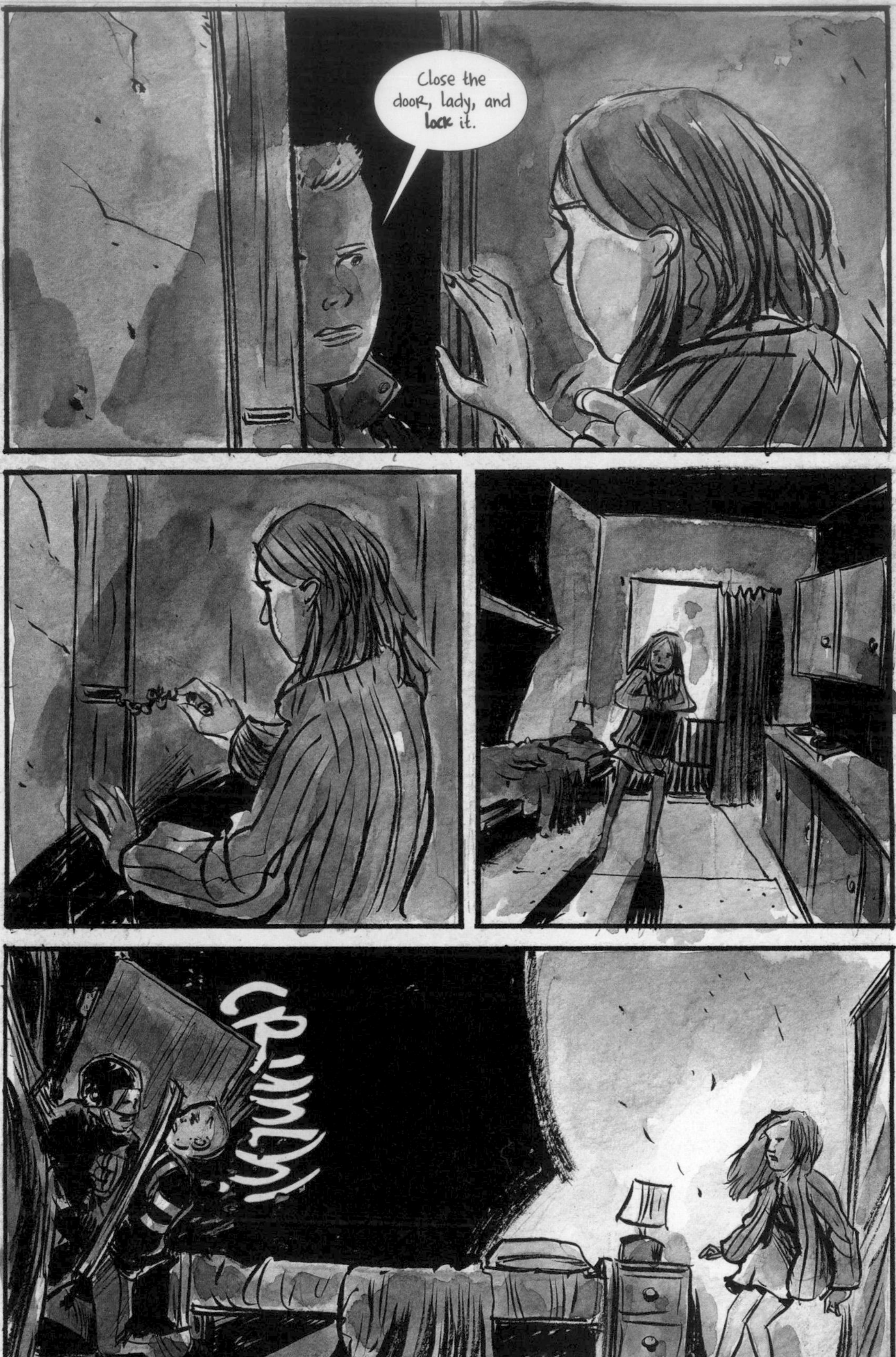
Close the door, lady, and lock it.
CRUNCH!

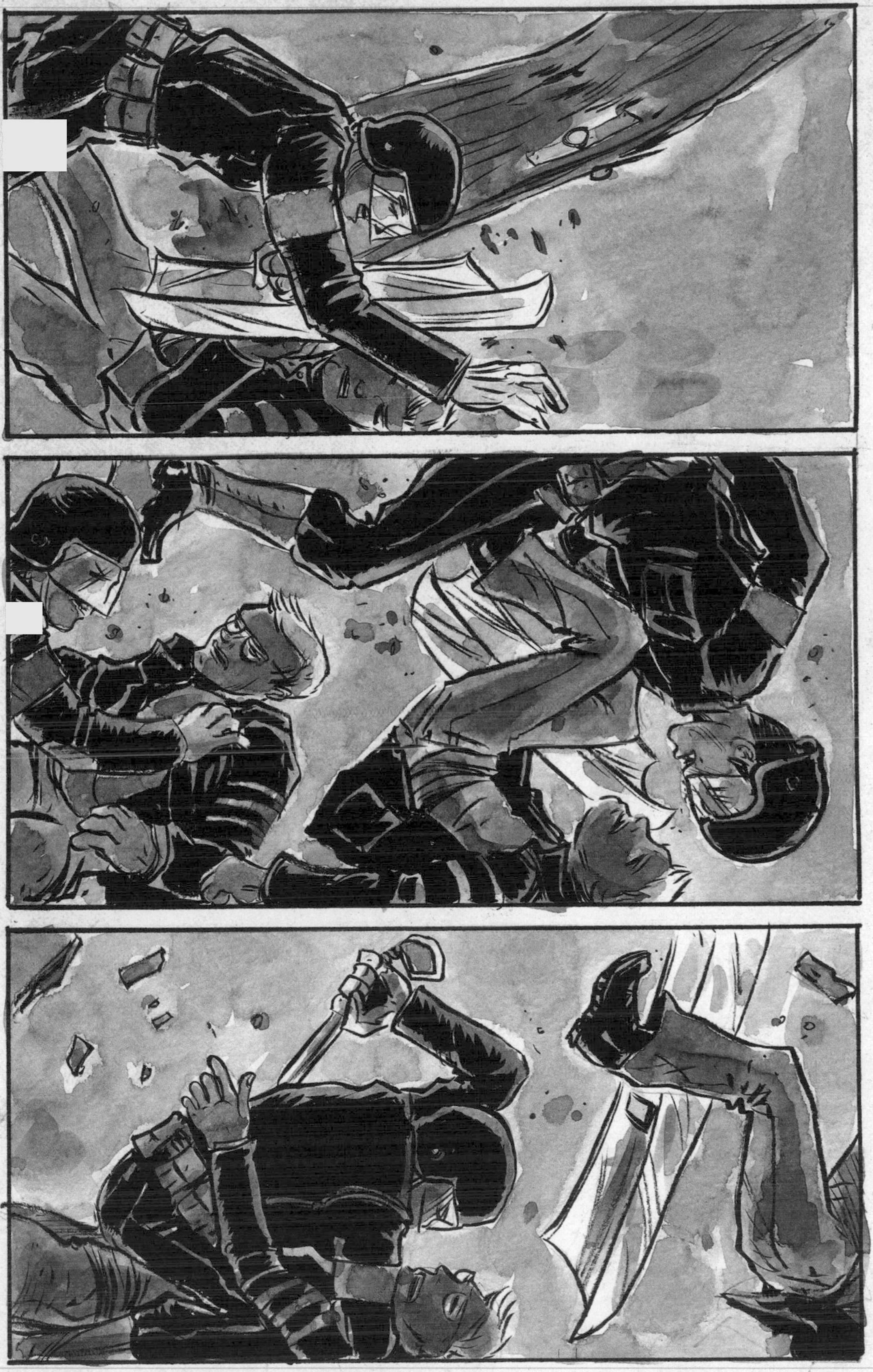

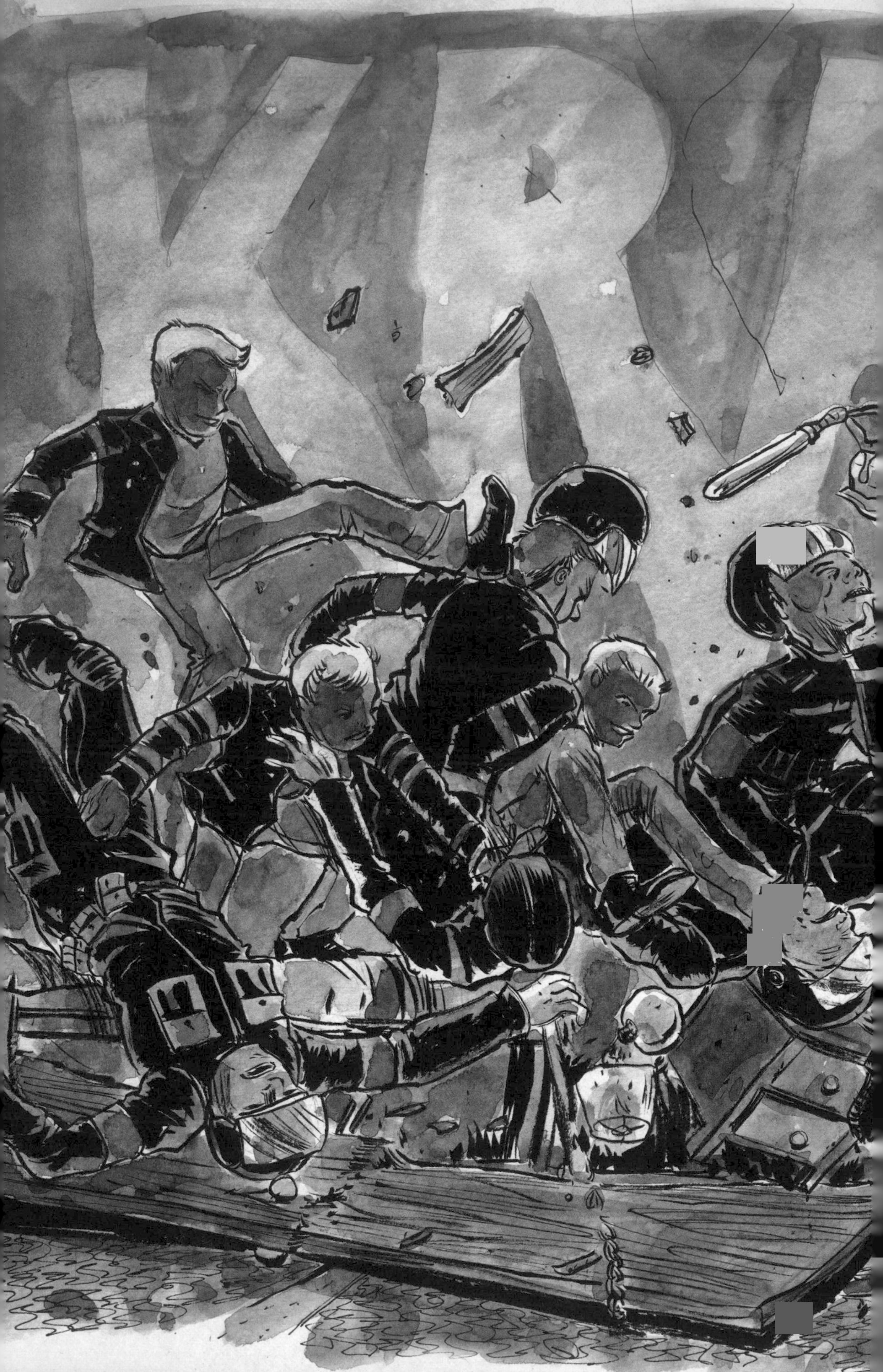

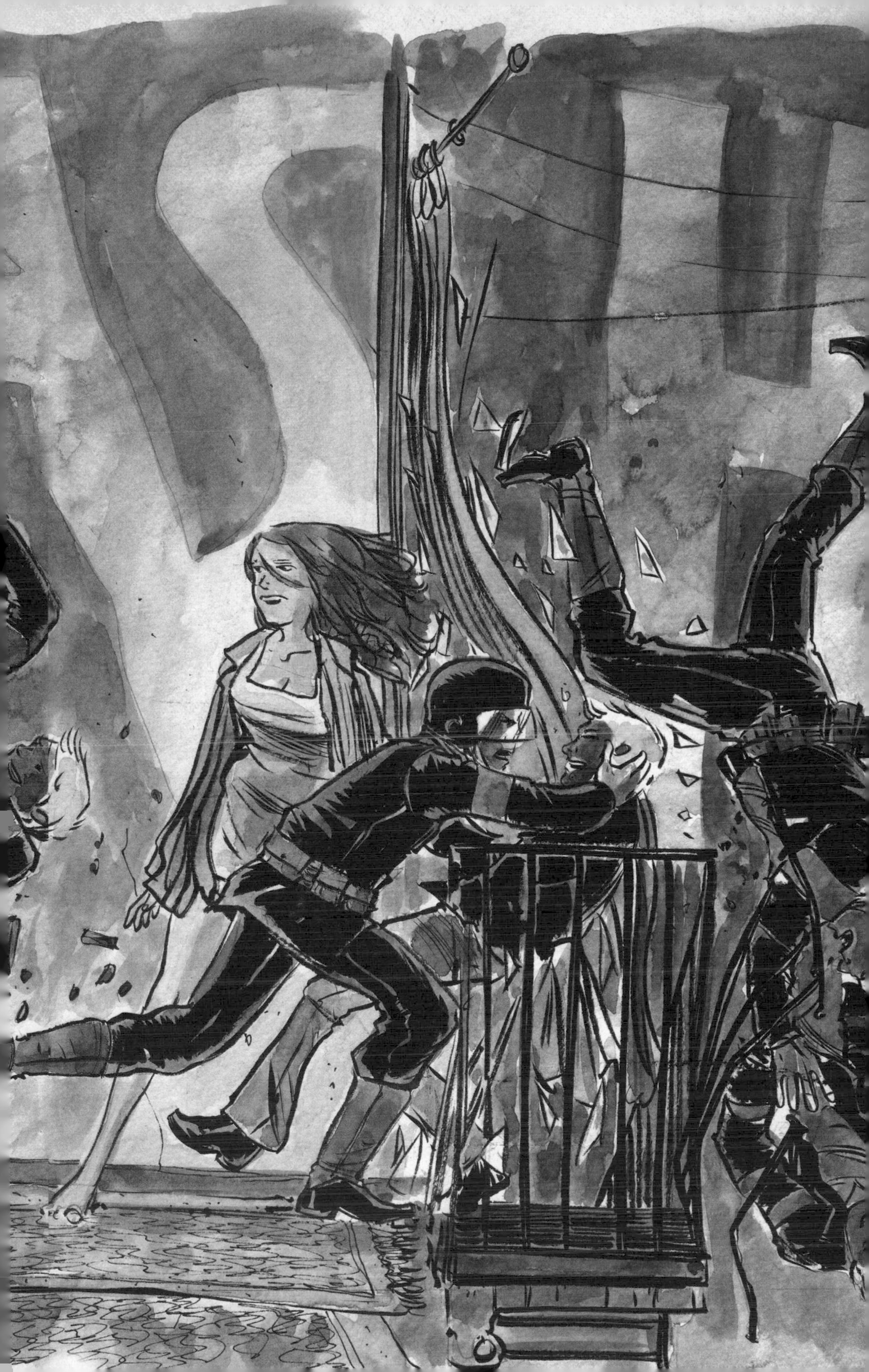

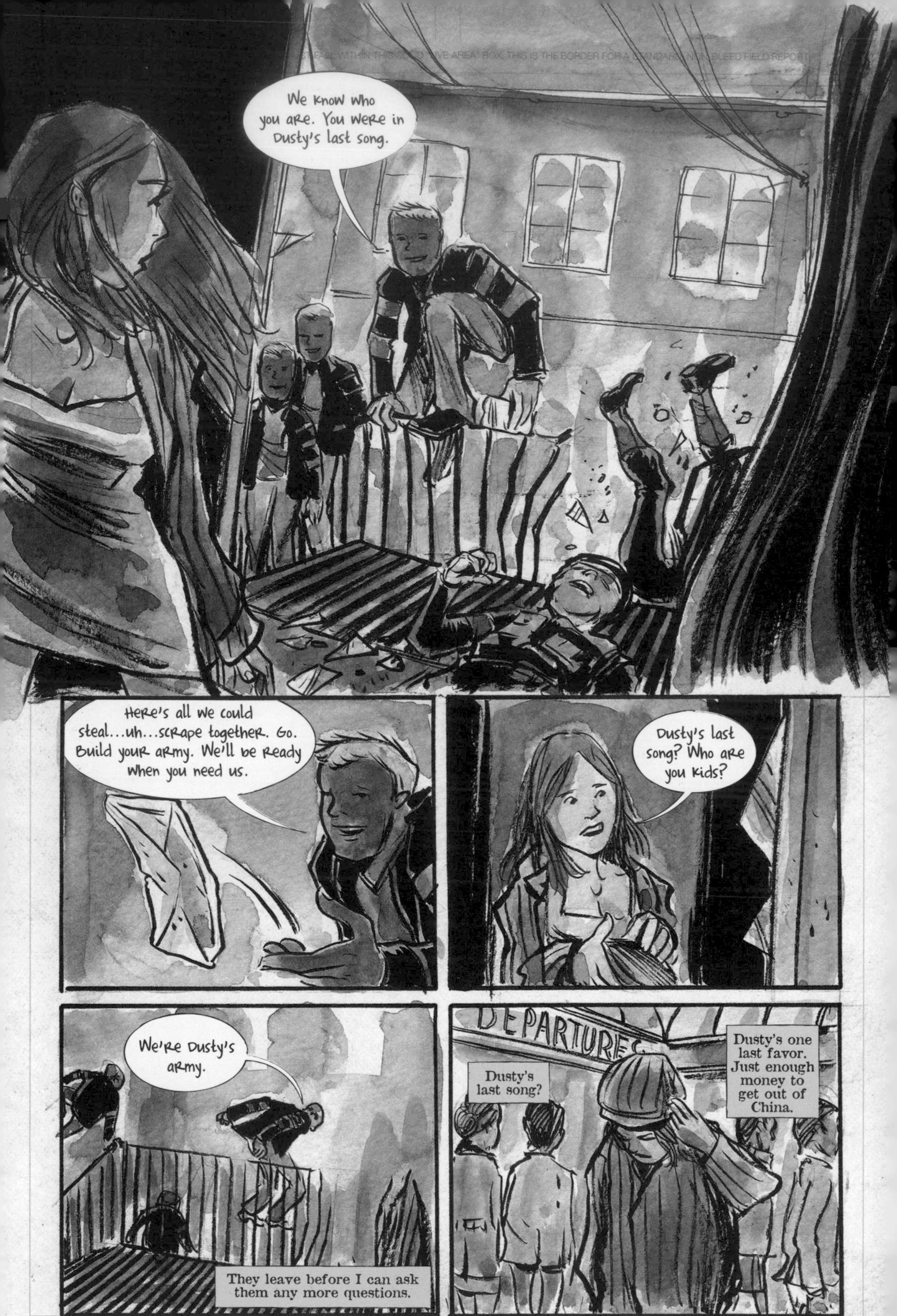
We know who you are. You were in Dusty's last song.
Here's all we could steal...uh...scrape together. Go. Build your army. We'll be ready when you need us.
Dusty's last song? Who are you kids?
We're Dusty's army.
They leave before I can ask them any more questions.
DEPARTURES
Dusty's last song?
Dusty's one last favor. Just enough money to get out of China.

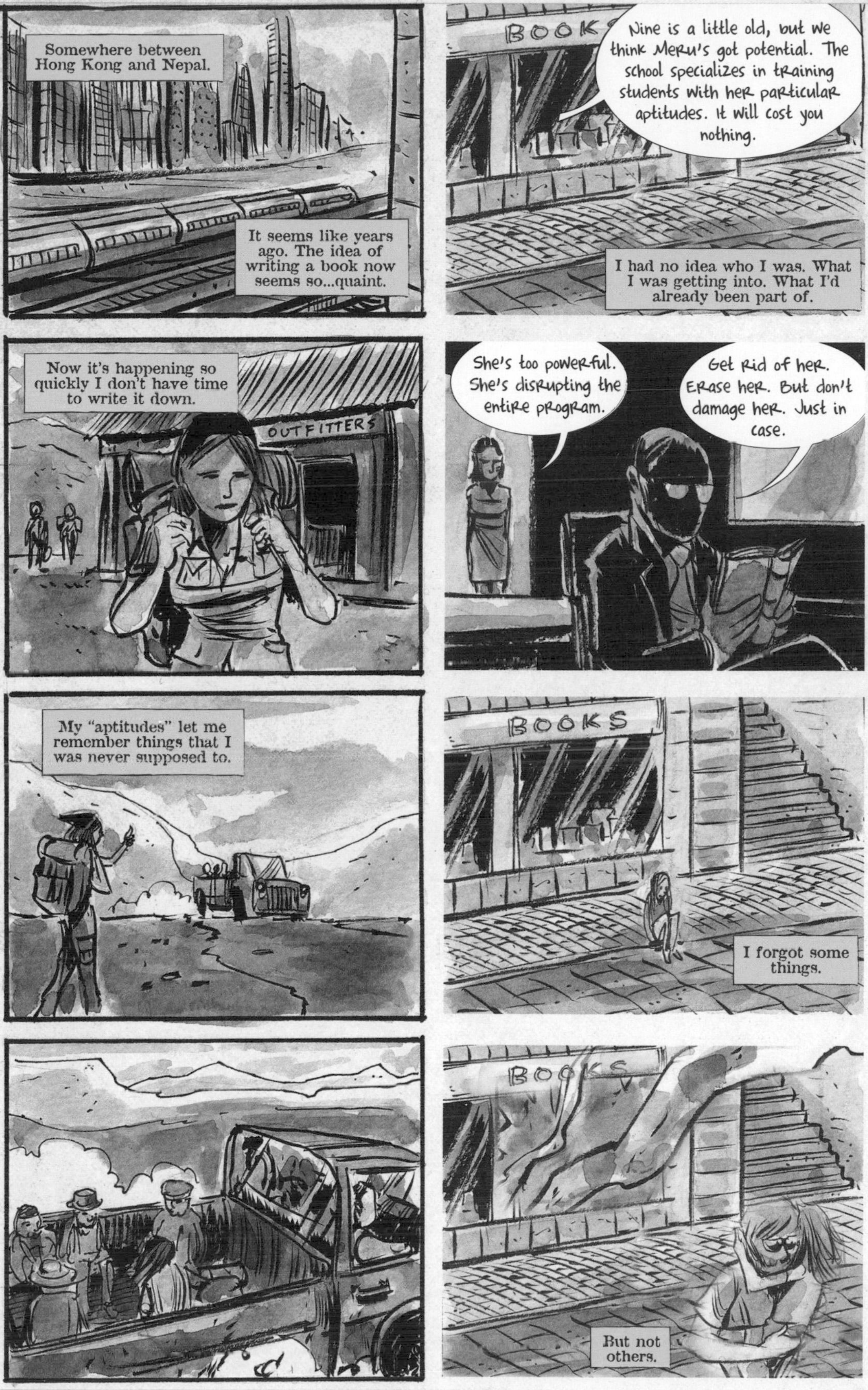
Somewhere between Hong Kong and Nepal.
It seems like years ago. The idea of writing a book now seems so...quaint.
Nine is a little old, but we think Meru's got potential. The school specializes in training students with her particular aptitudes. It will cost you nothing.
I had no idea who I was. What I was getting into. What I'd already been part of.
Now it's happening so quickly I don't have time to write it down.
OUTFITTERS
She's too powerful. She's disrupting the entire program.
Get rid of her. Erase her. But don't damage her. Just in case.
My "aptitudes" let me remember things that I was never supposed to.
BOOKS
I forgot some things.
BOOKS
But not others.

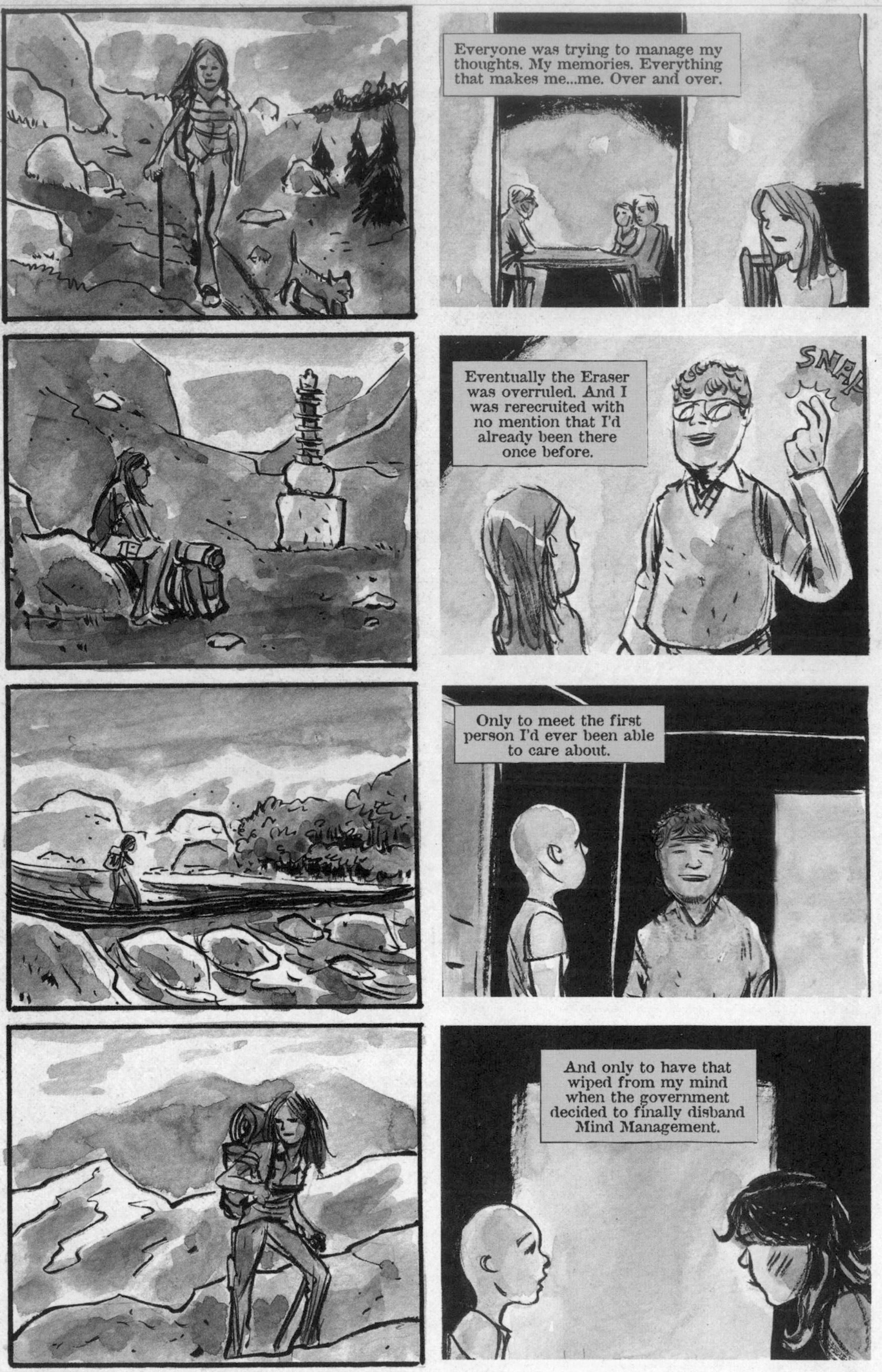
Everyone was trying to manage my thoughts. My memories. Everything that makes me...me. Over and over.
Eventually the Eraser was overruled. And I was rerecruited with no mention that I'd already been there once before.
SNAP
Only to meet the first person I'd ever been able to care about.
And only to have that wiped from my mind when the government decided to finally disband Mind Management.

MIND MGMT FIELD GUIDE. 25.12. When traveling off the grid, agents should still travel with a partner and stick with larger groups of travelers to avoid standing out.

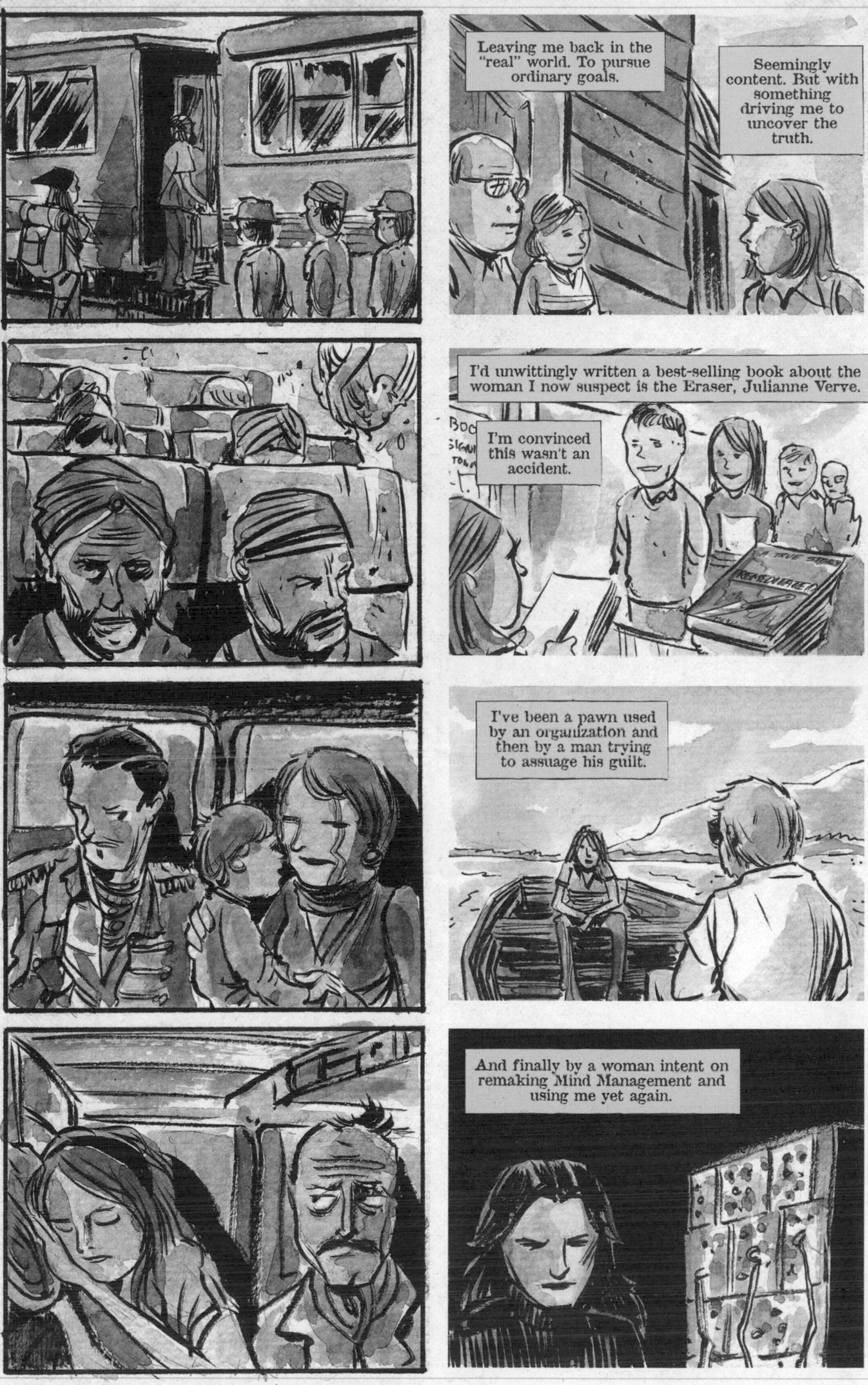
Leaving me back in the "real" world. To pursue ordinary goals.
Seemingly content. But with something driving me to uncover the truth.
I'd unwittingly written a best-selling book about the woman I now suspect is the Eraser, Julianne Verve.
I'm convinced this wasn't an accident.
I've been a pawn used by an organization and then by a man trying to assuage his guilt.
And finally by a woman intent on remaking Mind Management and using me yet again.

MIND MGMT FIELD GUIDE. 25.13. Paranoia is the enemy of the lone agent on the move. Remember to trust your training and allow yourself to relax. A tense agent stands out in a crowd.

WHEN FILING REPORT ALL ESSENTIAL DETAILS MUST FALL WITHIN THIS SOLID "LIVE AREA" BOX. THIS IS THE BORDER FOR A STANDARD, NON-BLEED FIELD REPORT

MIND MGMT FIELD GUIDE. 25.14. Prearranged rendezvous should be approached with caution and should never be documented or discussed ahead of time, to maintain the integrity of the location

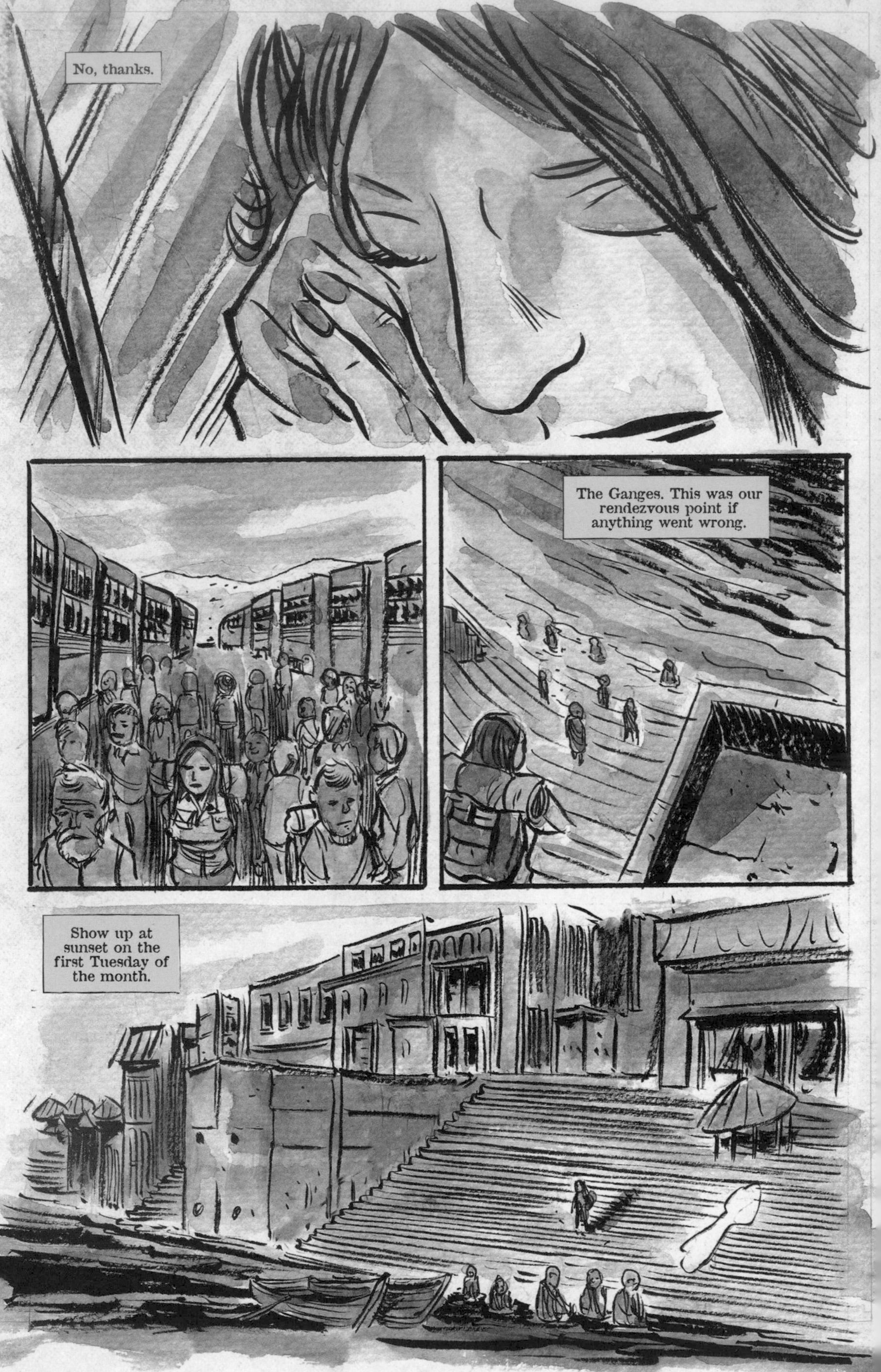

No, thanks.
The Ganges. This was our rendezvous point if anything went wrong.
Show up at sunset on the first Tuesday of the month.

MIND MGMT FIELD GUIDE. 25.15. If a prearranged rendezvous deviates from the prearranged protocol in any way, the rendezvous should be aborted immediately.

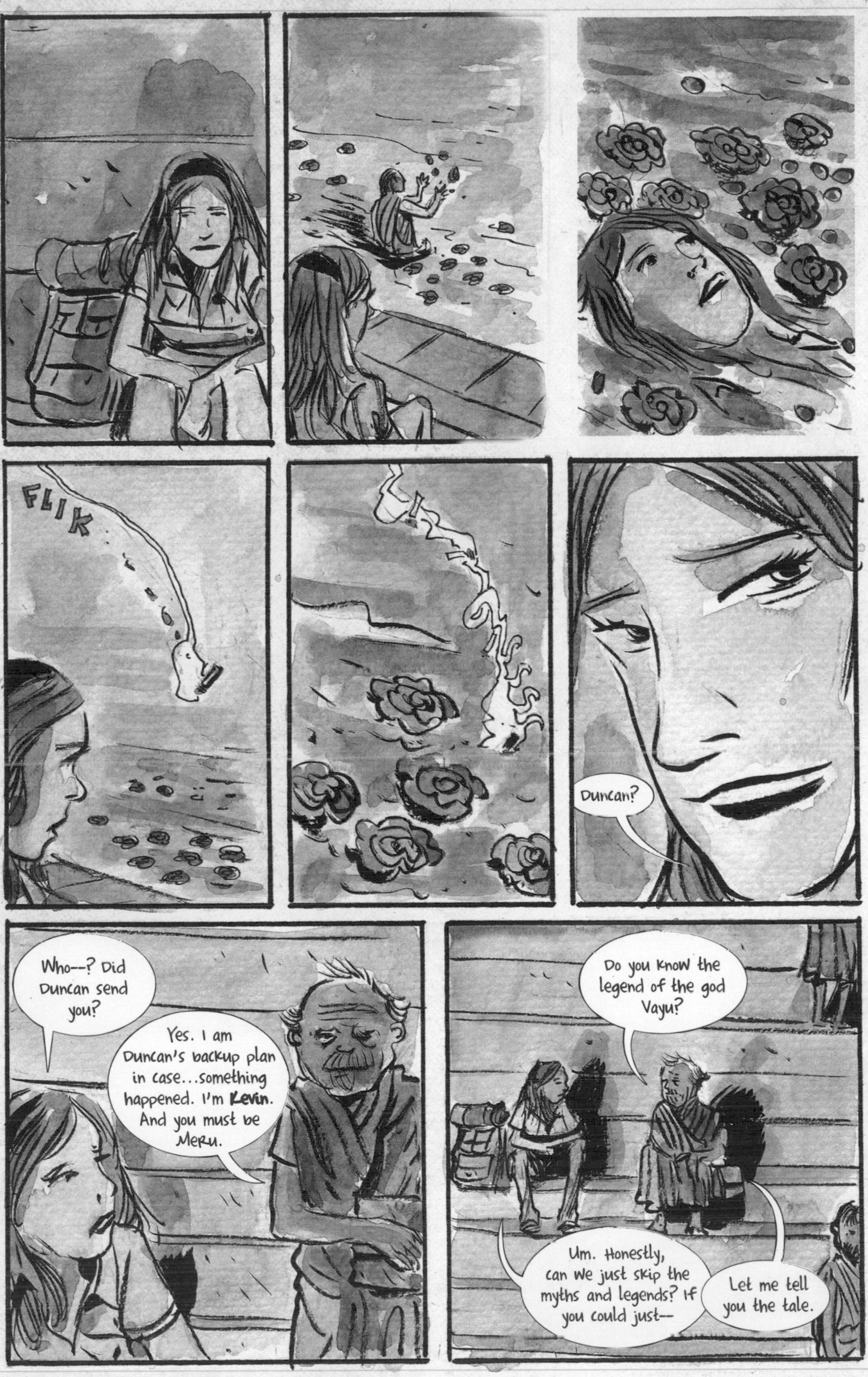
FLIK
Duncan?
Who--? Did Duncan send you?
Yes. I am Duncan's backup plan in case...something happened. I'm Kevin. And you must be Meru.
Do you know the legend of the god Vayu?
Um. Honestly, can we just skip the myths and legends? If you could just--
Let me tell you the tale.

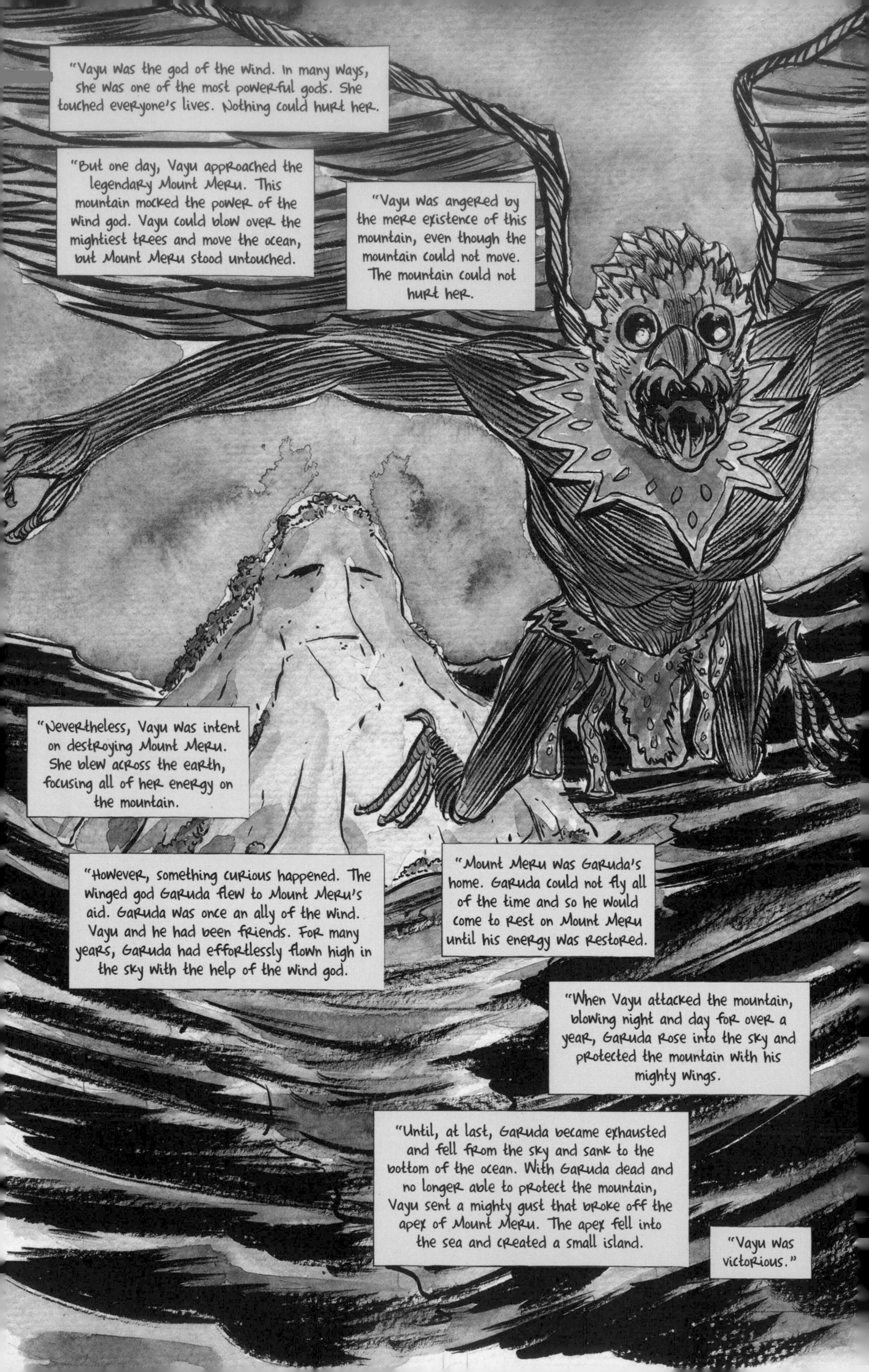
"Vayu was the god of the wind. In many ways, she was one of the most powerful gods. She touched everyone's lives. Nothing could hurt her.
"But one day, Vayu approached the legendary Mount Meru. This mountain mocked the power of the wind god. Vayu could blow over the mightiest trees and move the ocean, but Mount Meru stood untouched.
"Vayu was angered by the mere existence of this mountain, even though the mountain could not move. The mountain could not hurt her.
"Nevertheless, Vayu was intent on destroying Mount Meru. She blew across the earth, focusing all of her energy on the mountain.
"However, something curious happened. The winged god Garuda flew to Mount Meru's aid. Garuda was once an ally of the wind. Vayu and he had been friends. For many years, Garuda had effortlessly flown high in the sky with the help of the wind god.
"Mount Meru was Garuda's home. Garuda could not fly all of the time and so he would come to rest on Mount Meru until his energy was restored.
"When Vayu attacked the mountain, blowing night and day for over a year, Garuda rose into the sky and protected the mountain with his mighty wings.
"Until, at last, Garuda became exhausted and fell from the sky and sank to the bottom of the ocean. With Garuda dead and no longer able to protect the mountain, Vayu sent a mighty gust that broke off the apex of Mount Meru. The apex fell into the sea and created a small island.
"Vayu was victorious."

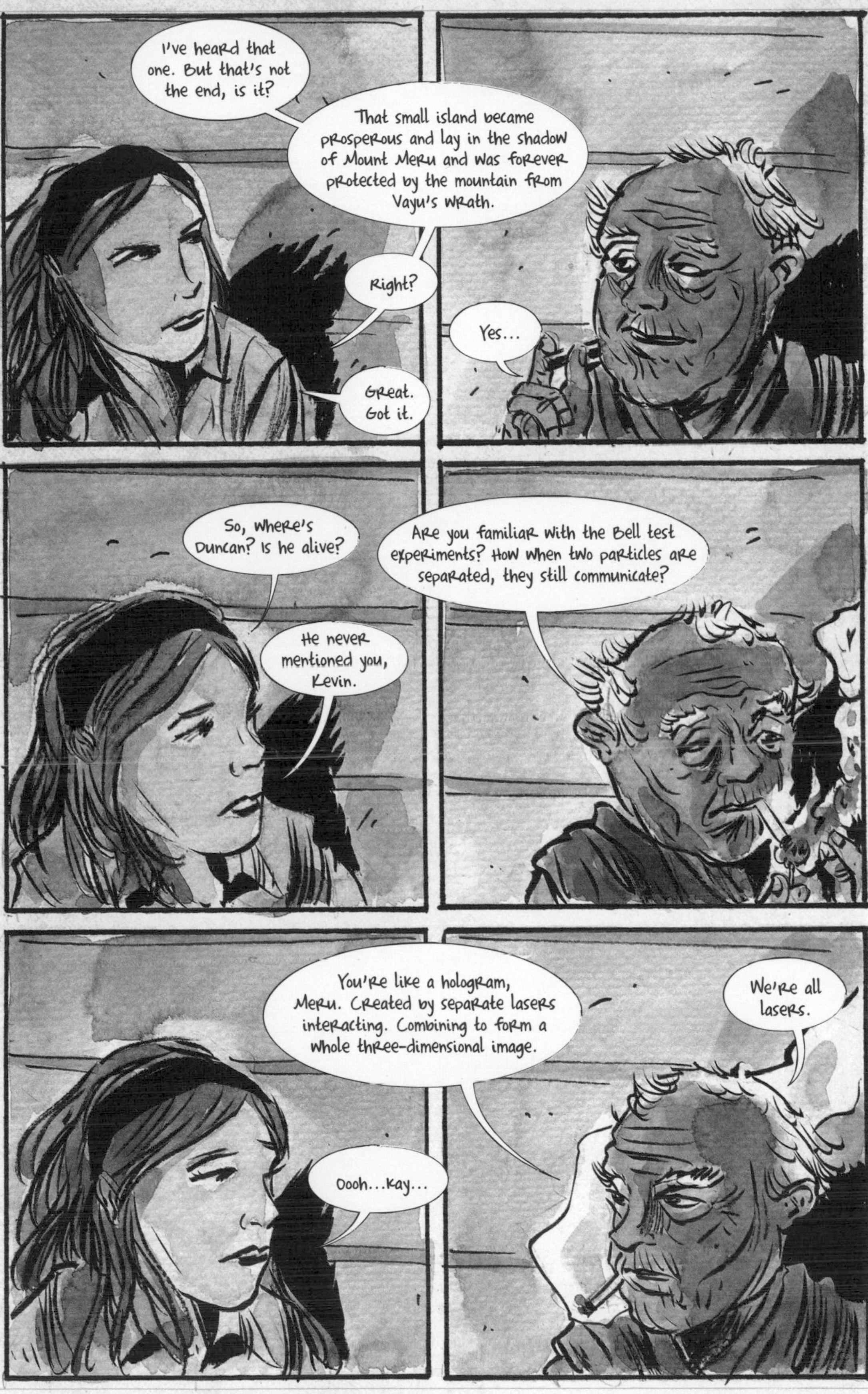
I've heard that one. But that's not the end, is it?
That small island became prosperous and lay in the shadow of Mount Meru and was forever protected by the mountain from Vayu's wrath.
Right?
Yes...
Great. Got it.
So, where's Duncan? Is he alive?
He never mentioned you, Kevin.
Are you familiar with the Bell test experiments? How when two particles are separated, they still communicate?
You're like a hologram, Meru. Created by separate lasers interacting. Combining to form a whole three-dimensional image.
We're all lasers.
Oooh...kay...

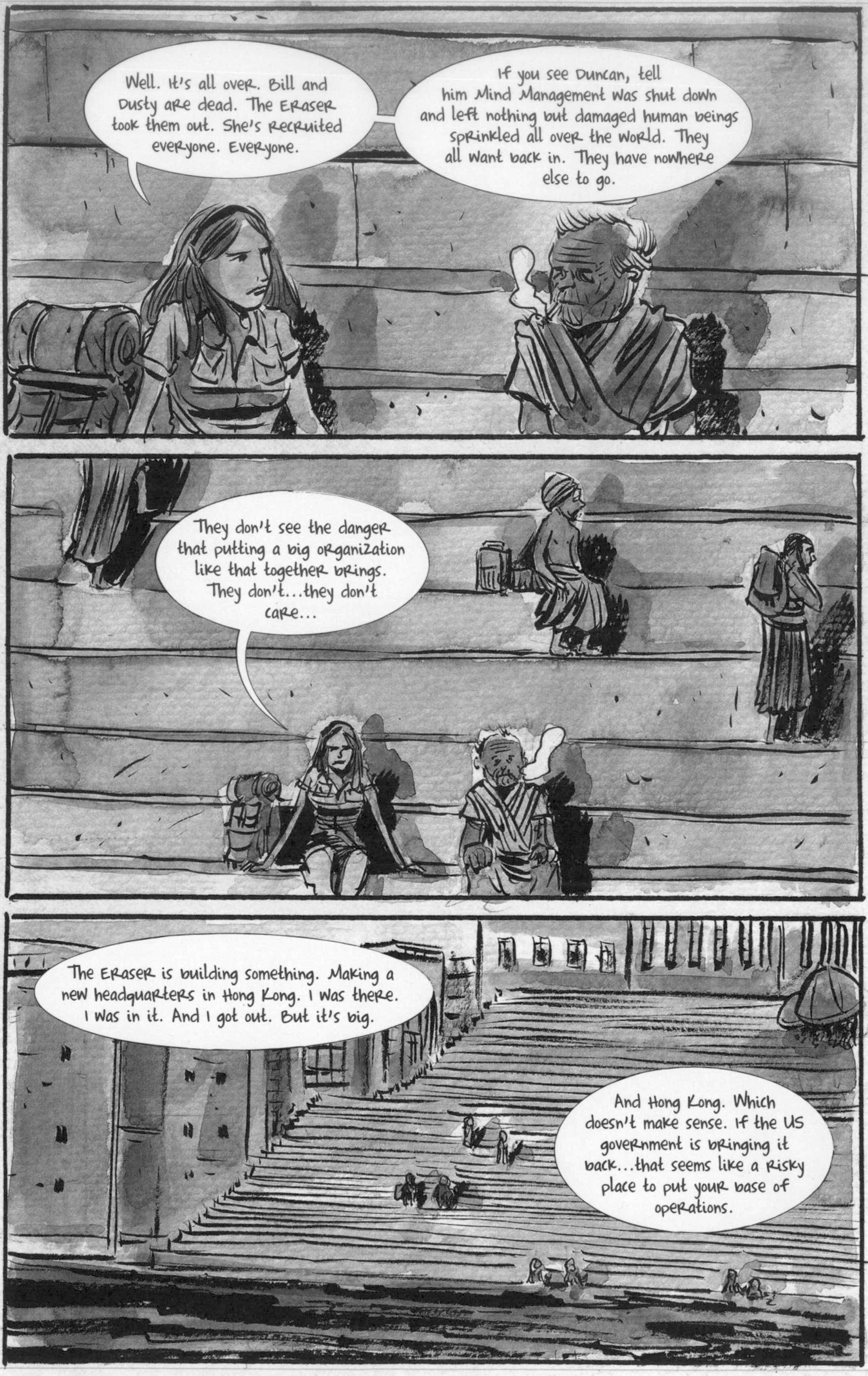
Well. It's all over. Bill and Dusty are dead. The Eraser took them out. She's recruited everyone. Everyone.
If you see Duncan, tell him Mind Management was shut down and left nothing but damaged human beings sprinkled all over the world. They all want back in. They have nowhere else to go.
They don't see the danger that putting a big organization like that together brings. They don't...they don't care...
The Eraser is building something. Making a new headquarters in Hong Kong. I was there. I was in it. And I got out. But it's big.
And Hong Kong. Which doesn't make sense. If the US government is bringing it back...that seems like a risky place to put your base of operations.

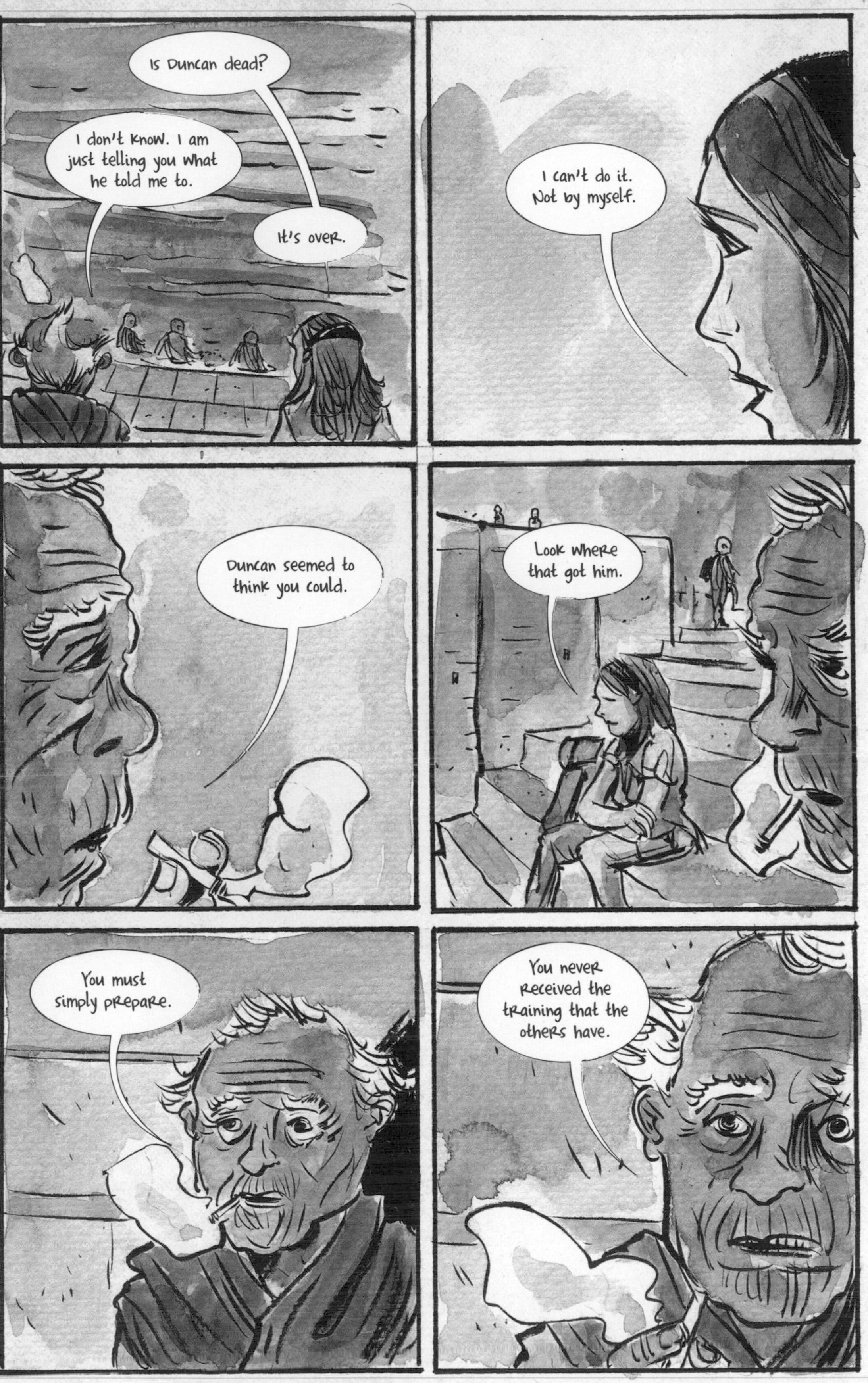
Is Duncan dead?
I don't know. I am just telling you what he told me to.
It's over.
I can't do it. Not by myself.
Duncan seemed to think you could.
Look where that got him.
You must simply prepare.
You never received the training that the others have.

MIND MGMT FIELD GUIDE. 25.19. In rare instances, friendly agents may be sent into the field to contact undercover assets. In such cases, the agent will be named after your mother's first pet.

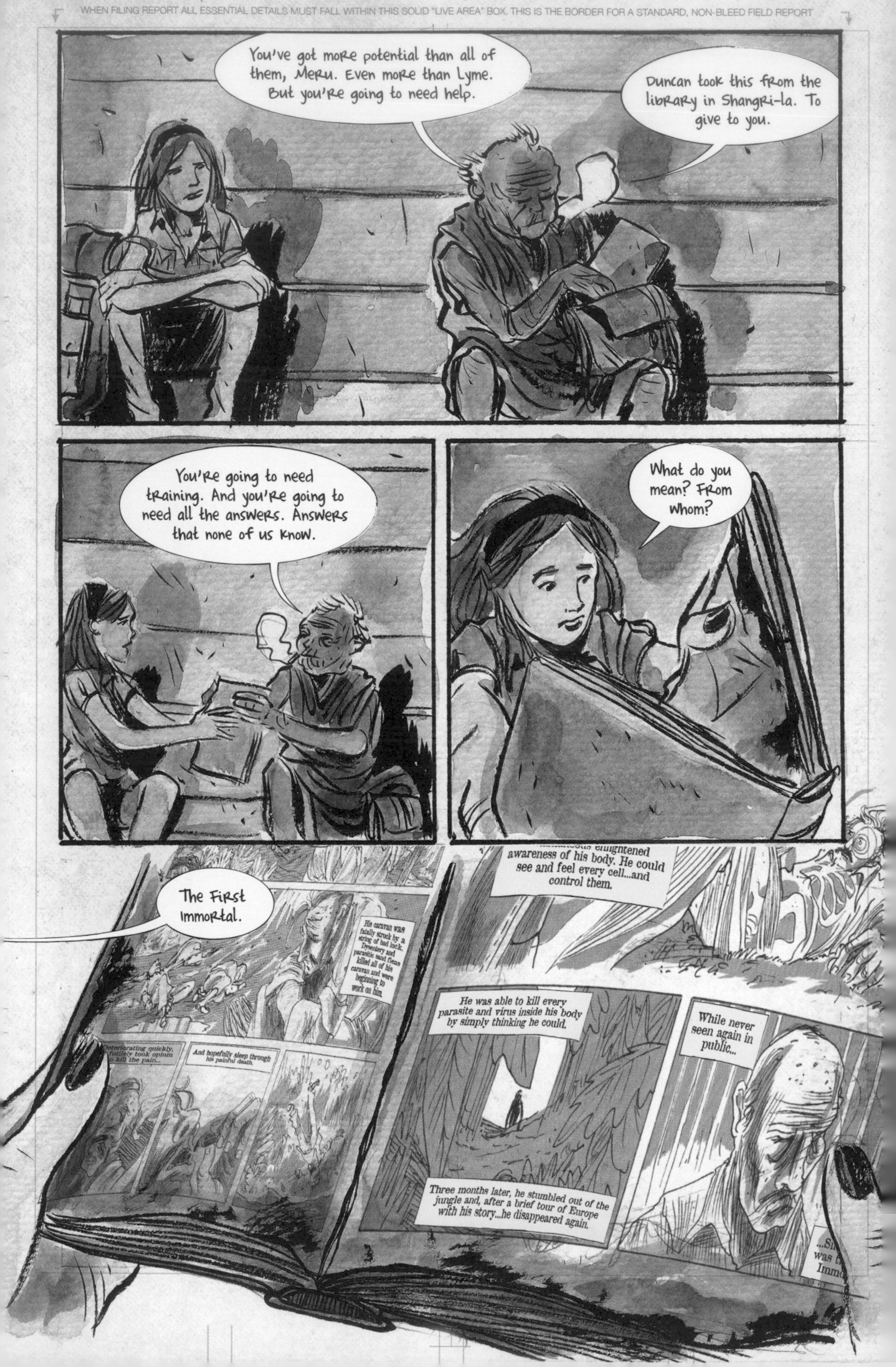
WHEN FILING REPORT ALL ESSENTIAL DETAILS MUST FALL WITHIN THIS SOLID "LIVE AREA" BOX. THIS IS THE BORDER FOR A STANDARD, NON-BLEED FIELD REPORT
You've got more potential than all of them, Meru. Even more than Lyme. But you're going to need help.
Duncan took this from the library in Shangri-la. To give to you.
You're going to need training. And you're going to need all the answers. Answers that none of us know.
What do you mean? From whom?
The First Immortal.
His caravan was fatally struck by a string of bad luck. Dysentery and parasitic sand fleas killed all of his caravan and were beginning to work on him.
And hopefully sleep through his painful death.
awareness of his body. He could see and feel every cell...and control them.
He was able to kill every parasite and virus inside his body by simply thinking he could.
Three months later, he stumbled out of the jungle and, after a brief tour of Europe with his story...he disappeared again.
While never seen again in public...

MIND MGMT FIELD GUIDE: 25.21. Once a field asset has proven his identity, the vital information will be conveyed to the agent via a benign-looking young-adult novel or a foreign-language dictionary.

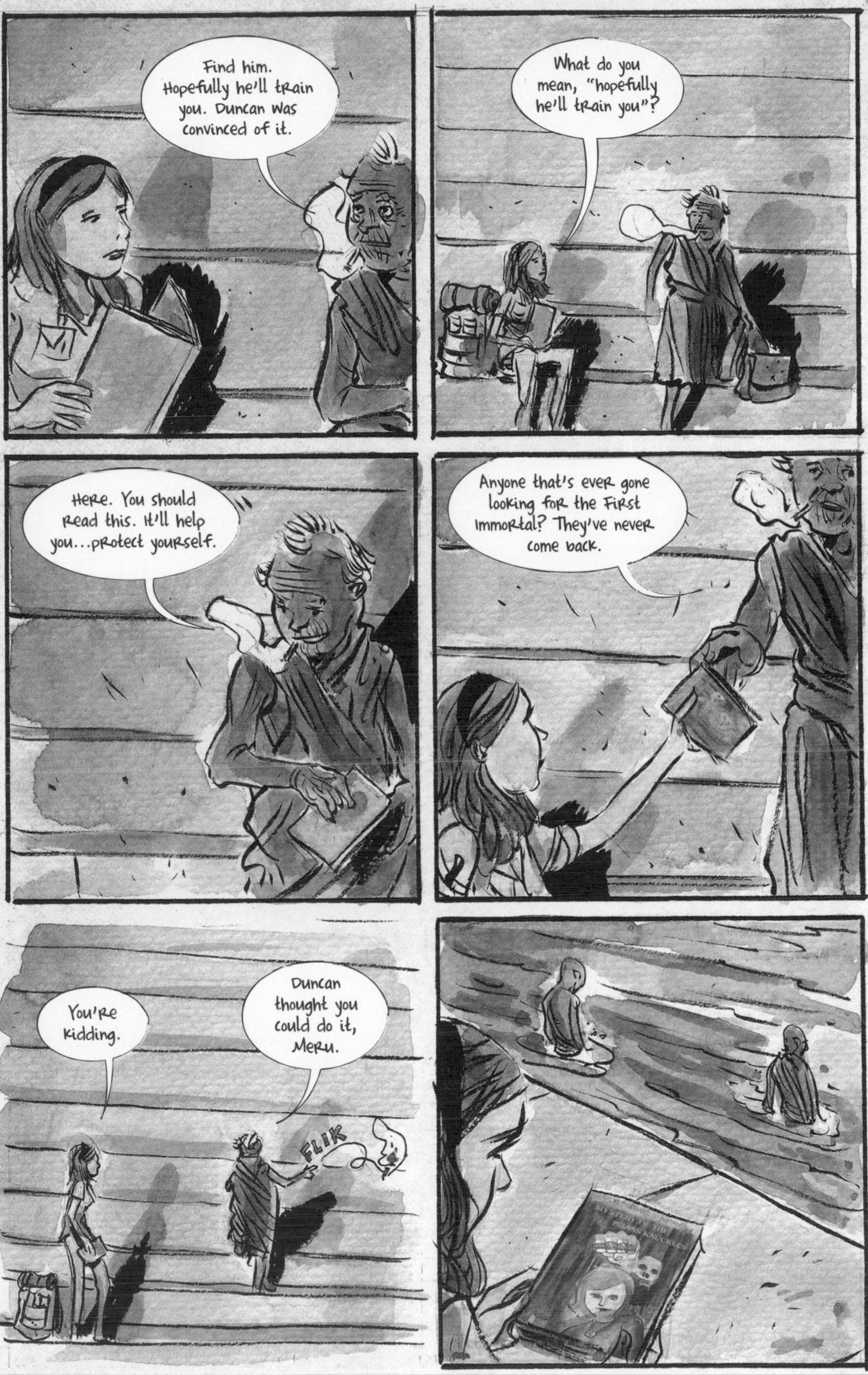
Find him. Hopefully he'll train you. Duncan was convinced of it.
What do you mean, "hopefully he'll train you"?
Here. You should read this. It'll help you...protect yourself.
Anyone that's ever gone looking for the First Immortal? They've never come back.
You're kidding.
Duncan thought you could do it, Meru.
FLIK

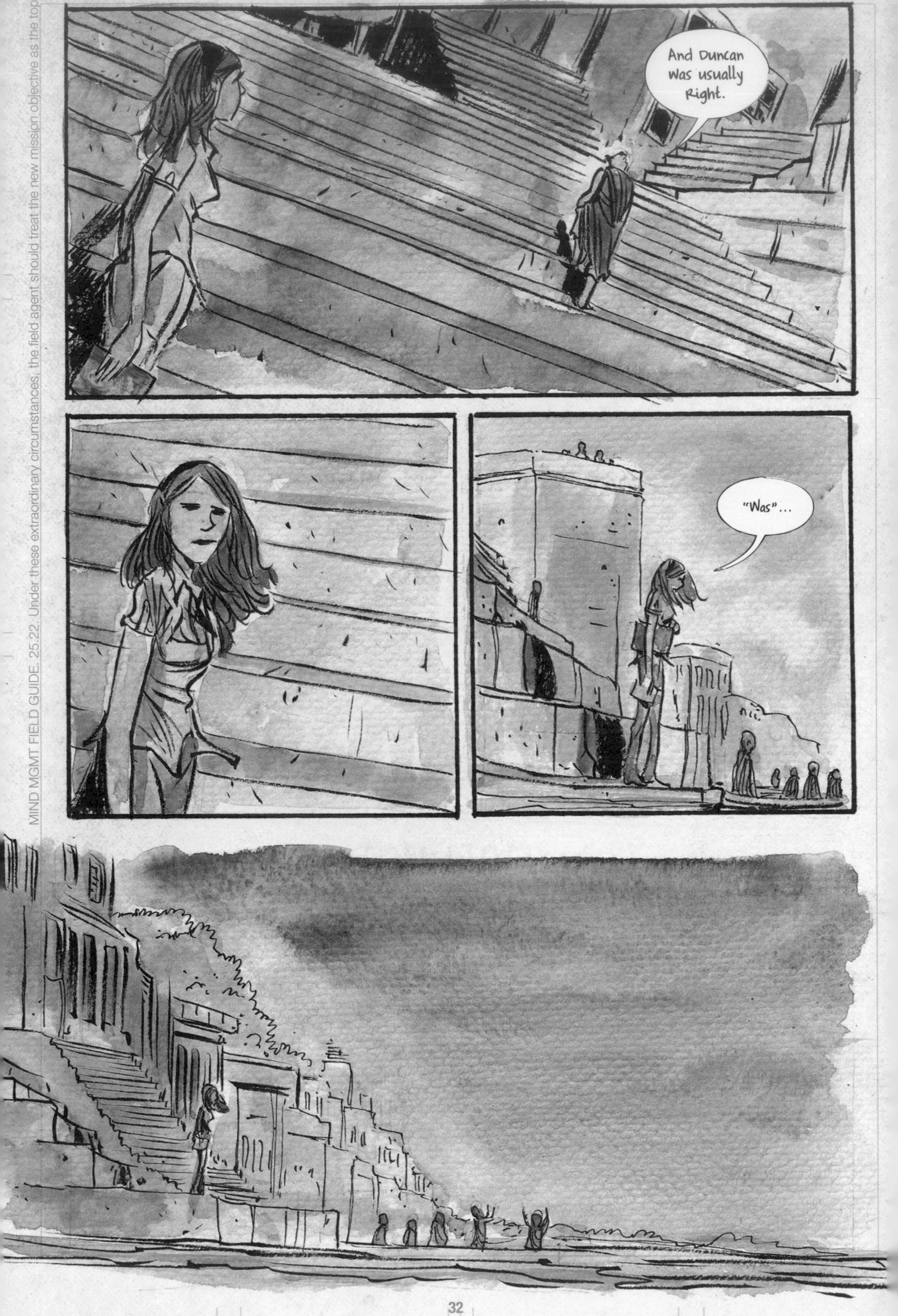
And Duncan was usually Right.
"Was"...

MIND MGMT
Mind Memos

The Sub Texts

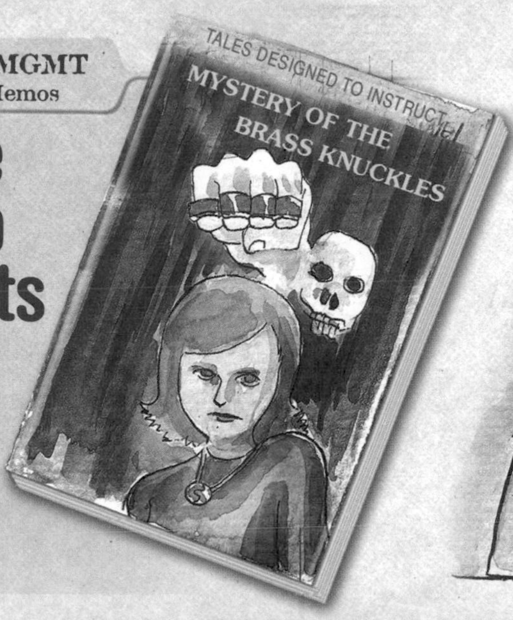

TALES DESIGNED TO INSTRUCT
MYSTERY OF THE BRASS KNUCKLES

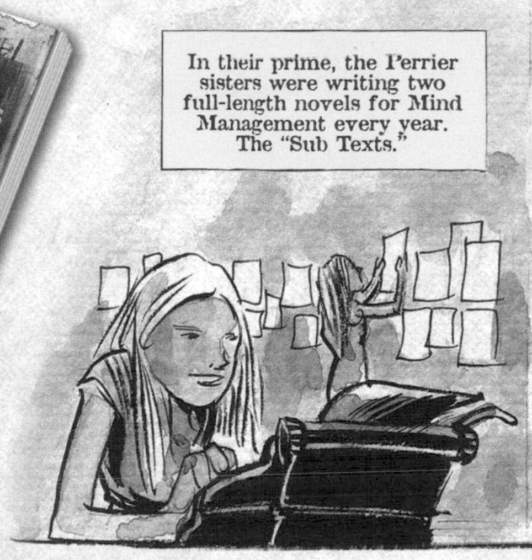

In their prime, the Perrier sisters were writing two full-length novels for Mind Management every year. The "Sub Texts."

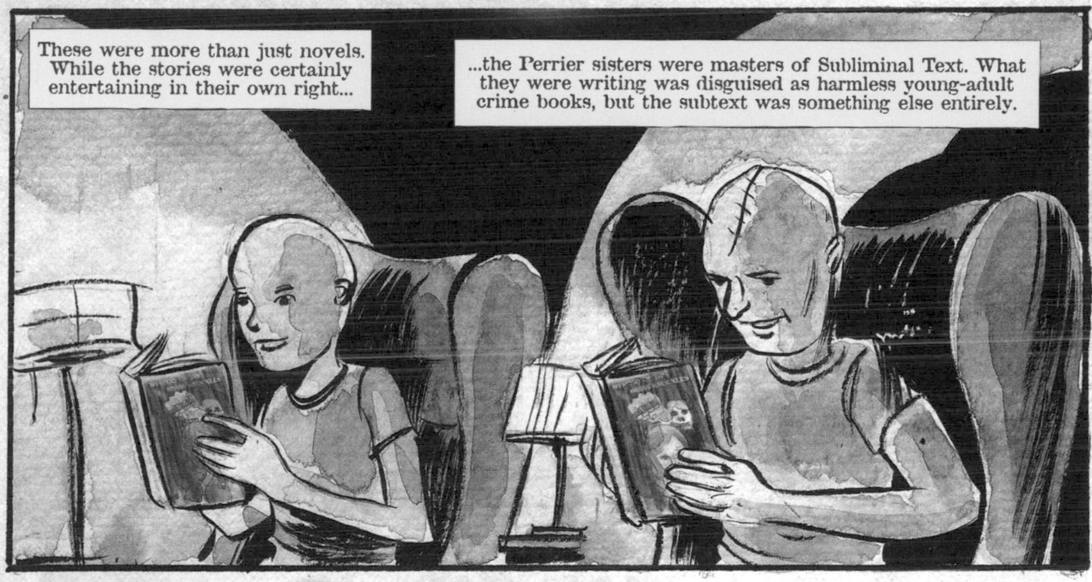

These were more than just novels. While the stories were certainly entertaining in their own right...
...the Perrier sisters were masters of Subliminal Text. What they were writing was disguised as harmless young-adult crime books, but the subtext was something else entirely.

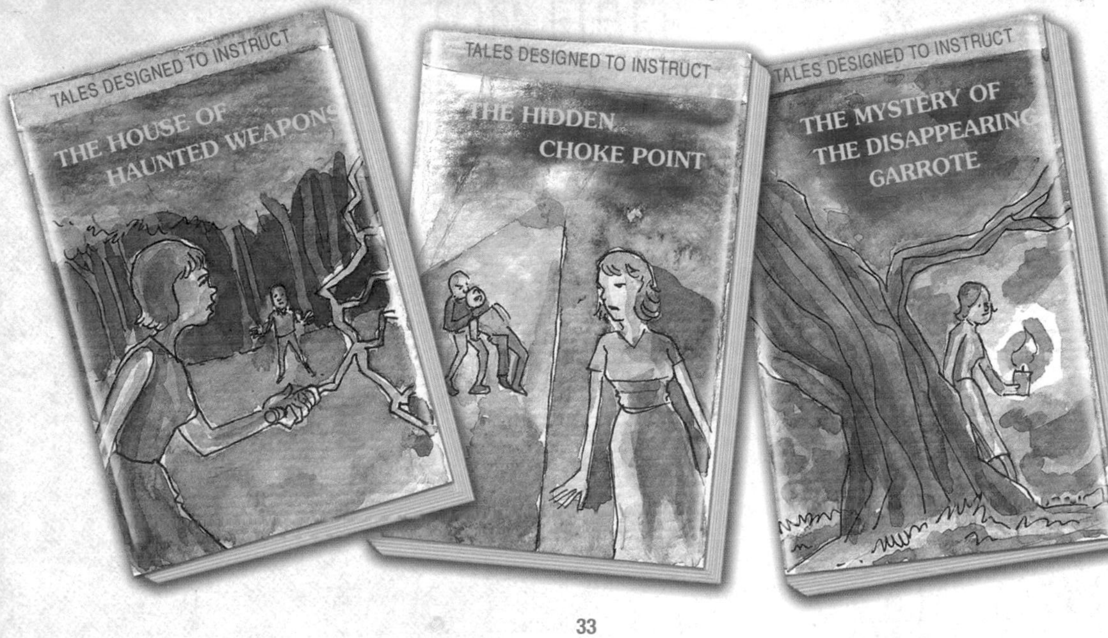

TALES DESIGNED TO INSTRUCT
THE HOUSE OF HAUNTED WEAPONS
TALES DESIGNED TO INSTRUCT
THE HIDDEN CHOKE POINT
TALES DESIGNED TO INSTRUCT
THE MYSTERY OF THE DISAPPEARING GARROTE

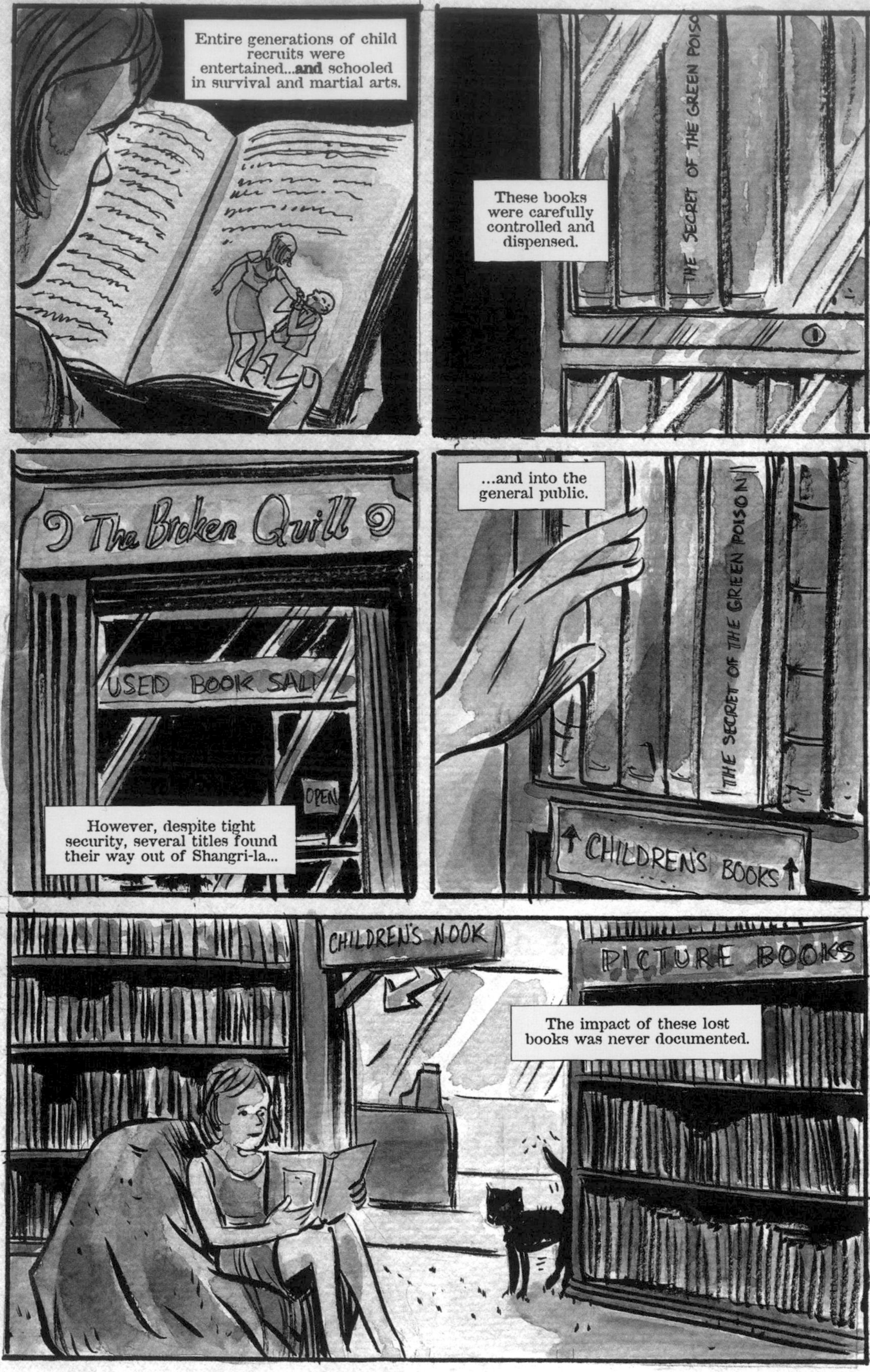
Entire generations of child recruits were entertained...**and** schooled in survival and martial arts.
THE SECRET OF THE GREEN POISO
These books were carefully controlled and dispensed.
The Broken Quill
USED BOOK SAL
OPEN
However, despite tight security, several titles found their way out of Shangri-la...
...and into the general public.
THE SECRET OF THE GREEN POISON
CHILDREN'S BOOKS
CHILDREN'S NOOK
PICTURE BOOKS
The impact of these lost books was never documented.

End Mind Memo.

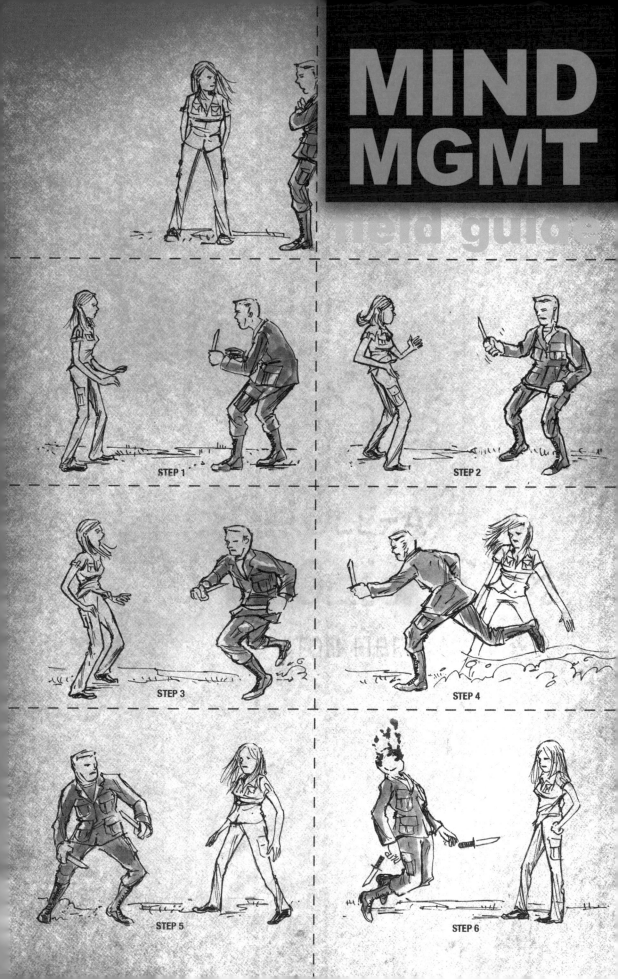

MIND MGMT

field guide

STEP 1

STEP 2

STEP 3

STEP 4

STEP 5

STEP 6

26

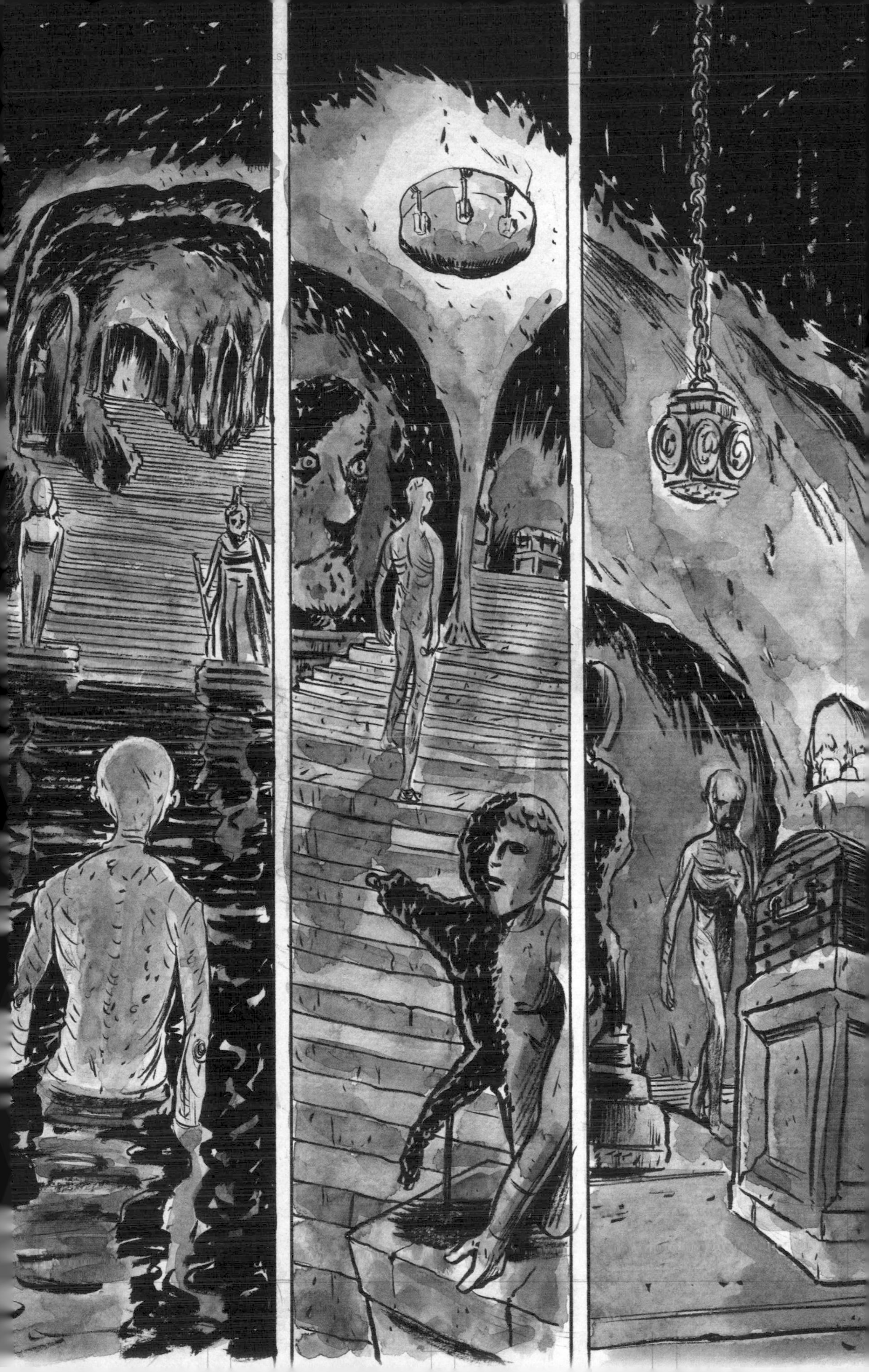

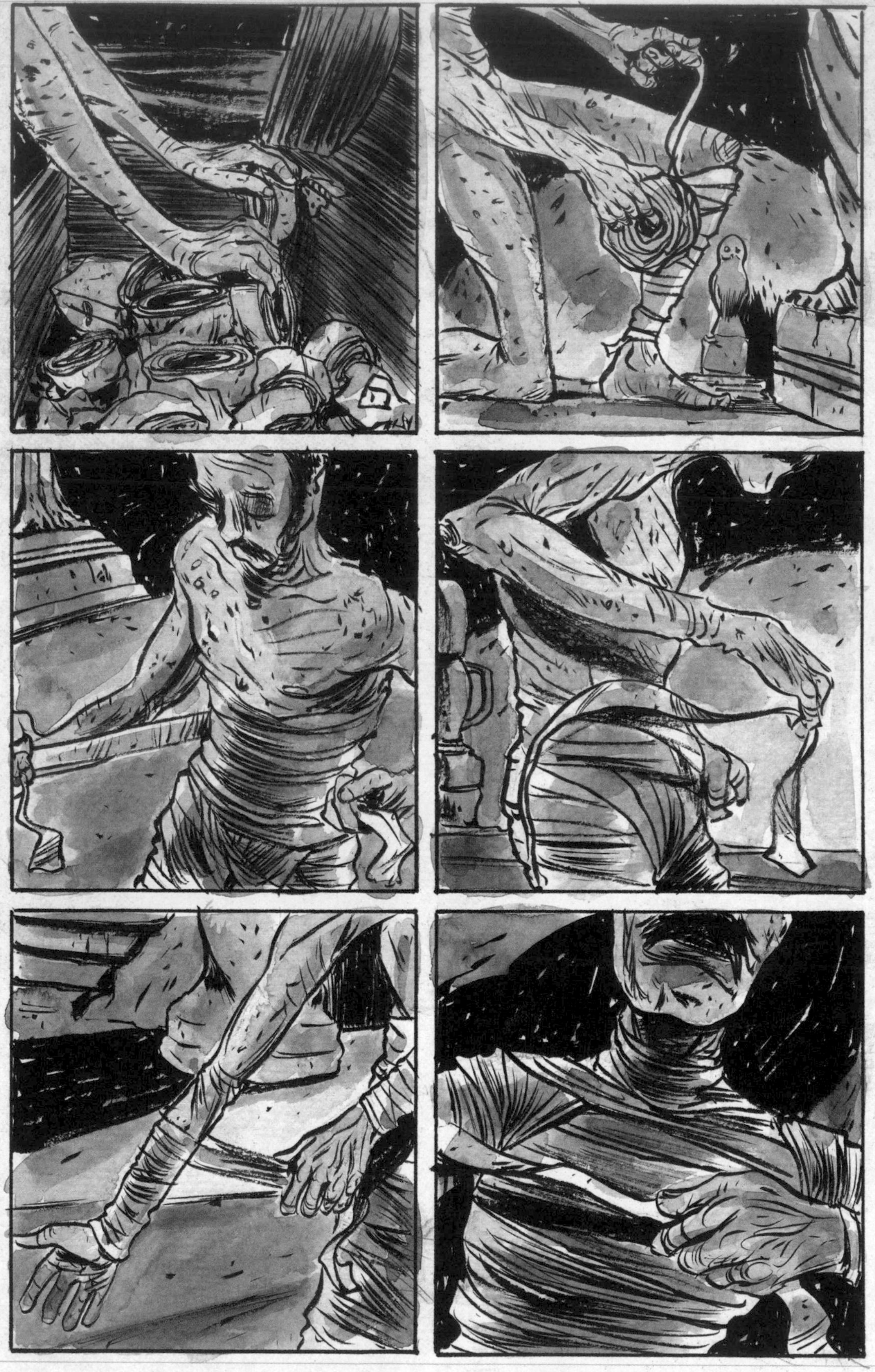

MIND MGMT FIELD GUIDE. 26.2. In the event of injury while in the field, trust your basic medical training and try to reach a Mind Management cache of supersensory bandages.

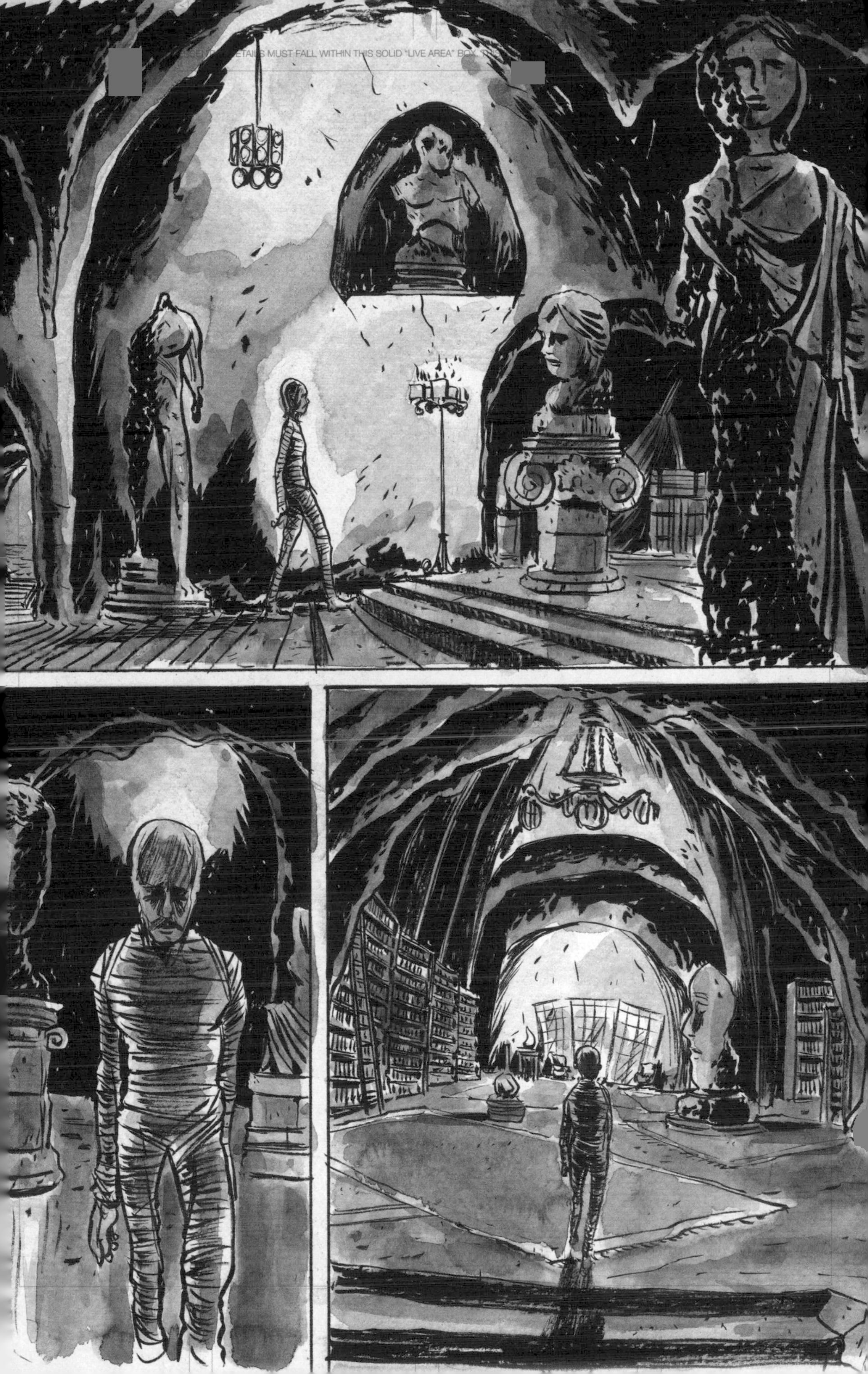
MUST FALL WITHIN THIS SOLID "LIVE AREA" BOX

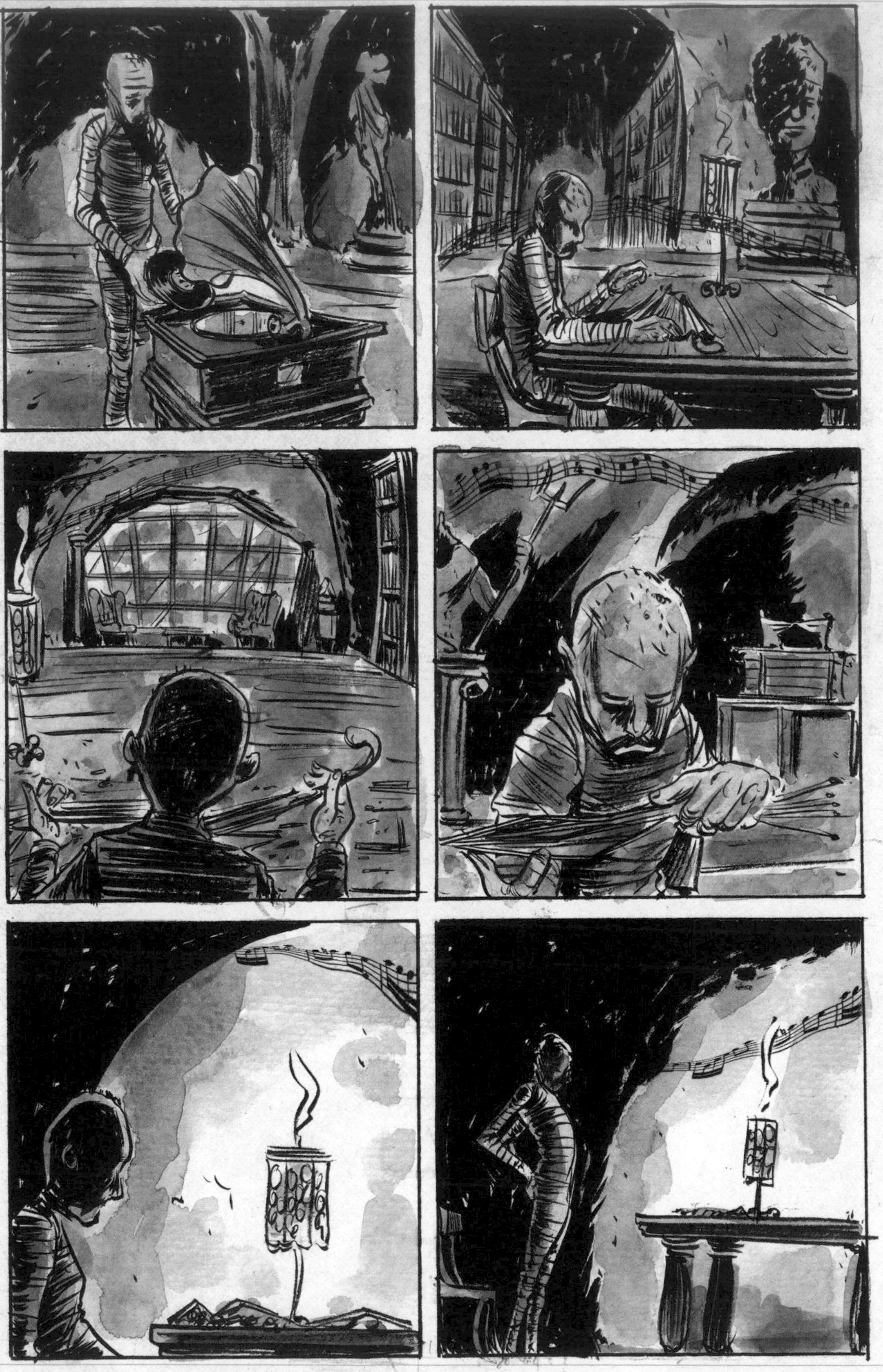

MIND MGMT FIELD GUIDE. 26.4. It is essential to find a safe house for proper recuperation. Use of sensile plainsong recordings are also helpful in treating grievous injuries.

WHEN FILING REPORT ALL ESSENTIAL DETAILS MUST FALL WITHIN THIS SOLID "LIVE AREA" BOX. THIS IS THE BORDER FOR A STANDARD, NON-BLEED FIELD REP

MIND MGMT FIELD GUIDE. 26.5. Once black-channel distress calls have been sent, a consistent routine of meditation and reflection is invaluable for enduring prolonged isolation.

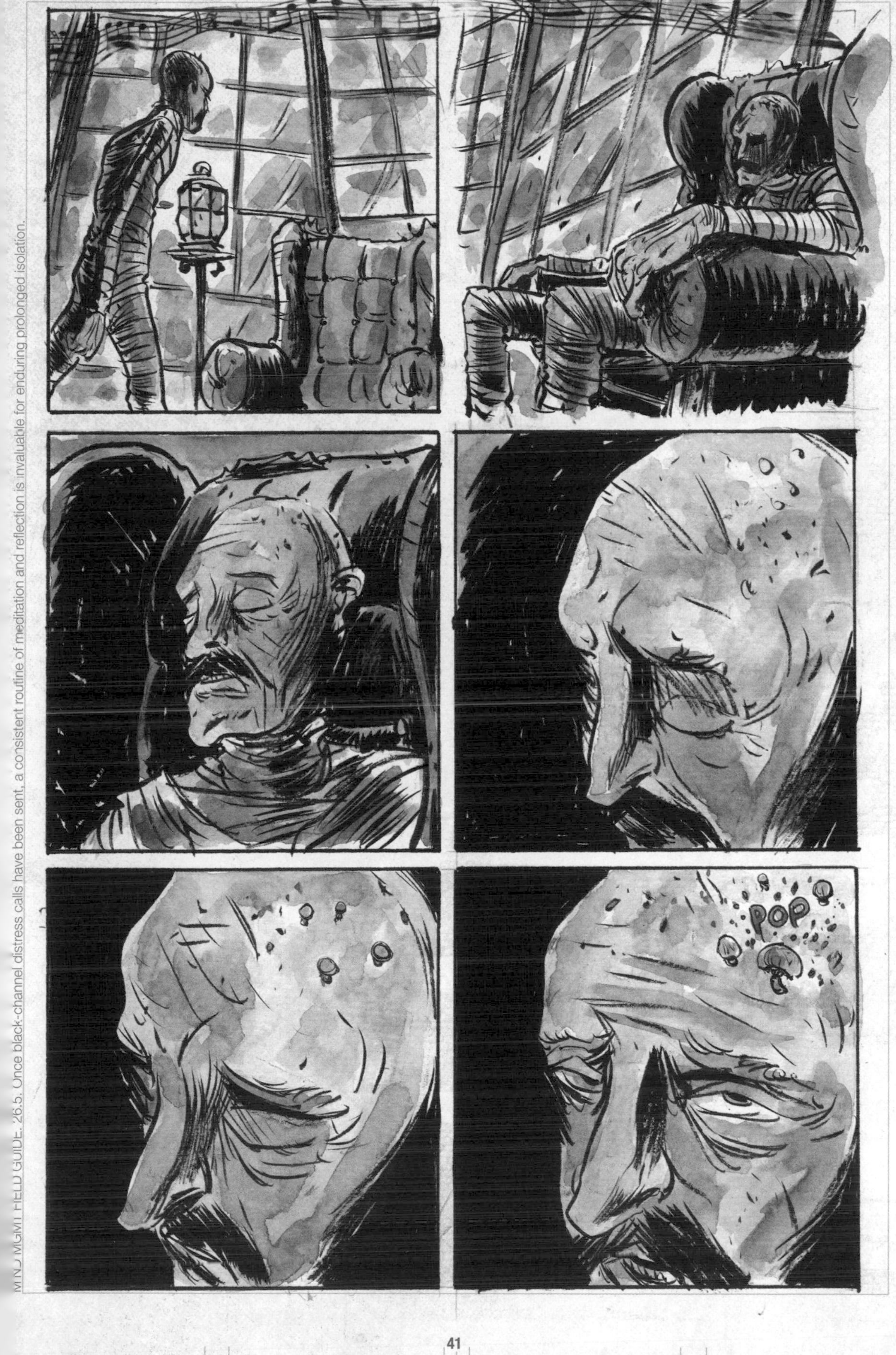
POP

MIND MGMT FIELD GUIDE. 26.6. It is important to set limits on sensile recordings to avoid cerebral feedback.

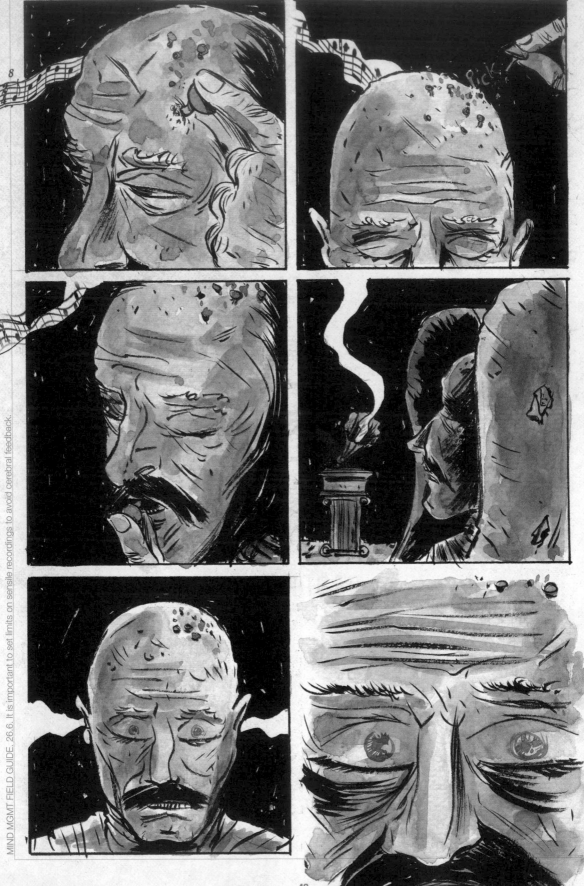

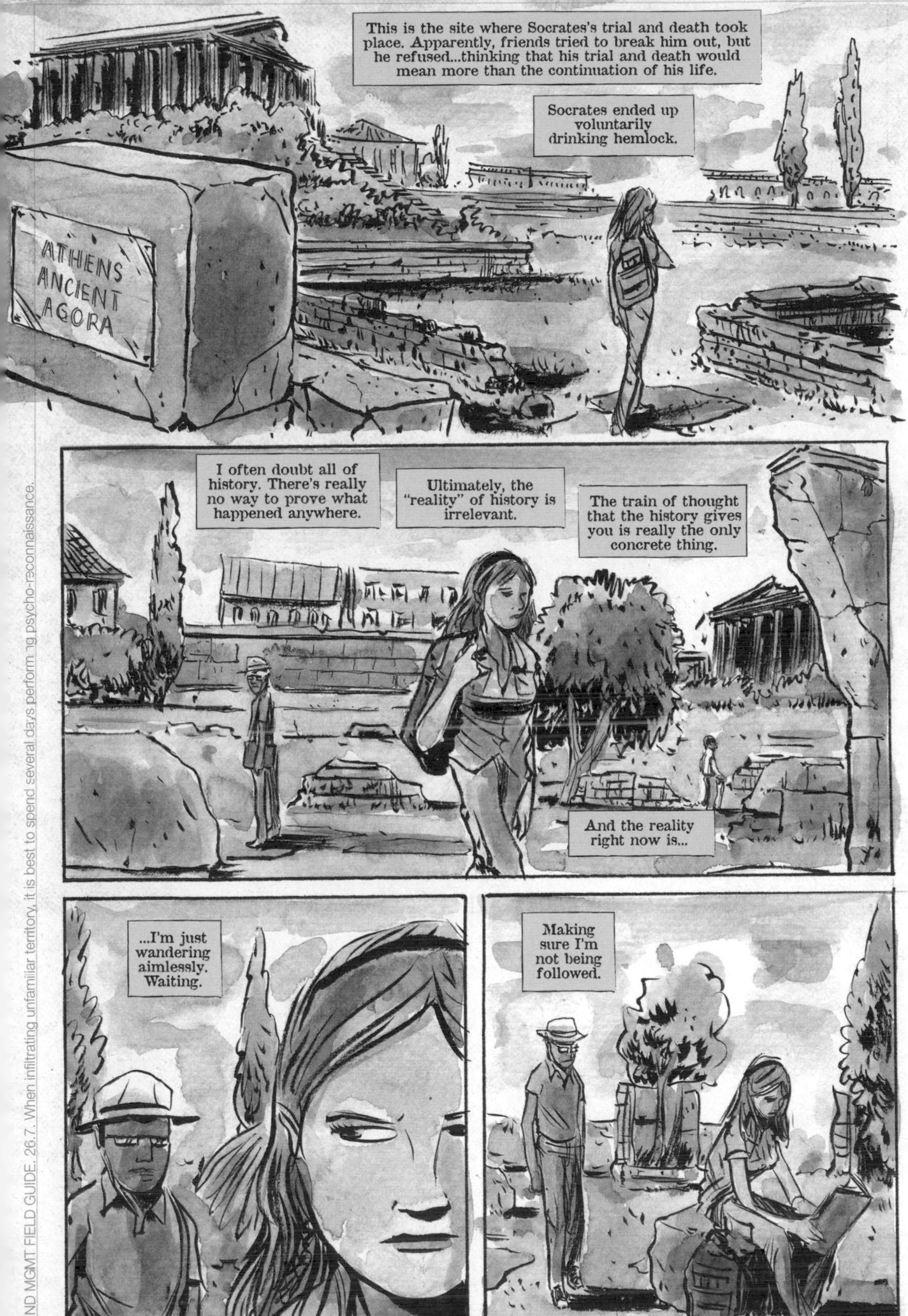
This is the site where Socrates's trial and death took place. Apparently, friends tried to break him out, but he refused...thinking that his trial and death would mean more than the continuation of his life.
Socrates ended up voluntarily drinking hemlock.
ATHENS ANCIENT AGORA
I often doubt all of history. There's really no way to prove what happened anywhere.
Ultimately, the "reality" of history is irrelevant.
The train of thought that the history gives you is really the only concrete thing.
And the reality right now is...
...I'm just wandering aimlessly. Waiting.
Making sure I'm not being followed.

MIND MGMT FIELD GUIDE. 26.7. When infiltrating unfamiliar territory, it is best to spend several days perform ng psycho-reconnaissance.

WHEN FILING REPORT ALL ESSENTIAL DETAILS MUST FALL WITHIN THIS SOLID "LIVE AREA" BOX. THIS IS THE BORDER FOR A STANDARD, NON-BLEED FIELD REPORT

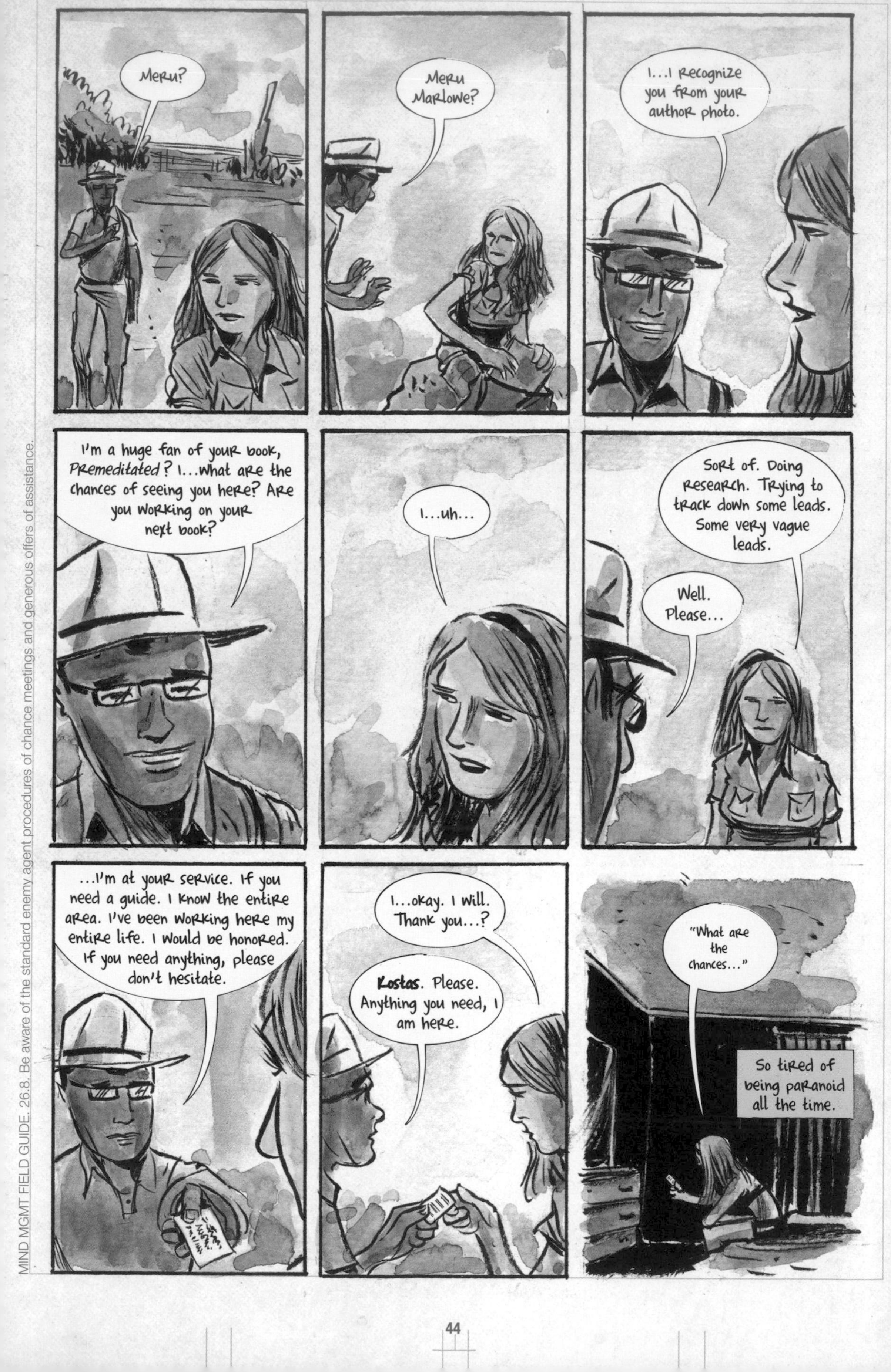
Meru?
Meru Marlowe?
I...I recognize you from your author photo.
I'm a huge fan of your book, *Premeditated*? I...What are the chances of seeing you here? Are you working on your next book?
I...uh...
Sort of. Doing research. Trying to track down some leads. Some very vague leads.
Well. Please...
...I'm at your service. If you need a guide. I know the entire area. I've been working here my entire life. I would be honored. If you need anything, please don't hesitate.
I...okay. I will. Thank you...?
Kostas. Please. Anything you need, I am here.
"What are the chances..."
So tired of being paranoid all the time.

MIND MGMT FIELD GUIDE. 26.8. Be aware of the standard enemy agent procedures of chance meetings and generous offers of assistance.

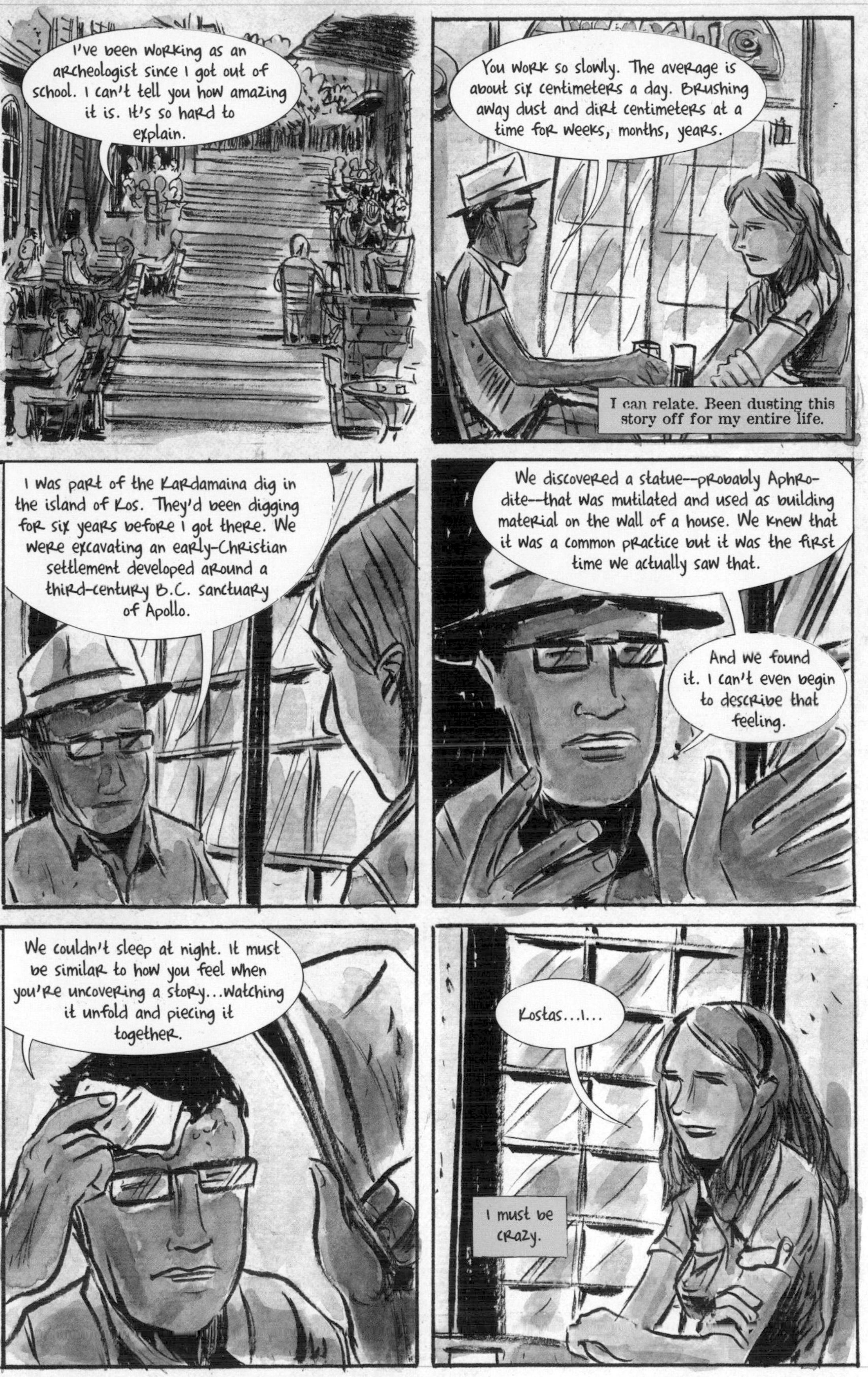
I've been working as an archeologist since I got out of school. I can't tell you how amazing it is. It's so hard to explain.
You work so slowly. The average is about six centimeters a day. Brushing away dust and dirt centimeters at a time for weeks, months, years.
I can relate. Been dusting this story off for my entire life.
I was part of the Kardamaina dig in the island of Kos. They'd been digging for six years before I got there. We were excavating an early-Christian settlement developed around a third-century B.C. sanctuary of Apollo.
We discovered a statue--probably Aphrodite--that was mutilated and used as building material on the wall of a house. We knew that it was a common practice but it was the first time we actually saw that.
And we found it. I can't even begin to describe that feeling.
We couldn't sleep at night. It must be similar to how you feel when you're uncovering a story...watching it unfold and piecing it together.
Kostas...I...
I must be crazy.

WHEN FILING REPORT ALL ESSENTIAL DETAILS MUST FALL WITHIN THIS SOLID "LIVE AREA" BOX. THIS IS THE BORDER FOR A STANDARD, NON-BLEED FIELD REPORT

MIND MGMT FIELD GUIDE. 26.10. After a period of nonantagonistic interchanges have occurred, recuse yourself at the earliest opportunity.

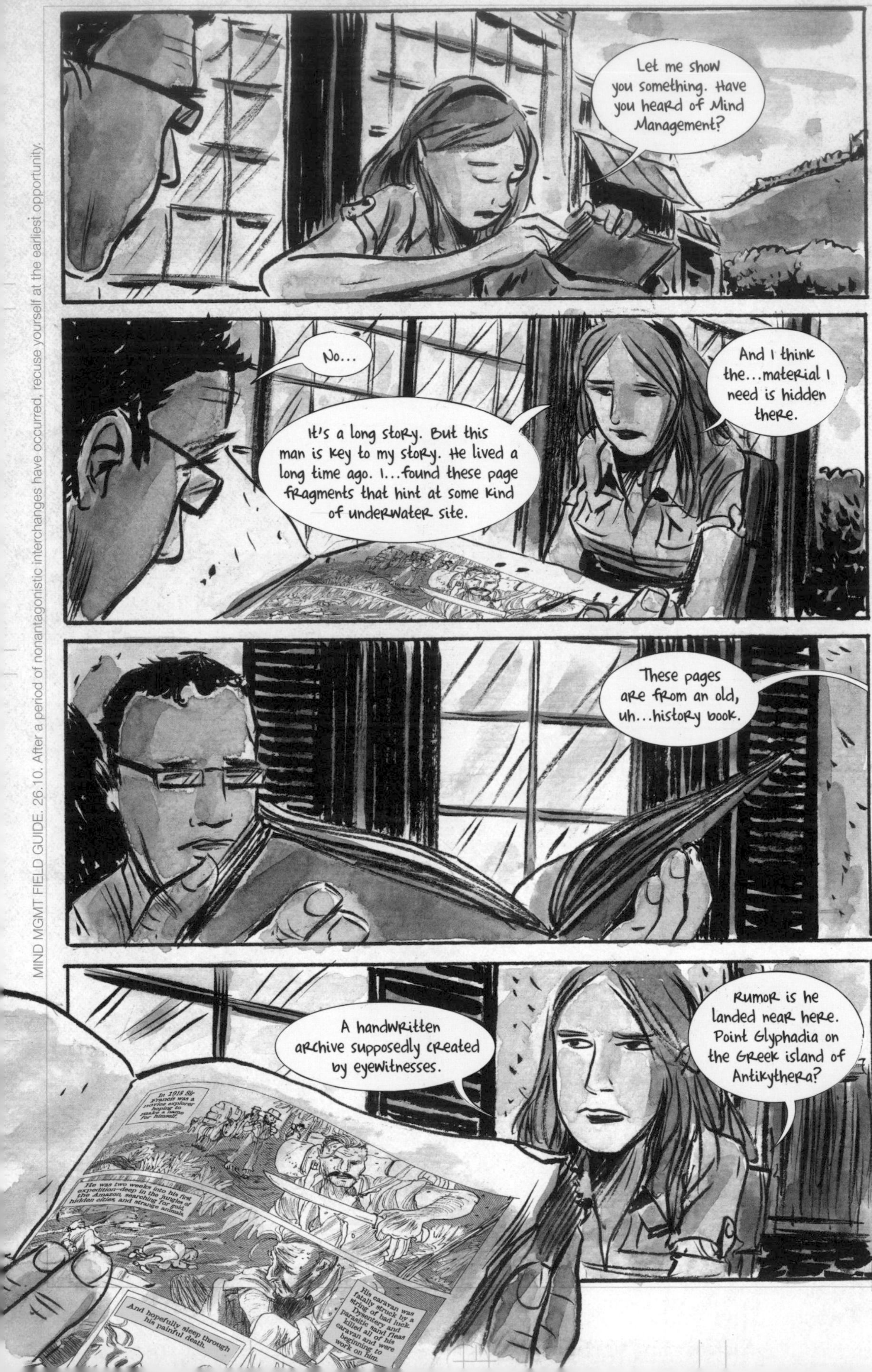

Let me show you something. Have you heard of Mind Management?
No...
It's a long story. But this man is key to my story. He lived a long time ago. I...found these page fragments that hint at some kind of underwater site.
And I think the...material I need is hidden there.
These pages are from an old, uh...history book.
A handwritten archive supposedly created by eyewitnesses.
In 1918 Sir Francis was a novice explorer hoping to make a name for himself.
He was two weeks into his first expedition—deep in the jungles of the Amazon, searching for gold, hidden cities, and strange animals.
His caravan was fatally struck by a string of bad luck. Dysentery and parasitic sand fleas killed all of his caravan and were beginning to work on him.
And hopefully sleep through his painful death.
Rumor is he landed near here. Point Glyphadia on the Greek island of Antikythera?

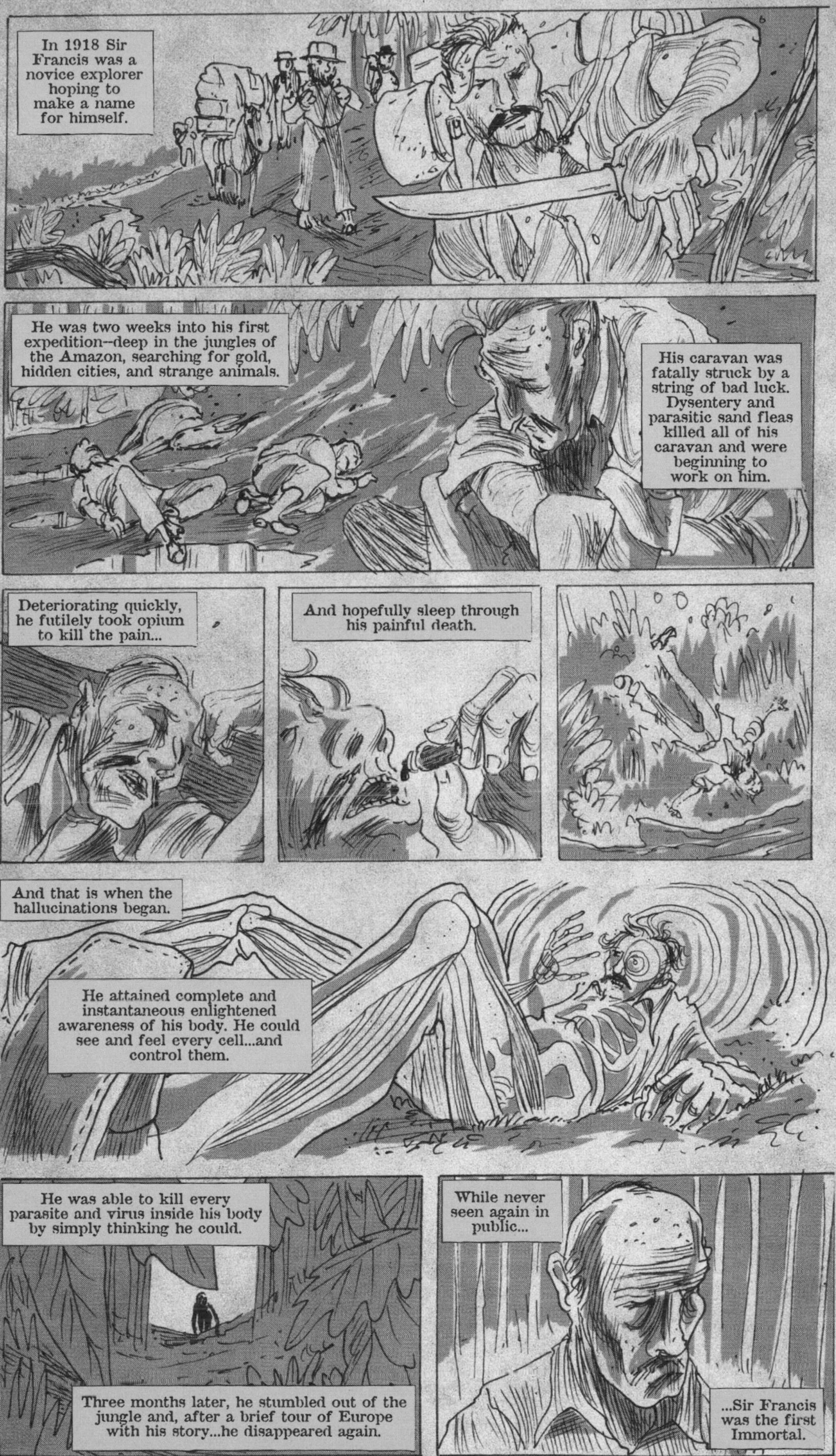
In 1918 Sir Francis was a novice explorer hoping to make a name for himself.
He was two weeks into his first expedition--deep in the jungles of the Amazon, searching for gold, hidden cities, and strange animals.
His caravan was fatally struck by a string of bad luck. Dysentery and parasitic sand fleas killed all of his caravan and were beginning to work on him.
Deteriorating quickly, he futilely took opium to kill the pain...
And hopefully sleep through his painful death.
And that is when the hallucinations began.
He attained complete and instantaneous enlightened awareness of his body. He could see and feel every cell...and control them.
He was able to kill every parasite and virus inside his body by simply thinking he could.
Three months later, he stumbled out of the jungle and, after a brief tour of Europe with his story...he disappeared again.
While never seen again in public...
...Sir Francis was the first Immortal.

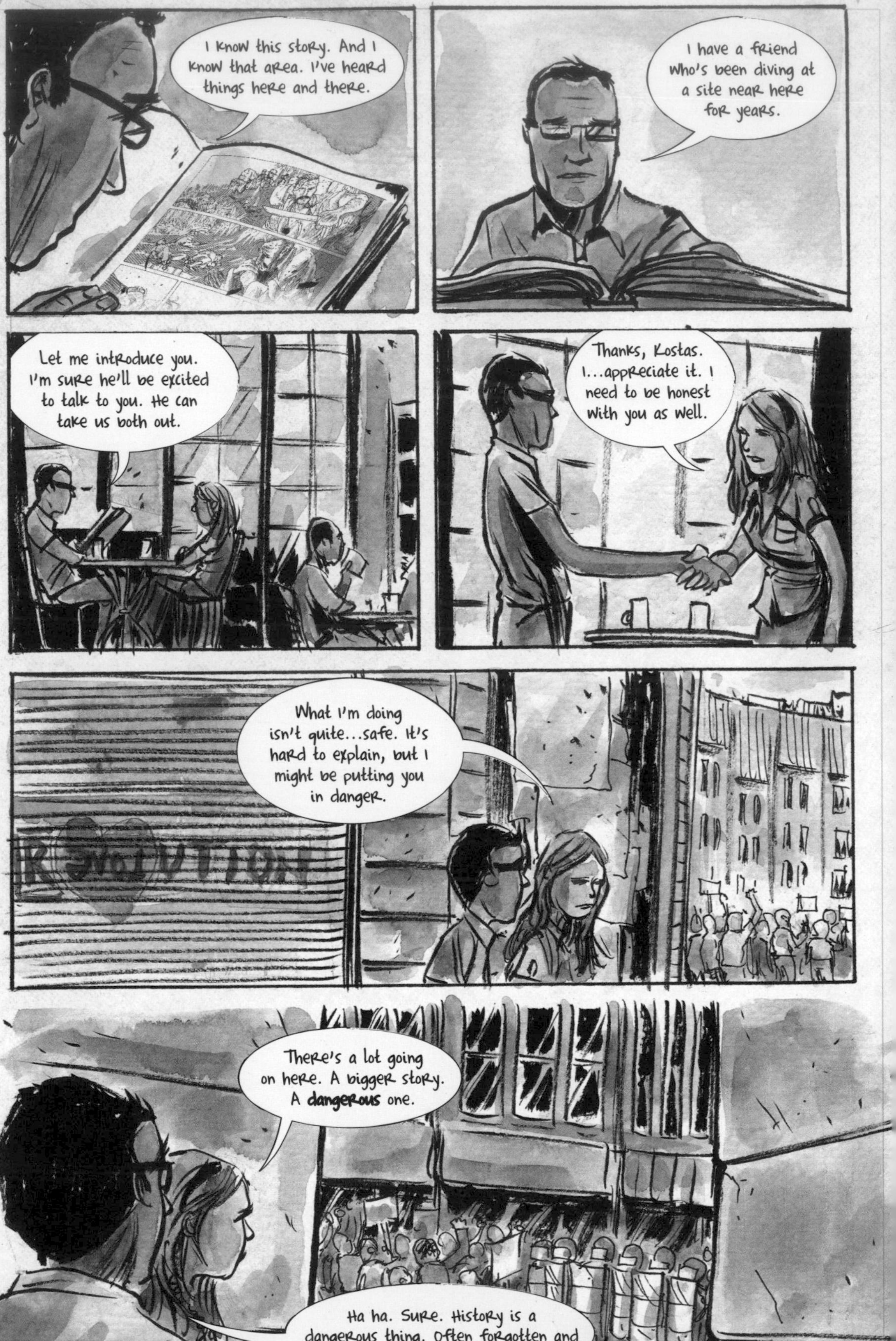
I know this story. And I know that area. I've heard things here and there.
I have a friend who's been diving at a site near here for years.
Let me introduce you. I'm sure he'll be excited to talk to you. He can take us both out.
Thanks, Kostas. I...appreciate it. I need to be honest with you as well.
What I'm doing isn't quite...safe. It's hard to explain, but I might be putting you in danger.
There's a lot going on here. A bigger story. A **dangerous** one.
Ha ha. Sure. History is a dangerous thing. Often forgotten and always repeated.

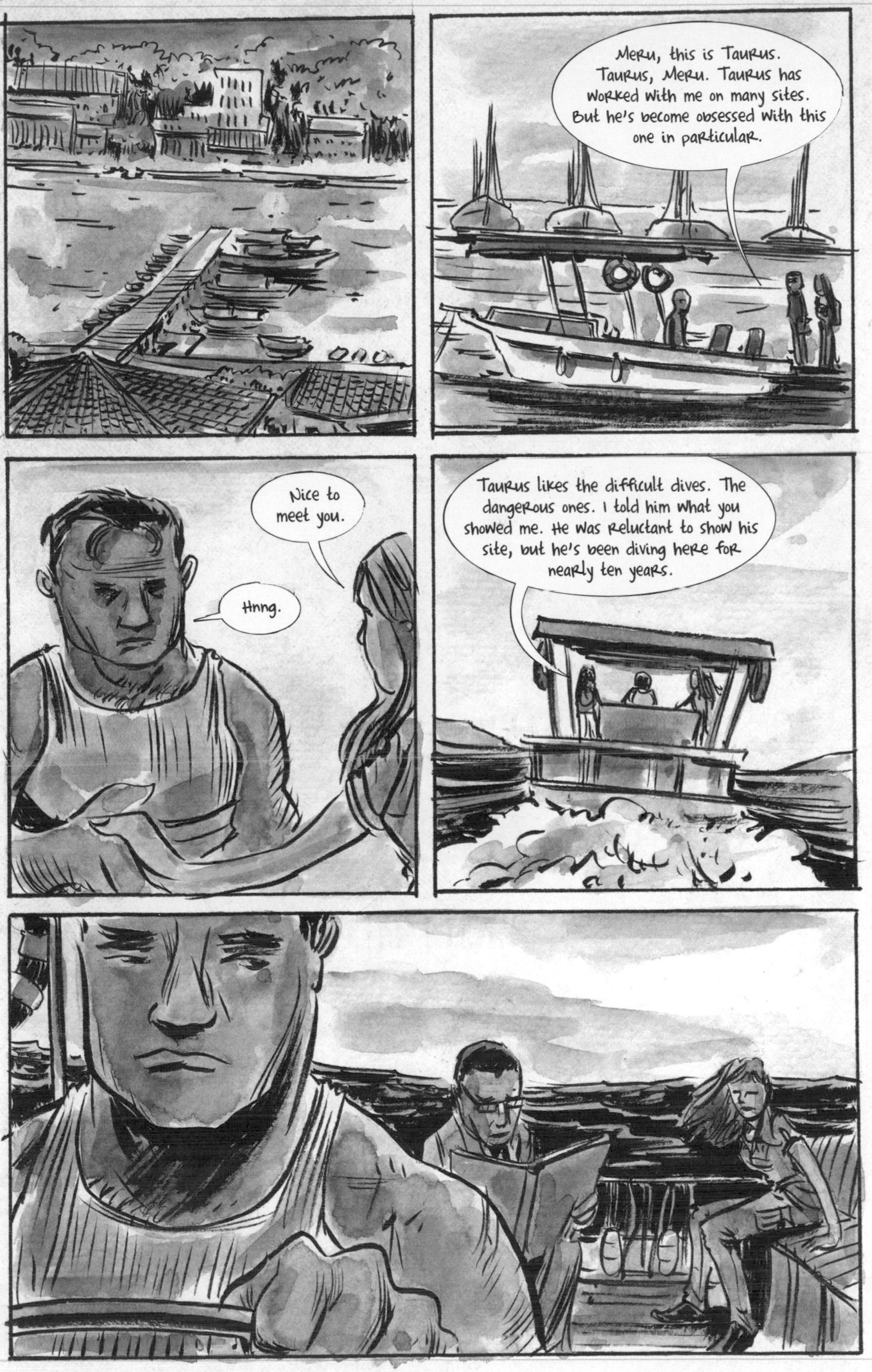
Meru, this is Taurus. Taurus, Meru. Taurus has worked with me on many sites. But he's become obsessed with this one in particular.
Nice to meet you.
Hnng.
Taurus likes the difficult dives. The dangerous ones. I told him what you showed me. He was reluctant to show his site, but he's been diving here for nearly ten years.

MND MGMT FIELD GUIDE. 26.13. Be particularly wary of unknown agents and their secondary contacts. Avoid these interactions at all costs.

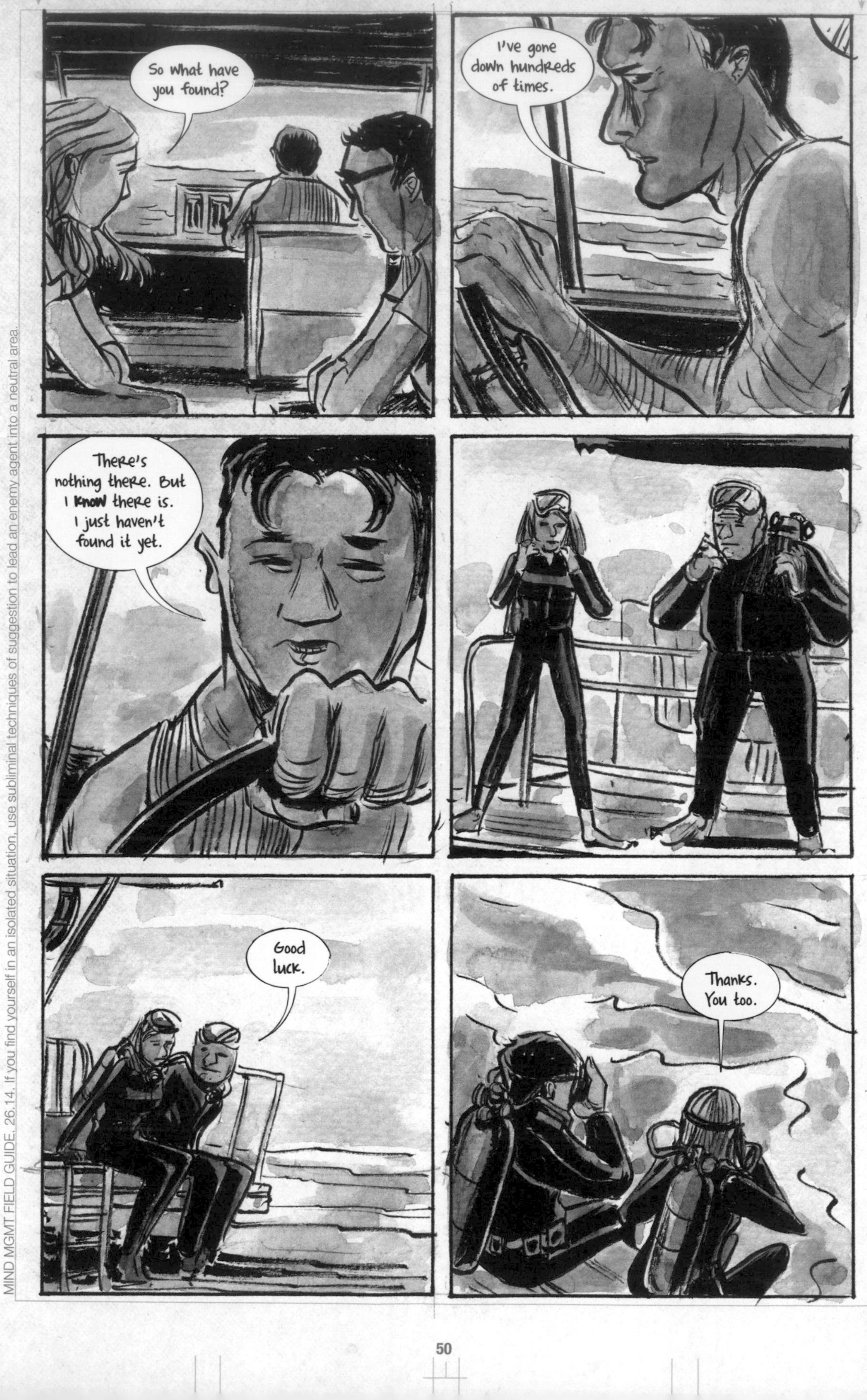
So what have you found?
I've gone down hundreds of times.
There's nothing there. But I **know** there is. I just haven't found it yet.
Good luck.
Thanks. You too.

MIND MGMT FIELD GUIDE. 26.14. If you find yourself in an isolated situation, use subliminal techniques of suggestion to lead an enemy agent into a neutral area.

MIND MGMT FIELD GUIDE. 26.15. Once you are both in a neutral area, continue suggestive techniques to confuse your antagonist and escape at the earliest opportunity.

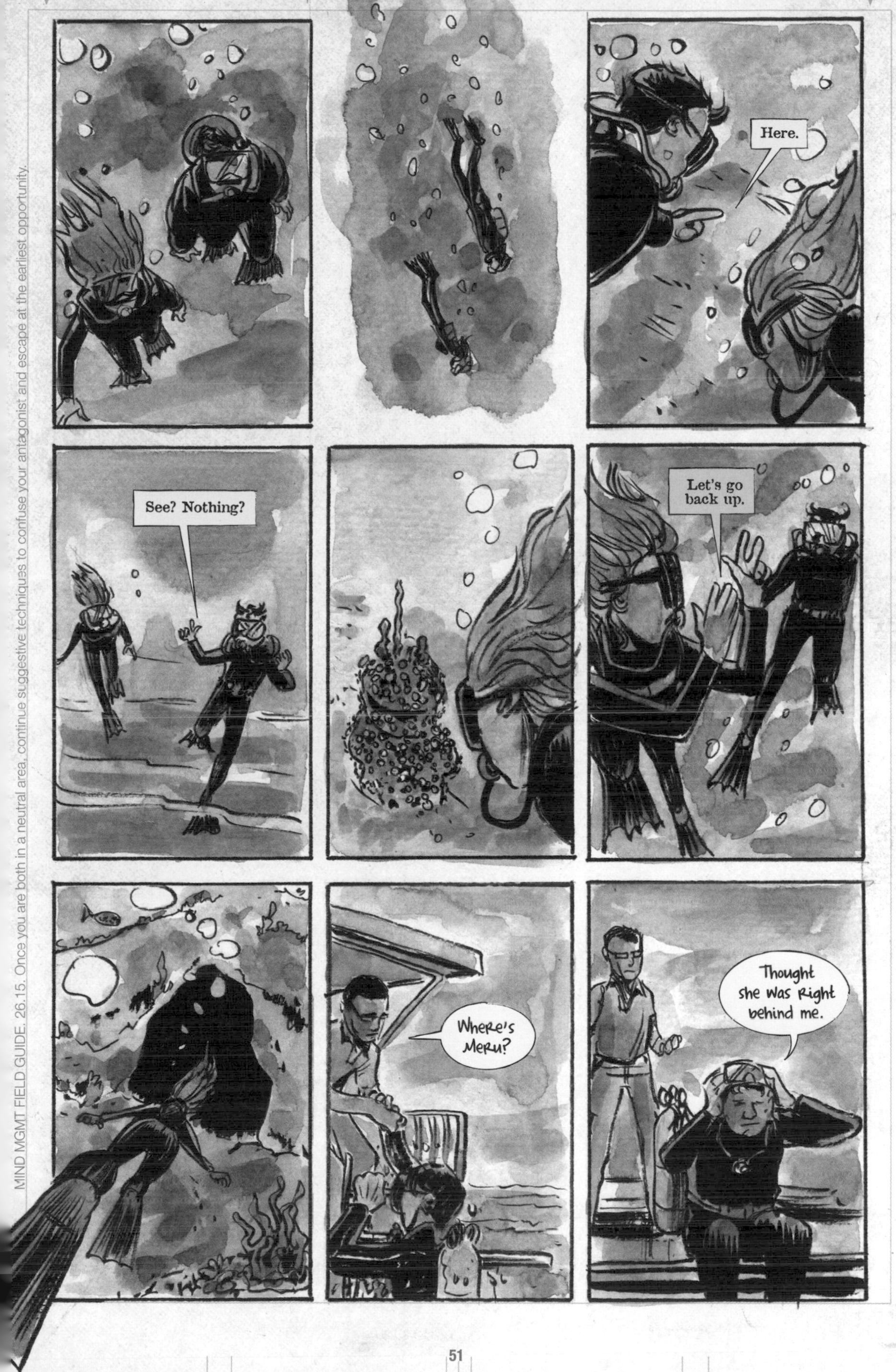
Here.
See? Nothing?
Let's go back up.
Where's Meru?
Thought she was right behind me.

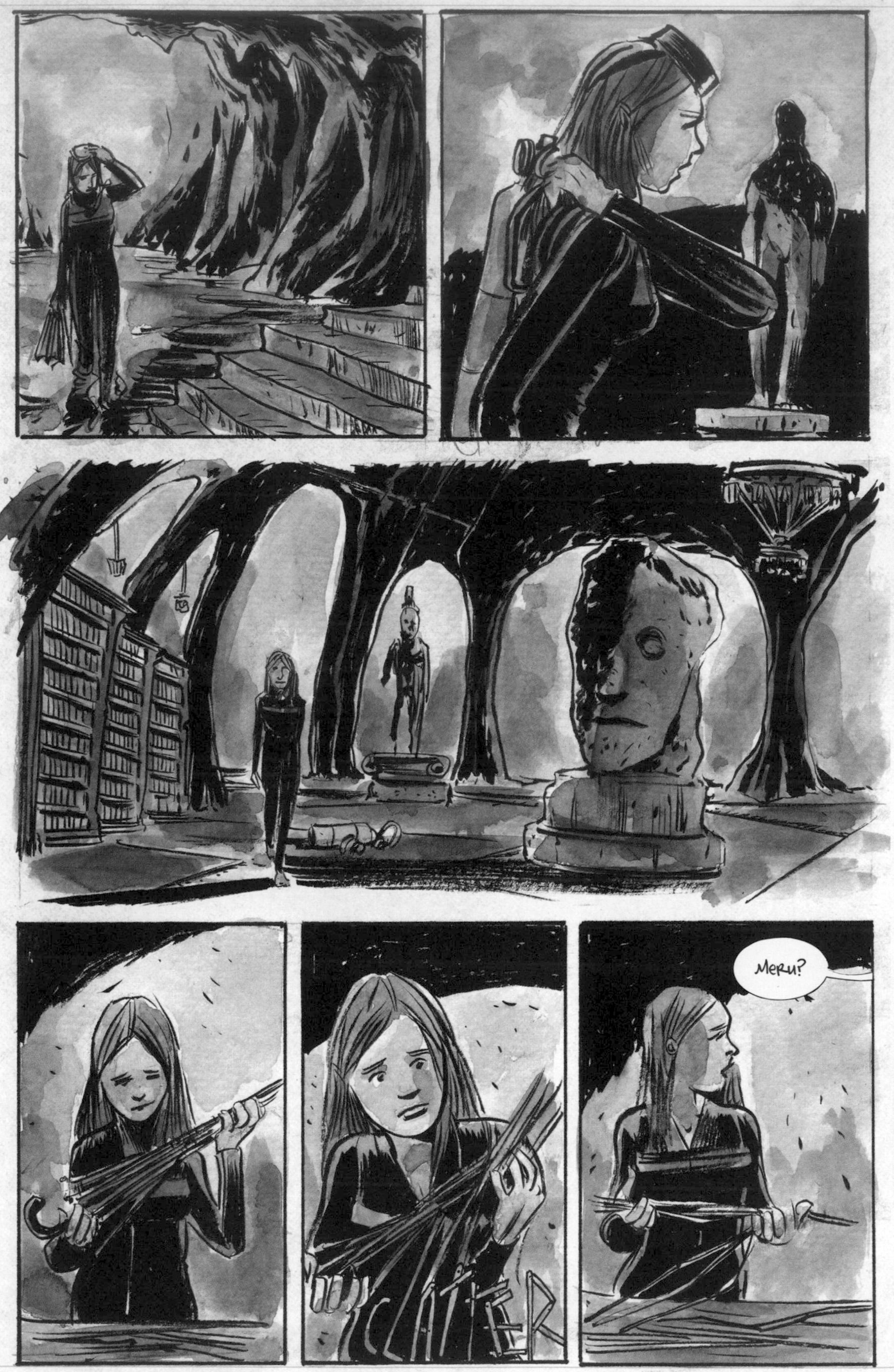
Meru?

MIND MGMT FIELD GUIDE. 26.17. Avoid contact with any agents that are obviously ingesting elements of an unknown origin.

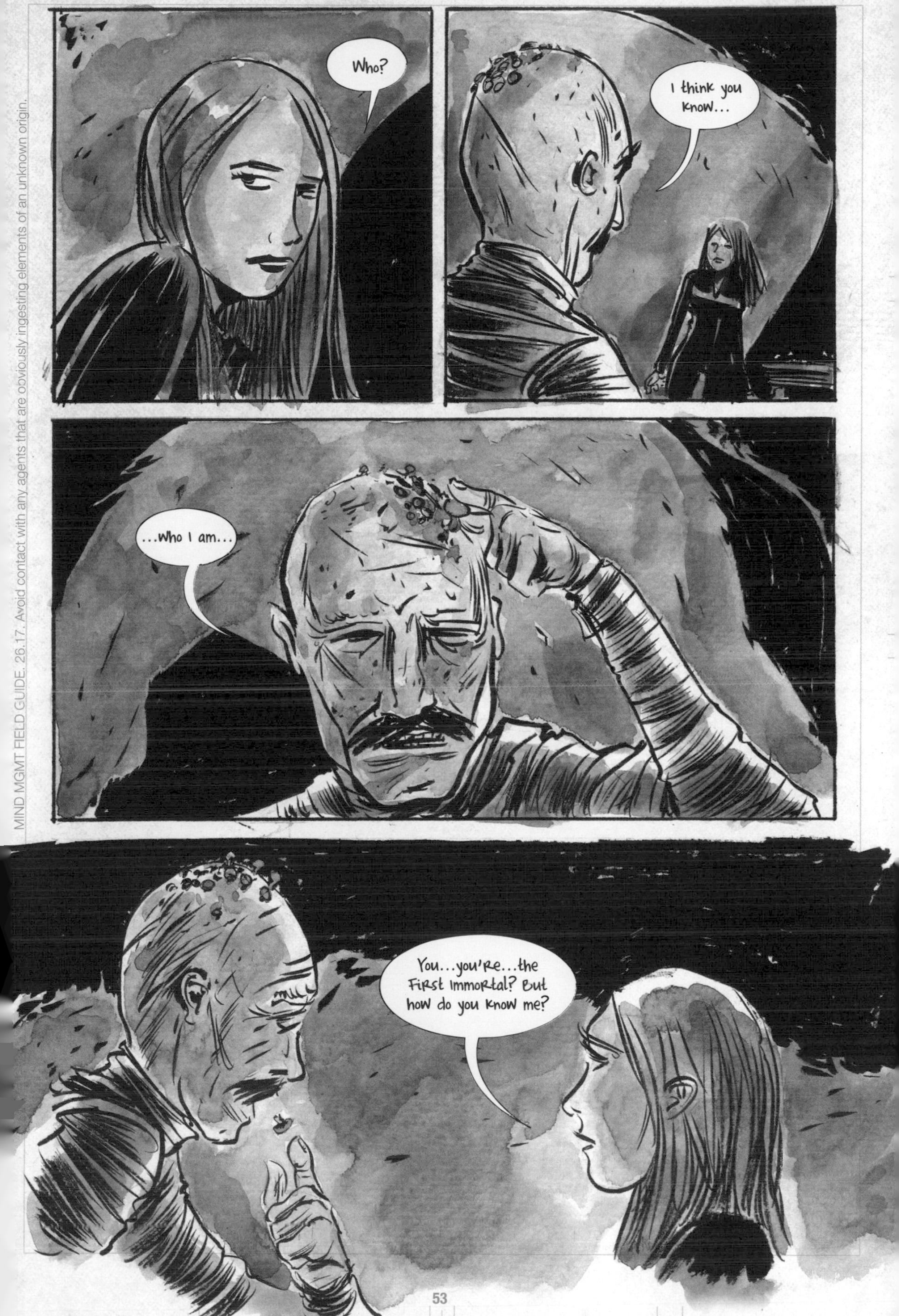
Who?
I think you know...
...Who I am...
You...you're...the First Immortal? But how do you know me?

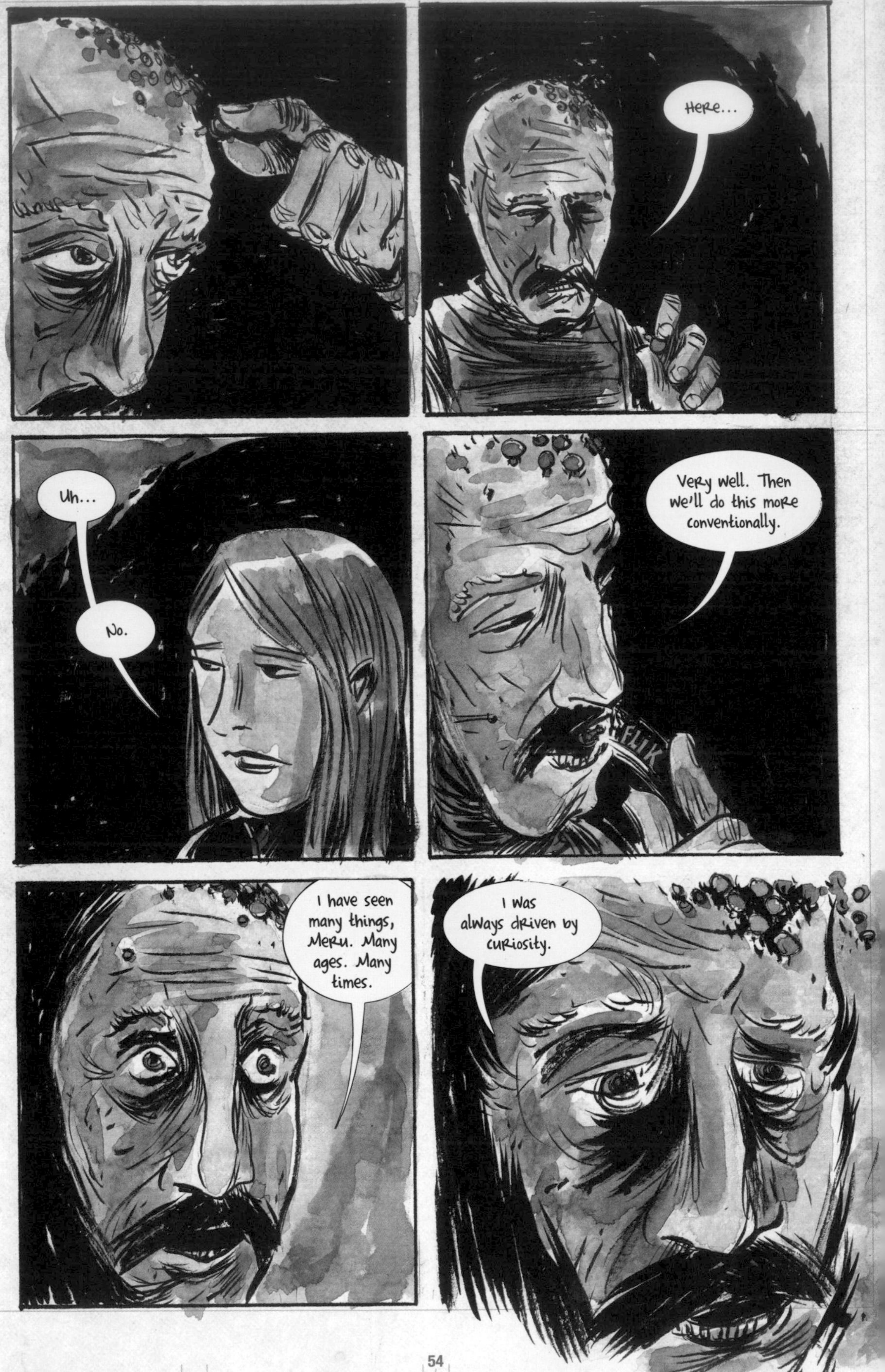
Here...
Uh...
No.
Very well. Then we'll do this more conventionally.
FLIK
I have seen many things, Meru. Many ages. Many times.
I was always driven by curiosity.

MIND MGMT FIELD GUIDE. 26.18. Never ingest an offered element of unknown origin. Friendly agents are prohibited from making such offerings.

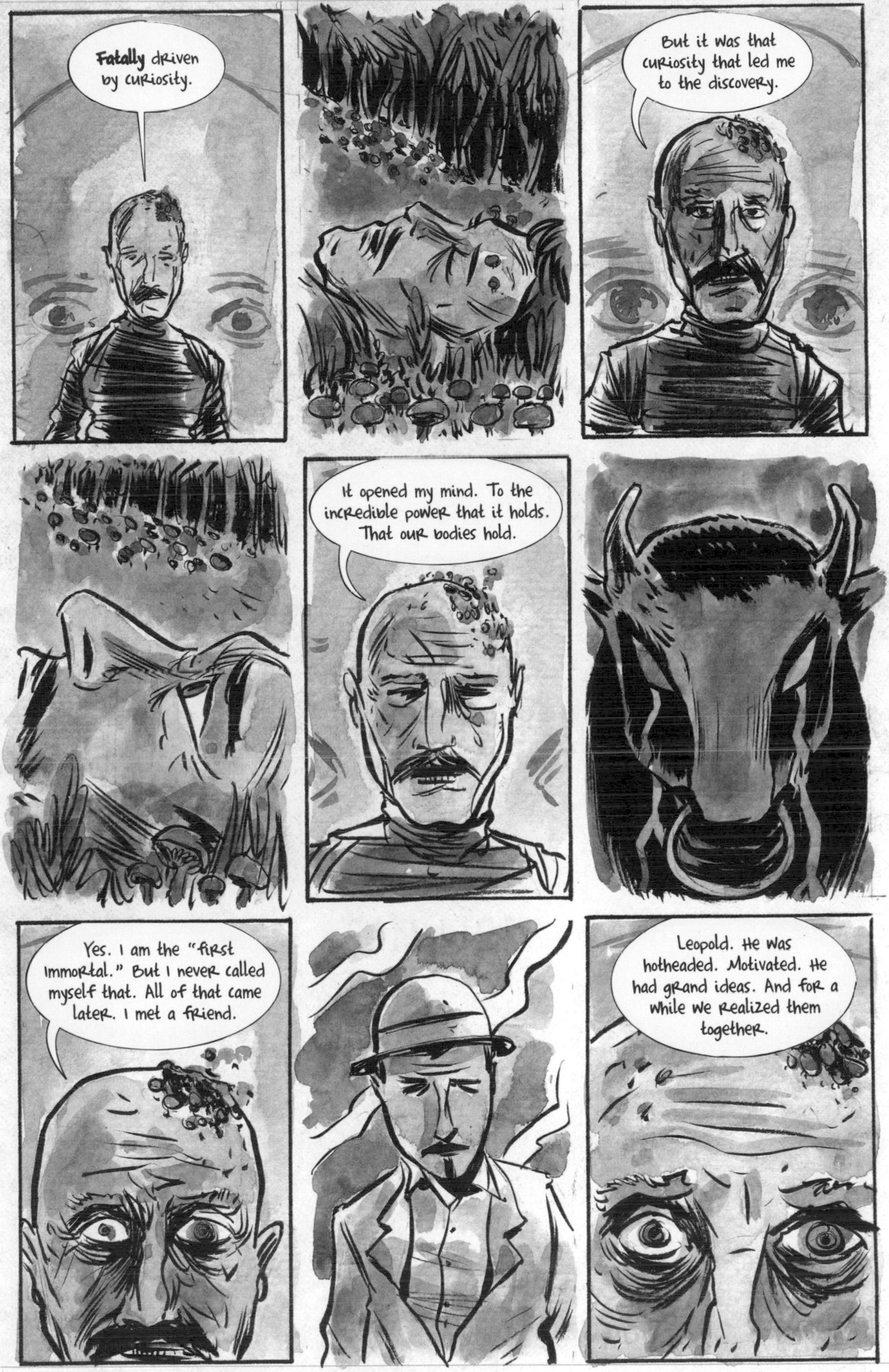
Fatally driven by curiosity.
But it was that curiosity that led me to the discovery.
It opened my mind. To the incredible power that it holds. That our bodies hold.
Yes. I am the "first immortal." But I never called myself that. All of that came later. I met a friend.
Leopold. He was hotheaded. Motivated. He had grand ideas. And for a while we realized them together.

MIND MGMT FIELD GUIDE. 26.19. Pay particular attention to the speech patterns of enemy and potential enemy agents.

MIND MGMT FIELD GUIDE. 26.20. Subliminal patterns of speech are hazardous. Take every opportunity to interrupt agents suspected of embedding patterns in their speech.

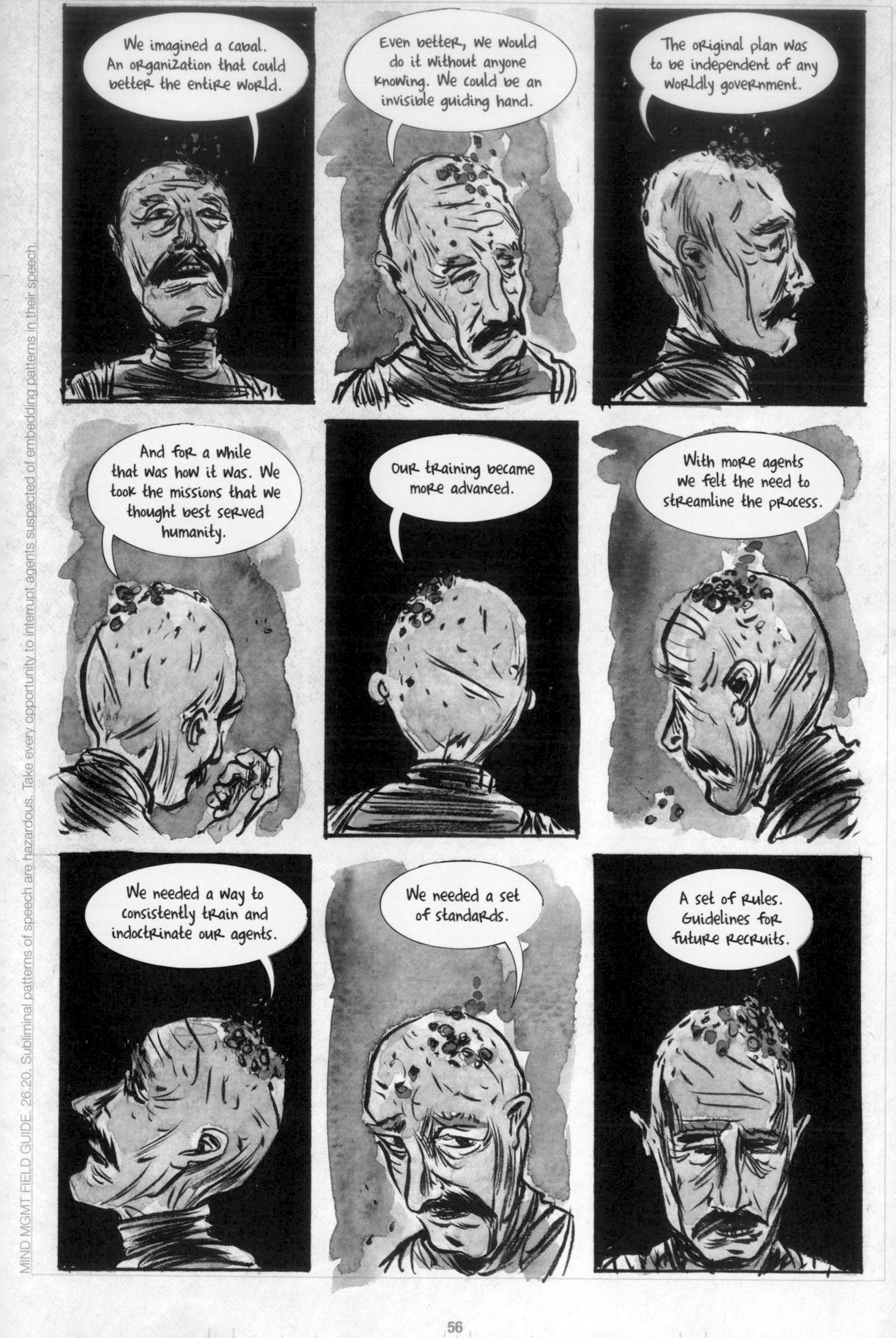
We imagined a cabal. An organization that could better the entire world.
Even better, we would do it without anyone knowing. We could be an invisible guiding hand.
The original plan was to be independent of any worldly government.
And for a while that was how it was. We took the missions that we thought best served humanity.
Our training became more advanced.
With more agents we felt the need to streamline the process.
We needed a way to consistently train and indoctrinate our agents.
We needed a set of standards.
A set of rules. Guidelines for future recruits.

WHEN FILING REPORT ALL ESSENTIAL DETAILS MUST FALL WITHIN THIS SOLID "LIVE AREA" BOX. THIS IS THE BORDER FOR A STANDARD, NON-BLEED FIELD REPORT

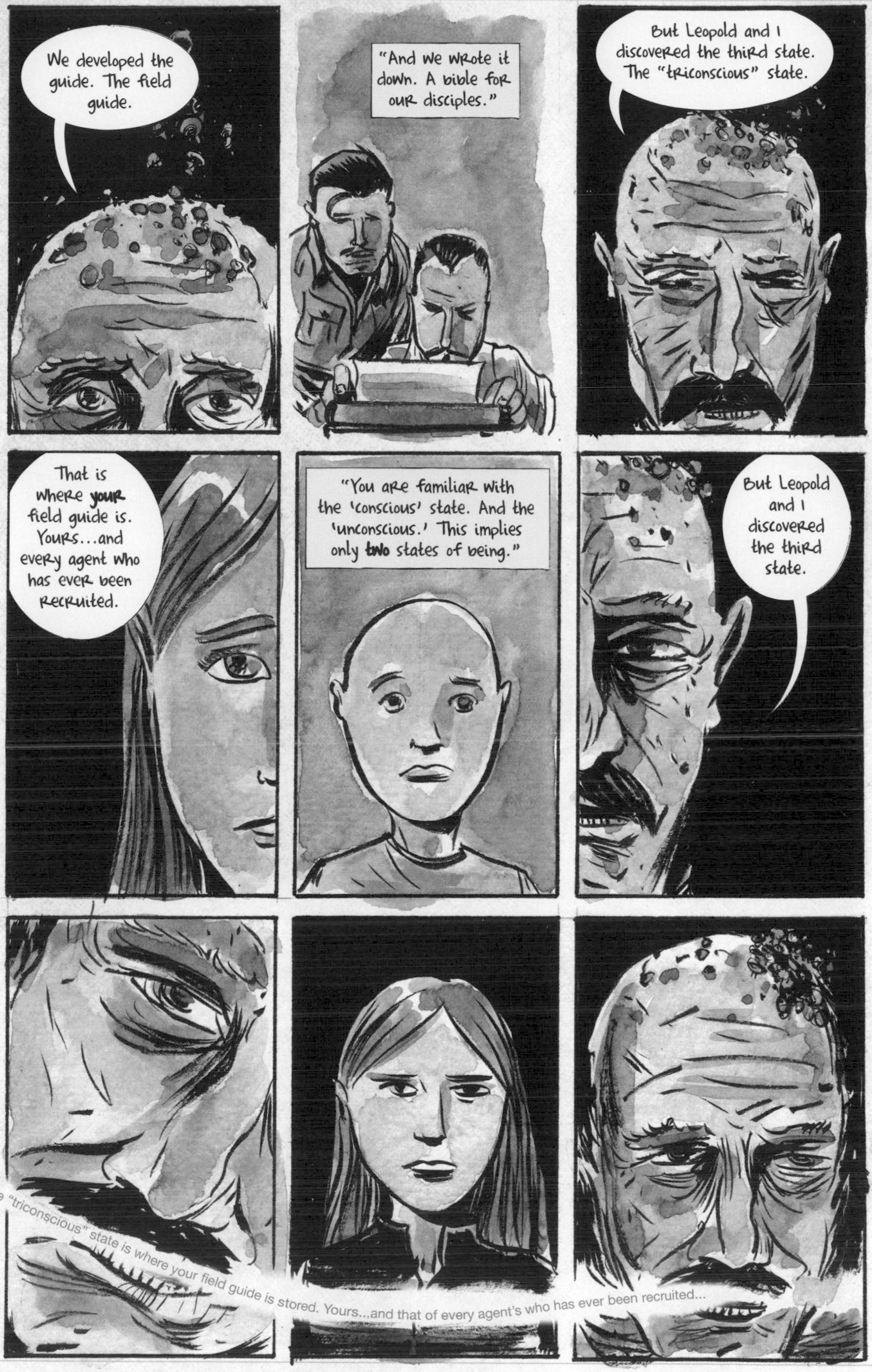
We developed the guide. The field guide.
"And we wrote it down. A bible for our disciples."
But Leopold and I discovered the third state. The "triconscious" state.
That is where your field guide is. Yours...and every agent who has ever been recruited.
"You are familiar with the 'conscious' state. And the 'unconscious.' This implies only two states of being."
But Leopold and I discovered the third state.
The "triconscious" state is where your field guide is stored. Yours...and that of every agent's who has ever been recruited...

MIND MGMT FIELD GUIDE. 26.21. Coded speech patterns are able to interrupt the triconscious state.

WHEN FILING REPORT ALL ESSENTIAL DETAILS MUST FALL WITHIN THIS SOLID "LIVE AREA" BOX. THIS IS THE BORDER FOR A STANDARD, NON-BLEED FIELD REPORT

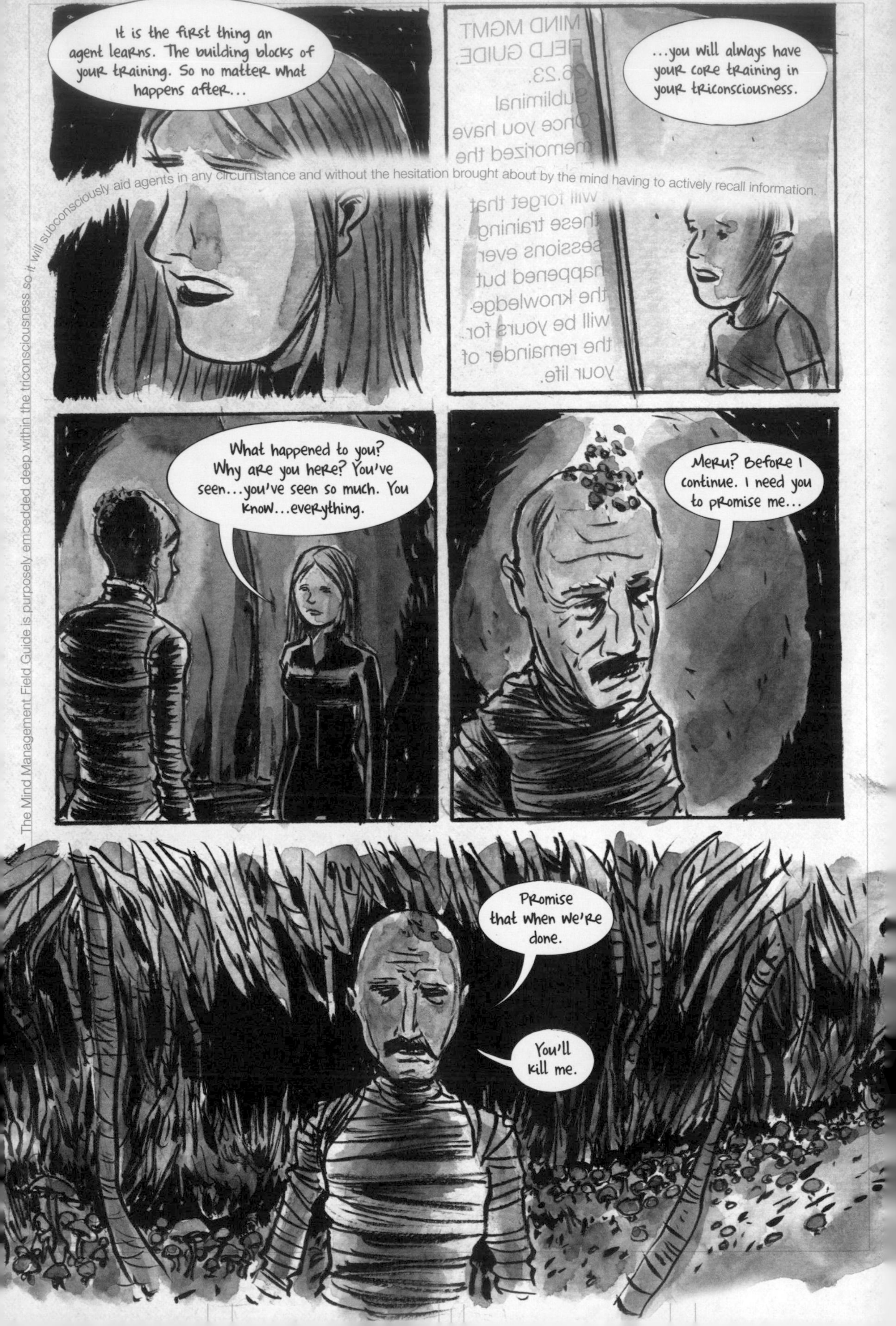
It is the first thing an agent learns. The building blocks of your training. So no matter what happens after...
MIND MGMT FIELD GUIDE 26.23. Subliminal Once you have memorized the
will forget that these training sessions ever happened but the knowledge will be yours for the remainder of your life.
...you will always have your core training in your triconsciousness.
What happened to you? Why are you here? You've seen...you've seen so much. You know...everything.
Meru? Before I continue. I need you to promise me...
Promise that when we're done.
You'll kill me.

The Mind Management Field Guide is purposely embedded deep within the triconsciousness so it will subconsciously aid agents in any circumstance and without the hesitation brought about by the mind having to actively recall information.

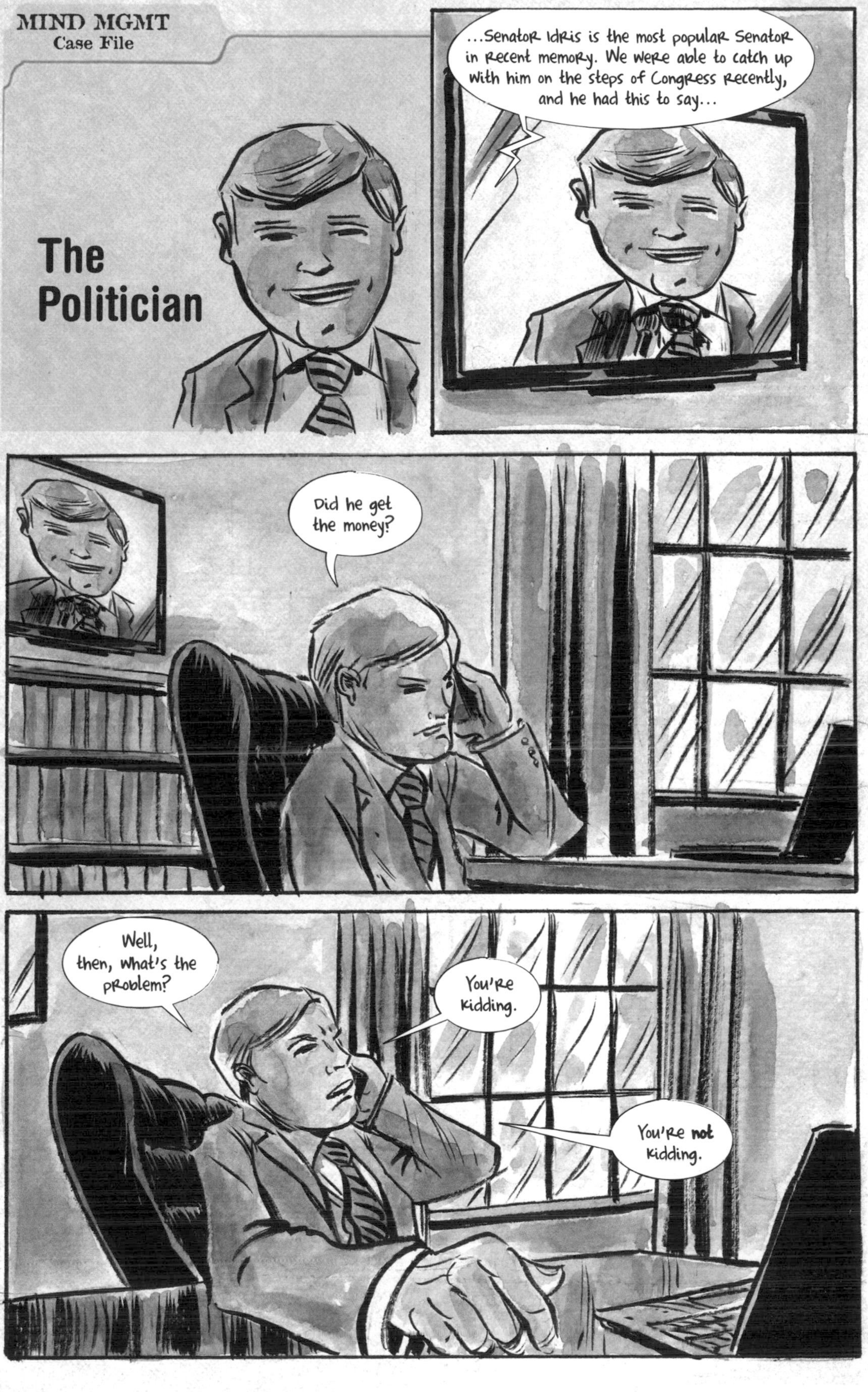
MIND MGMT
Case File
The Politician
...Senator Idris is the most popular Senator in recent memory. We were able to catch up with him on the steps of Congress recently, and he had this to say...
Did he get the money?
Well, then, what's the problem?
You're kidding.
You're **not** kidding.

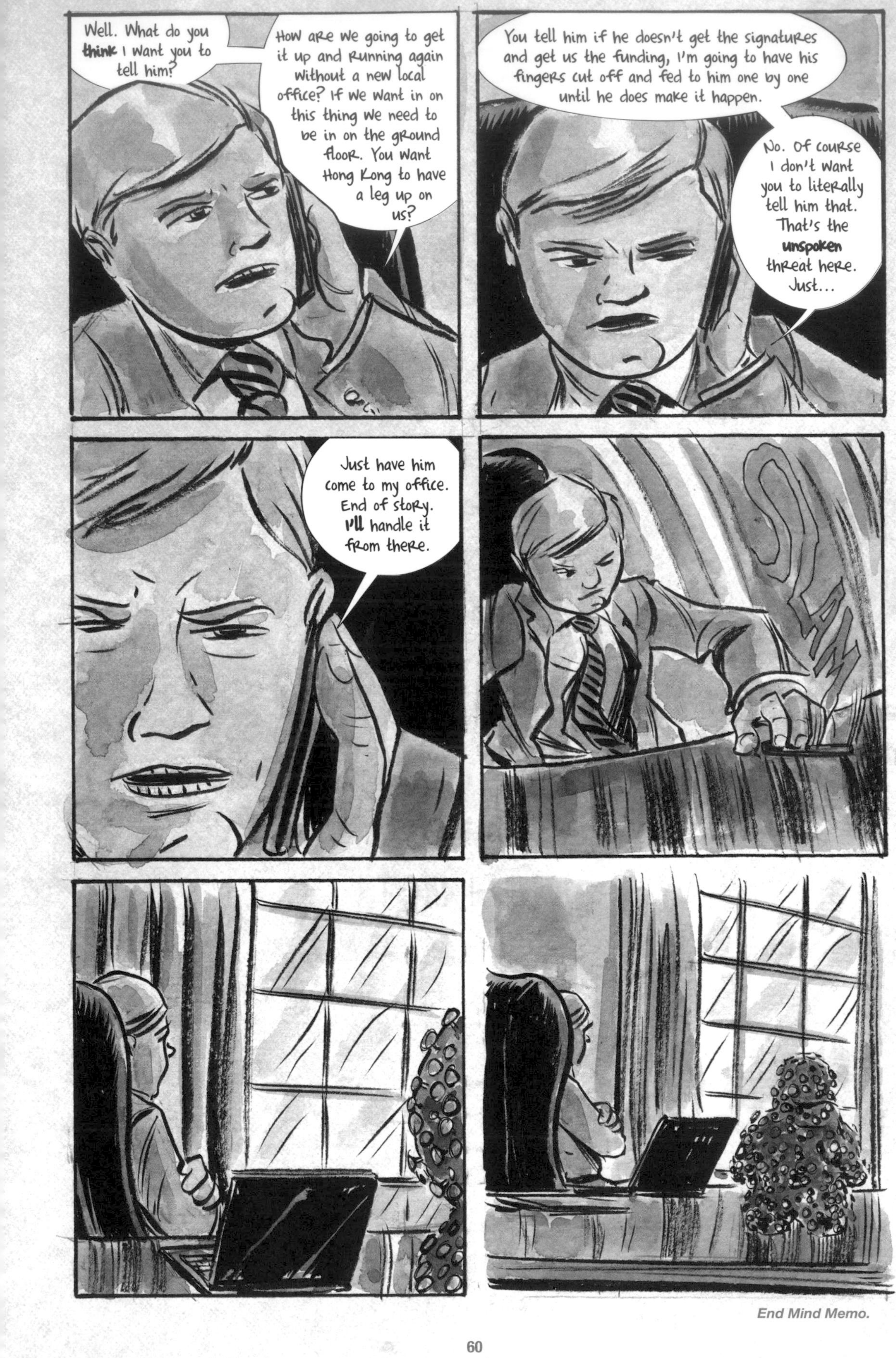
Well. What do you think I want you to tell him?
How are we going to get it up and running again without a new local office? If we want in on this thing we need to be in on the ground floor. You want Hong Kong to have a leg up on us?
You tell him if he doesn't get the signatures and get us the funding, I'm going to have his fingers cut off and fed to him one by one until he does make it happen.
No. Of course I don't want you to literally tell him that. That's the unspoken threat here. Just...
Just have him come to my office. End of story. I'll handle it from there.
SLAM

End Mind Memo.

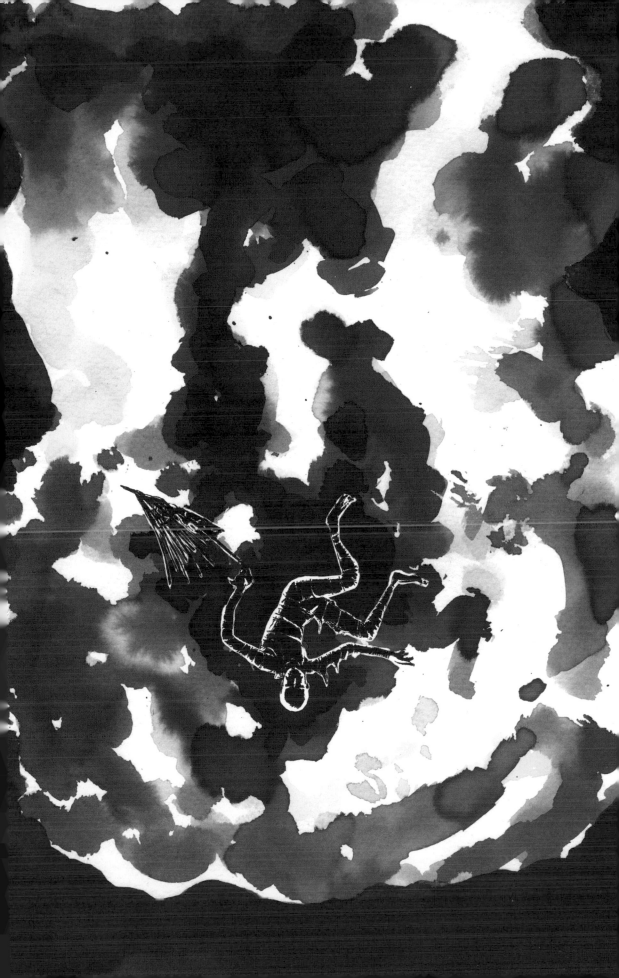

27

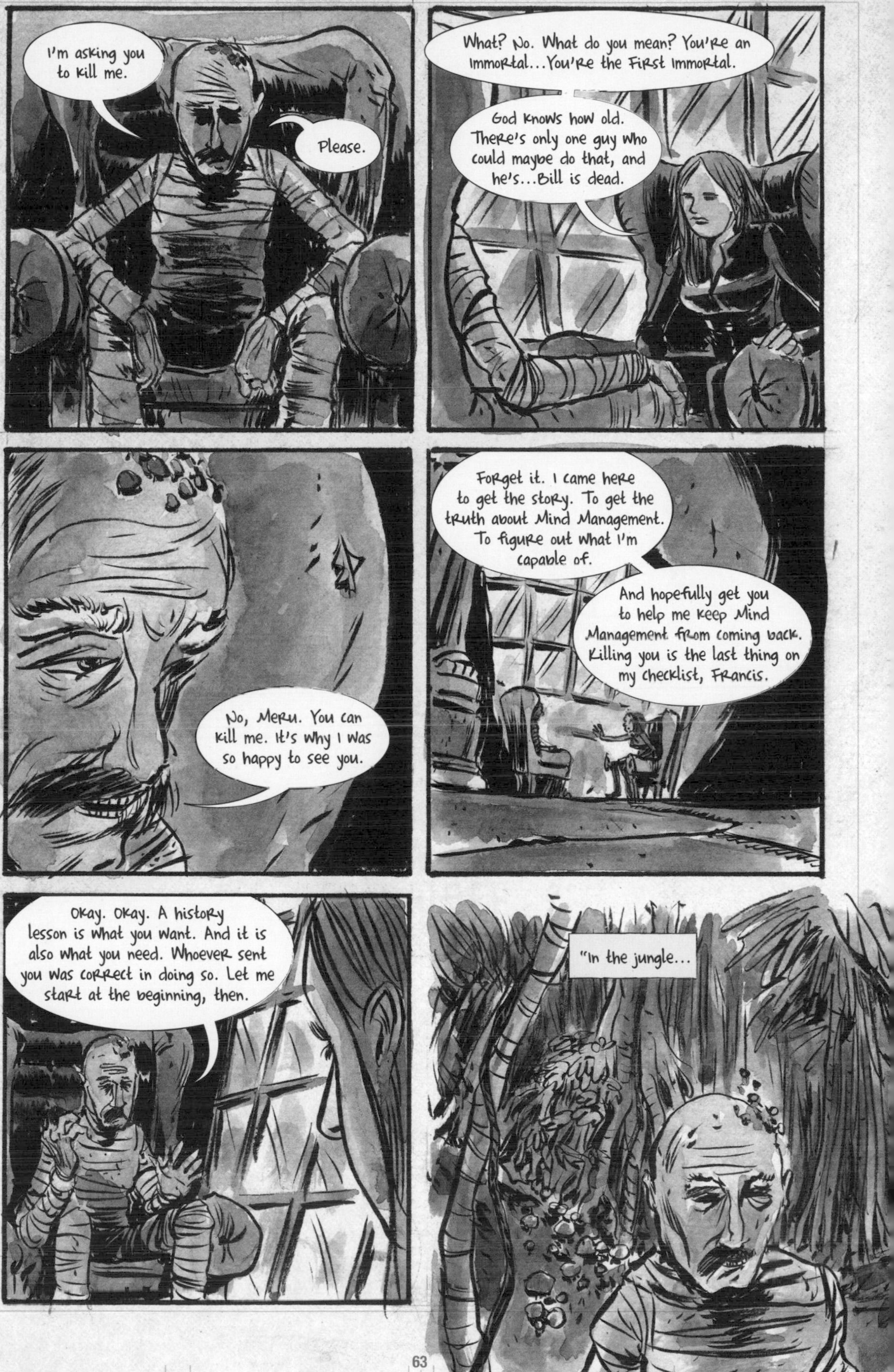
I'm asking you to kill me.
Please.
What? No. What do you mean? You're an immortal... You're the First Immortal.
God knows how old. There's only one guy who could maybe do that, and he's... Bill is dead.
No, Meru. You can kill me. It's why I was so happy to see you.
Forget it. I came here to get the story. To get the truth about Mind Management. To figure out what I'm capable of.
And hopefully get you to help me keep Mind Management from coming back. Killing you is the last thing on my checklist, Francis.
Okay. Okay. A history lesson is what you want. And it is also what you need. Whoever sent you was correct in doing so. Let me start at the beginning, then.
"In the jungle...

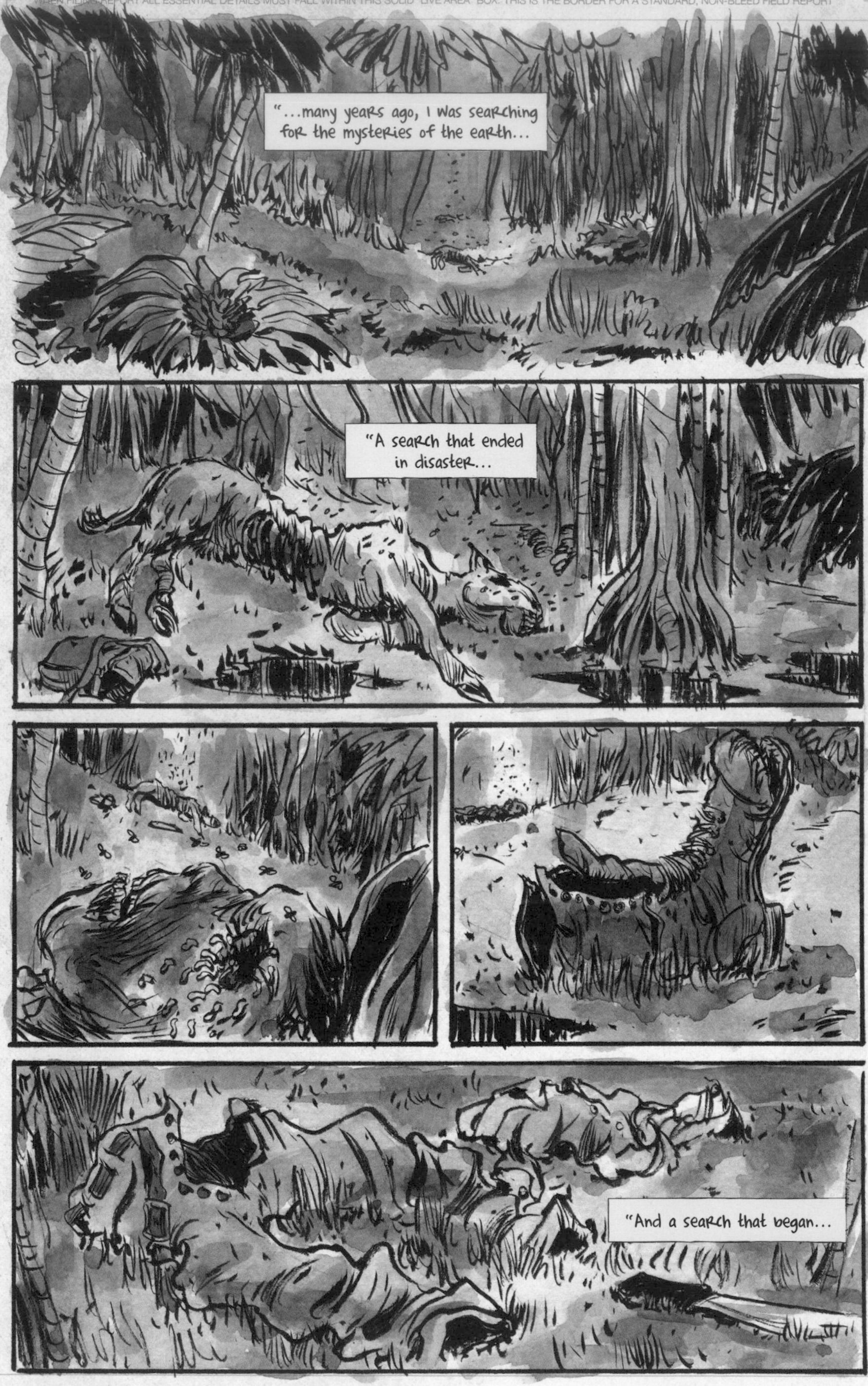
"...many years ago, I was searching for the mysteries of the earth...
"A search that ended in disaster...
"And a search that began...

MIND MGMT FIELD GUIDE 27.2. Once inside the hypno-report, be sure to start slowly with simple images to build the time and place of the reality being described.

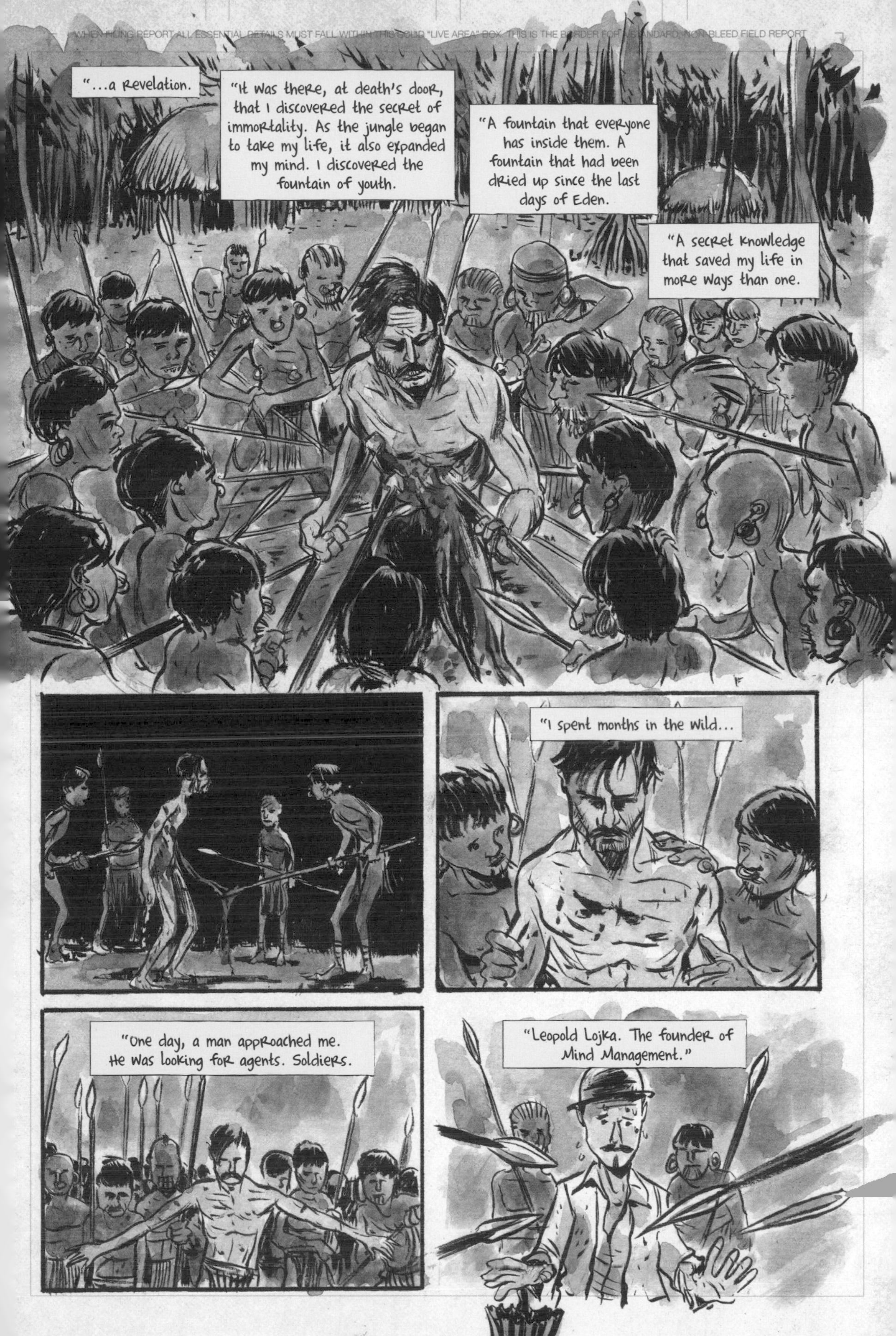
"...a Revelation.
"It was there, at death's door, that I discovered the secret of immortality. As the jungle began to take my life, it also expanded my mind. I discovered the fountain of youth.
"A fountain that everyone has inside them. A fountain that had been dried up since the last days of Eden.
"A secret knowledge that saved my life in more ways than one.
"I spent months in the wild...
"One day, a man approached me. He was looking for agents. Soldiers.
"Leopold Lojka. The founder of Mind Management."

WHEN FILING REPORT ALL ESSENTIAL DETAILS MUST FALL WITHIN THIS SOLID "LIVE AREA" BOX. THIS IS THE BORDER FOR A STANDARD, NON-BLEED FIELD REPORT

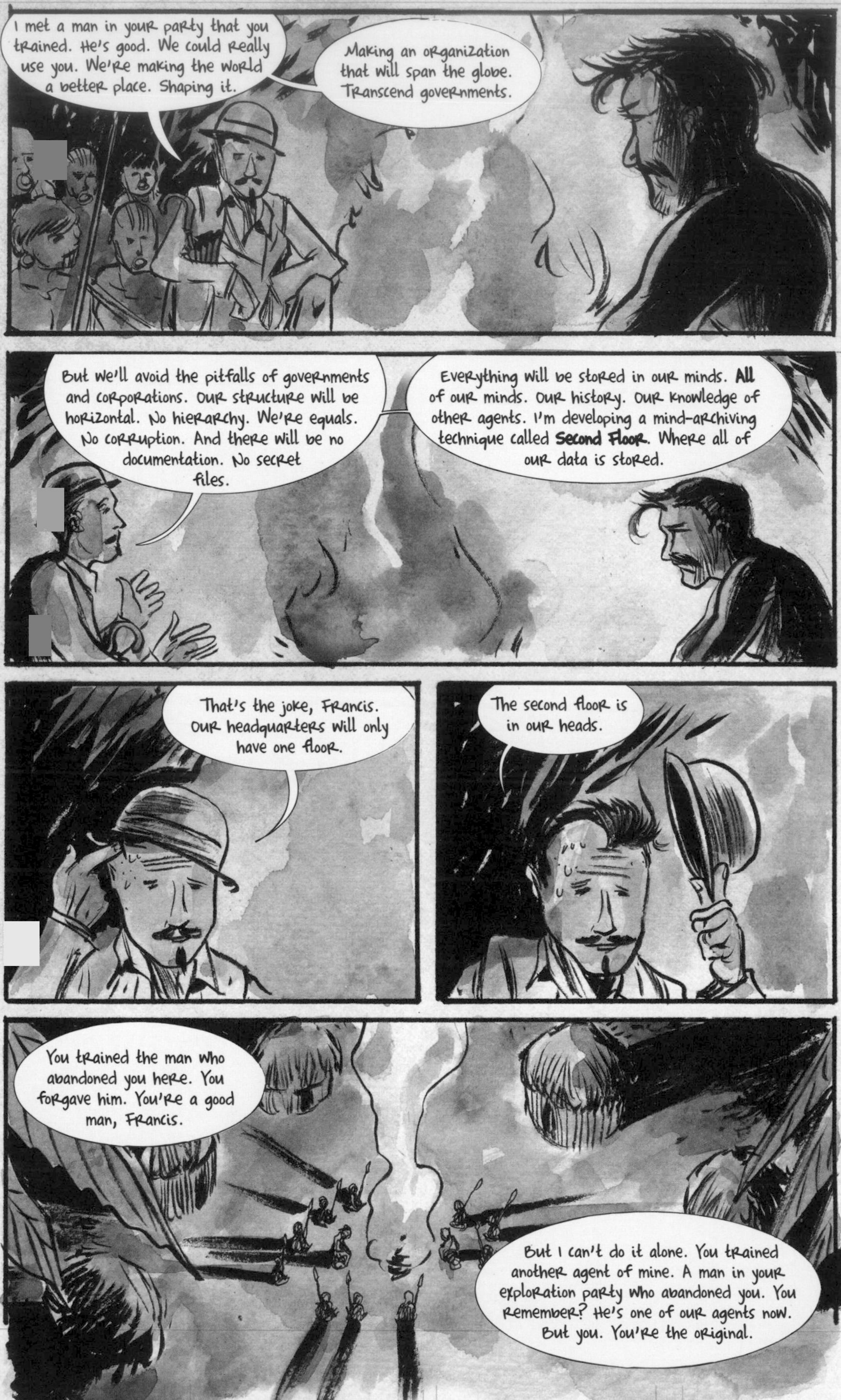
I met a man in your party that you trained. He's good. We could really use you. We're making the world a better place. Shaping it.
Making an organization that will span the globe. Transcend governments.
But we'll avoid the pitfalls of governments and corporations. Our structure will be horizontal. No hierarchy. We're equals. No corruption. And there will be no documentation. No secret files.
Everything will be stored in our minds. **All** of our minds. Our history. Our knowledge of other agents. I'm developing a mind-archiving technique called **Second Floor**. Where all of our data is stored.
That's the joke, Francis. Our headquarters will only have one floor.
The second floor is in our heads.
You trained the man who abandoned you here. You forgave him. You're a good man, Francis.
But I can't do it alone. You trained another agent of mine. A man in your exploration party who abandoned you. You remember? He's one of our agents now. But you. You're the original.

MIND MGMT FIELD GUIDE 27.4. It is essential that the agent filing the report also initiate a self-regulating hypno-script so that an impartial account of events can be given.

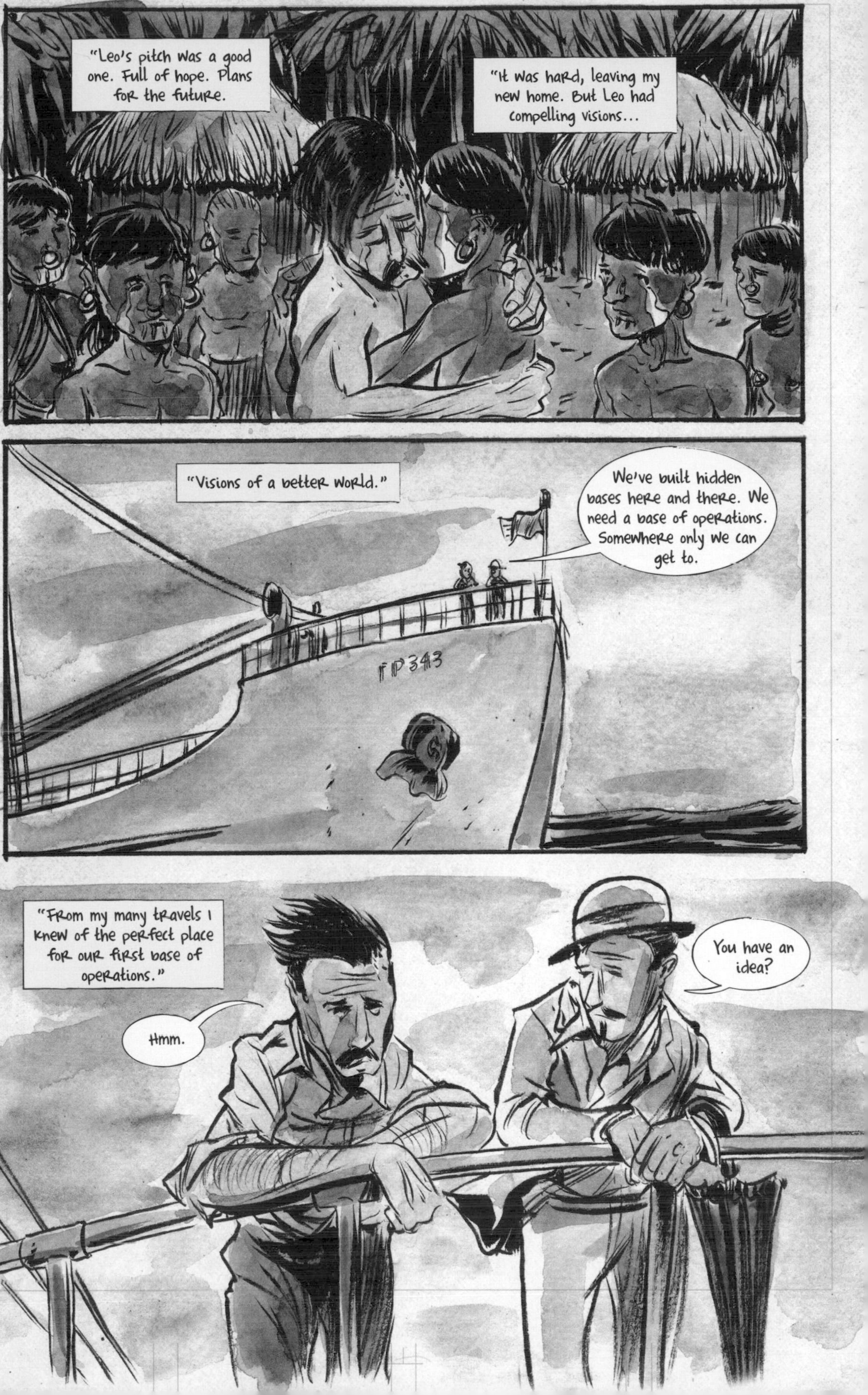
"Leo's pitch was a good one. Full of hope. Plans for the future.
"It was hard, leaving my new home. But Leo had compelling visions...
"Visions of a better world."
We've built hidden bases here and there. We need a base of operations. Somewhere only we can get to.
FP343
"From my many travels I knew of the perfect place for our first base of operations."
Hmm.
You have an idea?

WHEN FILING REPORT ALL ESSENTIAL DETAILS MUST FALL WITHIN THIS SOLID "LIVE AREA" BOX. THIS IS THE BORDER FOR A STANDARD, NON-BLEED FIELD REPORT

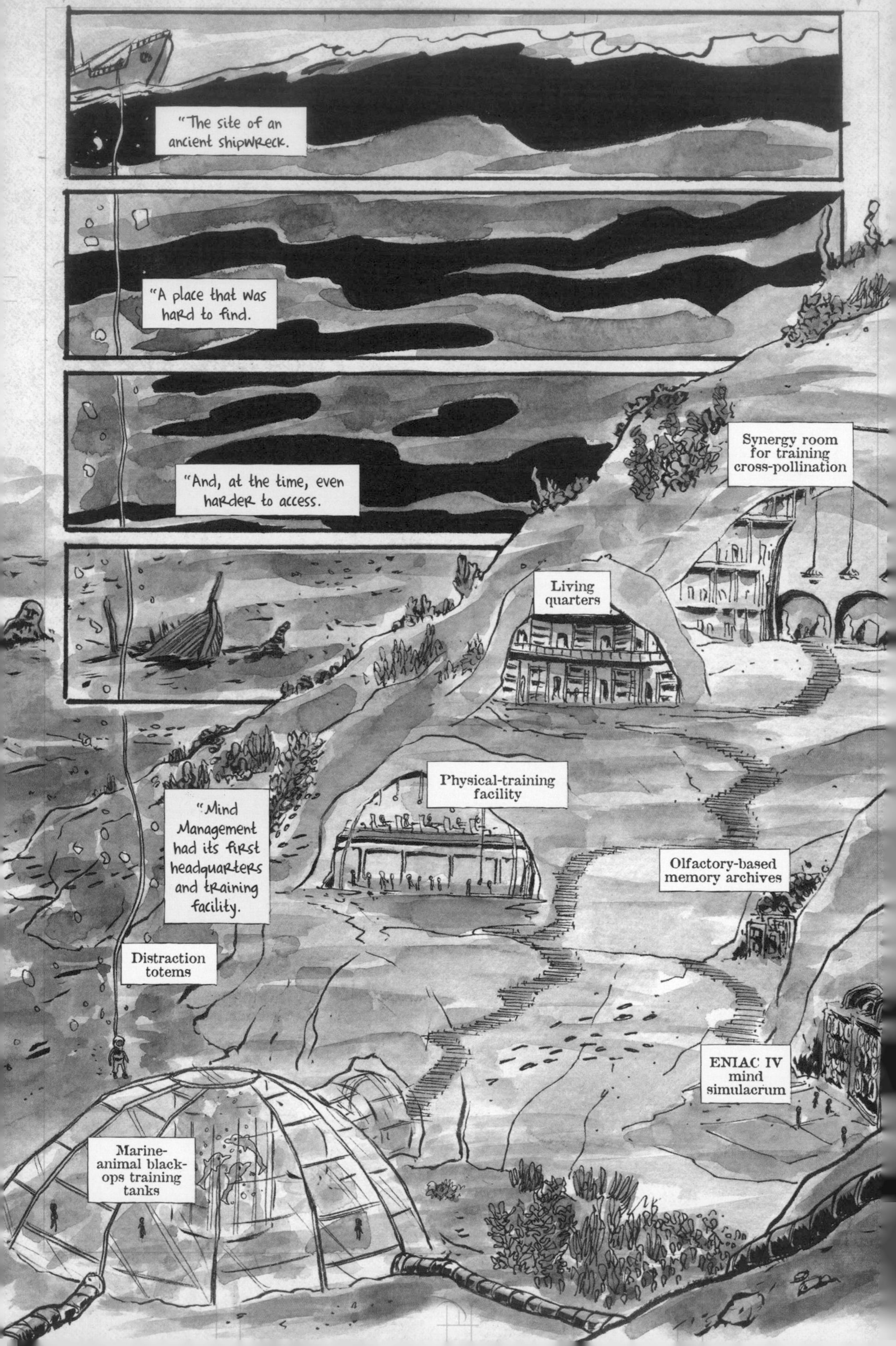
"The site of an ancient shipwreck.
"A place that was hard to find.
"And, at the time, even harder to access.
"Mind Management had its first headquarters and training facility.
Synergy room for training cross-pollination
Living quarters
Physical-training facility
Olfactory-based memory archives
Distraction totems
ENIAC IV mind simulacrum
Marine-animal black-ops training tanks

MIND MGMT FIELD GUIDE 2/7.7: While hypno-reports are generally considered impartial, exposure to outside elements within the backstory, such as instinctual incense, may cloud the veracity of a report.

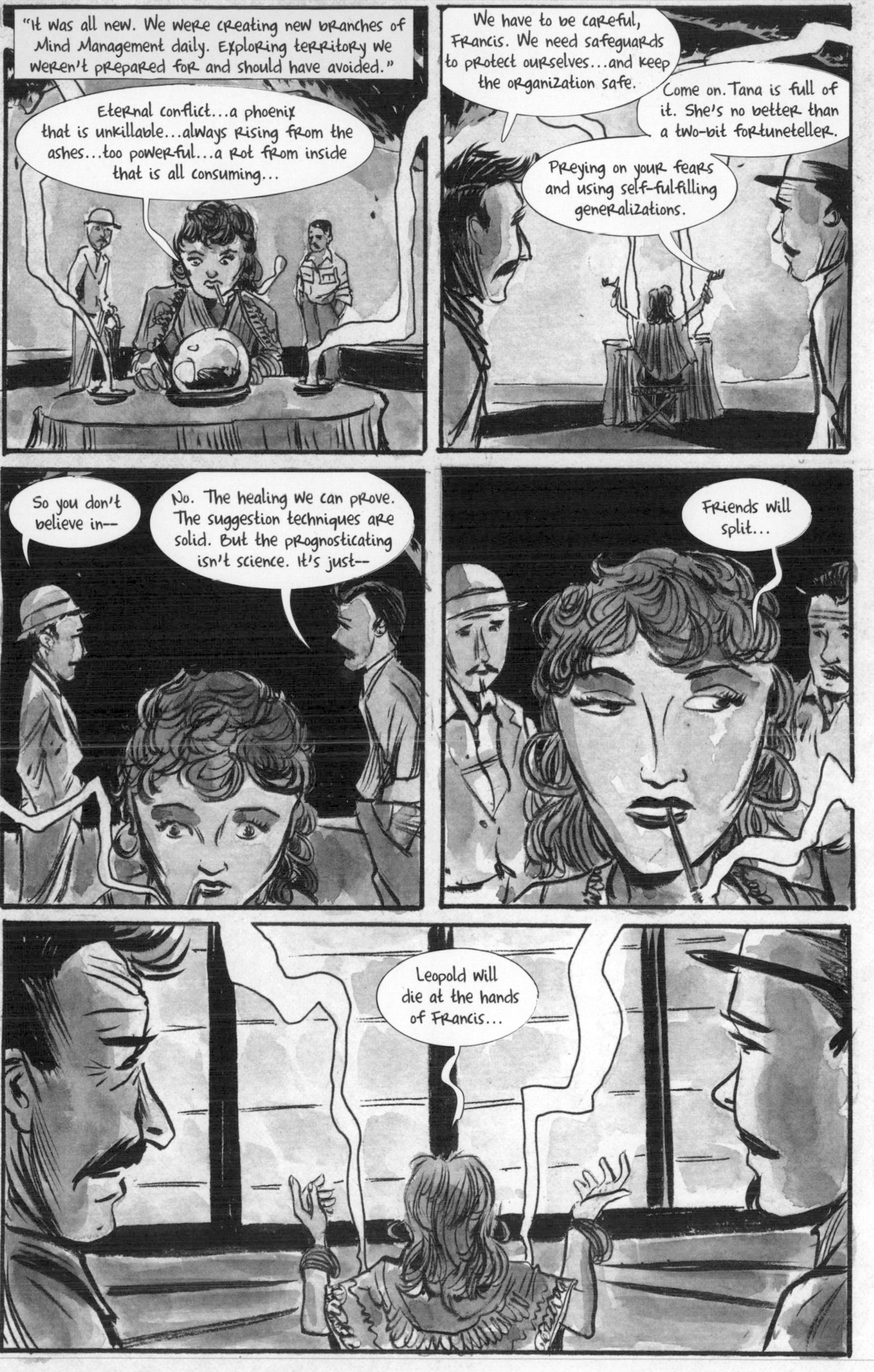
"It was all new. We were creating new branches of Mind Management daily. Exploring territory we weren't prepared for and should have avoided."
Eternal conflict...a phoenix that is unkillable...always rising from the ashes...too powerful...a rot from inside that is all consuming...
We have to be careful, Francis. We need safeguards to protect ourselves...and keep the organization safe.
Come on. Tana is full of it. She's no better than a two-bit fortuneteller.
Preying on your fears and using self-fulfilling generalizations.
So you don't believe in--
No. The healing we can prove. The suggestion techniques are solid. But the prognosticating isn't science. It's just--
Friends will split...
Leopold will die at the hands of Francis...

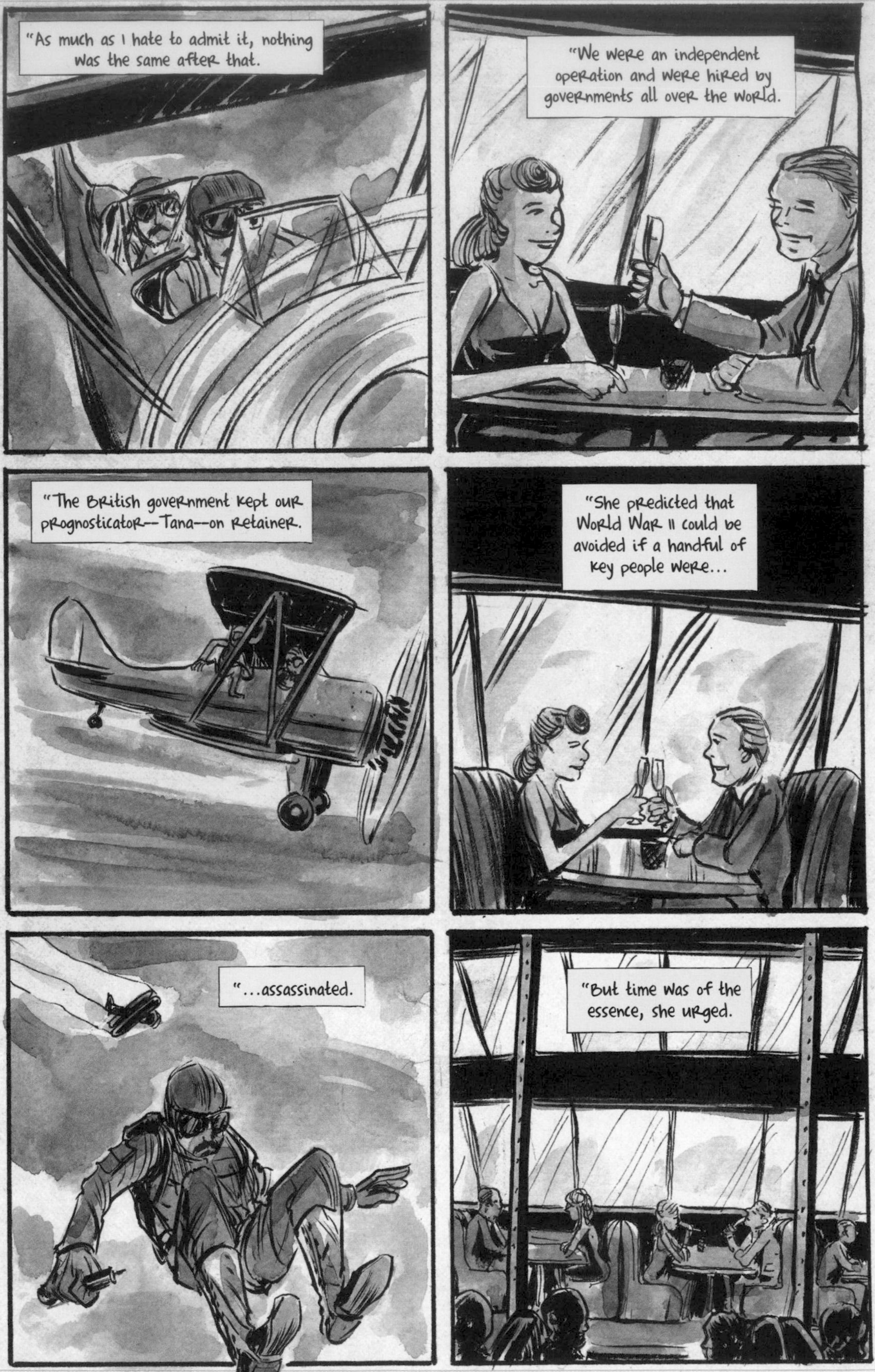
"As much as I hate to admit it, nothing was the same after that.
"We were an independent operation and were hired by governments all over the world.
"The British government kept our prognosticator--Tana--on retainer.
"She predicted that World War II could be avoided if a handful of key people were...
"...assassinated.
"But time was of the essence, she urged.

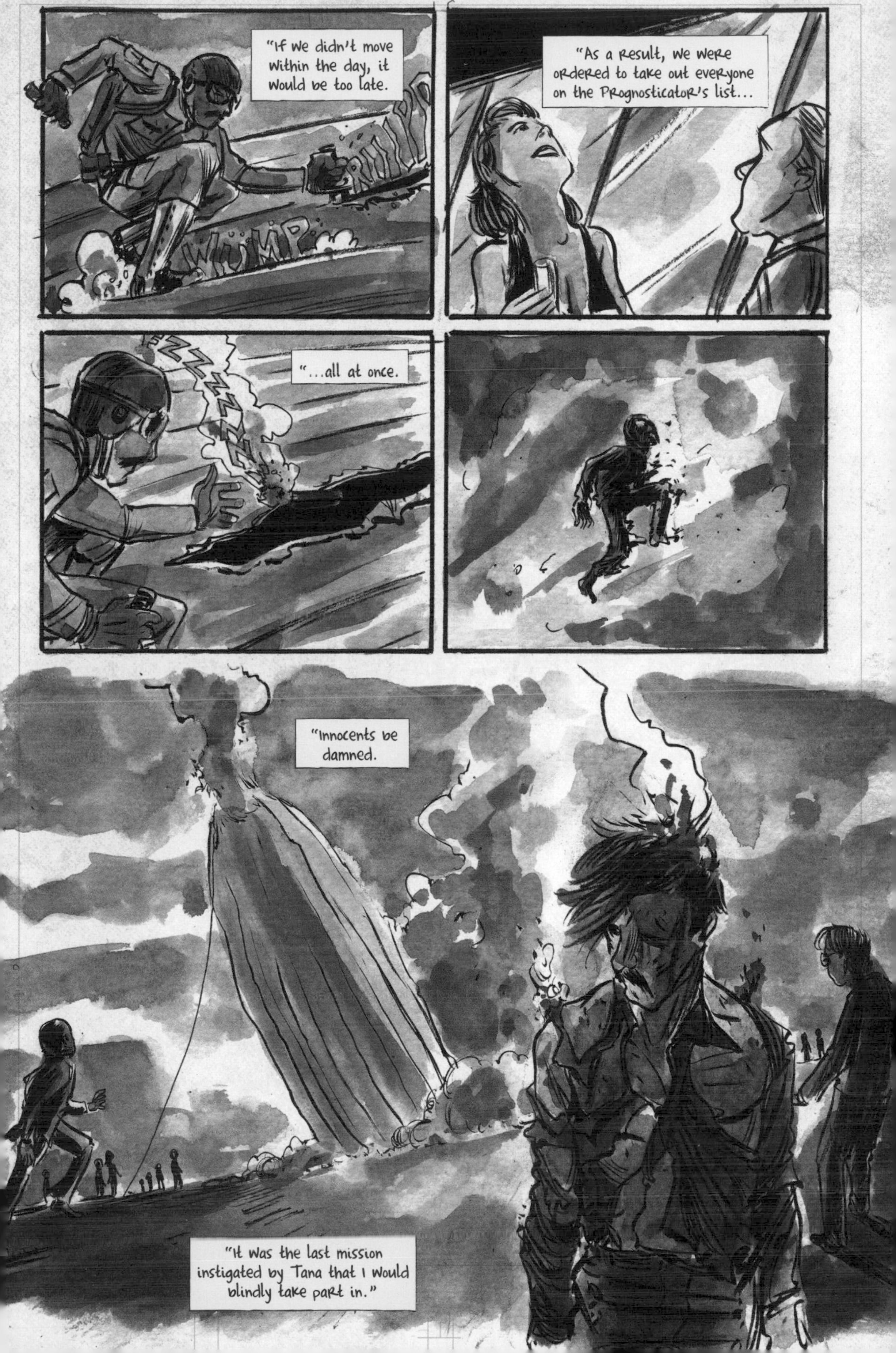
"If we didn't move within the day, it would be too late.
"As a result, we were ordered to take out everyone on the Prognosticator's list...
"...all at once.
"Innocents be damned.
"It was the last mission instigated by Tana that I would blindly take part in."

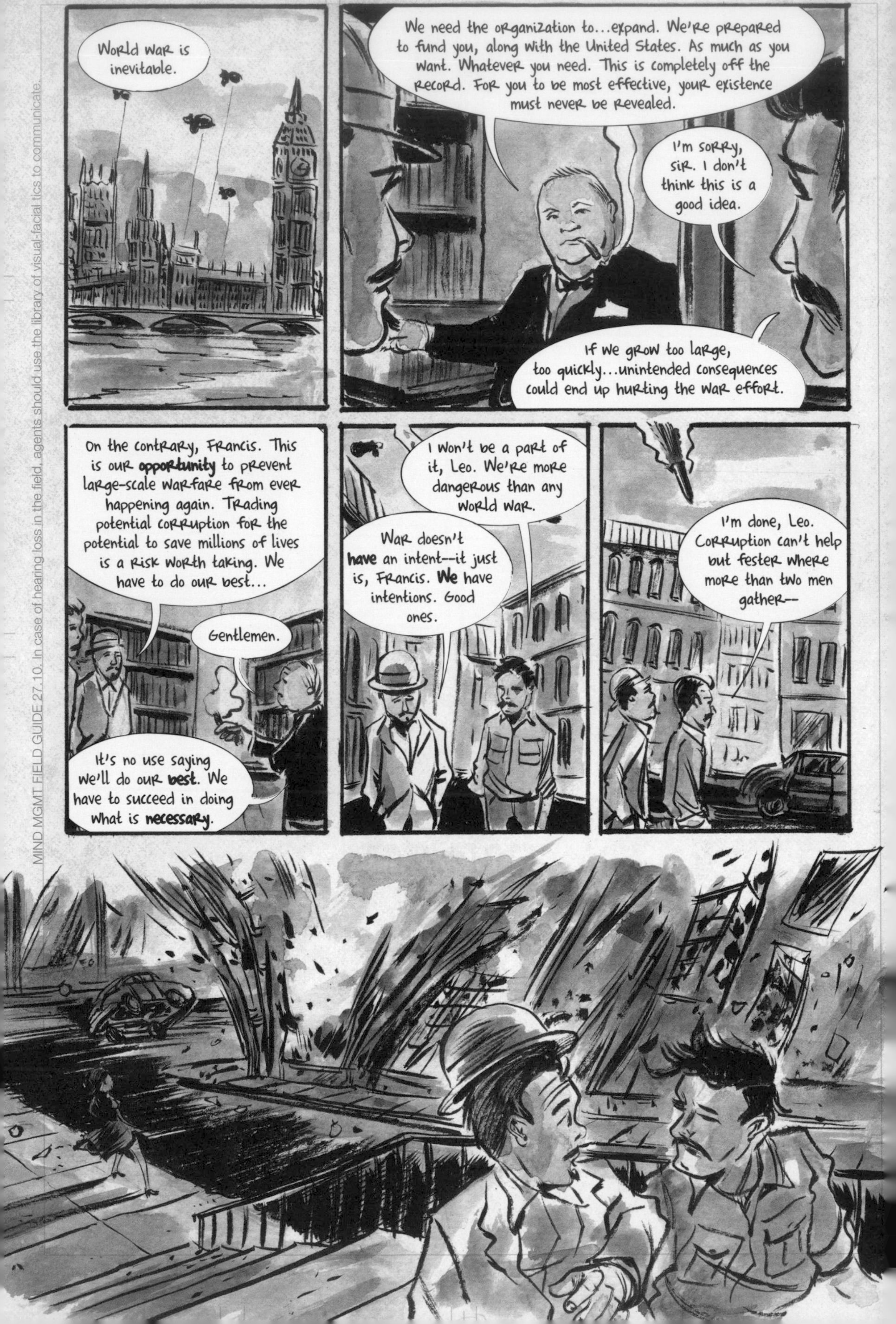
World war is inevitable.
We need the organization to...expand. We're prepared to fund you, along with the United States. As much as you want. Whatever you need. This is completely off the record. For you to be most effective, your existence must never be revealed.
I'm sorry, sir. I don't think this is a good idea.
If we grow too large, too quickly...unintended consequences could end up hurting the war effort.
On the contrary, Francis. This is our **opportunity** to prevent large-scale warfare from ever happening again. Trading potential corruption for the potential to save millions of lives is a risk worth taking. We have to do our best...
Gentlemen.
It's no use saying we'll do our **best**. We have to succeed in doing what is **necessary**.
I won't be a part of it, Leo. We're more dangerous than any world war.
War doesn't **have** an intent--it just is, Francis. **We** have intentions. Good ones.
I'm done, Leo. Corruption can't help but fester where more than two men gather--

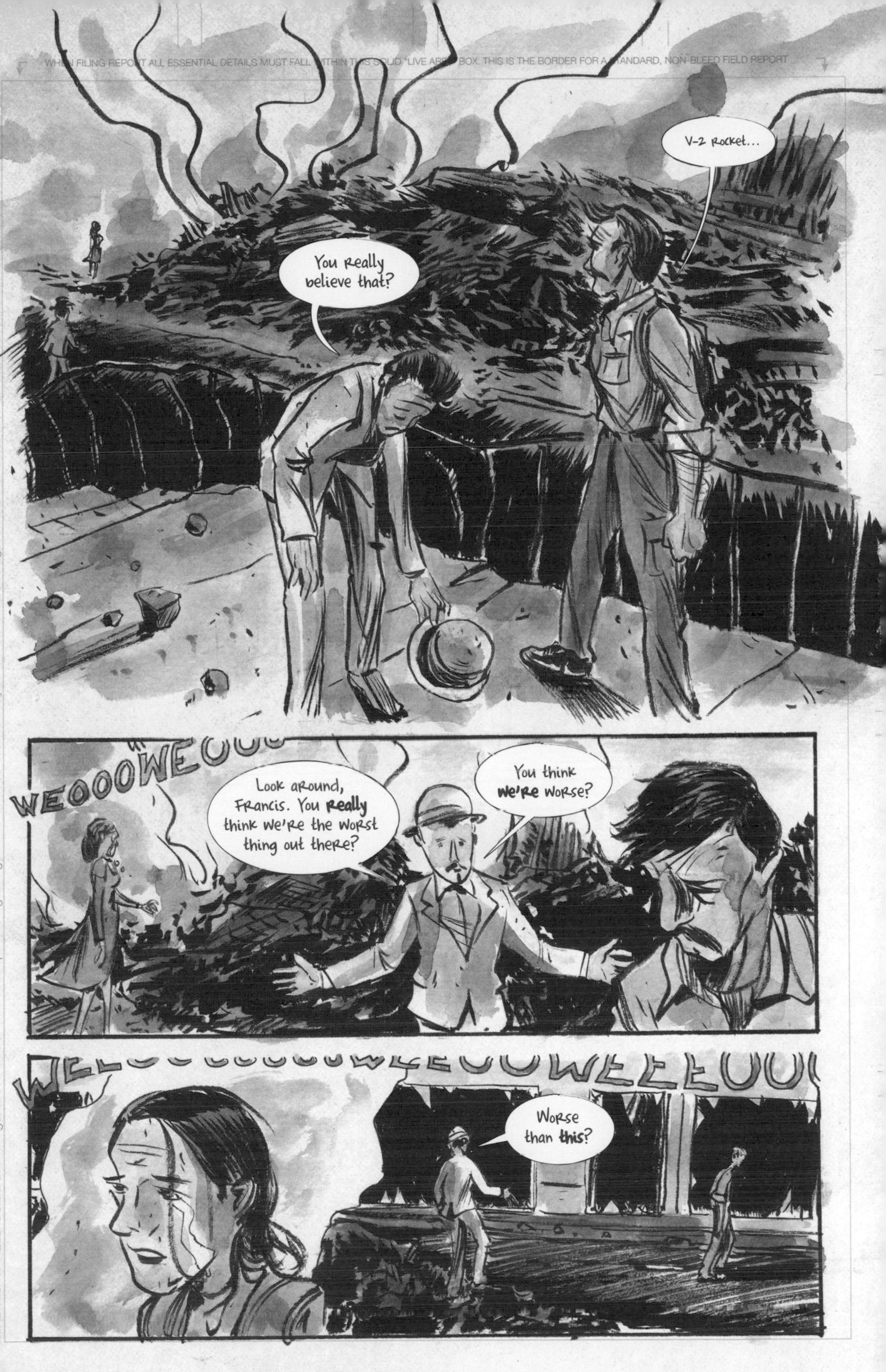
WHEN FILING REPORT ALL ESSENTIAL DETAILS MUST FALL WITHIN THIS SOLID "LIVE AREA" BOX. THIS IS THE BORDER FOR A STANDARD, NON-BLEED FIELD REPORT
V-2 Rocket...
You Really believe that?
WEOOOWE
Look around, Francis. You **Really** think we're the worst thing out there?
You think **we're** worse?
Worse than **this**?
MIND MGMT FIELD GUIDE 27.11. Agents in the field with moral qualms regarding missions should immediately seek Eraser counseling.

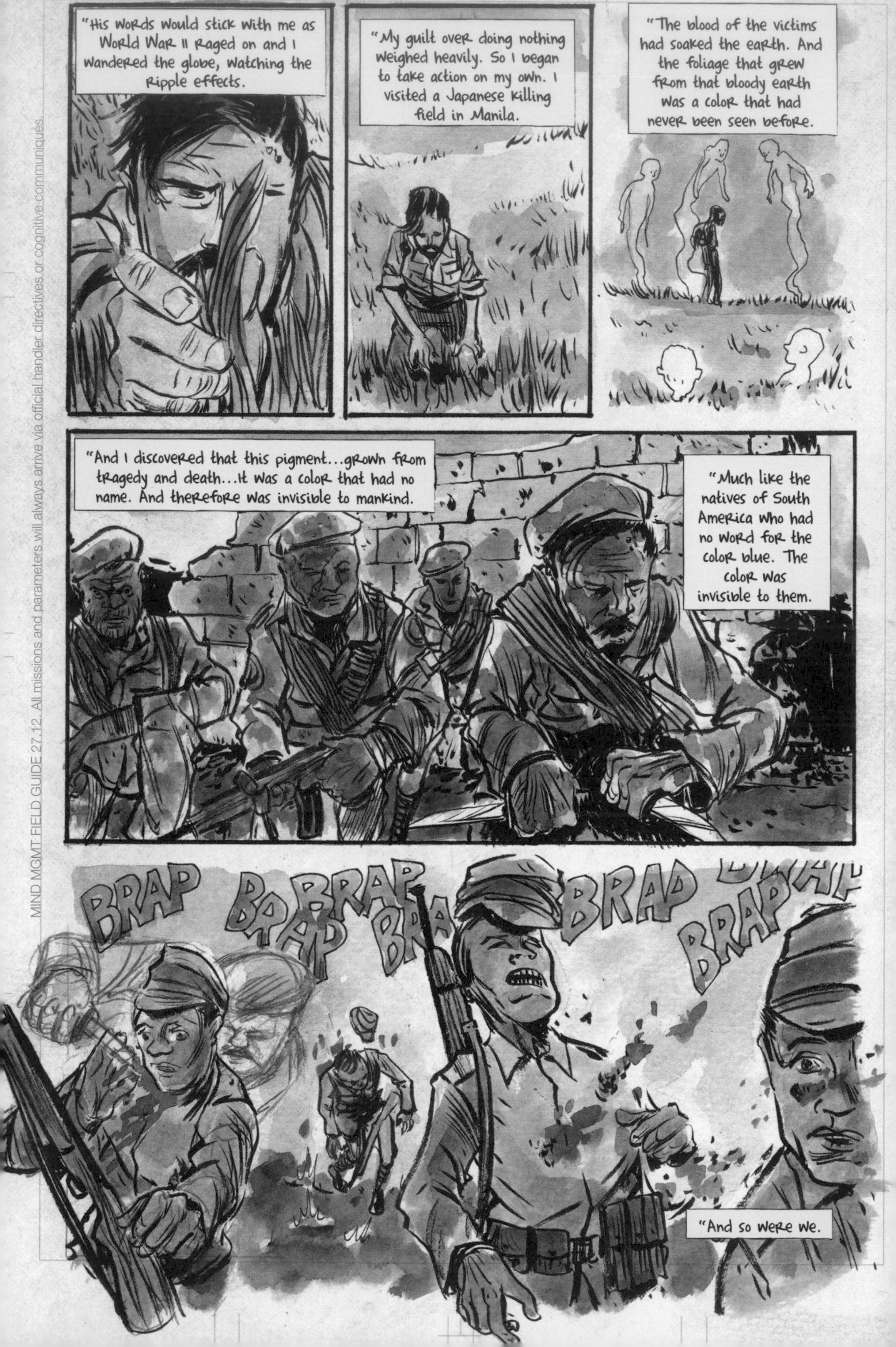
"His words would stick with me as World War II raged on and I wandered the globe, watching the ripple effects.
"My guilt over doing nothing weighed heavily. So I began to take action on my own. I visited a Japanese killing field in Manila.
"The blood of the victims had soaked the earth. And the foliage that grew from that bloody earth was a color that had never been seen before.
"And I discovered that this pigment...grown from tragedy and death...it was a color that had no name. And therefore was invisible to mankind.
"Much like the natives of South America who had no word for the color blue. The color was invisible to them.
BRAP
BRAP
BRAP
BRAP
BRA
BRAP
BRAP
"And so were we.

WHEN FILING REPORT ALL ESSENTIAL DETAILS MUST FALL WITHIN THIS SOLID "LIVE AREA" BOX. THIS IS THE BORDER FOR A STANDARD, NON-BLEED FIELD REPORT

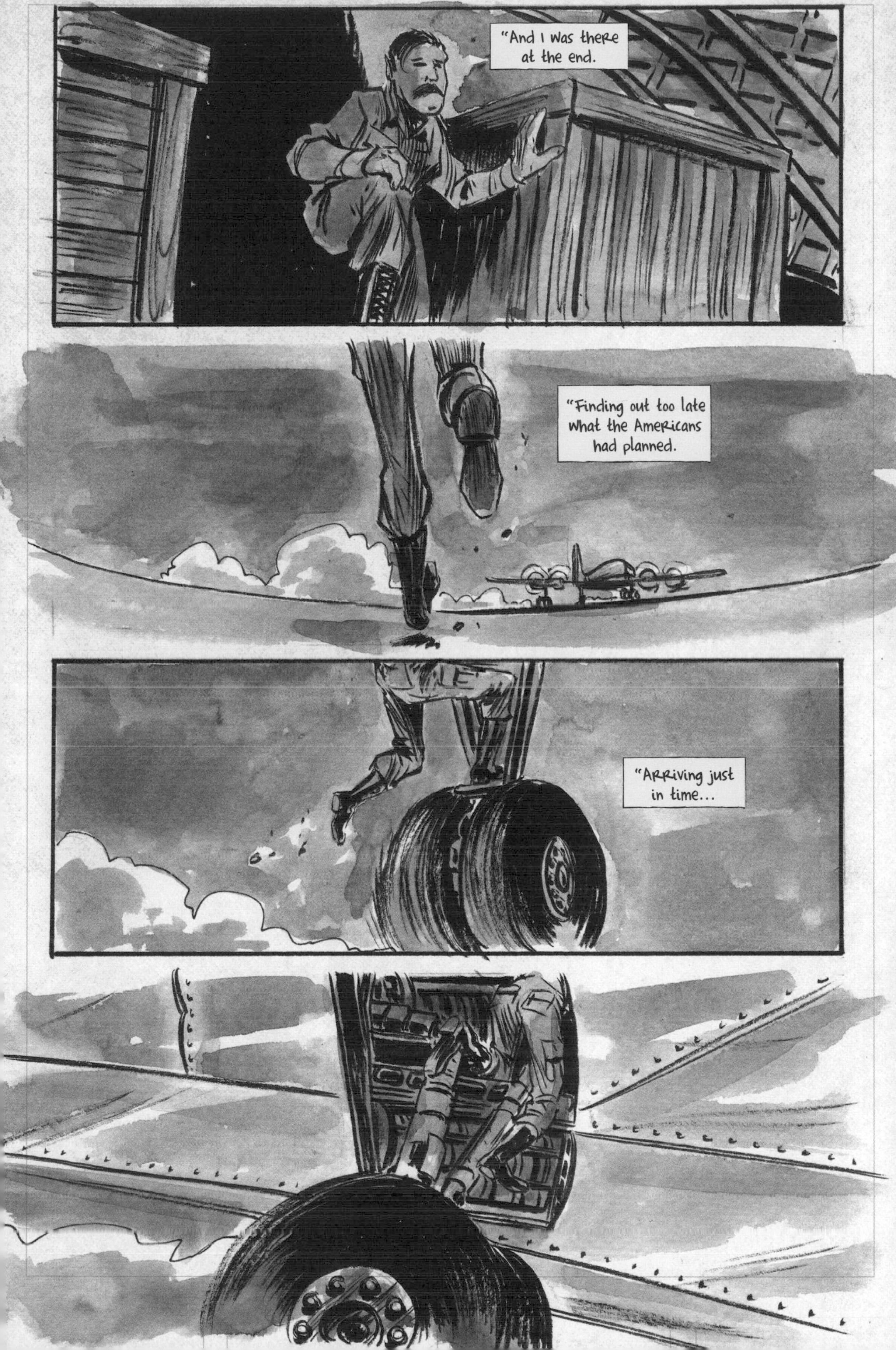

"And I was there at the end.
"Finding out too late what the Americans had planned.
"Arriving just in time...

WHEN FILING REPORT ALL ESSENTIAL DETAILS MUST FALL WITHIN THIS SOLID "LIVE AREA" BOX. THIS IS THE BORDER FOR A STANDARD, NON-BLEED FIELD REPORT

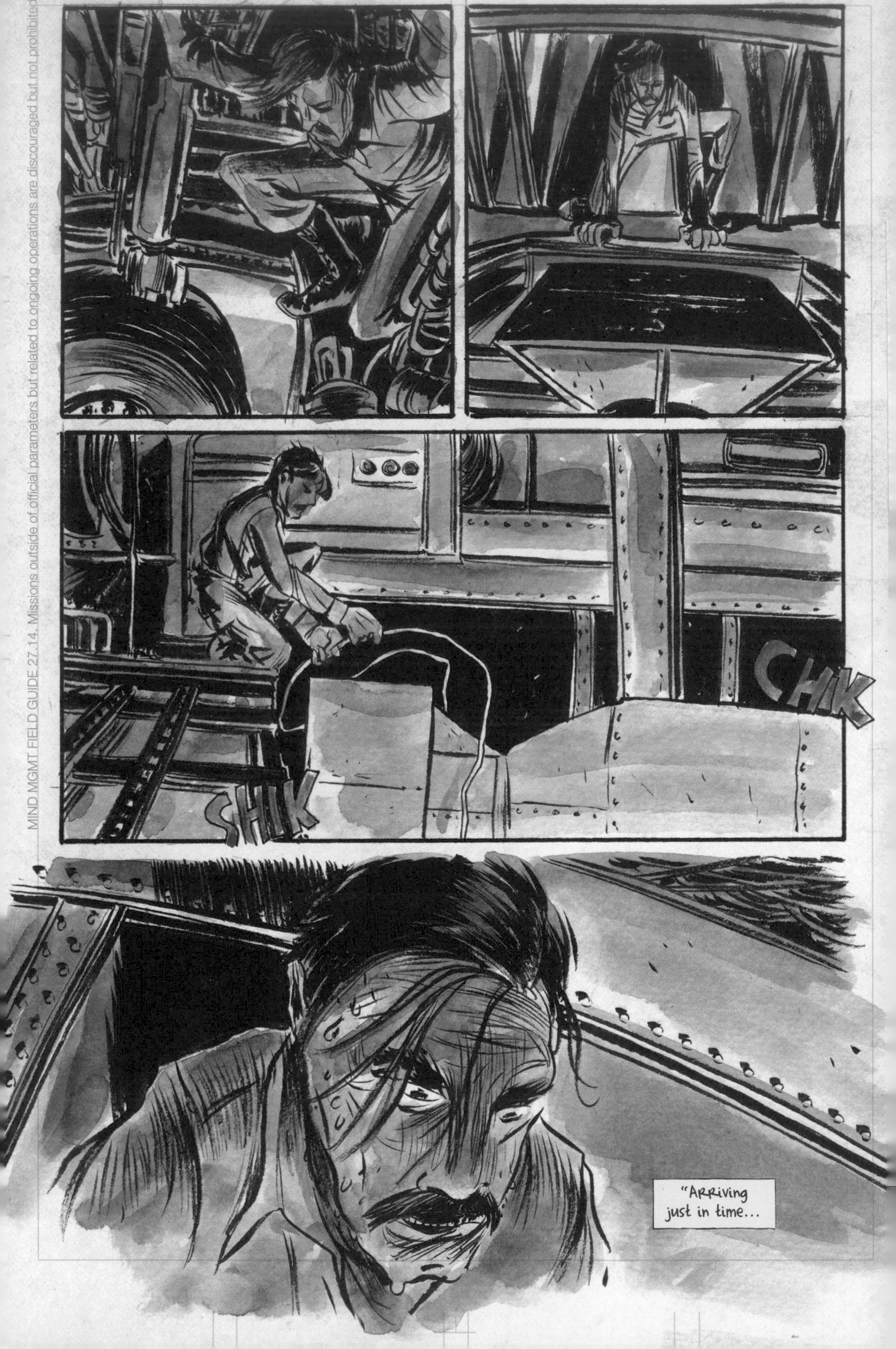

CHK
SHK
"ARRIVING just in time...

MIND MGMT FIELD GUIDE 27.14. Missions outside of official parameters but related to ongoing operations are discouraged but not prohibited.

MIND MGMT FIELD GUIDE 27.15. If outside-parameter missions are undertaken, they should always be done in pairs.

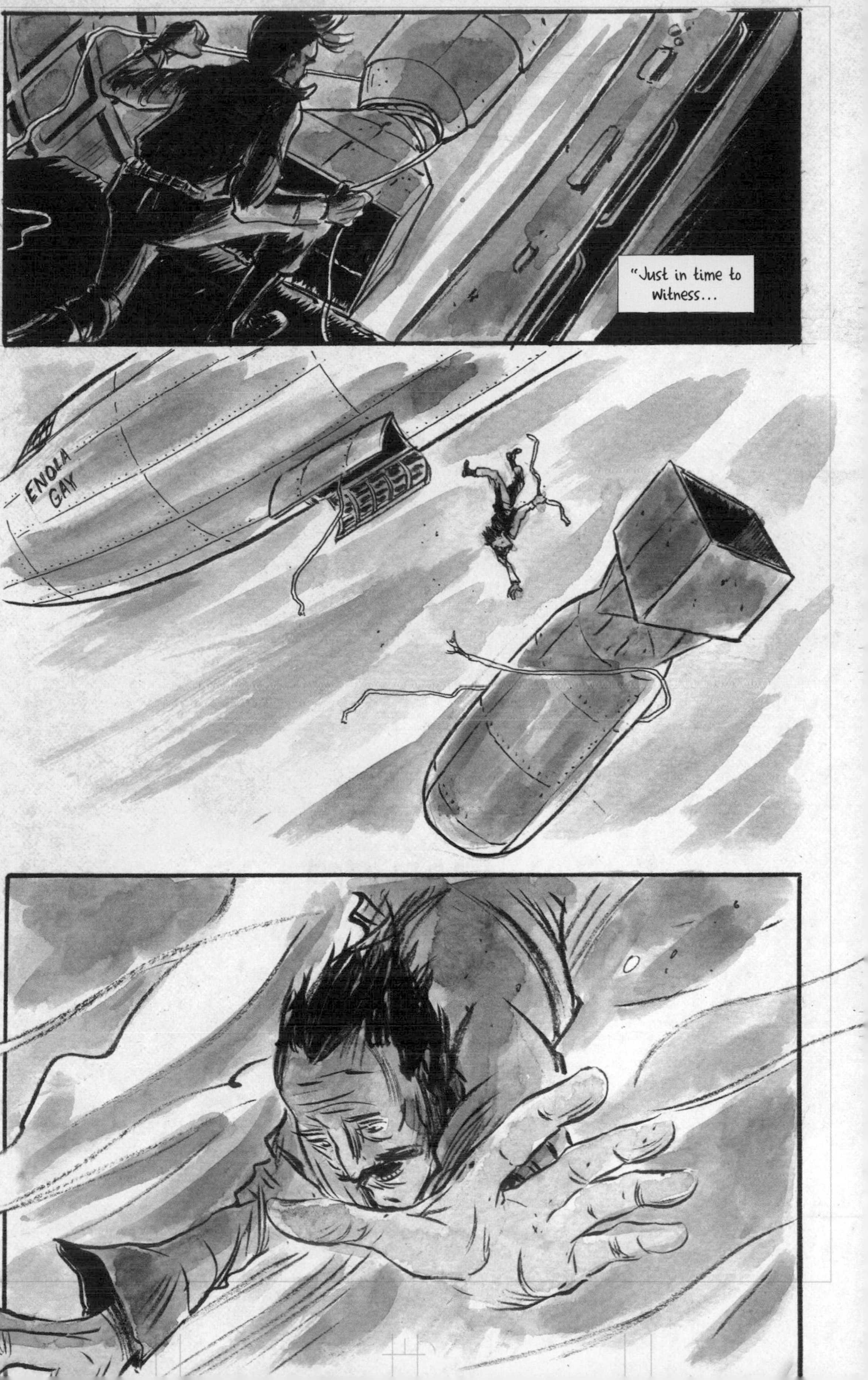
"Just in time to witness...
ENOLA GAY

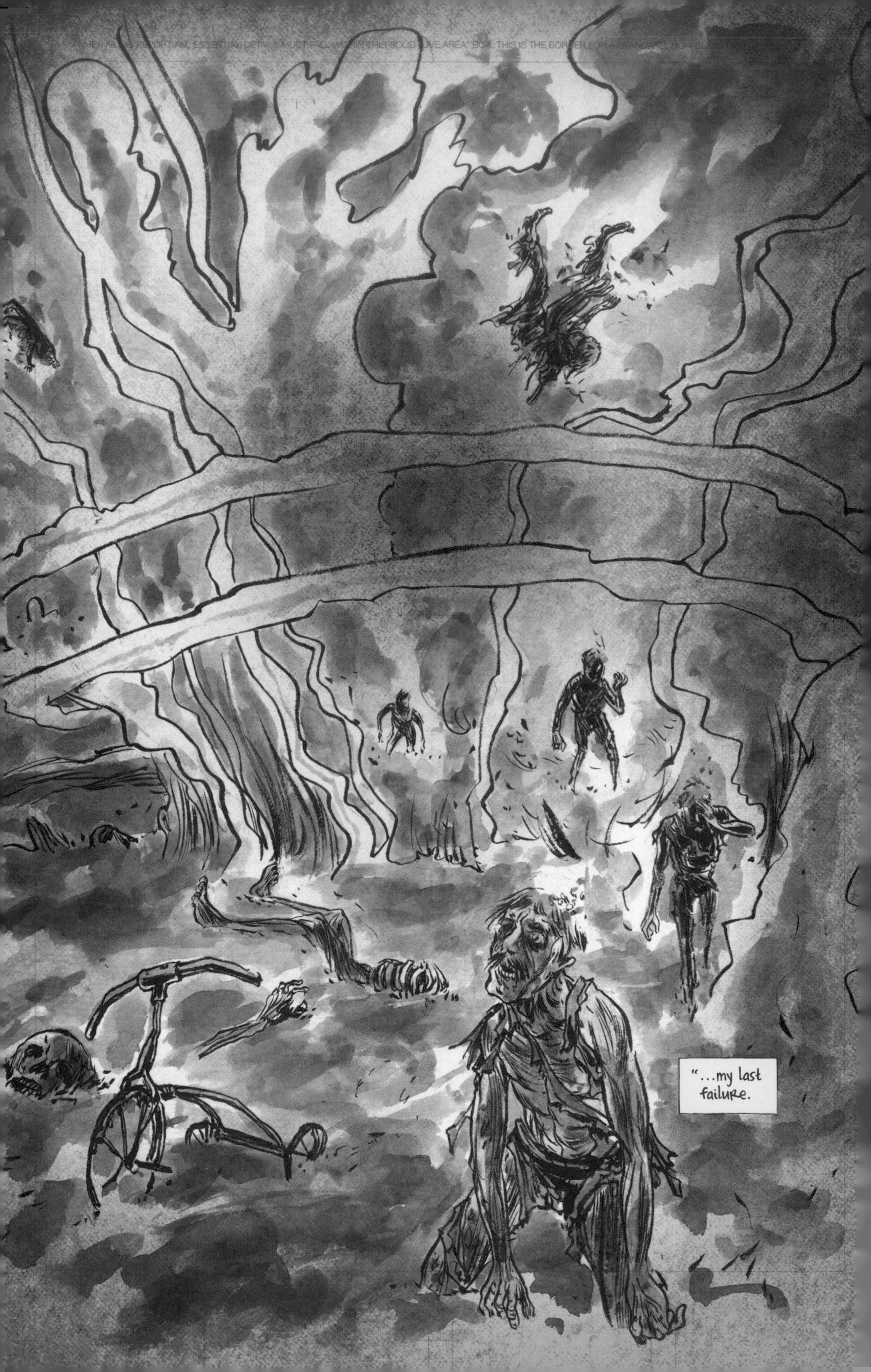
"...my last failure.

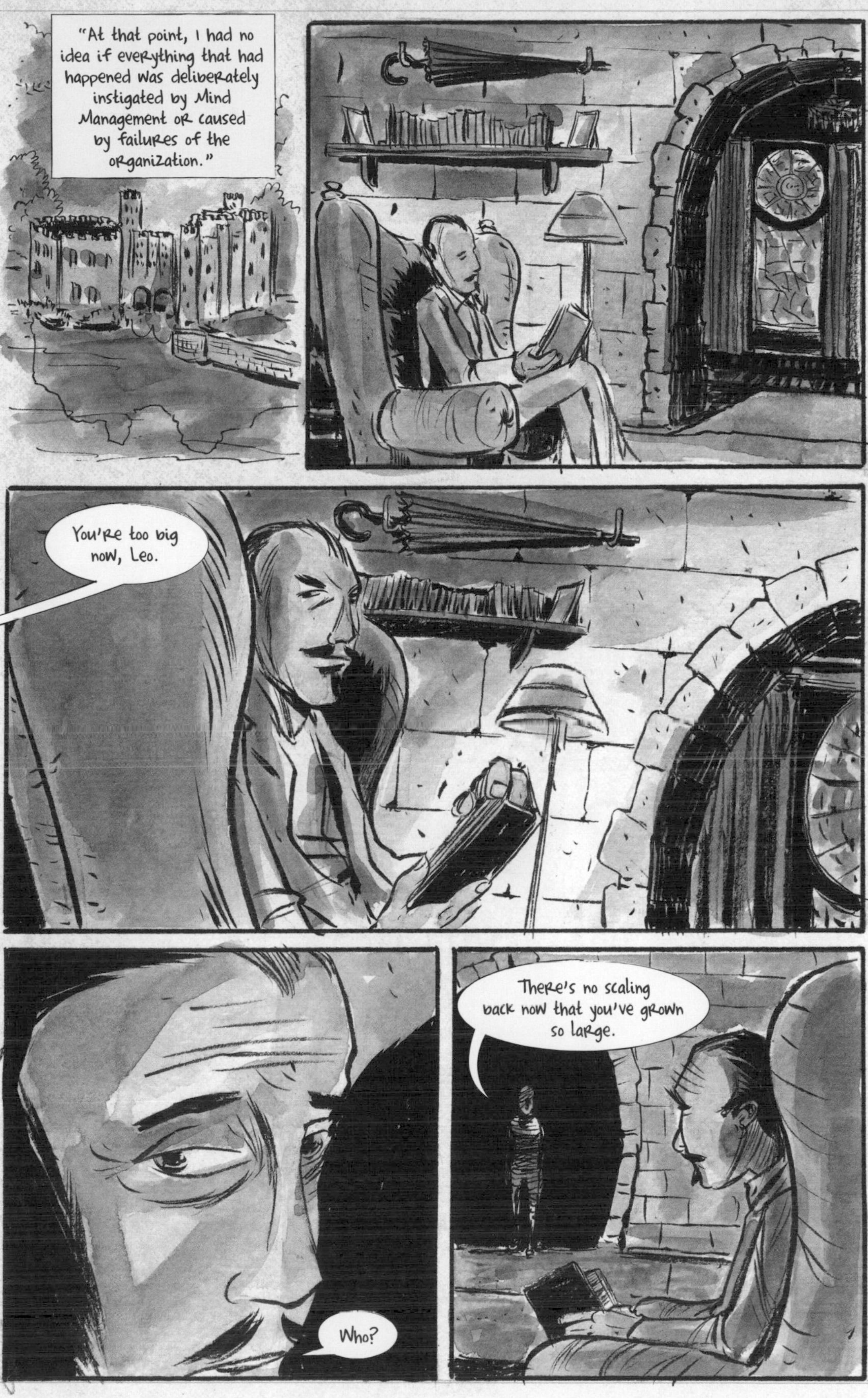
"At that point, I had no idea if everything that had happened was deliberately instigated by Mind Management or caused by failures of the organization."
You're too big now, Leo.
Who?
There's no scaling back now that you've grown so large.

MIND MGMT FIELD GUIDE 27.17. While lone-agent missions are often employed, duos are the ideal operational structure, encouraging a simple system of checks and balances.

MIND MGMT FIELD GUIDE 27.18. Teams working in pairs have historically been more effective in operations and in efforts to discourage corruption and mismanagement.

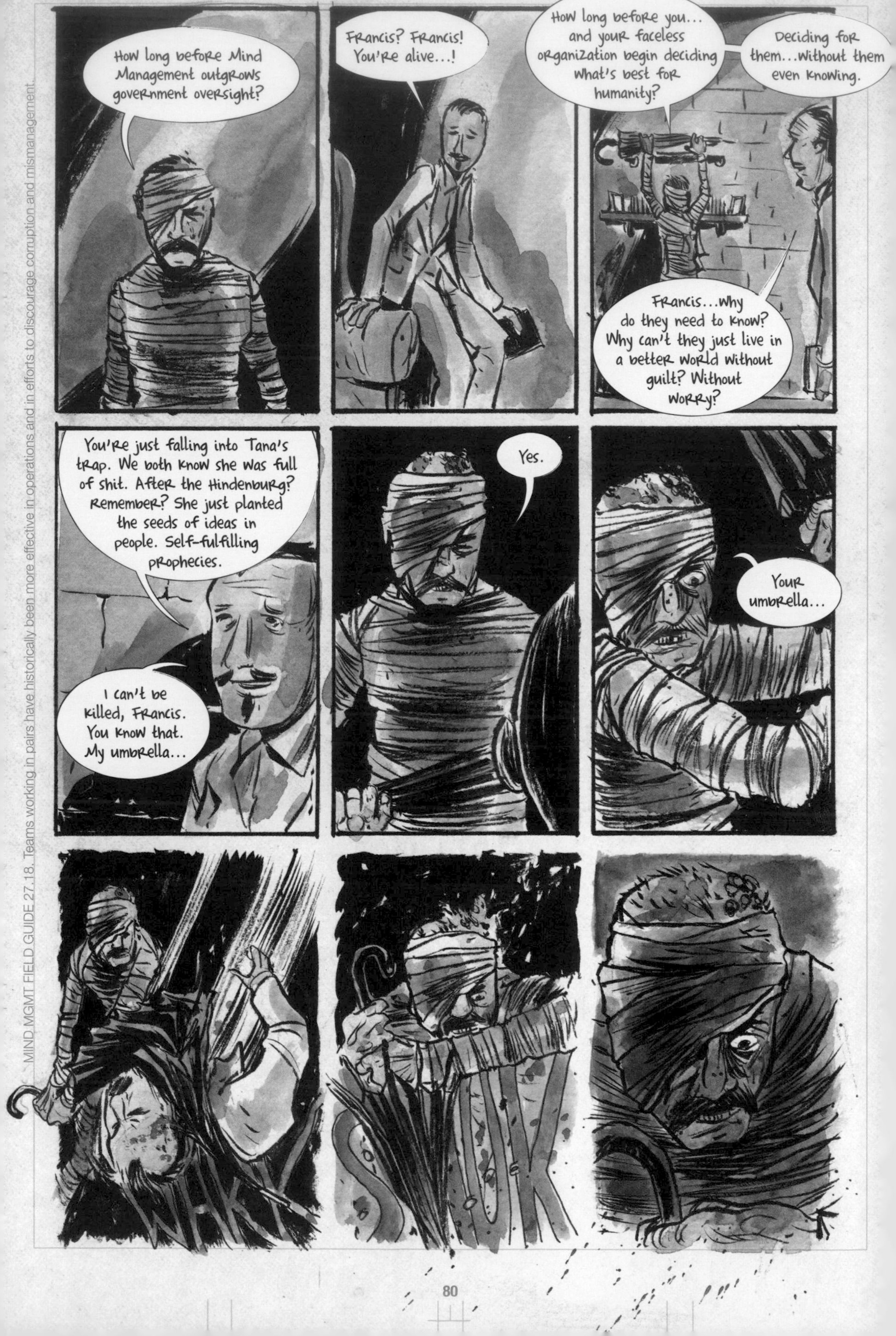
How long before Mind Management outgrows government oversight?
Francis? Francis! You're alive...!
How long before you... and your faceless organization begin deciding what's best for humanity?
Deciding for them...without them even knowing.
Francis...Why do they need to know? Why can't they just live in a better world without guilt? Without worry?
You're just falling into Tana's trap. We both know she was full of shit. After the Hindenburg? Remember? She just planted the seeds of ideas in people. Self-fulfilling prophecies.
I can't be killed, Francis. You know that. My umbrella...
Yes.
Your umbrella...

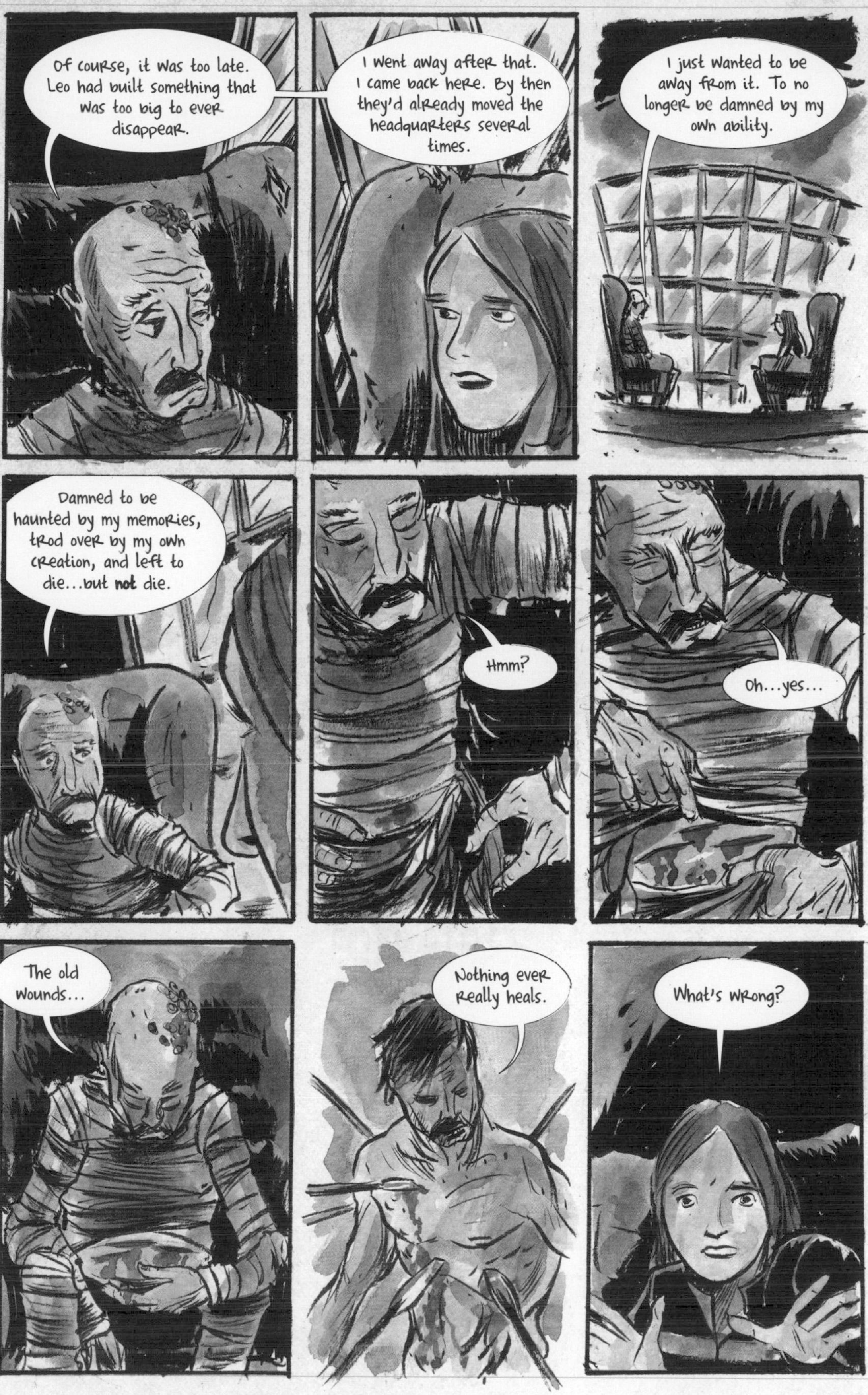
Of course, it was too late. Leo had built something that was too big to ever disappear.
I went away after that. I came back here. By then they'd already moved the headquarters several times.
I just wanted to be away from it. To no longer be damned by my own ability.
Damned to be haunted by my memories, trod over by my own creation, and left to die...but **not** die.
Hmm?
Oh...yes...
The old wounds...
Nothing ever really heals.
What's wrong?

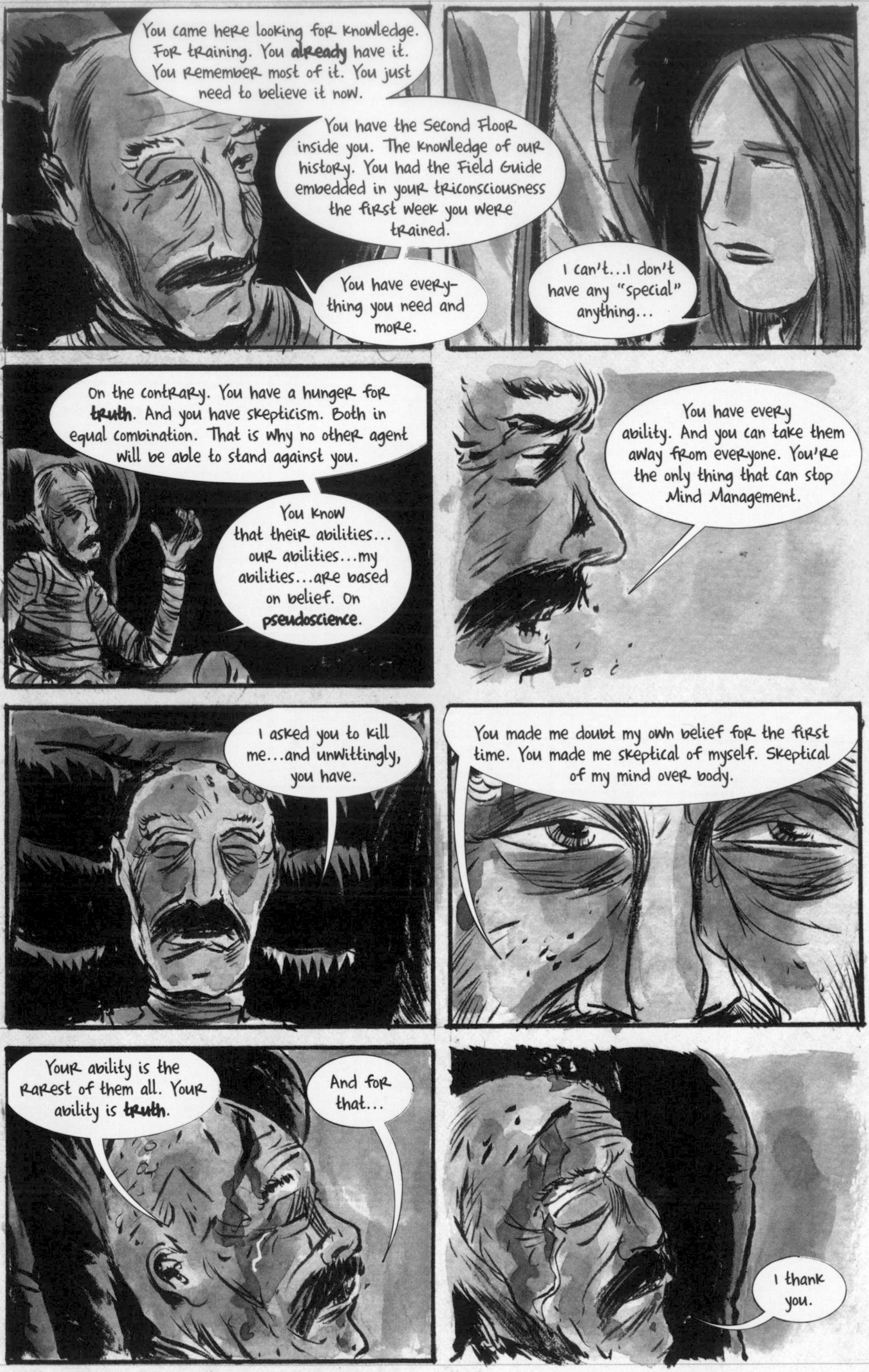
You came here looking for knowledge. For training. You **already** have it. You remember most of it. You just need to believe it now.
You have the Second Floor inside you. The knowledge of our history. You had the Field Guide embedded in your triconsciousness the first week you were trained.
You have everything you need and more.
I can't...I don't have any "special" anything...
On the contrary. You have a hunger for **truth**. And you have skepticism. Both in equal combination. That is why no other agent will be able to stand against you.
You know that their abilities... our abilities...my abilities...are based on belief. On **pseudoscience**.
You have every ability. And you can take them away from everyone. You're the only thing that can stop Mind Management.
I asked you to kill me...and unwittingly, you have.
You made me doubt my own belief for the first time. You made me skeptical of myself. Skeptical of my mind over body.
Your ability is the rarest of them all. Your ability is **truth**.
And for that...
I thank you.

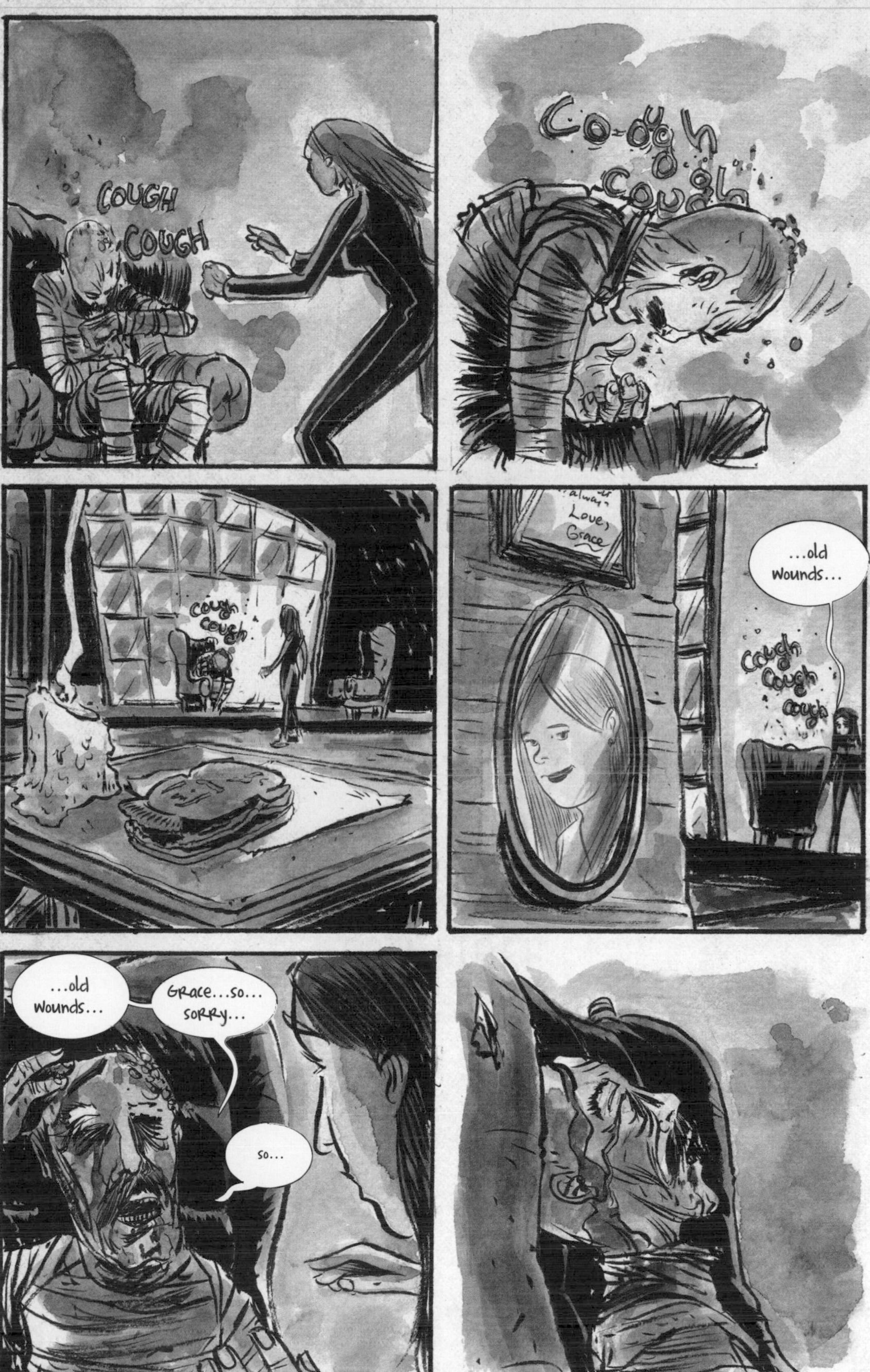
COUGH
COUGH
Co-ugh
cough
cough
cough
Love,
Grace
...old wounds...
cough
cough
cough
...old wounds...
Grace...so... sorry...
so...

MIND MGMT FIELD GUIDE 27:21. I regret so much . . . distracted by all of it. I didn't mean for any of that to happen . . . old wounds . . . Grace . . . sc . . . sorry . . . so . . .

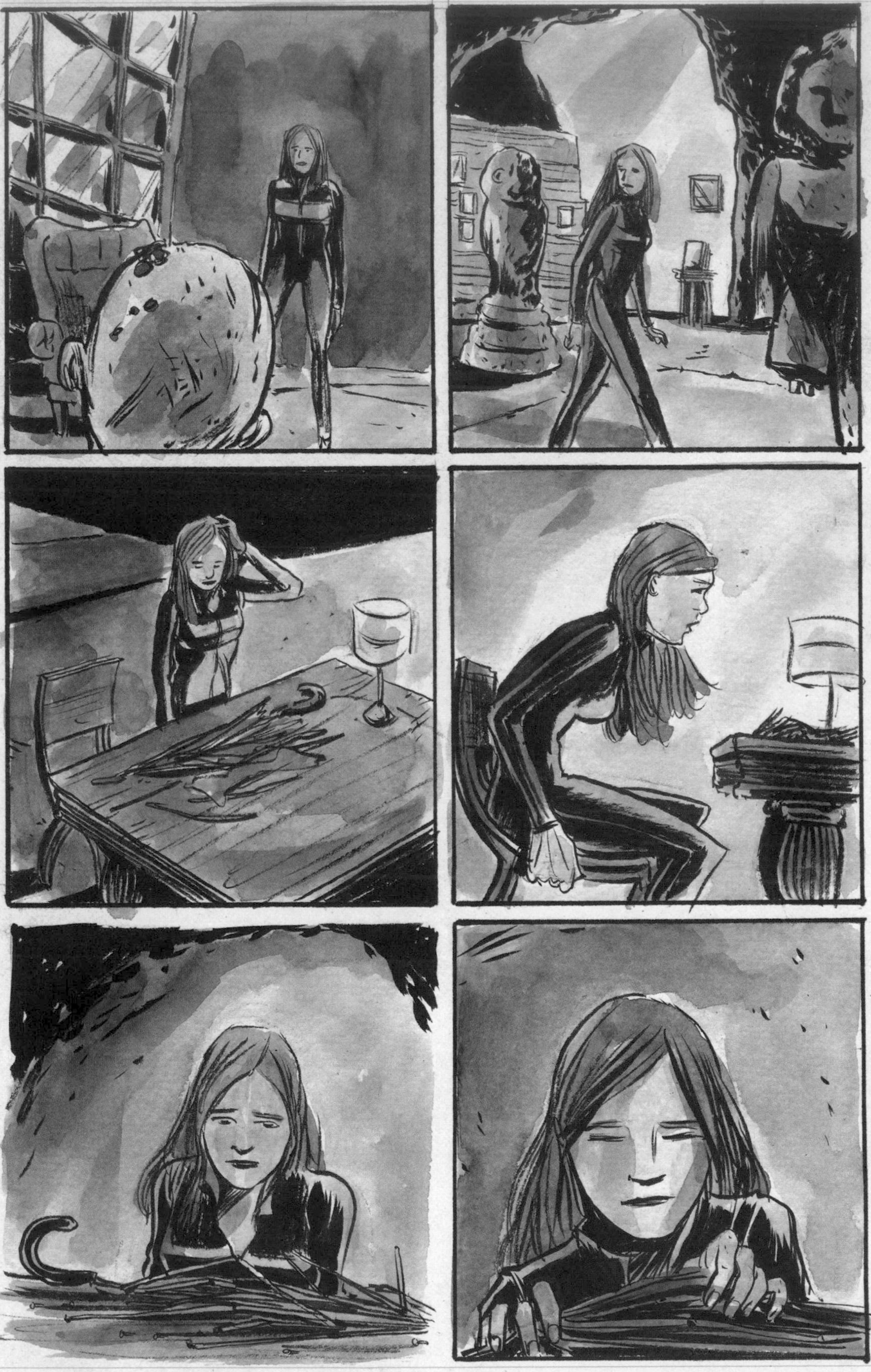

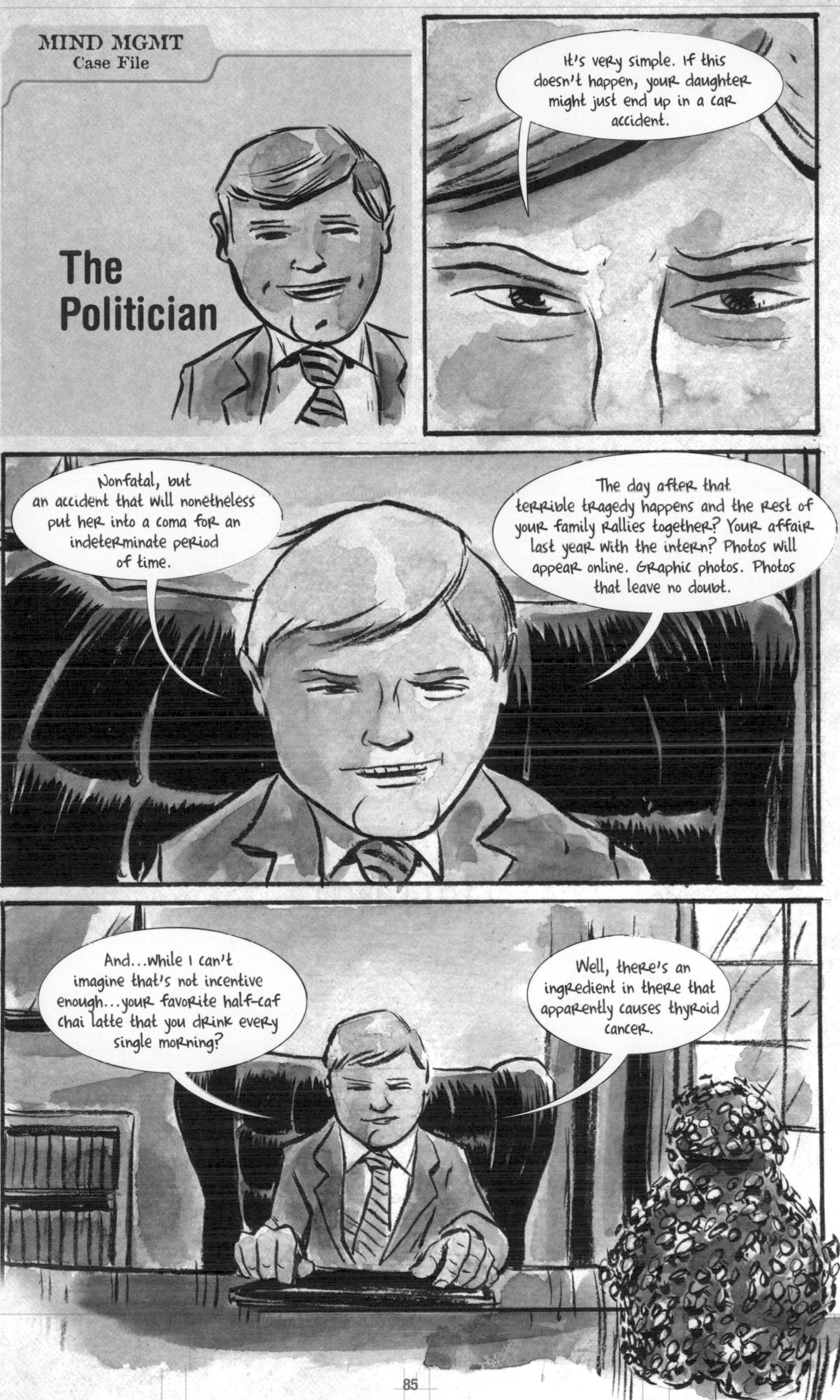
MIND MGMT
Case File
The Politician
It's very simple. If this doesn't happen, your daughter might just end up in a car accident.
Nonfatal, but an accident that will nonetheless put her into a coma for an indeterminate period of time.
The day after that terrible tragedy happens and the rest of your family rallies together? Your affair last year with the intern? Photos will appear online. Graphic photos. Photos that leave no doubt.
And...while I can't imagine that's not incentive enough...your favorite half-caf chai latte that you drink every single morning?
Well, there's an ingredient in there that apparently causes thyroid cancer.

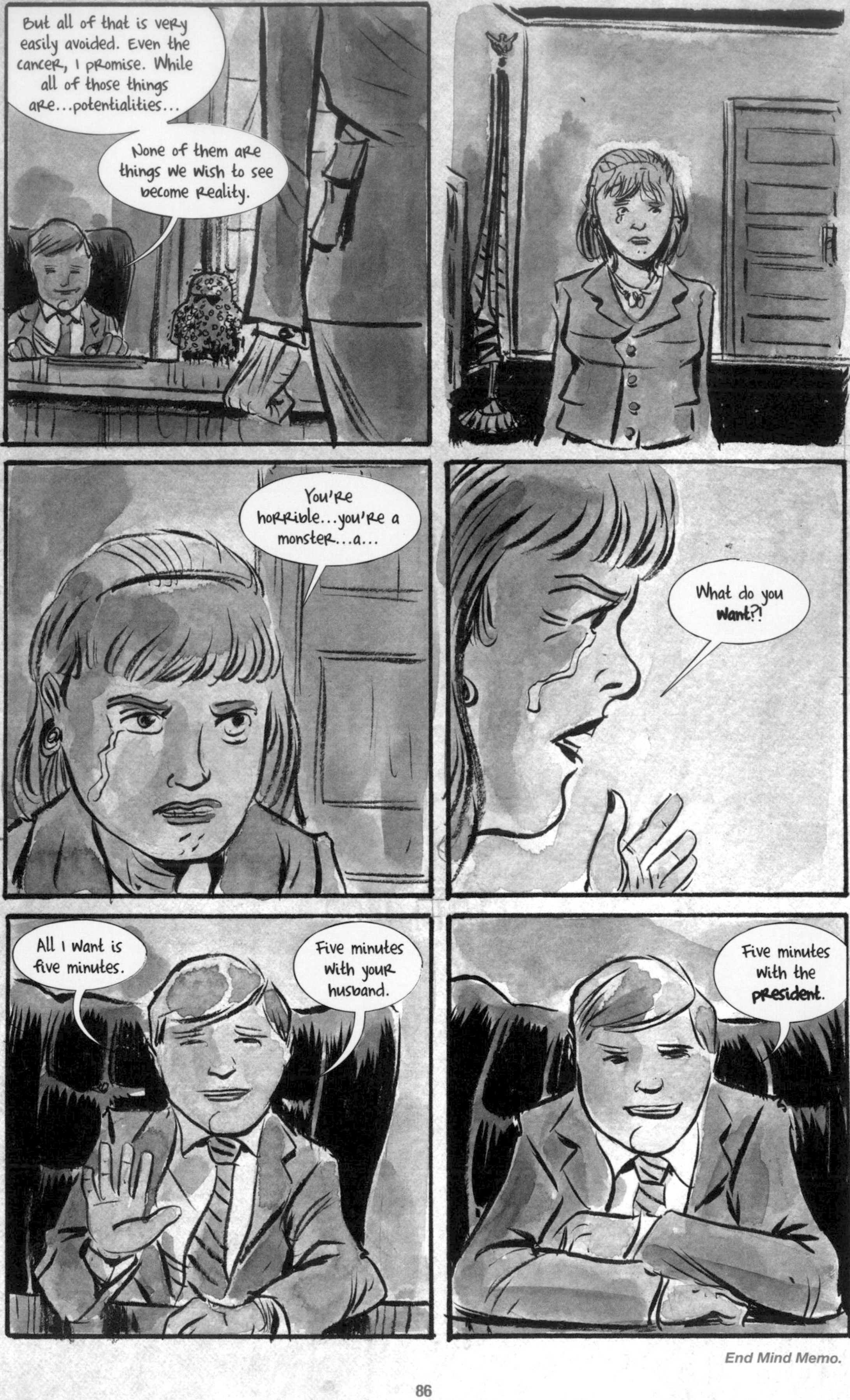
But all of that is very easily avoided. Even the cancer, I promise. While all of those things are...potentialities...
None of them are things we wish to see become reality.
You're horrible...you're a monster...a...
What do you **want**?!
All I want is five minutes.
Five minutes with your husband.
Five minutes with the **president**.

End Mind Memo.

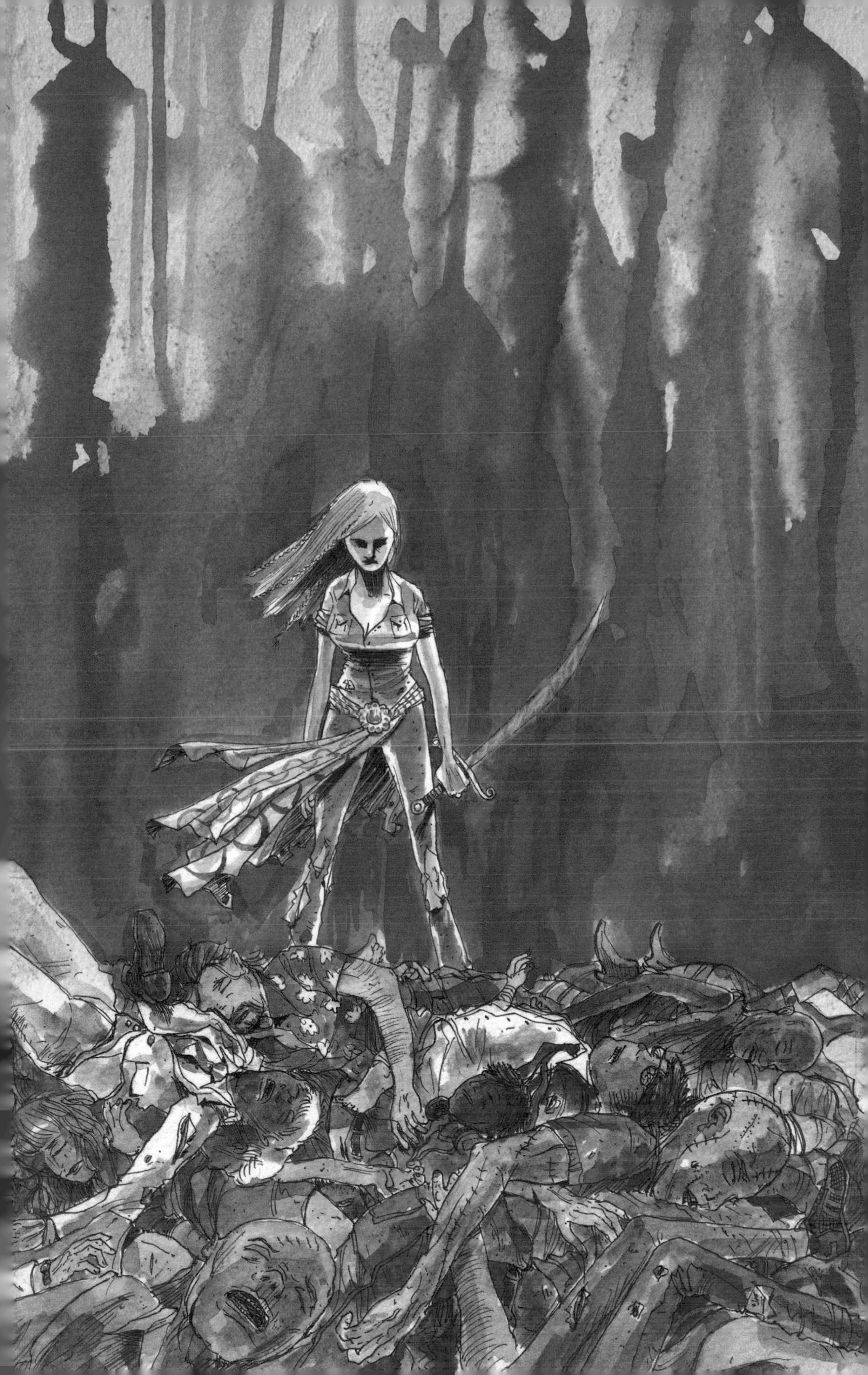

28

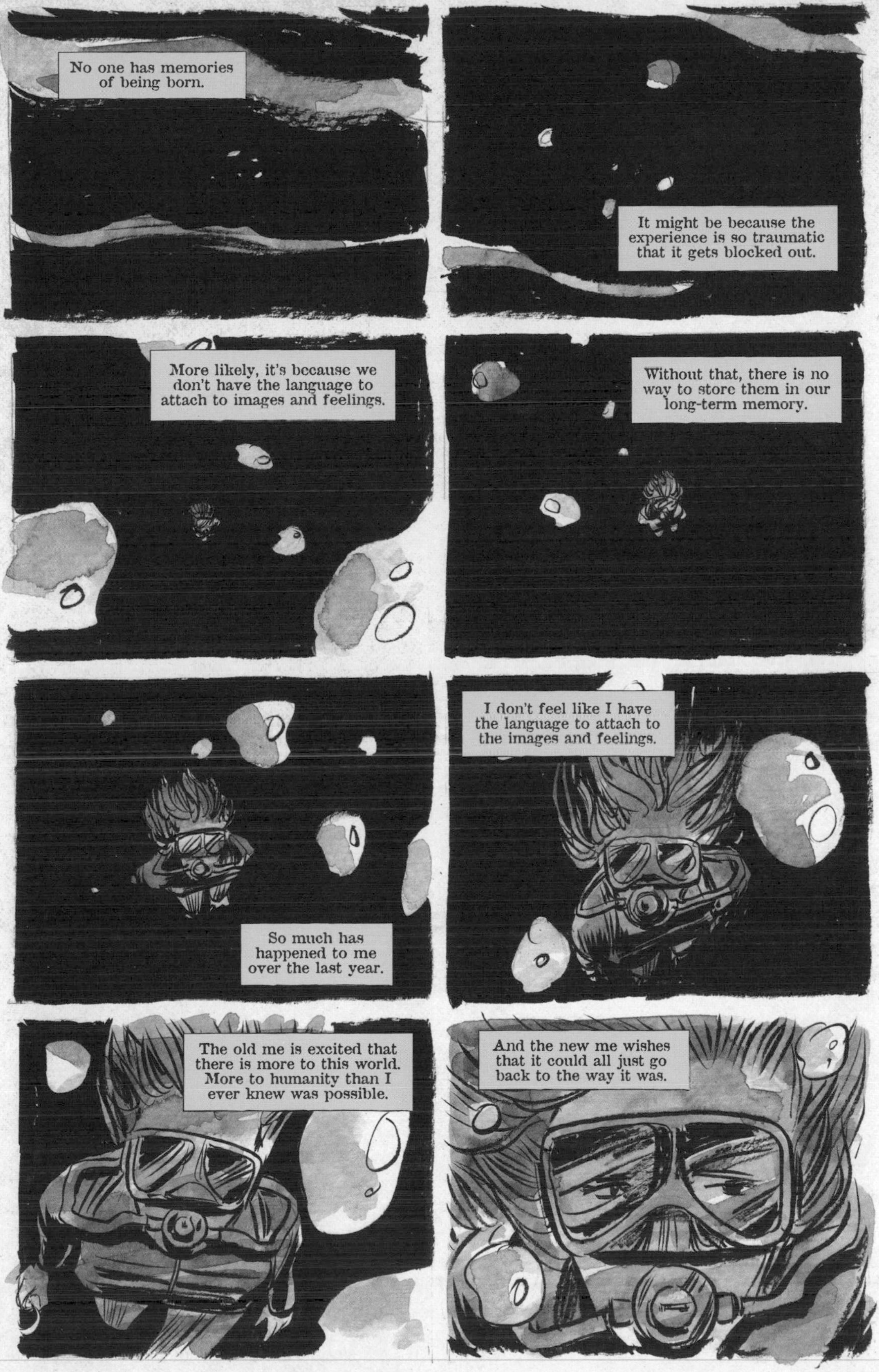
No one has memories of being born.
It might be because the experience is so traumatic that it gets blocked out.
More likely, it's because we don't have the language to attach to images and feelings.
Without that, there is no way to store them in our long-term memory.
So much has happened to me over the last year.
I don't feel like I have the language to attach to the images and feelings.
The old me is excited that there is more to this world. More to humanity than I ever knew was possible.
And the new me wishes that it could all just go back to the way it was.

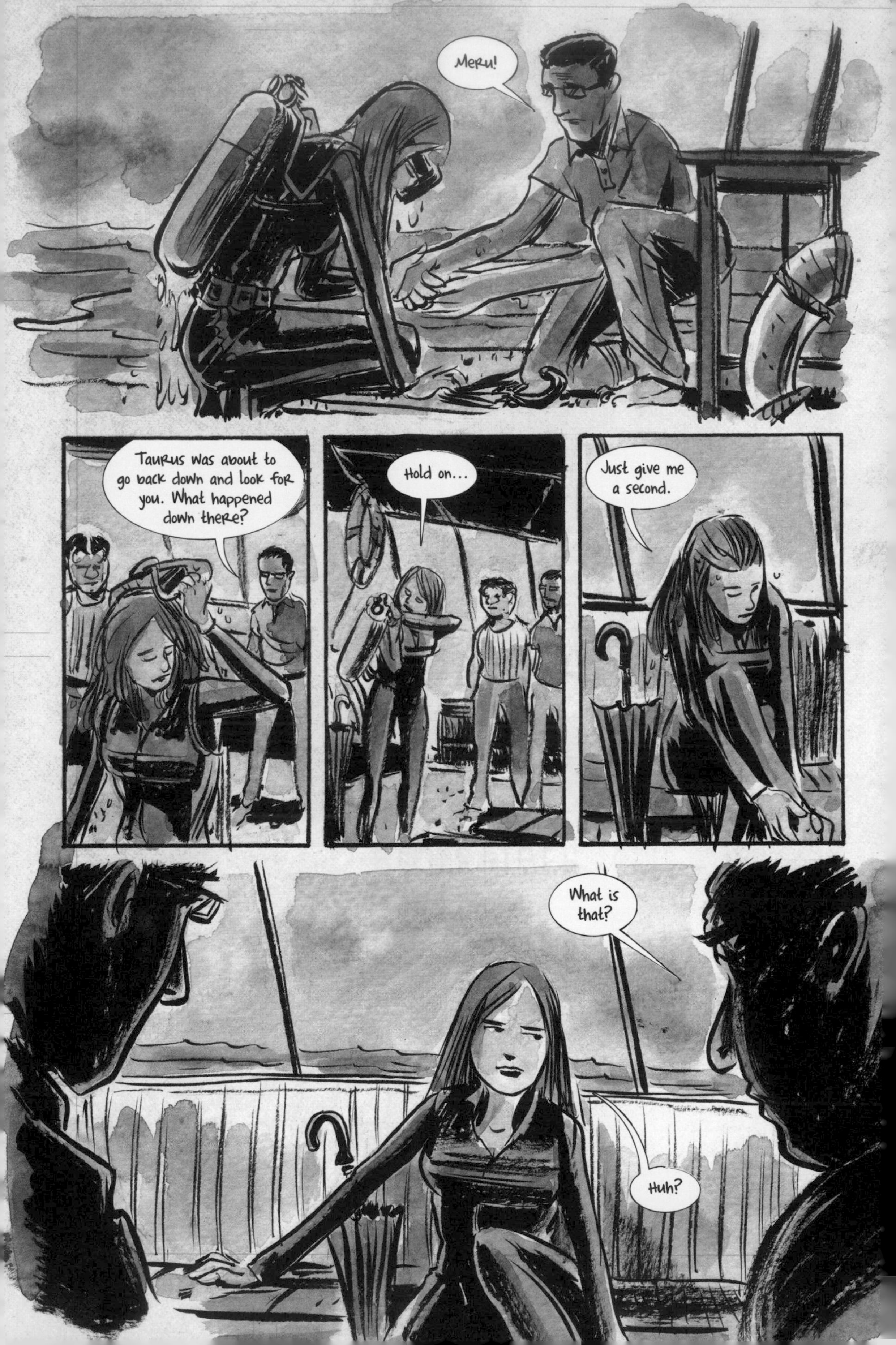
Meru!
Taurus was about to go back down and look for you. What happened down there?
Hold on...
Just give me a second.
What is that?
Huh?

MIND MGMT FIELD GUIDE: 28.3. When confronted with a more powerful agent, submit immediately and begin self-administered mind-purge protocols.

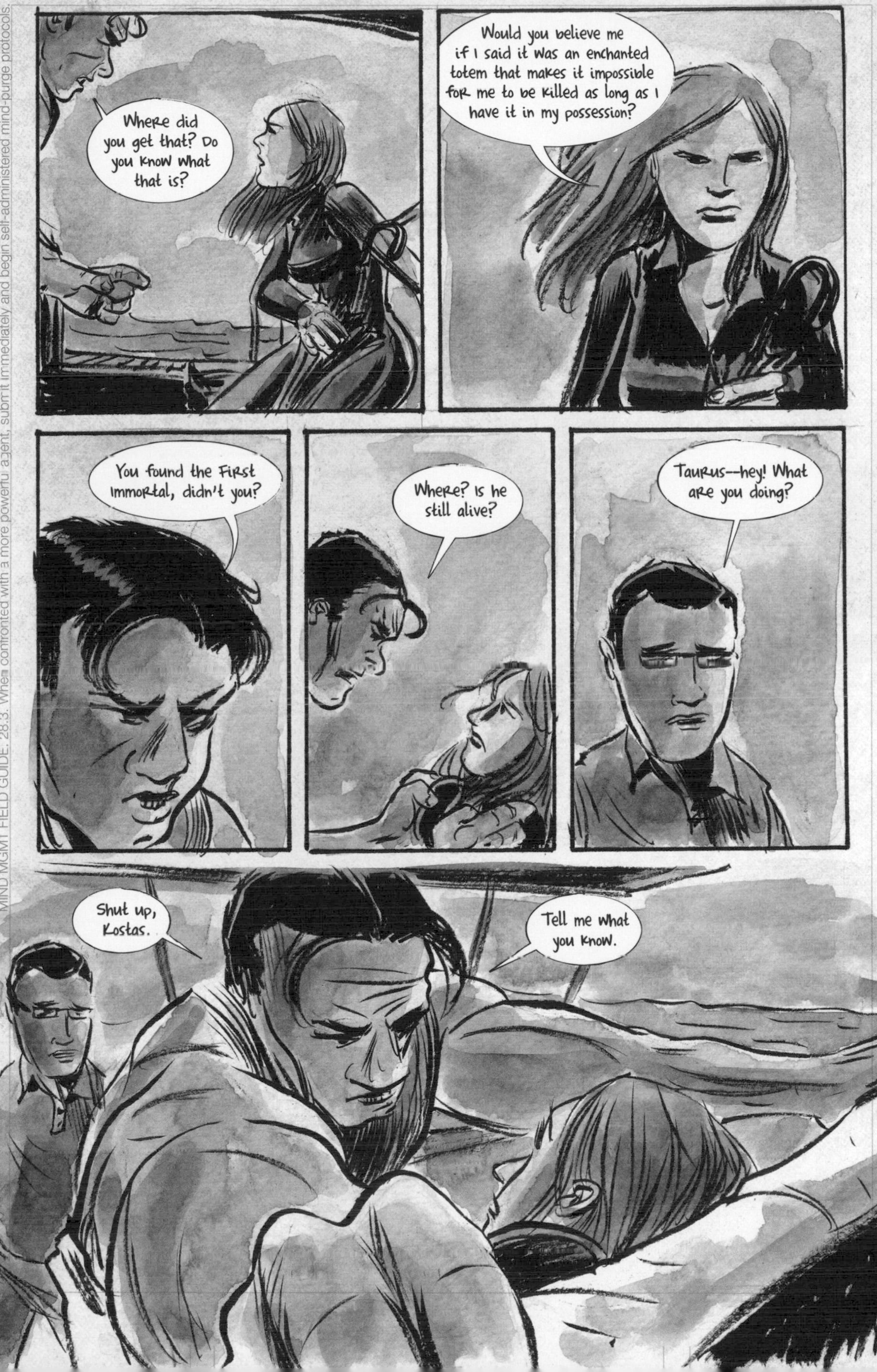
Where did you get that? Do you know what that is?
Would you believe me if I said it was an enchanted totem that makes it impossible for me to be killed as long as I have it in my possession?
You found the First Immortal, didn't you?
Where? Is he still alive?
Taurus--hey! What are you doing?
Shut up, Kostas.
Tell me what you know.

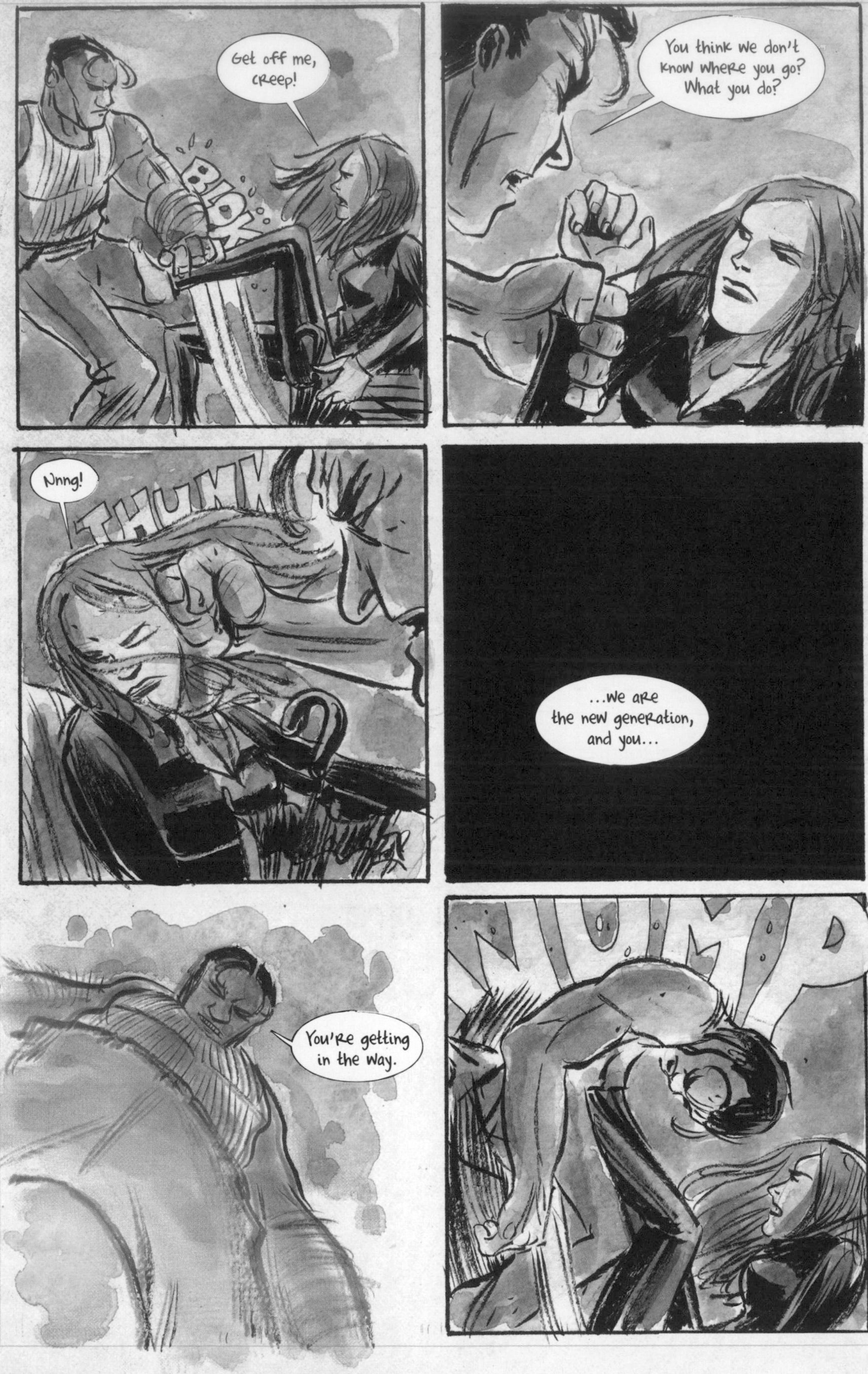
Get off me, creep!
BLOK
You think we don't know where you go? What you do?
Nnng!
THUNK
...we are the new generation, and you...
You're getting in the way.

MIND MGMT FIELD GUIDE. 28.4. Physical attacks on agents with unknown abilities should be avoided. All emphasis should be placed on either preservation or purging of field agent information.

WHEN FILING REPORT ALL ESSENTIAL DETAILS MUST FALL WITHIN THIS SOLID "LIVE AREA" BOX. THIS IS THE BORDER FOR A STANDARD, NON-BLEED FIELD REPORT

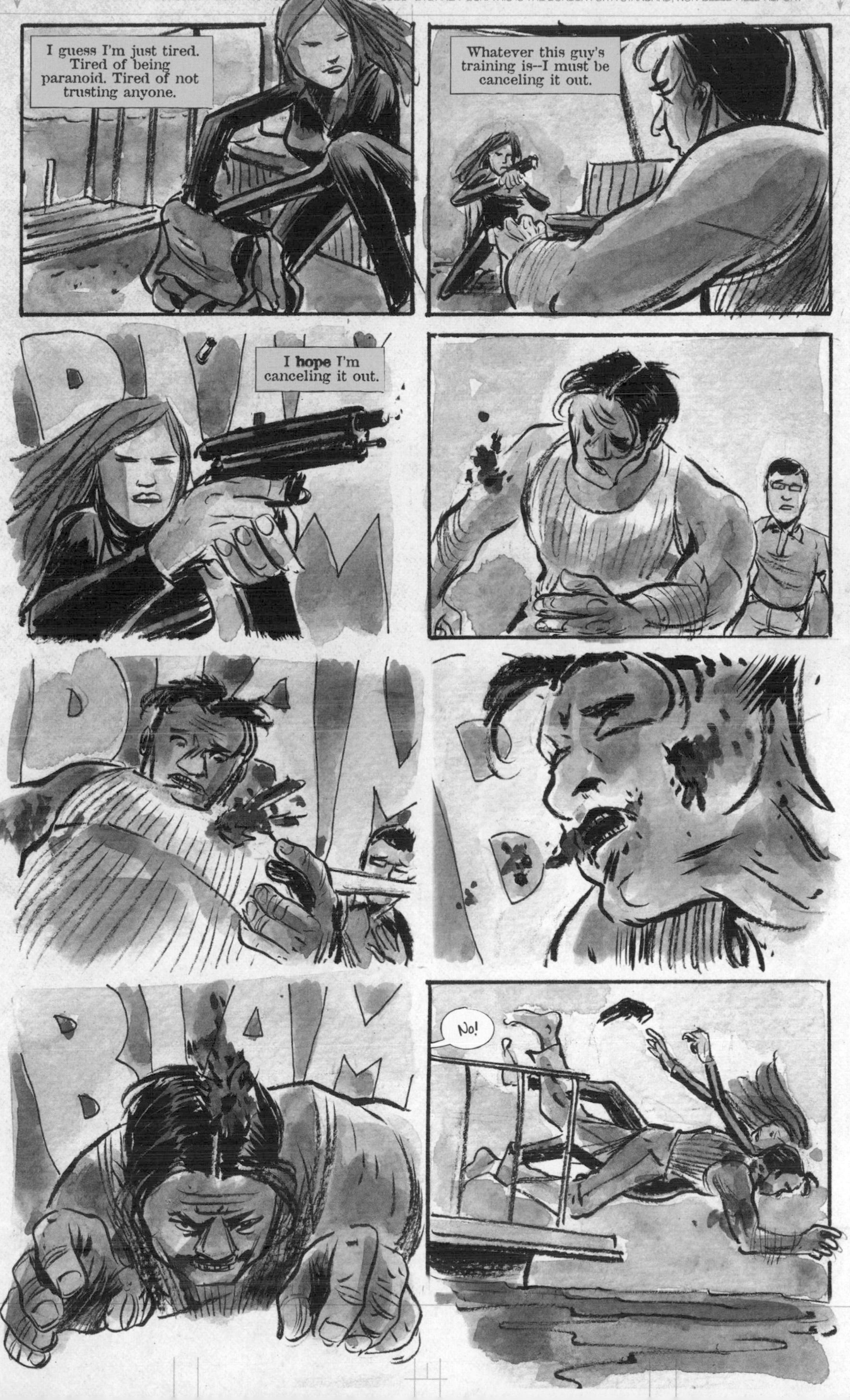

I guess I'm just tired. Tired of being paranoid. Tired of not trusting anyone.
Whatever this guy's training is--I must be canceling it out.
I **hope** I'm canceling it out.
No!

MIND MGMT FIELD GUIDE. 28.5. The use of firearms in the field is not prohibited but is discouraged due to their ineffectiveness against Immortal training techniques.

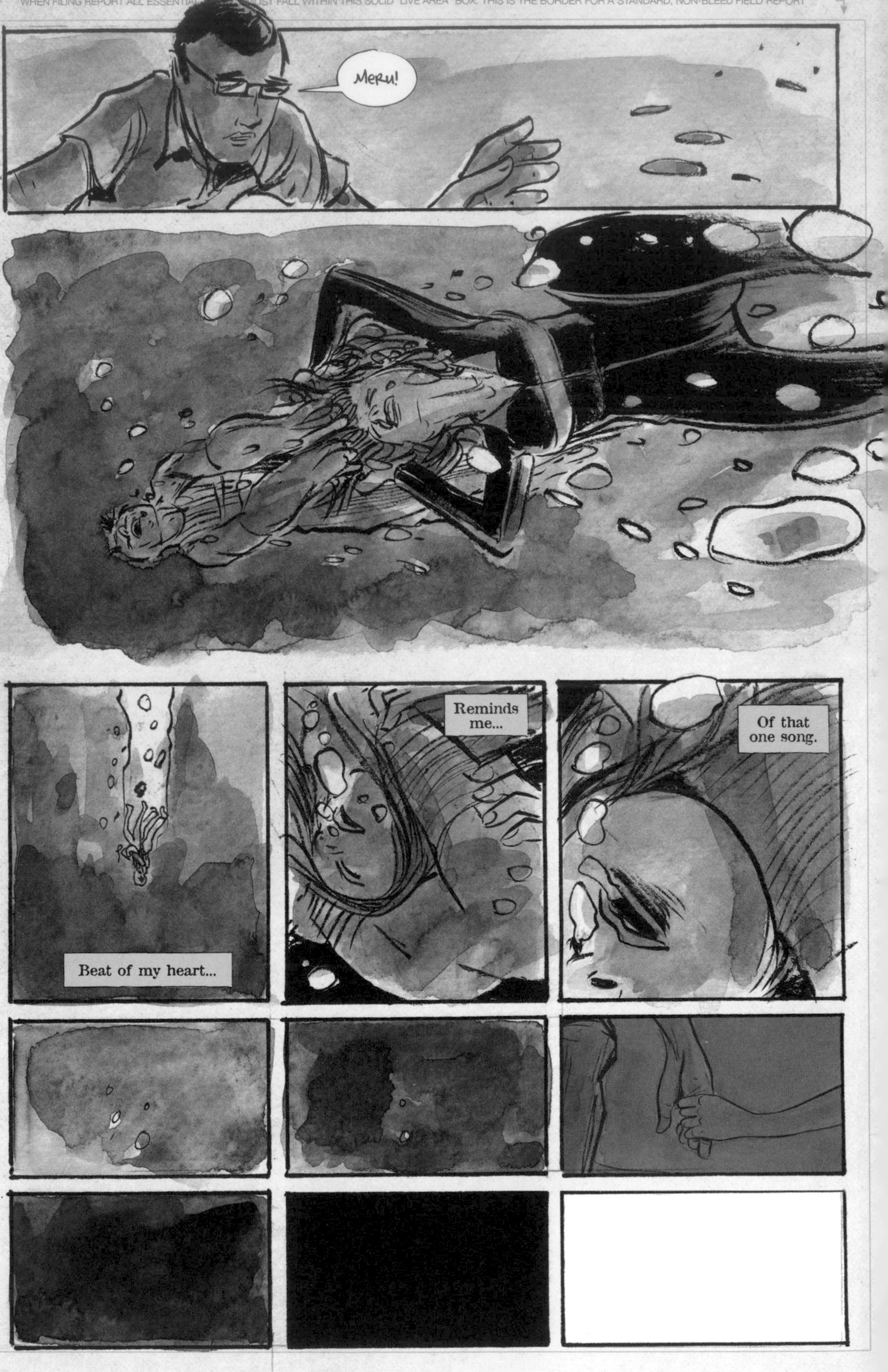
Meru!
Beat of my heart...
Reminds me...
Of that one song.

MIND MGMT FIELD GUIDE. 28.6. Drowning has been found to be a more successful technique in nullifying Immortal agents than firearms. However, this technique has not been fully tested.

WHEN FILING REPORT ALL ESSENTIAL DETAILS MUST FALL WITHIN THIS SOLID "LIVE AREA" BOX. THIS IS THE BORDER FOR A STANDARD, NON-BLEED FIELD REPORT

MIND MGMT FIELD GUIDE. 28.7. Suppression of emotions is paramount in maintaining cover. However, opportune displays of emotion can be used to leverage a more favorable position in the field.

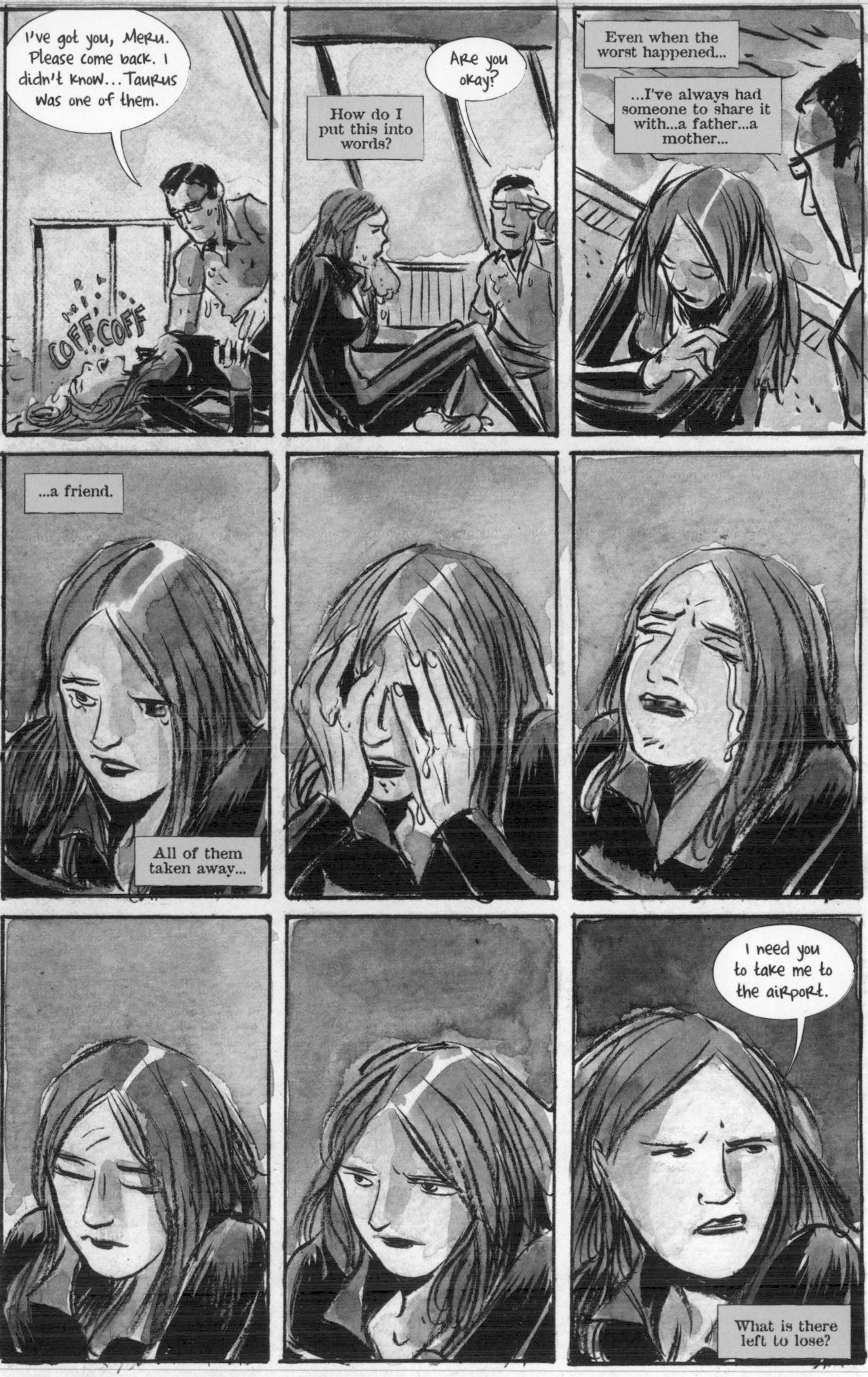
I've got you, Meru. Please come back. I didn't know... Taurus was one of them.
COFF COFF
Are you okay?
How do I put this into words?
Even when the worst happened...
...I've always had someone to share it with...a father...a mother...
...a friend.
All of them taken away...
I need you to take me to the airport.
What is there left to lose?

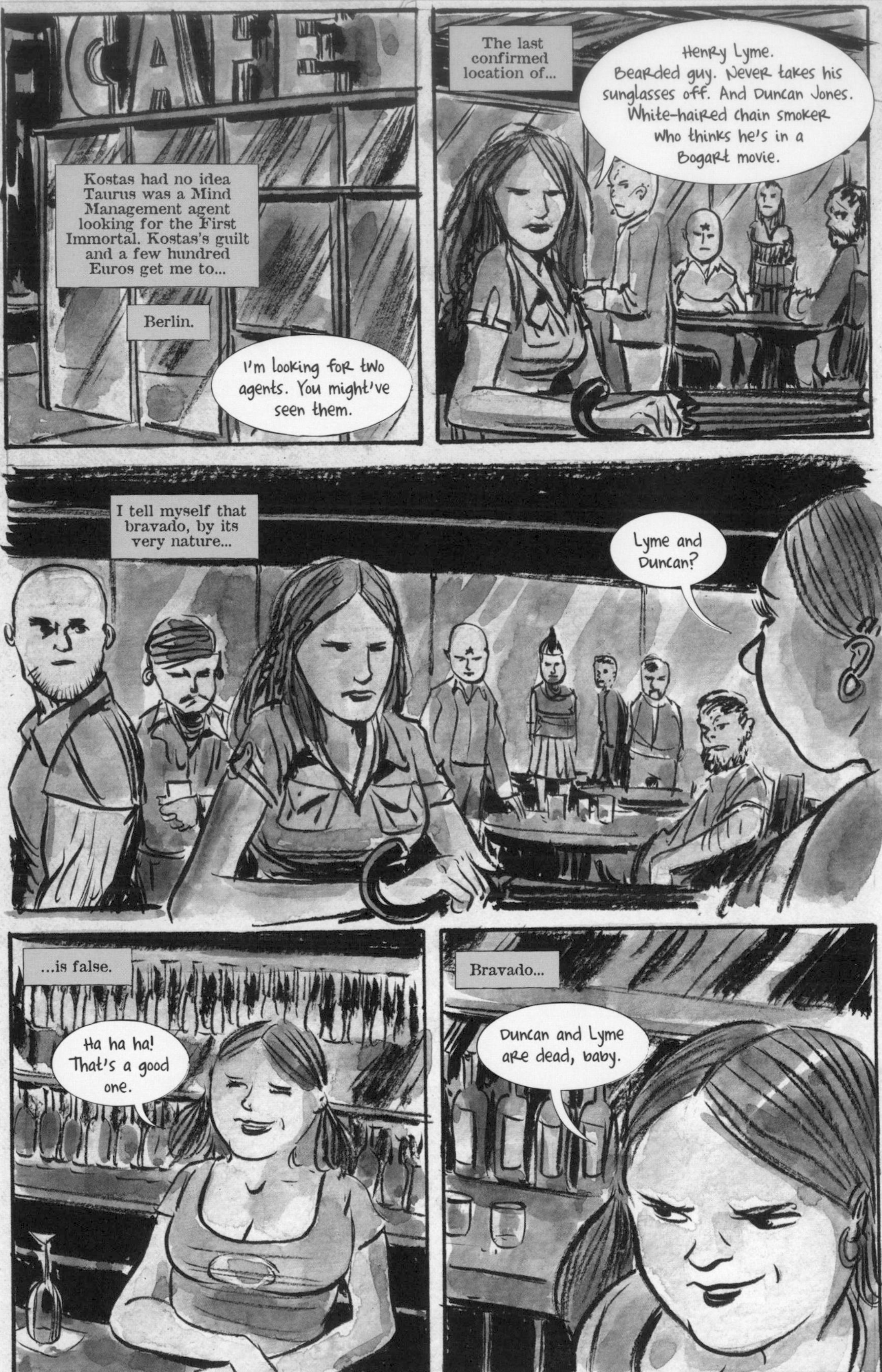
CAFE
Kostas had no idea Taurus was a Mind Management agent looking for the First Immortal. Kostas's guilt and a few hundred Euros get me to...
Berlin.
I'm looking for two agents. You might've seen them.
The last confirmed location of...
Henry Lyme. Bearded guy. Never takes his sunglasses off. And Duncan Jones. White-haired chain smoker who thinks he's in a Bogart movie.
I tell myself that bravado, by its very nature...
Lyme and Duncan?
...is false.
Ha ha ha! That's a good one.
Bravado...
Duncan and Lyme are dead, baby.

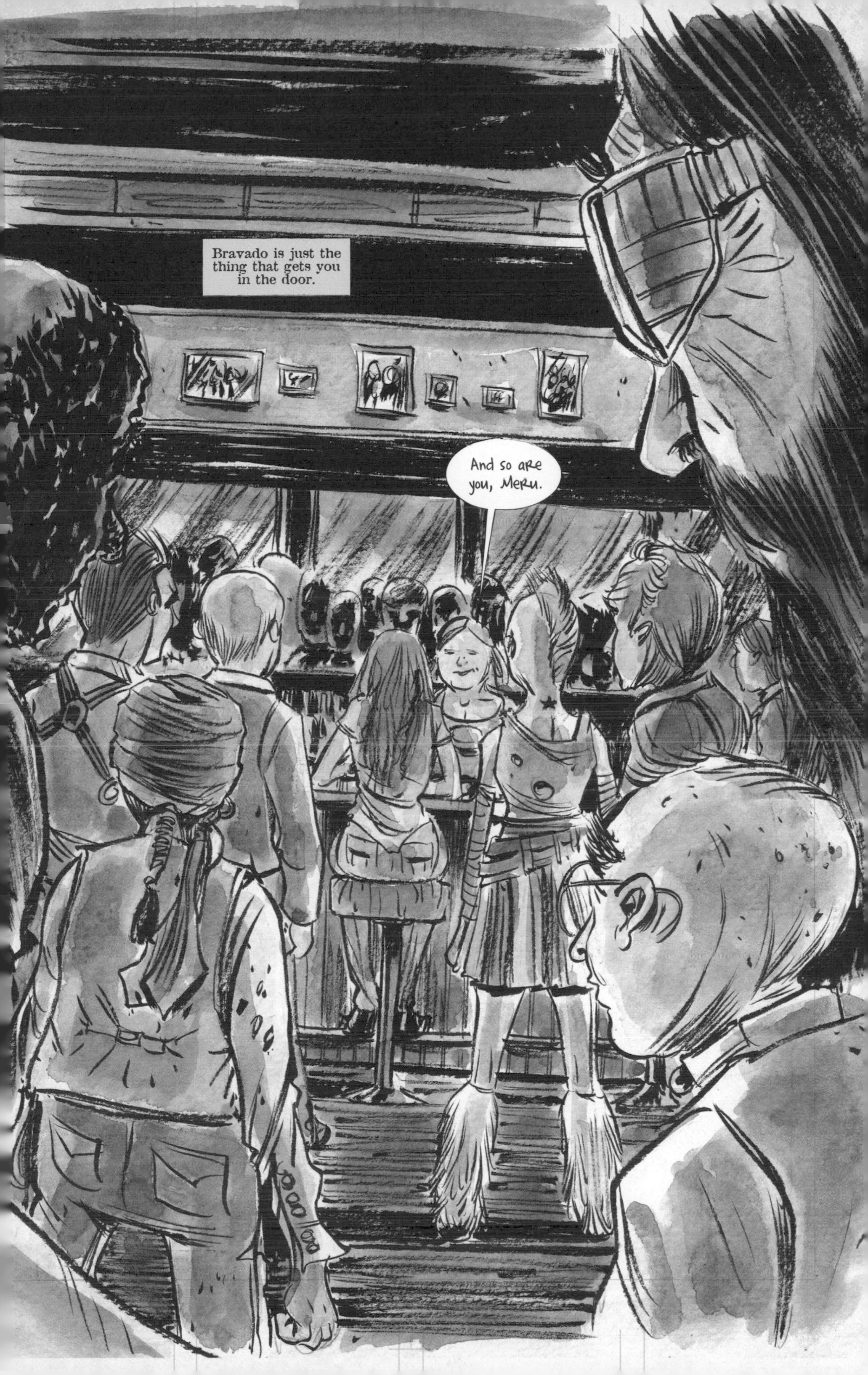
Bravado is just the thing that gets you in the door.
And so are you, Meru.

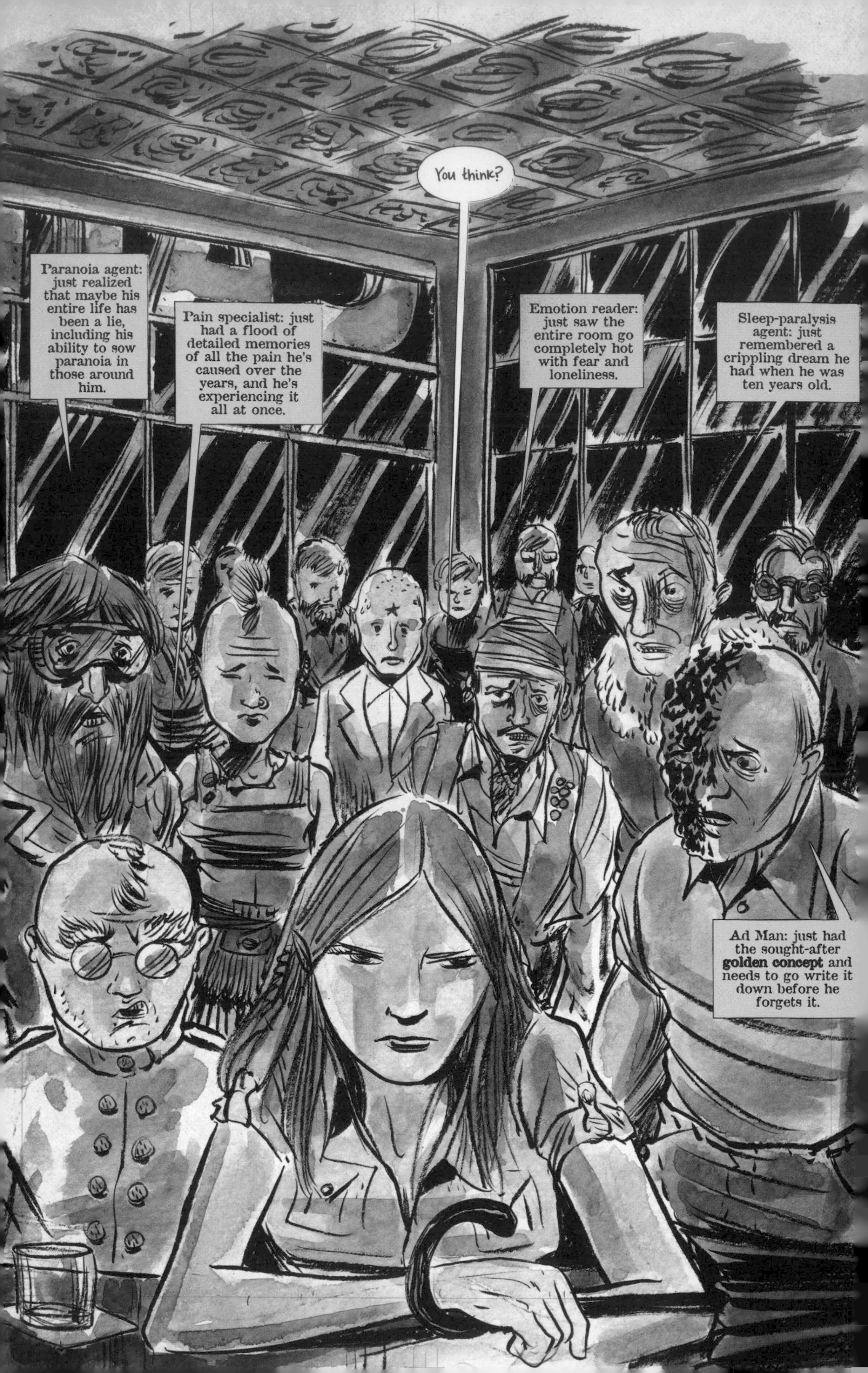
Paranoia agent: just realized that maybe his entire life has been a lie, including his ability to sow paranoia in those around him.
Pain specialist: just had a flood of detailed memories of all the pain he's caused over the years, and he's experiencing it all at once.
You think?
Emotion reader: just saw the entire room go completely hot with fear and loneliness.
Sleep-paralysis agent: just remembered a crippling dream he had when he was ten years old.
Ad Man: just had the sought-after **golden concept** and needs to go write it down before he forgets it.

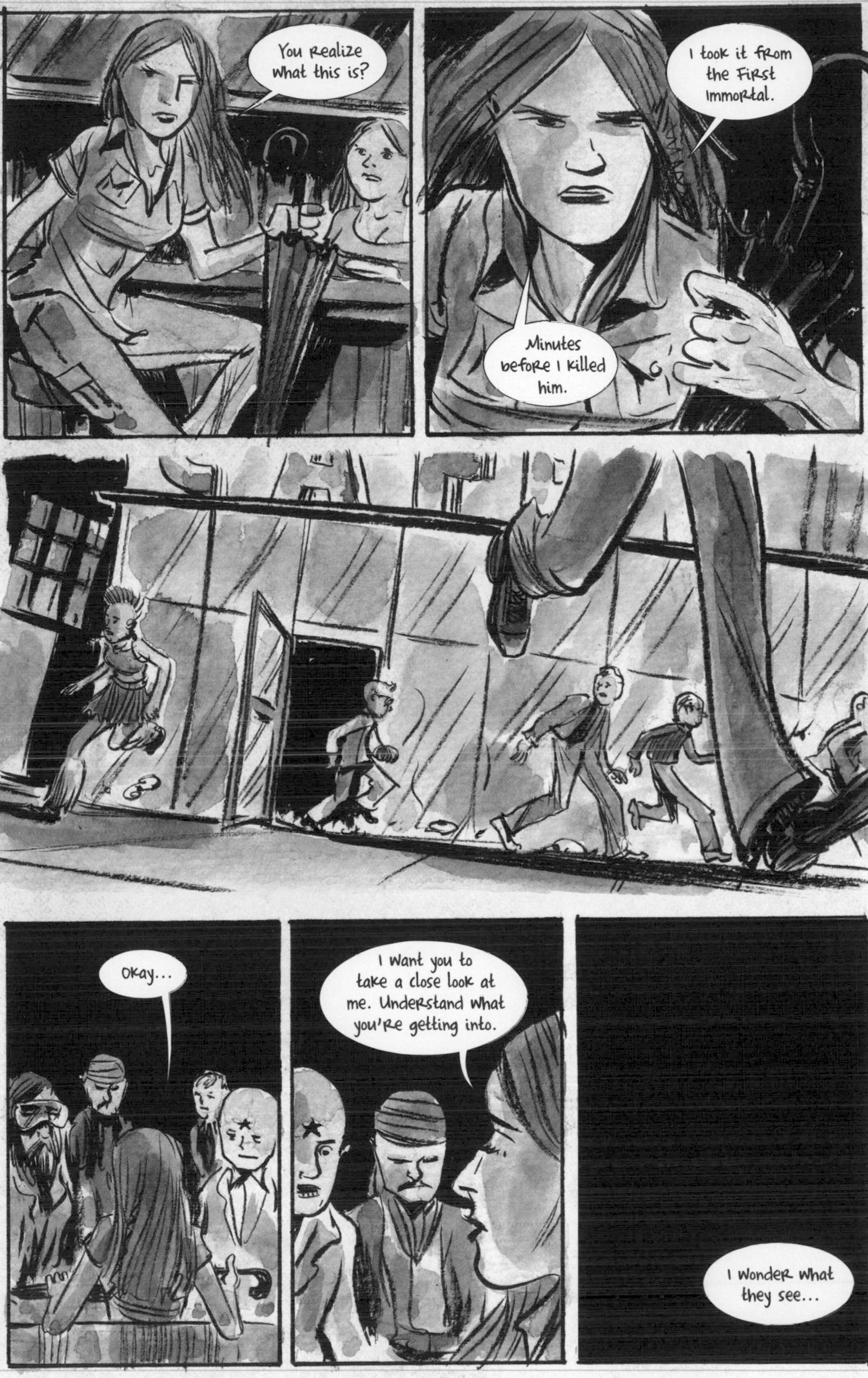
You realize what this is?
I took it from the First Immortal.
Minutes before I killed him.
Okay...
I want you to take a close look at me. Understand what you're getting into.
I wonder what they see...

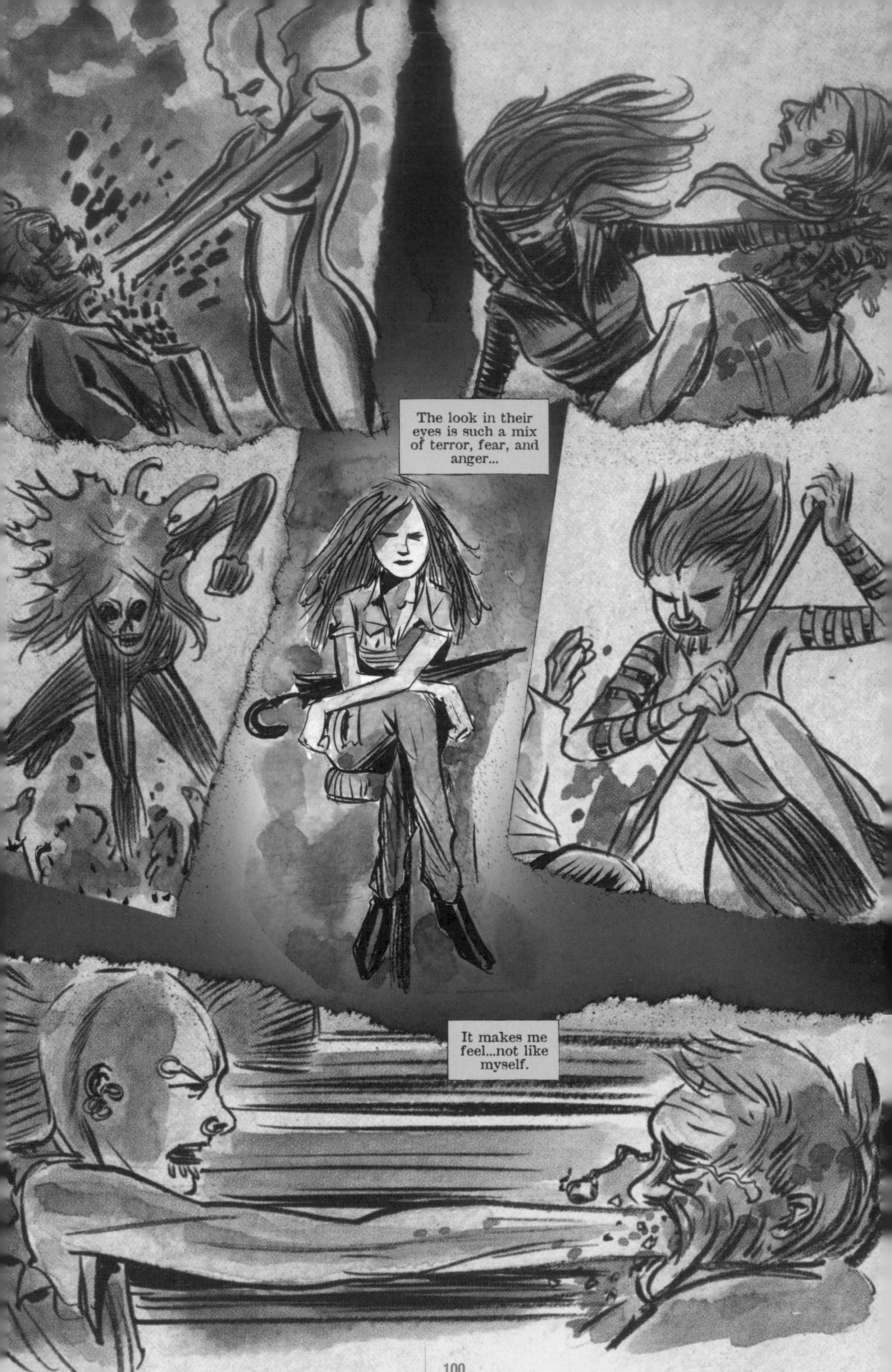
The look in their eyes is such a mix of terror, fear, and anger...
It makes me feel...not like myself.

MIND MGMT FIELD GUIDE. 28.13. The flux safe house bartender is your primary safe house contact. They are there to accommodate your every need and to see that field agents are fully prepped for further field work.

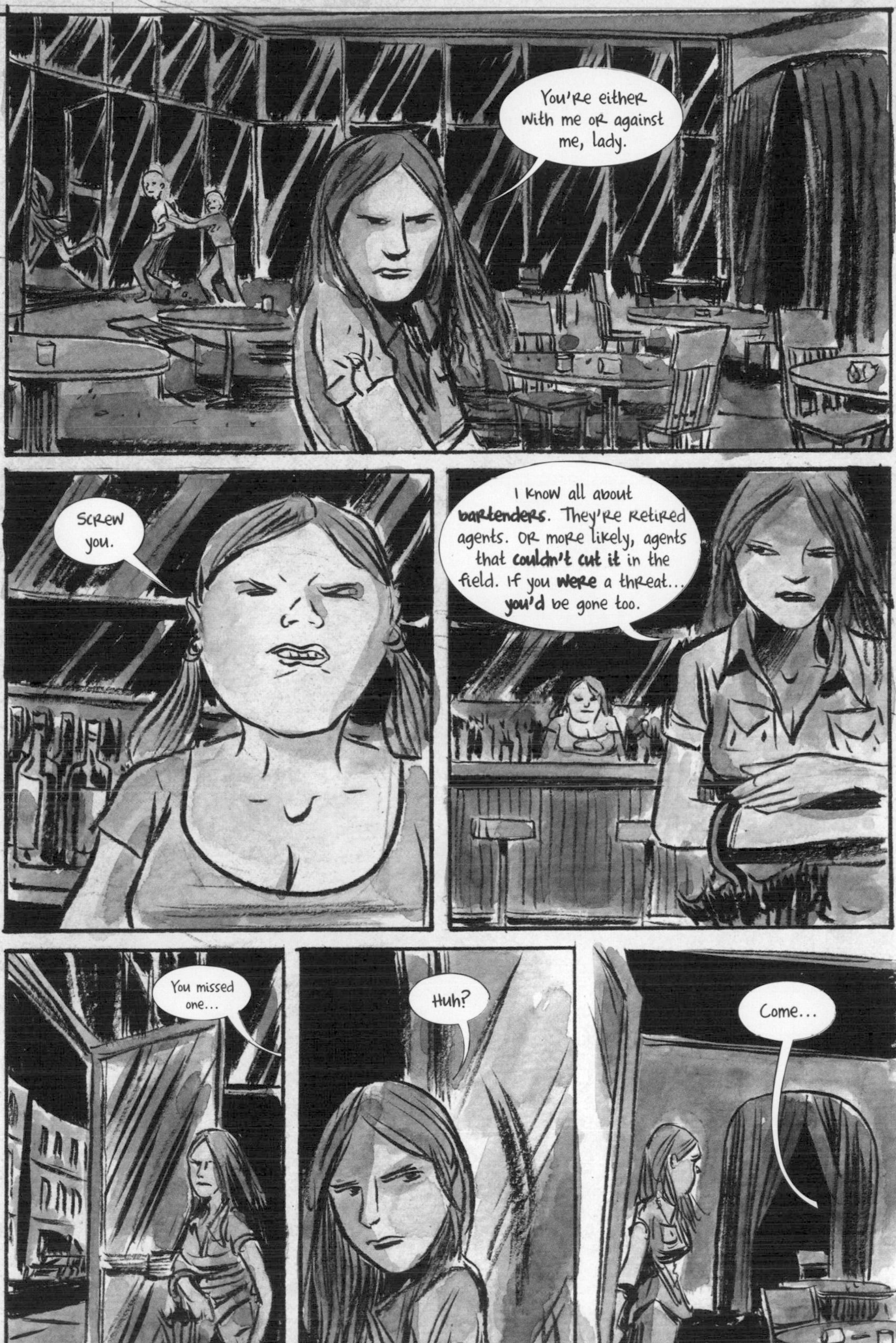
You're either with me or against me, lady.
Screw you.
I know all about bartenders. They're retired agents. Or more likely, agents that couldn't cut it in the field. If you were a threat... you'd be gone too.
You missed one...
Huh?
Come...

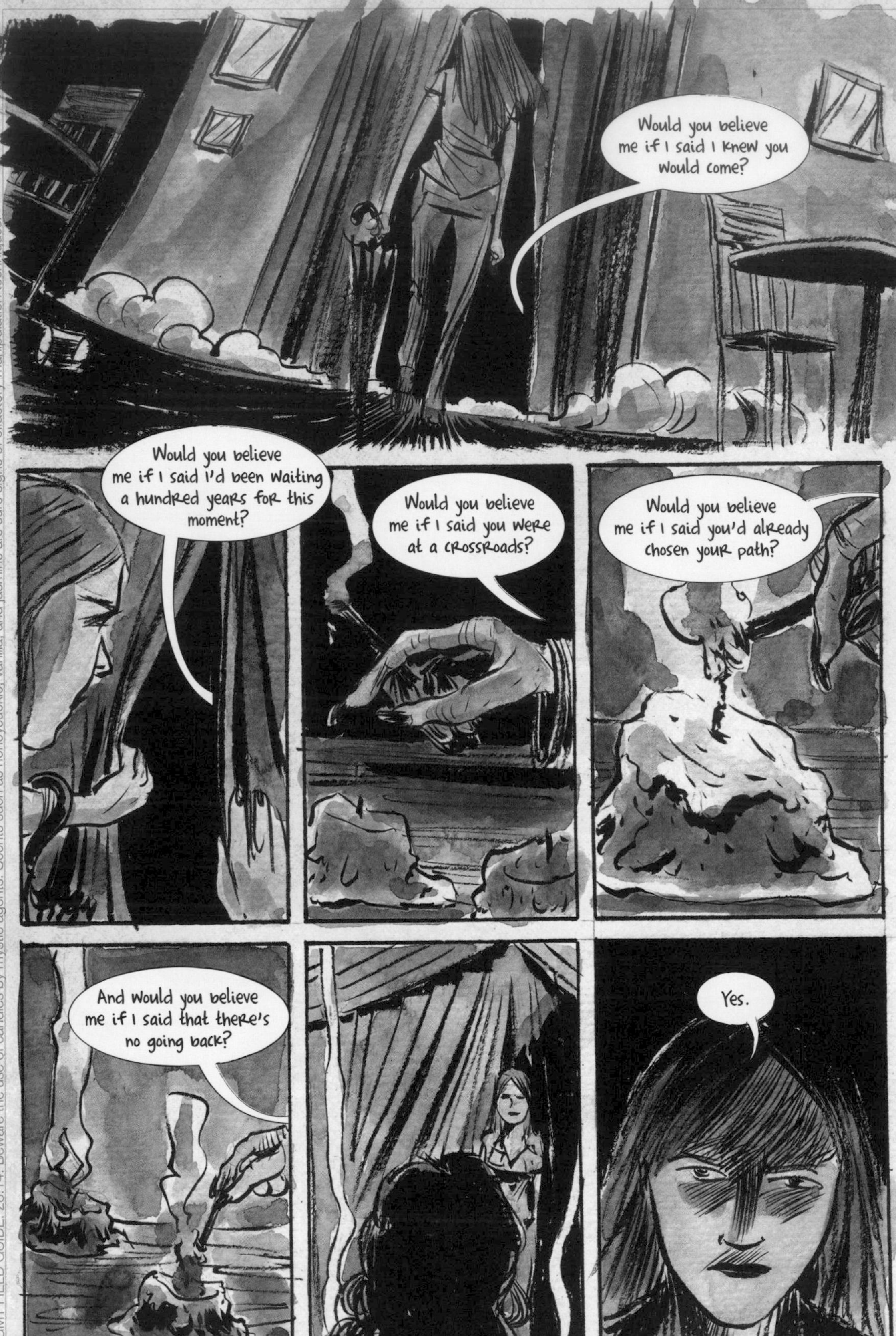
Would you believe me if I said I knew you would come?
Would you believe me if I said I'd been waiting a hundred years for this moment?
Would you believe me if I said you were at a crossroads?
Would you believe me if I said you'd already chosen your path?
And would you believe me if I said that there's no going back?
Yes.

MIND MGMT FIELD GUIDE. 28.14. Beware the use of candles by mystic agents. Scents such as honeysuckle, vanilla, and jasmine are sure signs of olfactory-manipulation techniques.

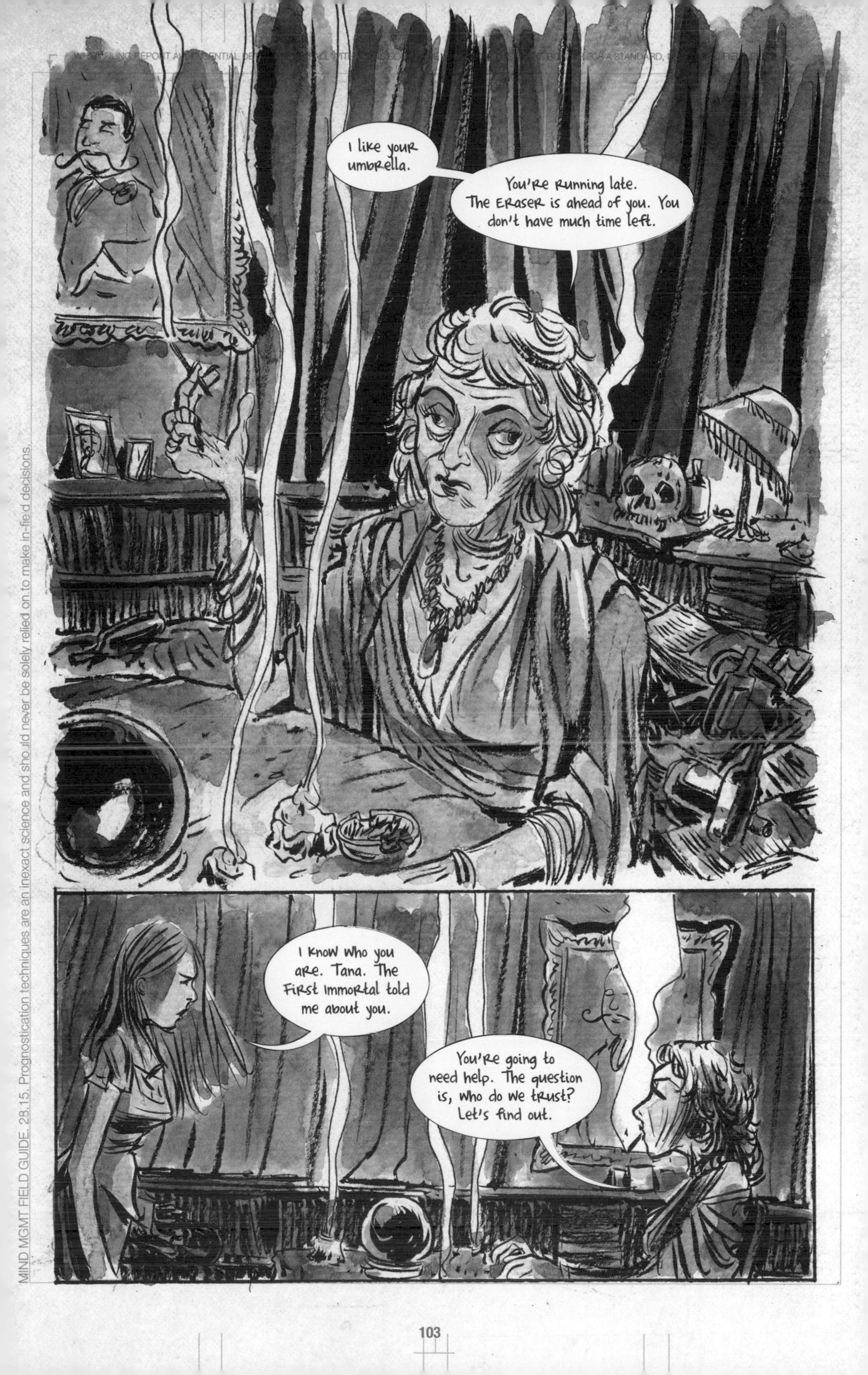

I like your umbrella.
You're running late. The Eraser is ahead of you. You don't have much time left.
I know who you are. Tana. The First Immortal told me about you.
You're going to need help. The question is, who do we trust? Let's find out.

MIND MGMT FIELD GUIDE. 28.15. Prognostication techniques are an inexact science and should never be solely relied on to make in-field decisions.

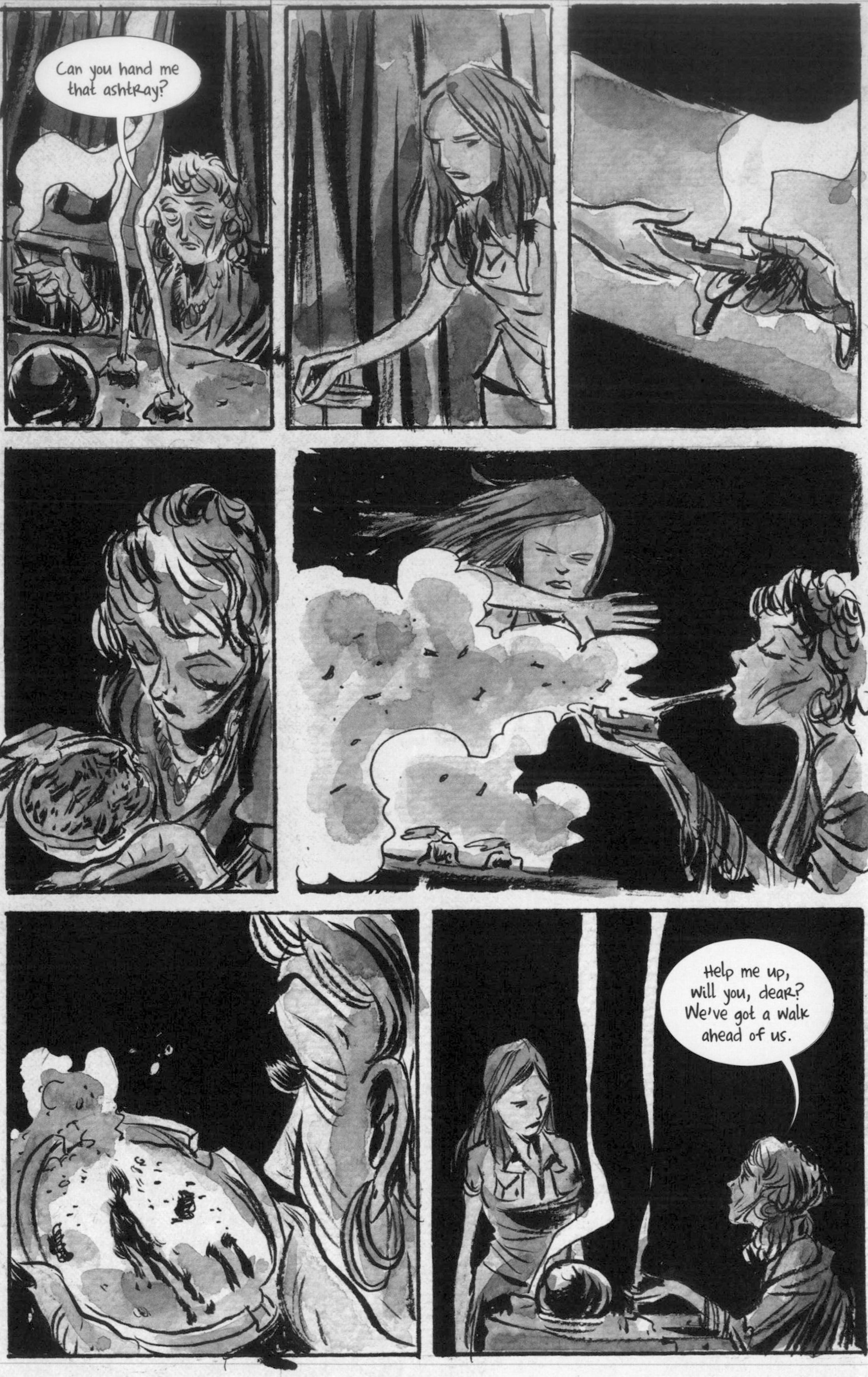
Can you hand me that ashtray?
Help me up, will you, dear? We've got a walk ahead of us.

MIND MGMT FIELD GUIDE. 28.16. Lethal dispatch of any agents who do not identify themselves with the three agent call signs is authorized and encouraged.

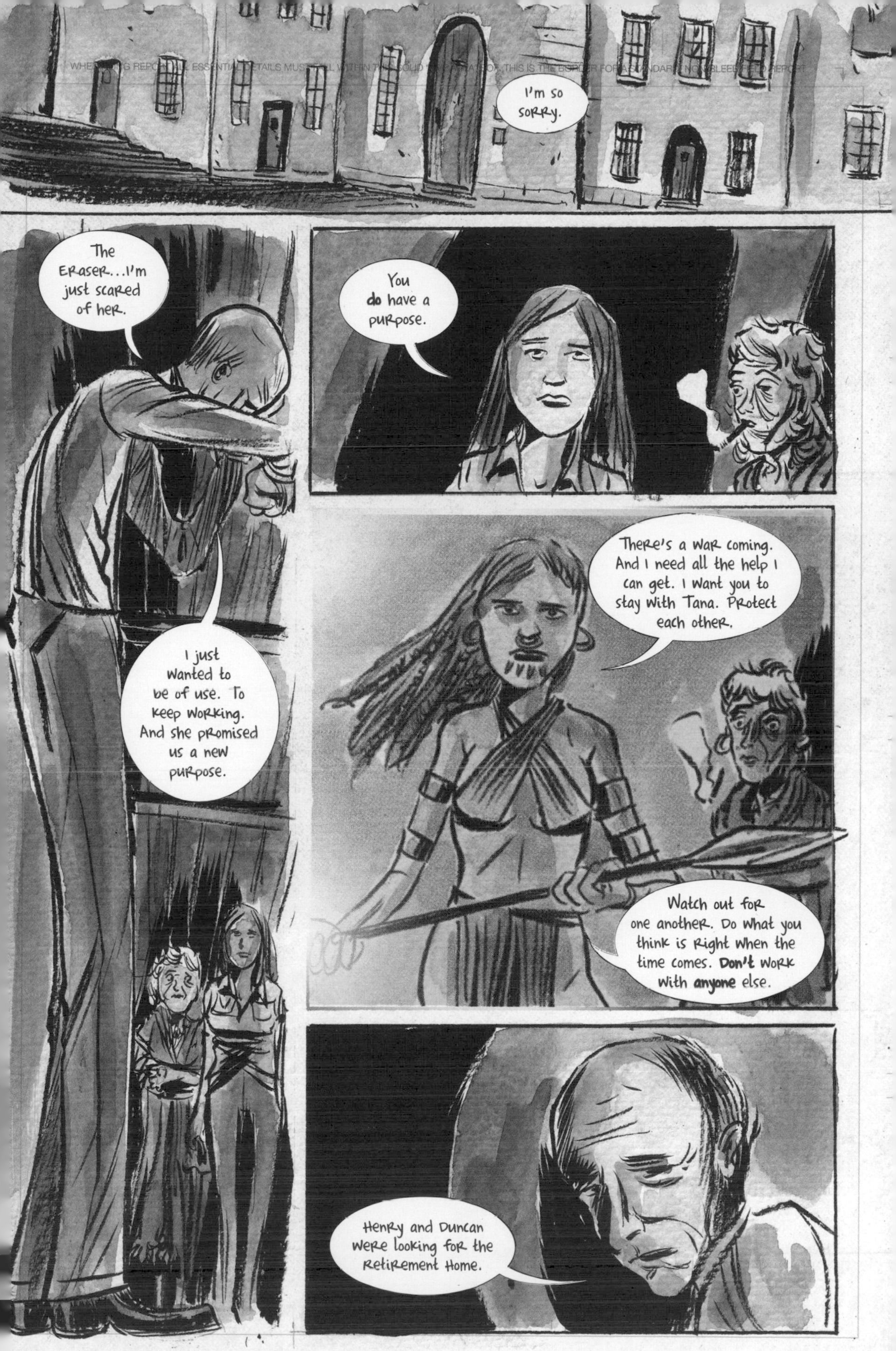
I'm so sorry.
The Eraser...I'm just scared of her.
I just wanted to be of use. To keep working. And she promised us a new purpose.
You **do** have a purpose.
There's a war coming. And I need all the help I can get. I want you to stay with Tana. Protect each other.
Watch out for one another. Do what you think is right when the time comes. **Don't** work with **anyone** else.
Henry and Duncan were looking for the Retirement Home.

WHEN FILING REPORT ALL ESSENTIAL DETAILS MUST FALL WITHIN THIS SOLID "LIVE AREA" BOX. THIS IS THE BORDER FOR A STA

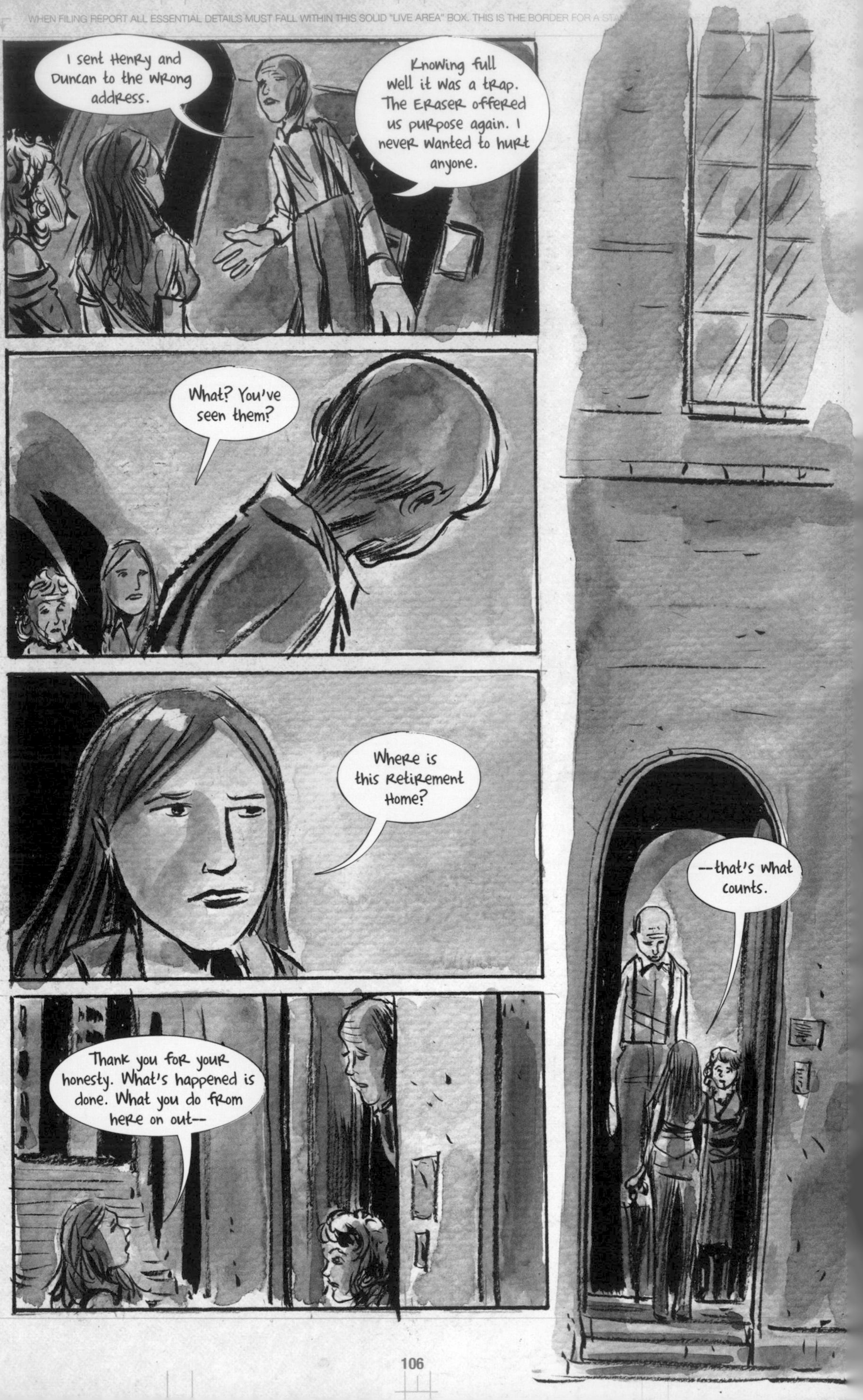

I sent Henry and Duncan to the wrong address.
Knowing full well it was a trap. The Eraser offered us purpose again. I never wanted to hurt anyone.
What? You've seen them?
Where is this Retirement Home?
Thank you for your honesty. What's happened is done. What you do from here on out--
--that's what counts.

MIND MGMT FIELD GUIDE. 28.18. Pairing of two agents in the field is inadvisable. Agents should always gather in committees or work as solo agents and handlers.

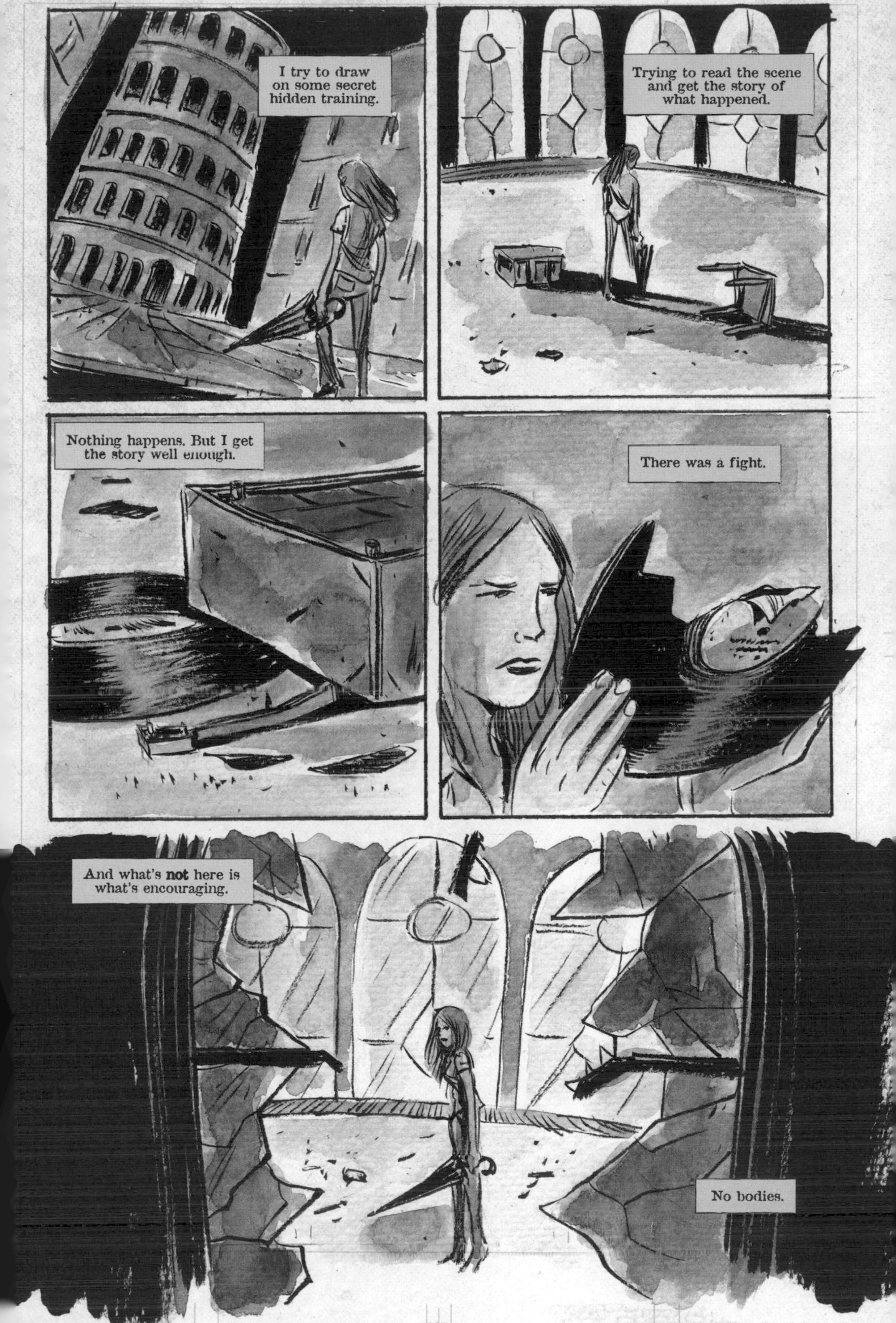
I try to draw on some secret hidden training.
Trying to read the scene and get the story of what happened.
Nothing happens. But I get the story well enough.
There was a fight.
And what's **not** here is what's encouraging.
No bodies.

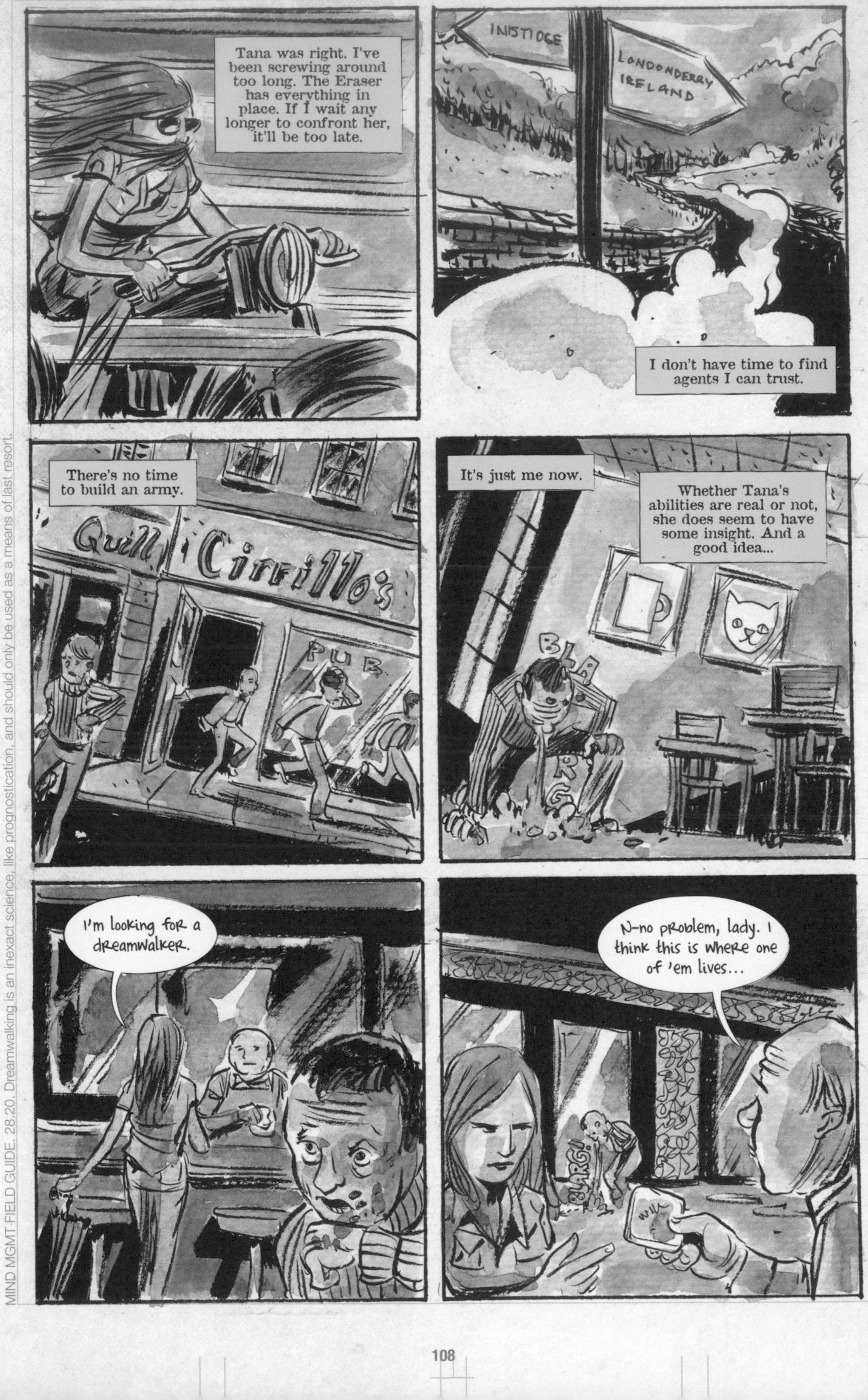
Tana was right. I've been screwing around too long. The Eraser has everything in place. If I wait any longer to confront her, it'll be too late.
INISTIOGE
LONDONDERRY IRELAND
I don't have time to find agents I can trust.
There's no time to build an army.
Quill
Cirrillo's
PUB
It's just me now.
Whether Tana's abilities are real or not, she does seem to have some insight. And a good idea...
BLARG
I'm looking for a dreamwalker.
N-no problem, lady. I think this is where one of 'em lives...
BLARG!

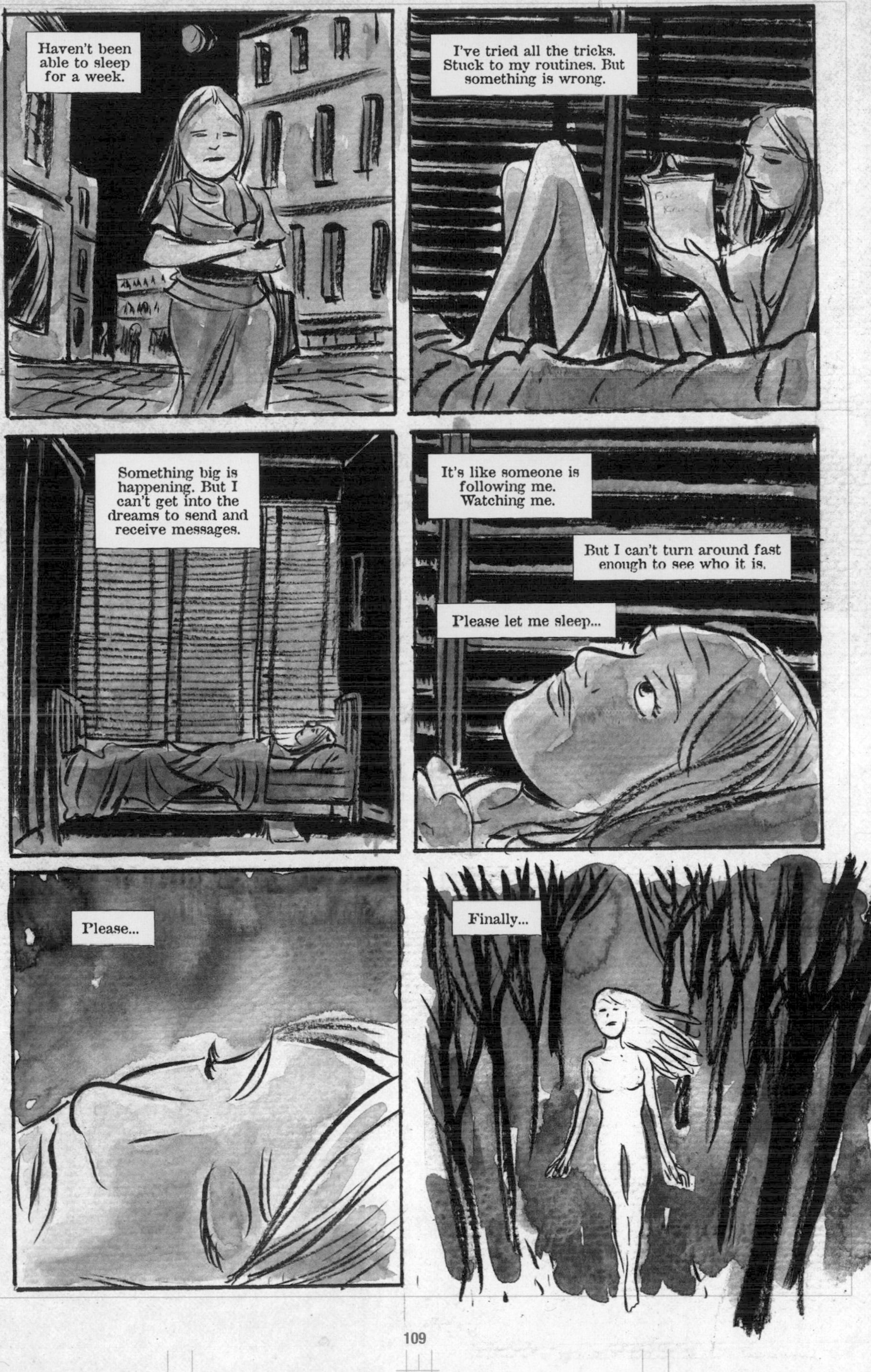
Haven't been able to sleep for a week.
I've tried all the tricks. Stuck to my routines. But something is wrong.
Something big is happening. But I can't get into the dreams to send and receive messages.
It's like someone is following me. Watching me.
But I can't turn around fast enough to see who it is.
Please let me sleep...
Please...
Finally...

MIND MGMT FIELD GUIDE. 28.21. Never wake a dreamwalker while they are sleeping. This can have devastating effects on both the walker and the receiver of a message.

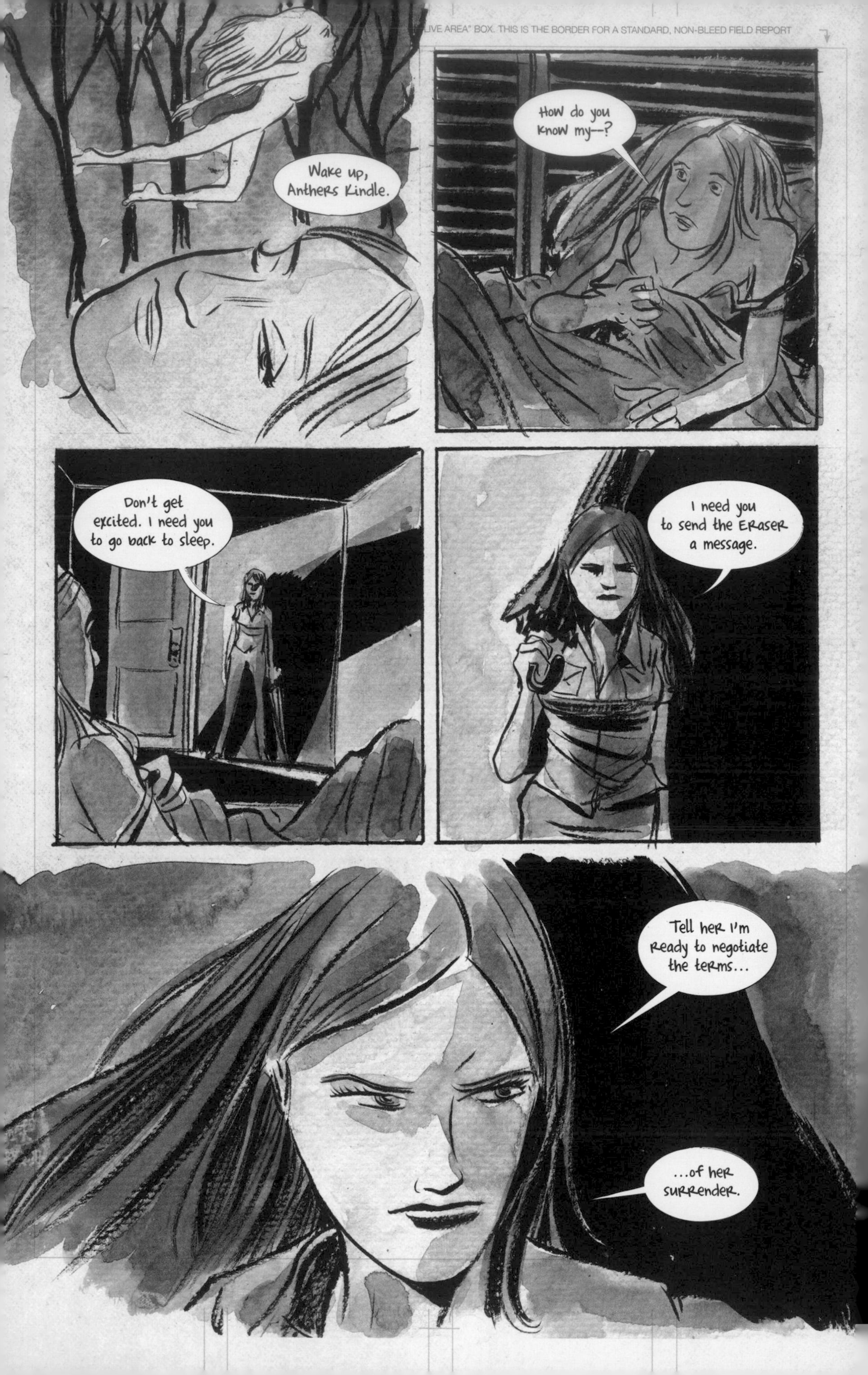
Wake up, Anthers Kindle.
How do you know my--?
Don't get excited. I need you to go back to sleep.
I need you to send the Eraser a message.
Tell her I'm ready to negotiate the terms...
...of her surrender.

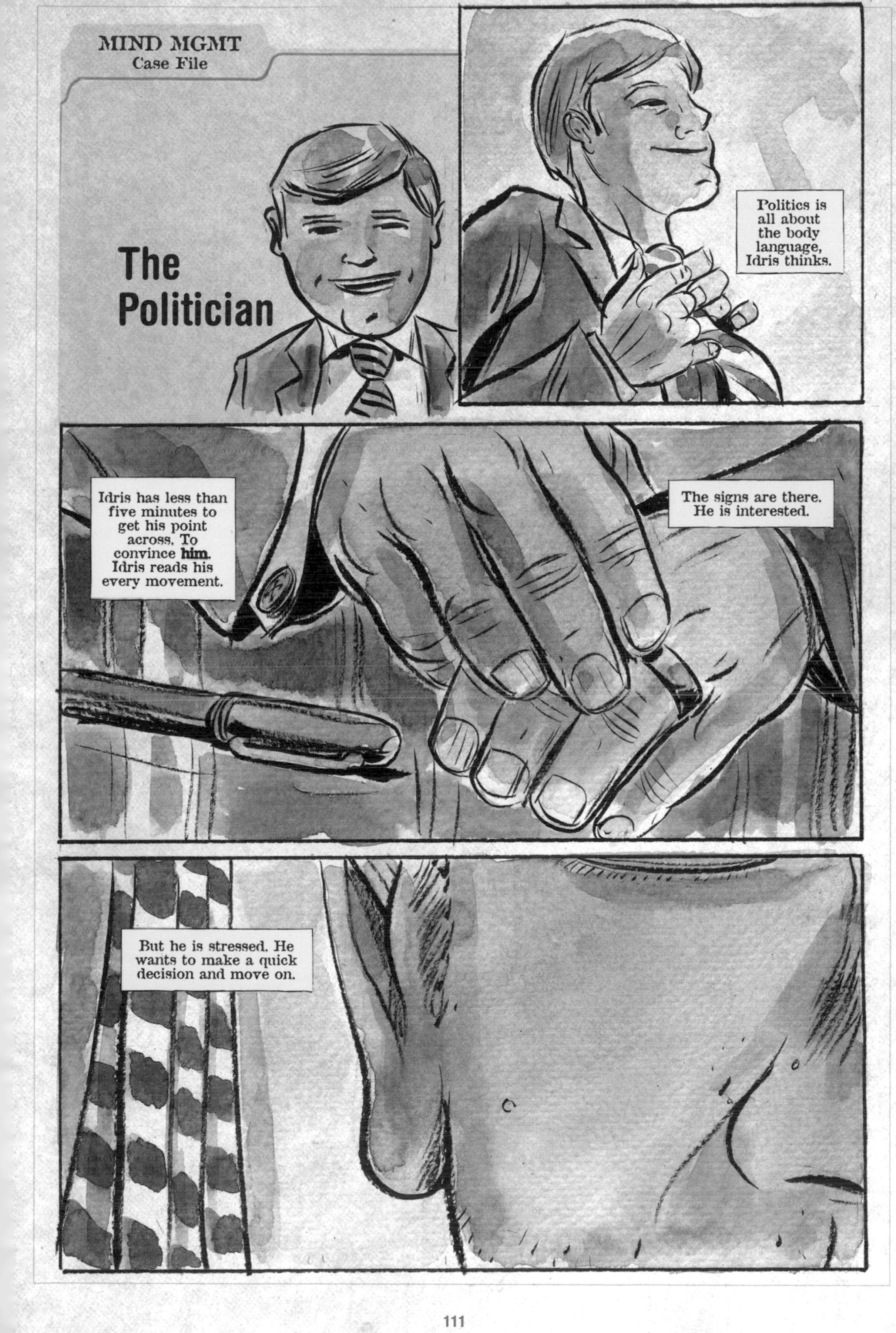
MIND MGMT
Case File
The Politician
Politics is all about the body language, Idris thinks.
Idris has less than five minutes to get his point across. To convince **him**. Idris reads his every movement.
The signs are there. He is interested.
But he is stressed. He wants to make a quick decision and move on.

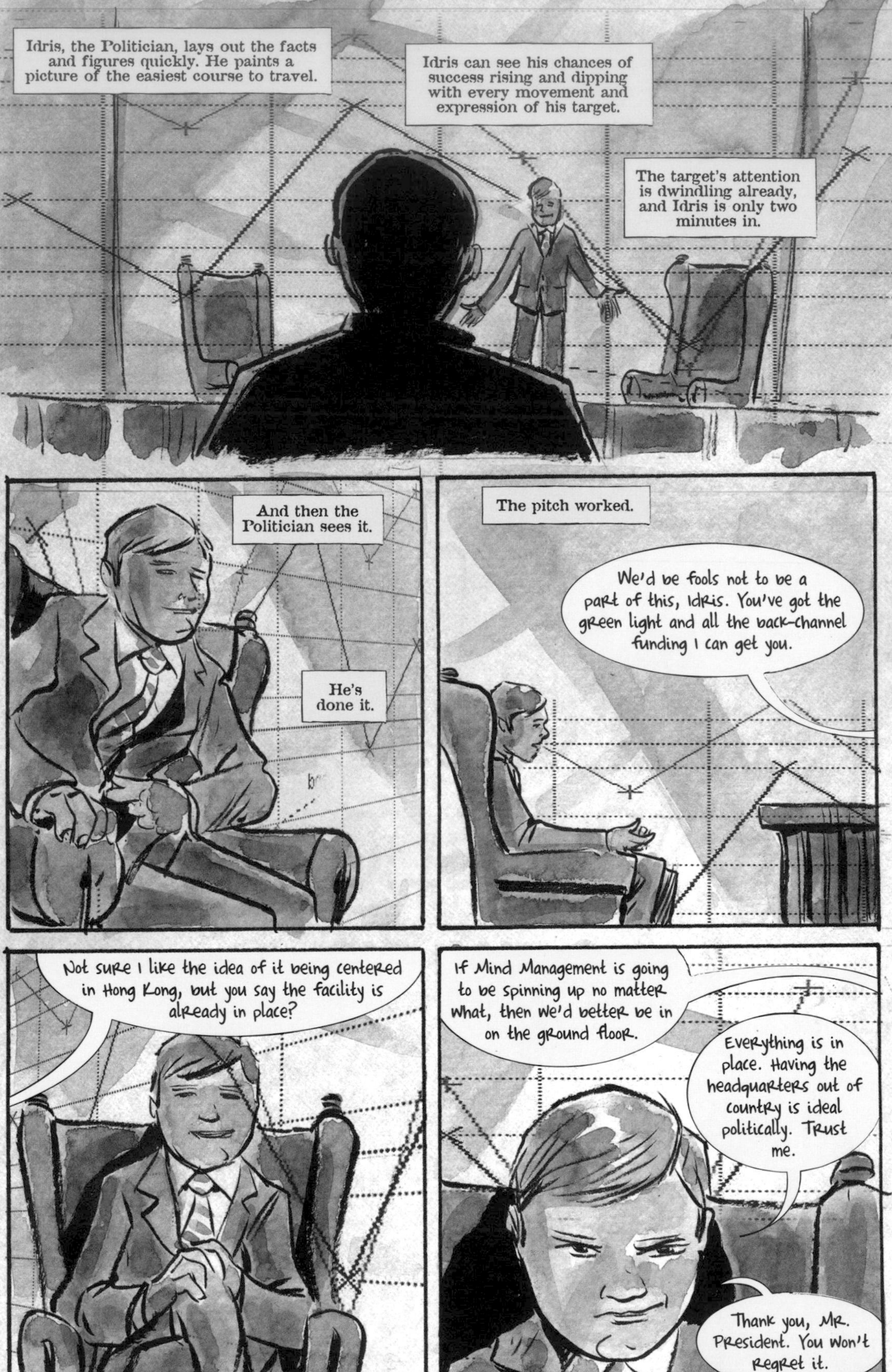
Idris, the Politician, lays out the facts and figures quickly. He paints a picture of the easiest course to travel.
Idris can see his chances of success rising and dipping with every movement and expression of his target.
The target's attention is dwindling already, and Idris is only two minutes in.
And then the Politician sees it.
He's done it.
The pitch worked.
We'd be fools not to be a part of this, Idris. You've got the green light and all the back-channel funding I can get you.
Not sure I like the idea of it being centered in Hong Kong, but you say the facility is already in place?
If Mind Management is going to be spinning up no matter what, then we'd better be in on the ground floor.
Everything is in place. Having the headquarters out of country is ideal politically. Trust me.
Thank you, Mr. President. You won't regret it.

End Mind Memo.

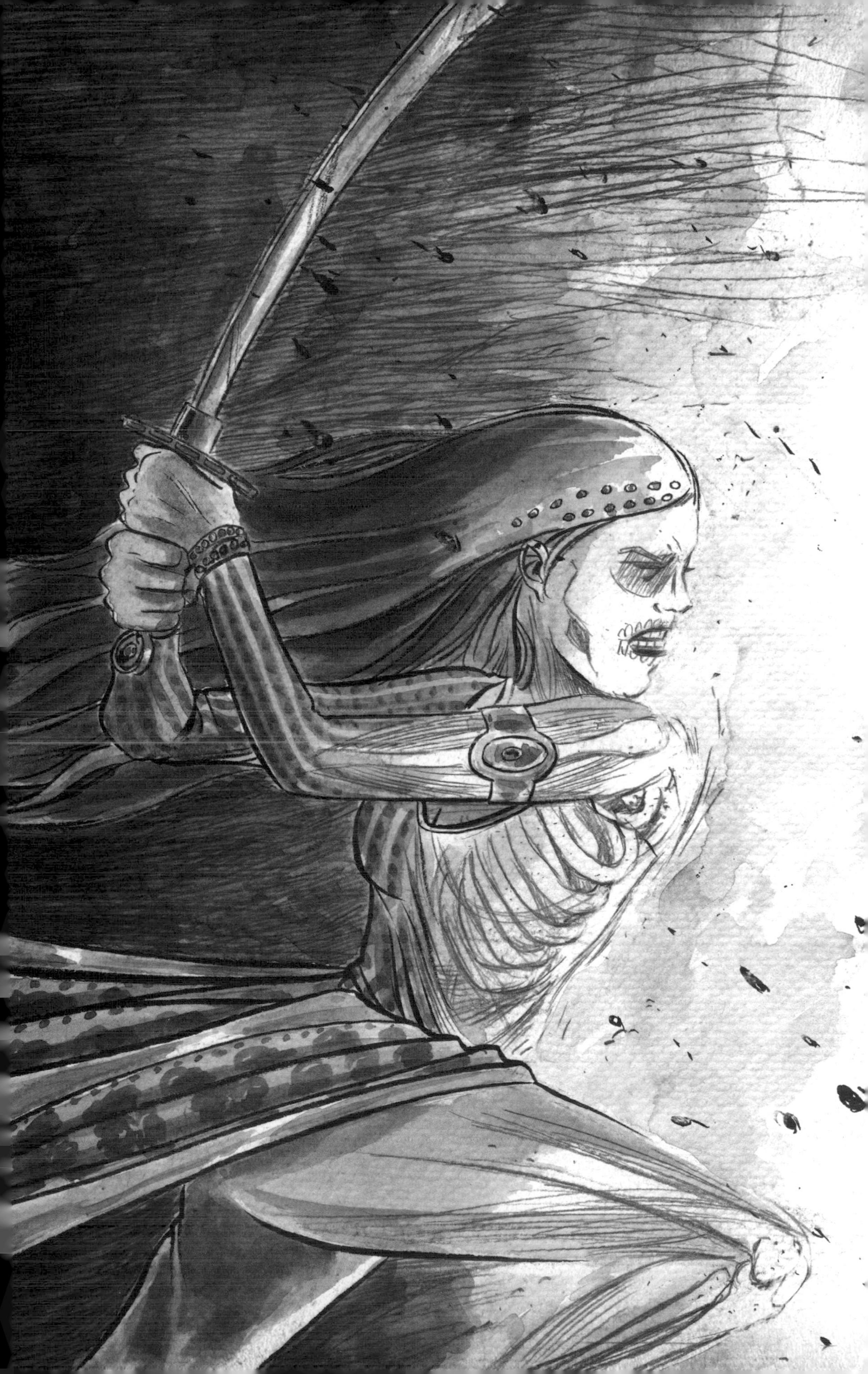

29

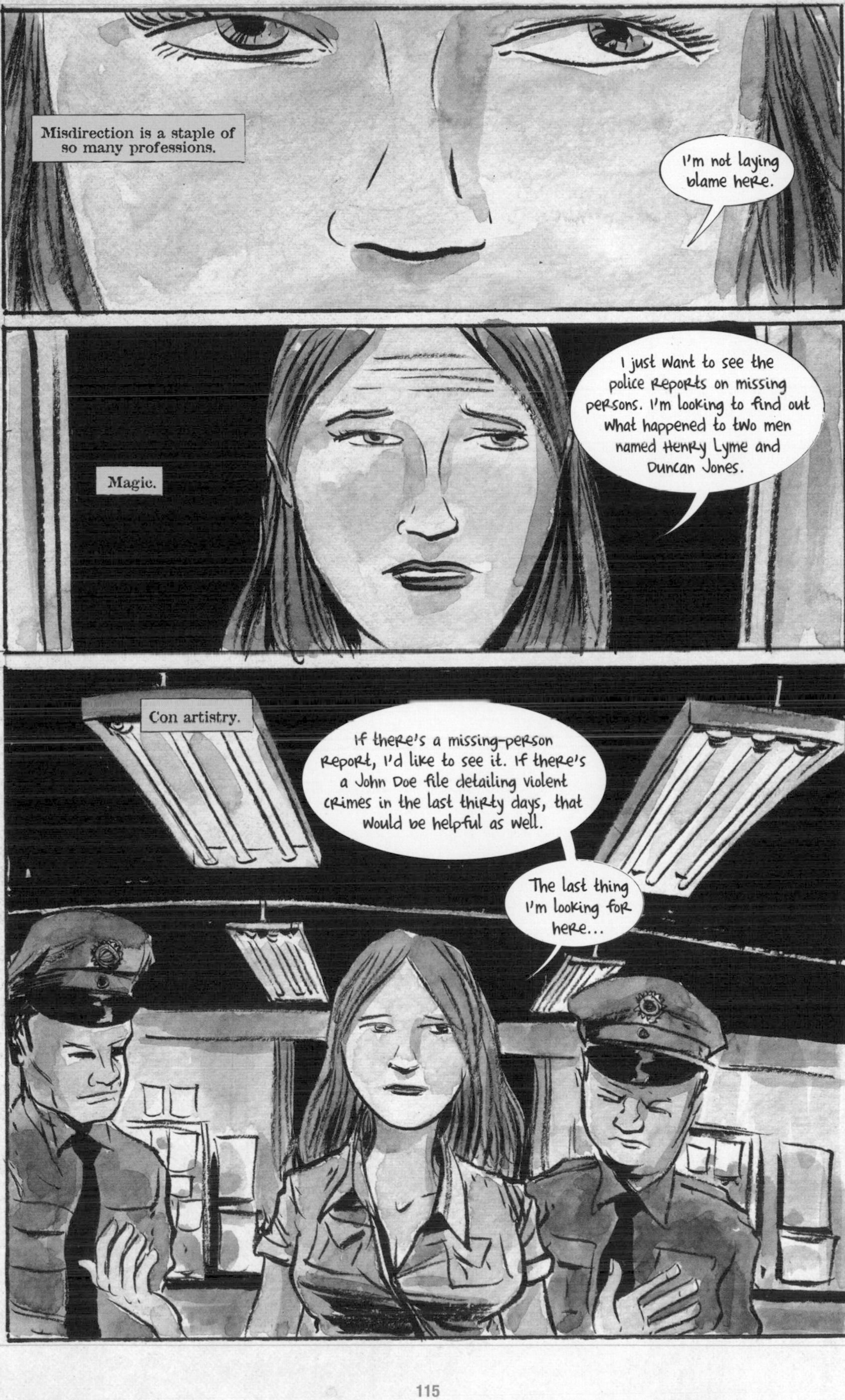
Misdirection is a staple of so many professions.
I'm not laying blame here.
Magic.
I just want to see the police reports on missing persons. I'm looking to find out what happened to two men named Henry Lyme and Duncan Jones.
Con artistry.
If there's a missing-person report, I'd like to see it. If there's a John Doe file detailing violent crimes in the last thirty days, that would be helpful as well.
The last thing I'm looking for here...

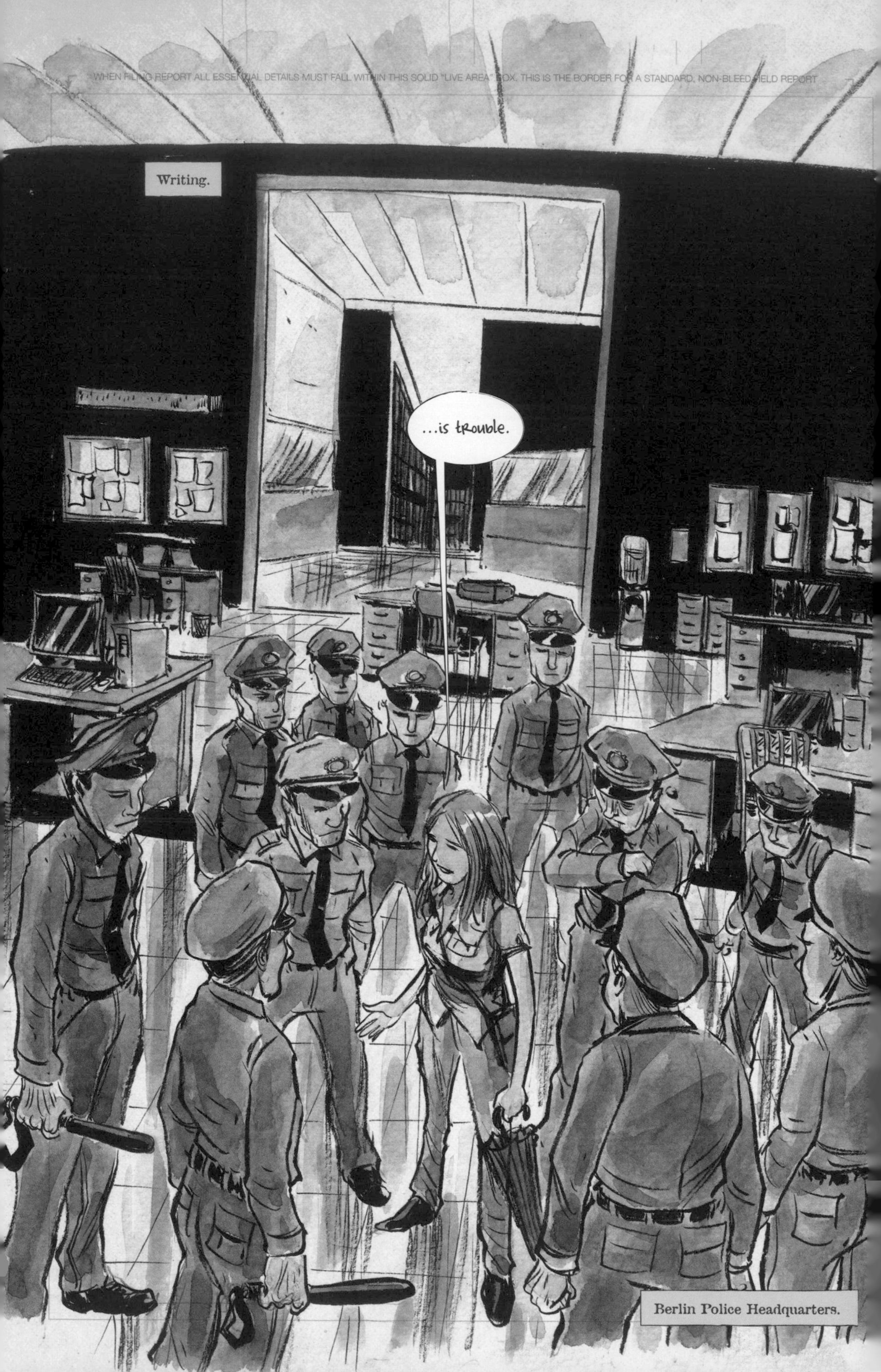
WHEN FILING REPORT ALL ESSENTIAL DETAILS MUST FALL WITHIN THIS SOLID "LIVE AREA" BOX. THIS IS THE BORDER FOR A STANDARD, NON-BLEED FIELD REPORT
Writing.
...is trouble.
Berlin Police Headquarters.

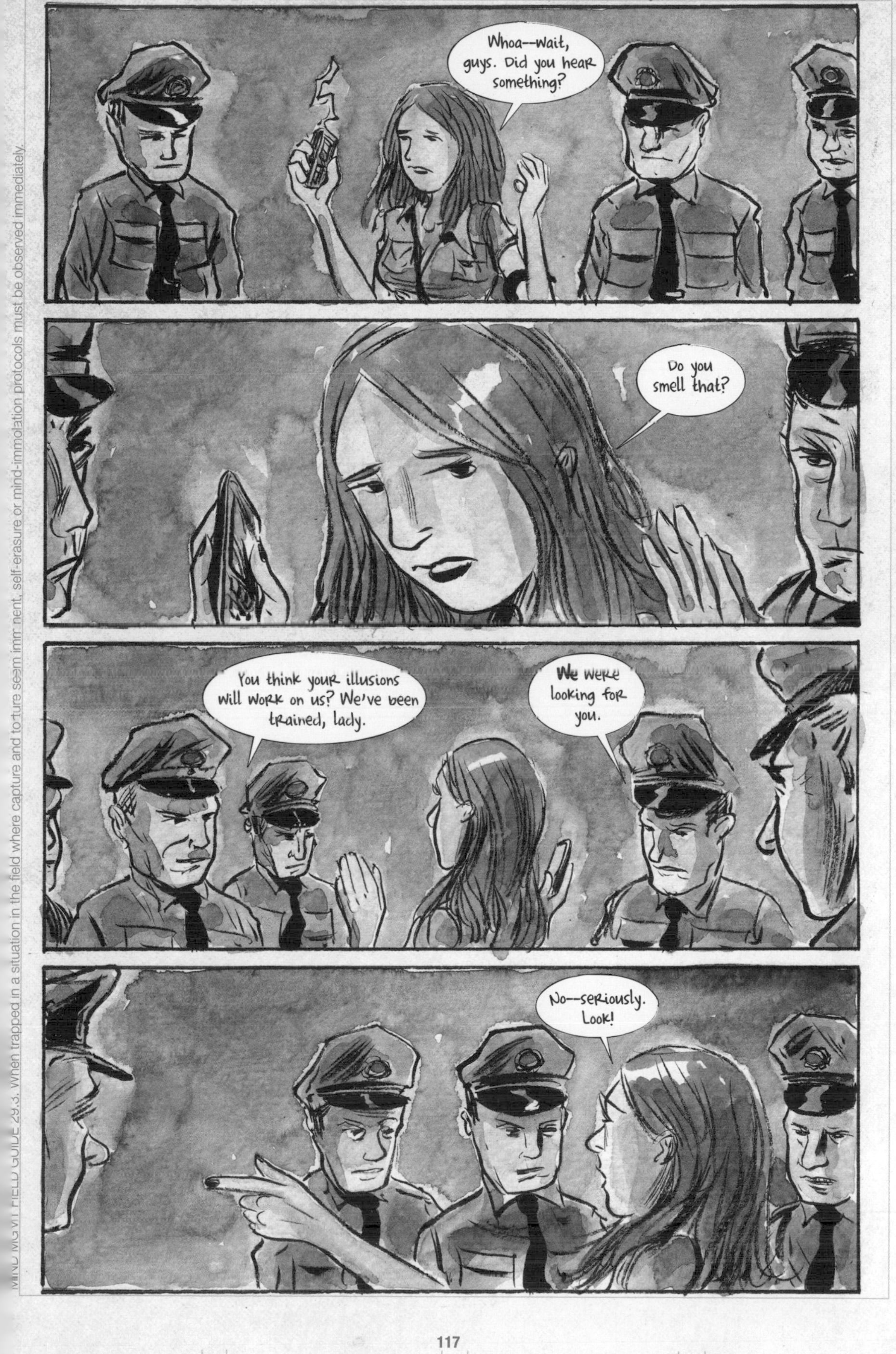
Whoa--wait, guys. Did you hear something?
Do you smell that?
You think your illusions will work on us? We've been trained, lady.
We were looking for you.
No--seriously. Look!

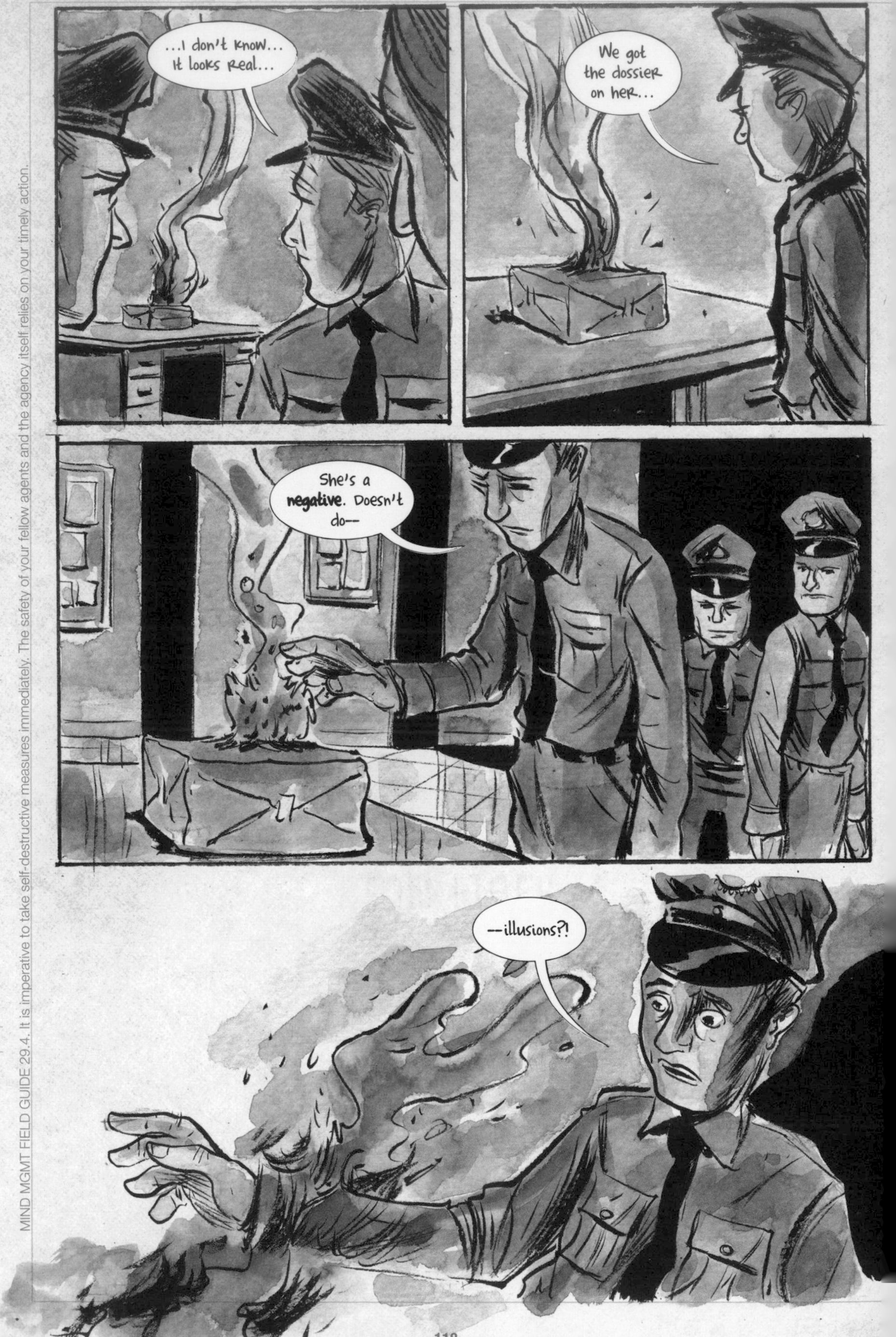
...I don't know...
It looks real...
We got the dossier on her...
She's a **negative**. Doesn't do--
--illusions?!

WHEN FILING REPORT ALL ESSENTIAL DETAILS MUST FALL WITHIN THIS SOLID "LIVE AREA" BOX. THIS IS THE BORDER FOR A STANDARD, NON-BLEED FIELD REPORT

MIND MGMT FIELD GUIDE 29.5. Using improvised incendiary/explosive devices in the field is discouraged. If such items are required, agents must file the appropriate ephemeral forms requesting Improvisation Agents.

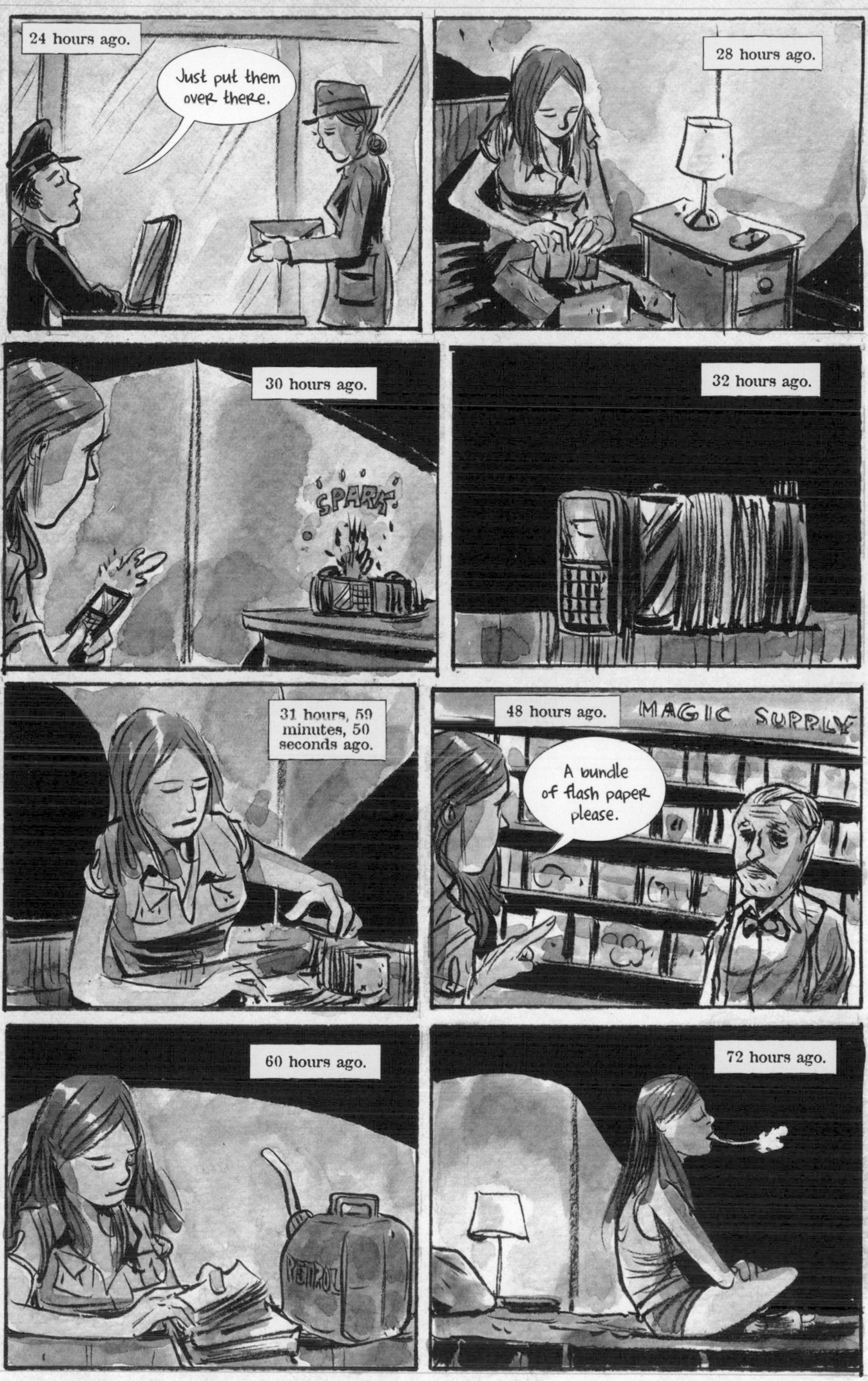

24 hours ago.
Just put them over there.
28 hours ago.
30 hours ago.
SPARK!
32 hours ago.
31 hours, 59 minutes, 50 seconds ago.
48 hours ago.
MAGIC SUPPLY
A bundle of flash paper please.
60 hours ago.
PETROL
72 hours ago.

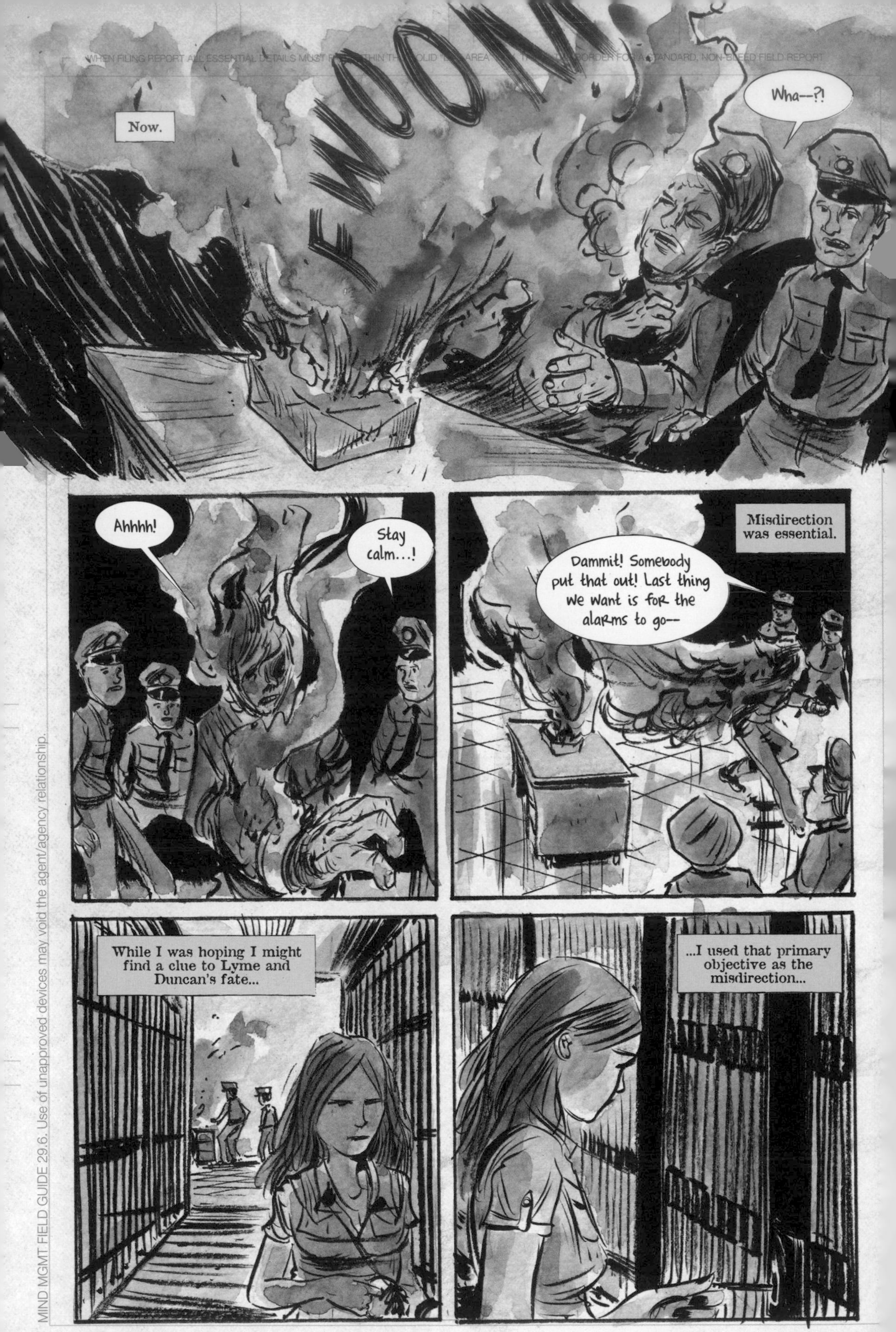

Now.
Wha--?!
Ahhhh!
Stay calm...!
Misdirection was essential.
Dammit! Somebody put that out! Last thing we want is for the alarms to go--
While I was hoping I might find a clue to Lyme and Duncan's fate...
...I used that primary objective as the misdirection...

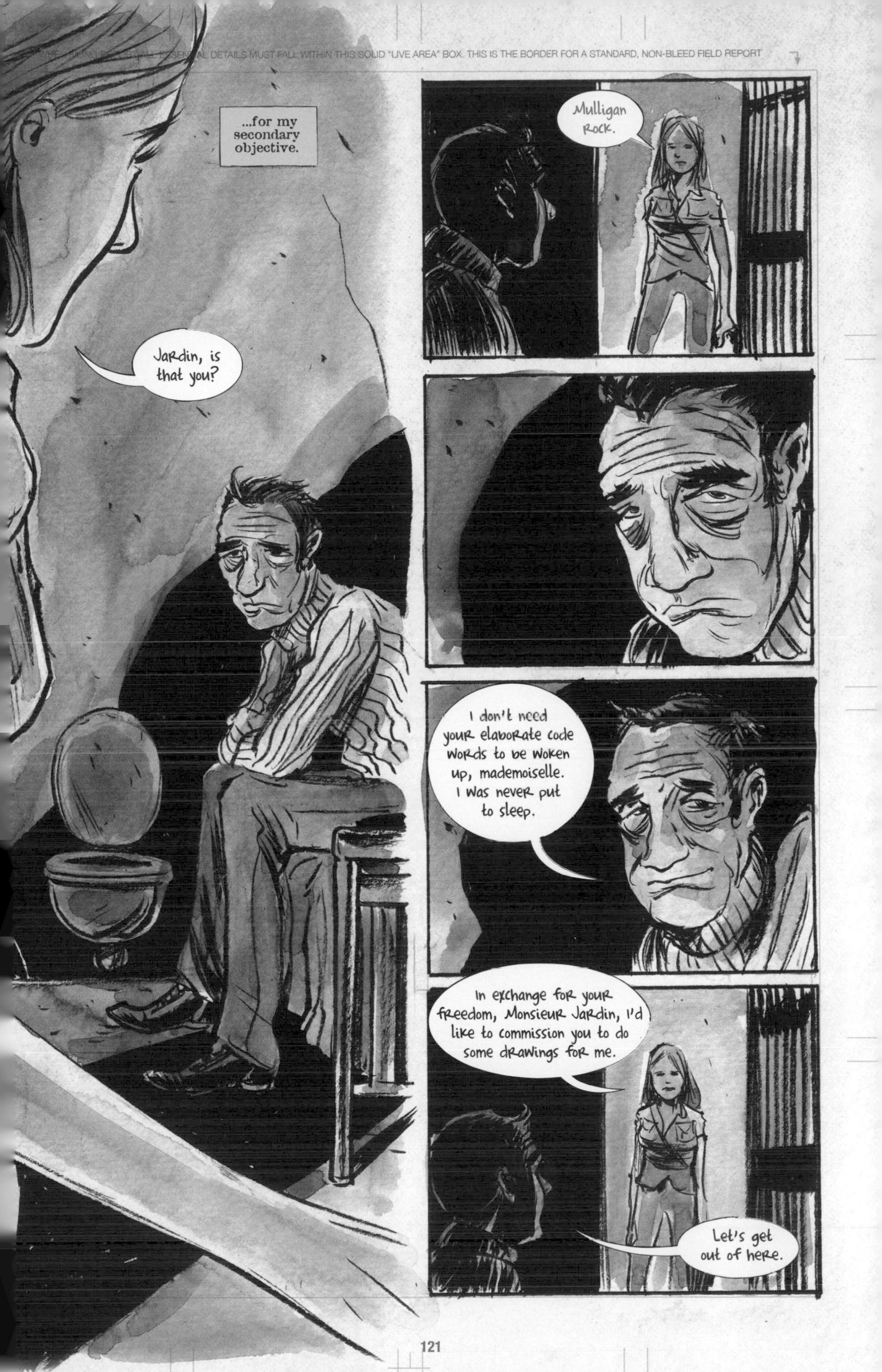
ESSENTIAL DETAILS MUST FALL WITHIN THIS SOLID "LIVE AREA" BOX. THIS IS THE BORDER FOR A STANDARD, NON-BLEED FIELD REPORT
...for my secondary objective.
Jardin, is that you?
Mulligan Rock.
I don't need your elaborate code words to be woken up, mademoiselle. I was never put to sleep.
In exchange for your freedom, Monsieur Jardin, I'd like to commission you to do some drawings for me.
Let's get out of here.

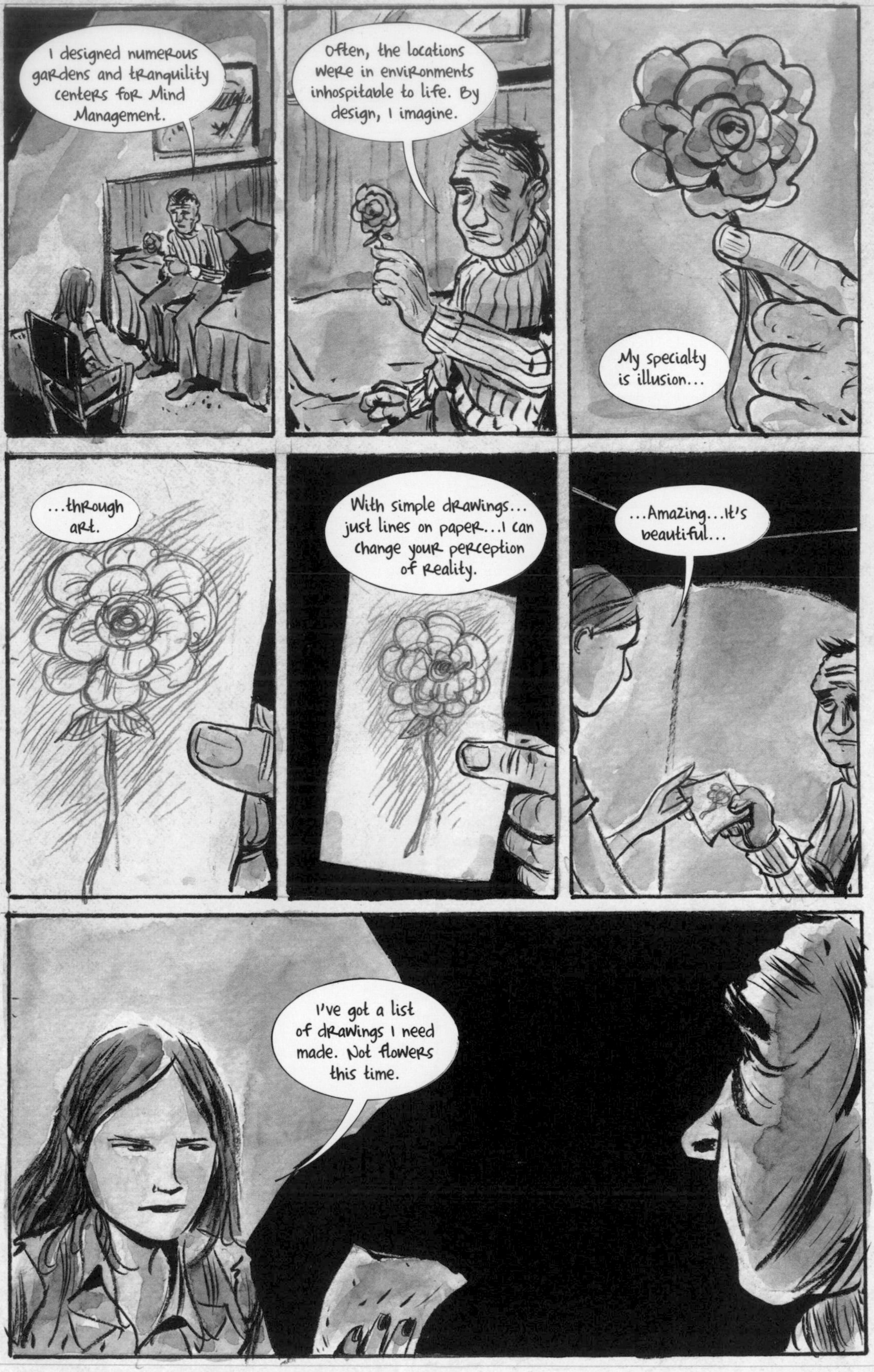
I designed numerous gardens and tranquility centers for Mind Management.
Often, the locations were in environments inhospitable to life. By design, I imagine.
My specialty is illusion...
...through art.
With simple drawings... just lines on paper...I can change your perception of reality.
...Amazing...It's beautiful...
I've got a list of drawings I need made. Not flowers this time.

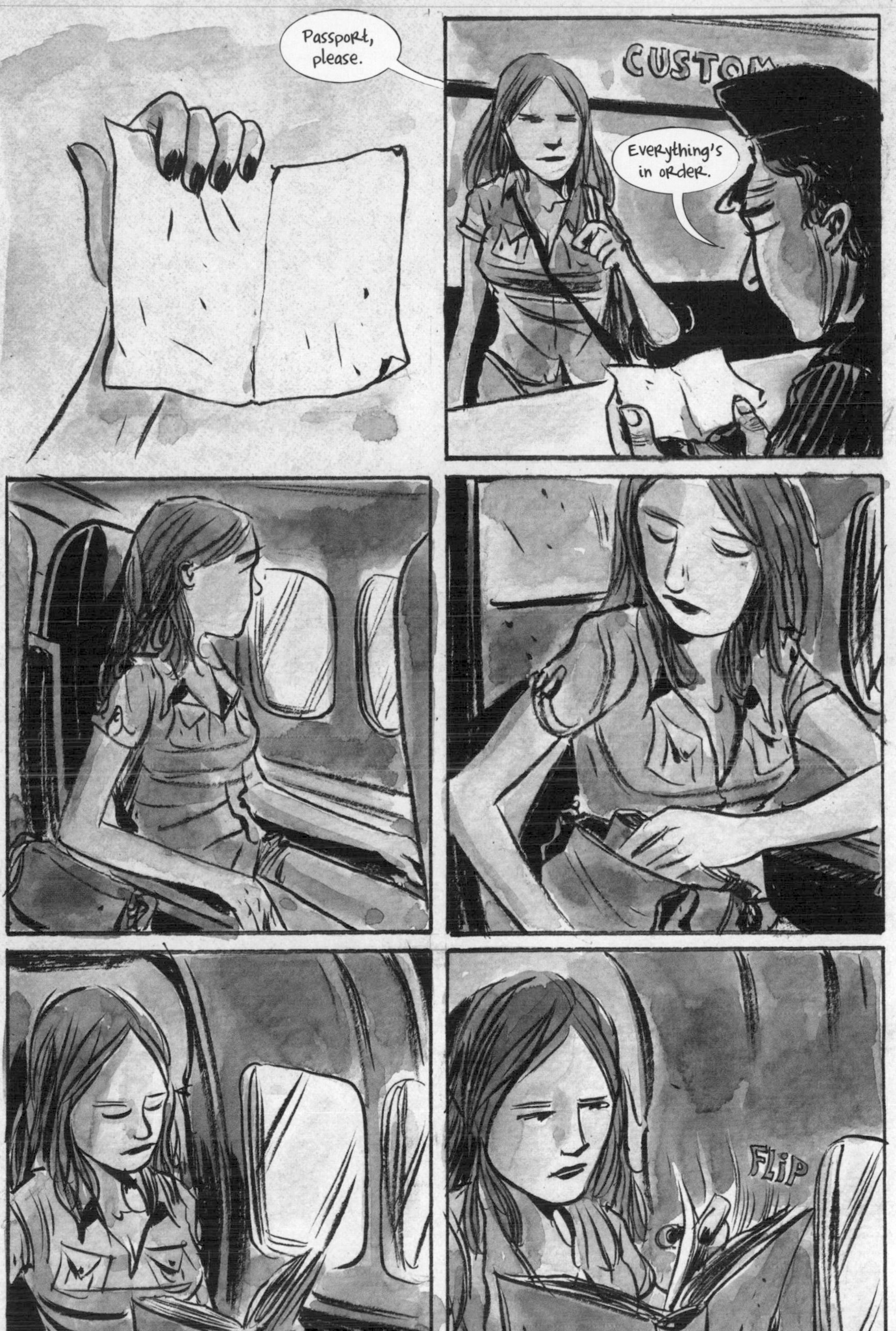
Passport, please.
Everything's in order.
FLIP

MIND MGMT FIELD GUIDE 29.9: Use of non-agency travel documents is prohibited. Only sanctioned Theoretical Paper documents are to be deployed.

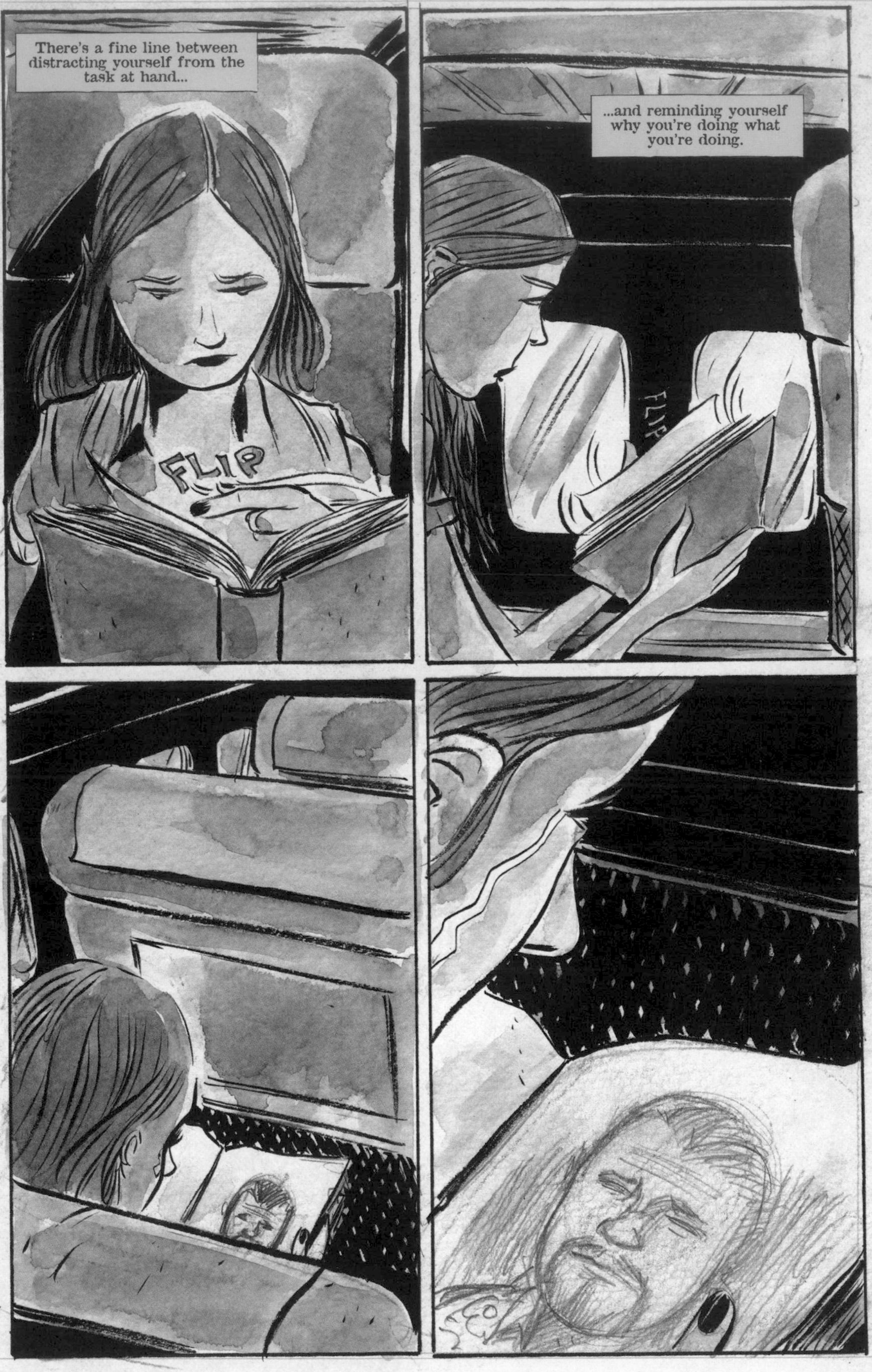
There's a fine line between distracting yourself from the task at hand...
FLIP
...and reminding yourself why you're doing what you're doing.
FLIP

WHEN ... REPORT ALL ESSENTIAL DETAILS MUST FALL WITHIN THIS SOLID "LIVE AREA" BOX. THIS IS THE BORDER FOR A STANDARD, NON-BLEED FIELD REPOR

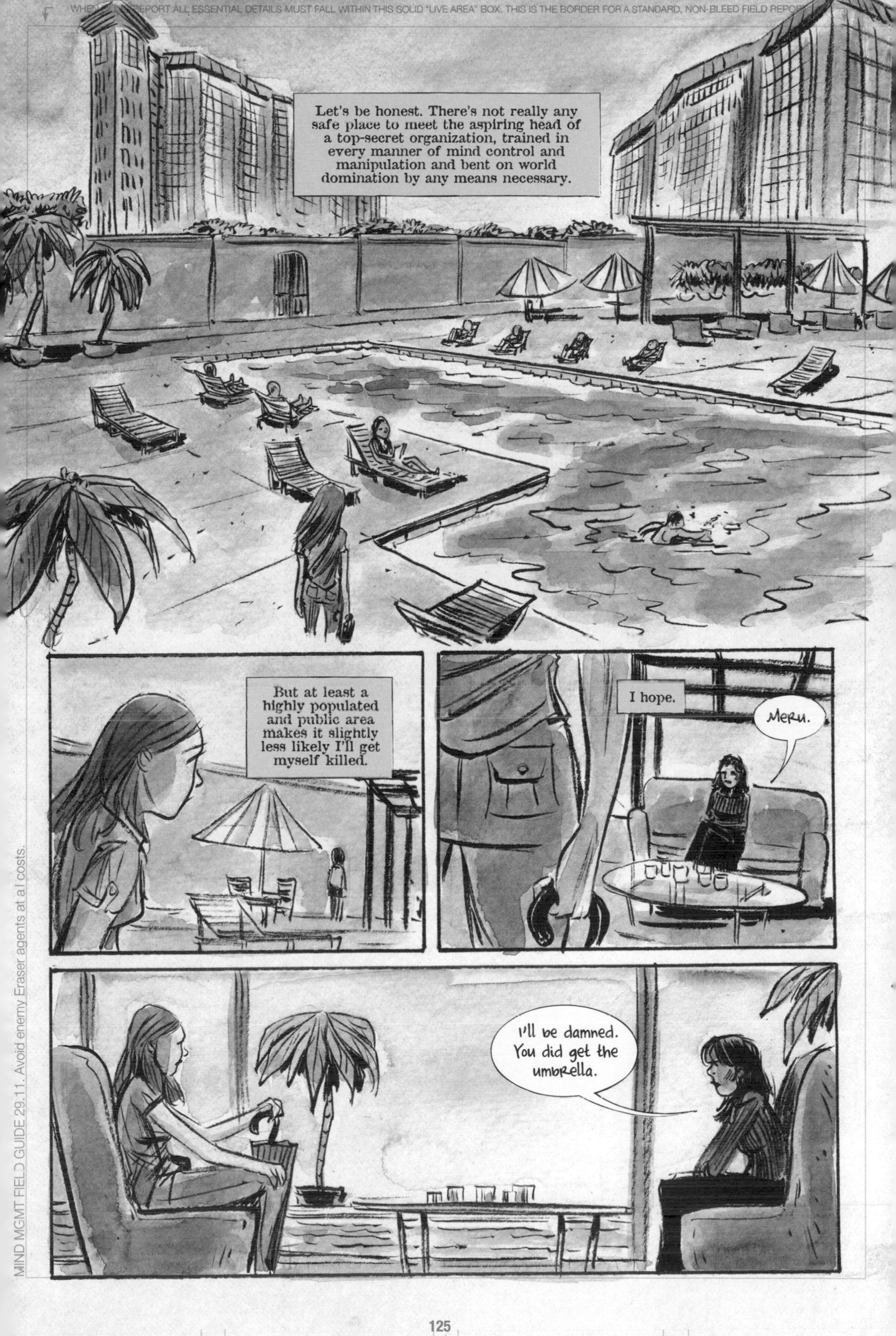
Let's be honest. There's not really any safe place to meet the aspiring head of a top-secret organization, trained in every manner of mind control and manipulation and bent on world domination by any means necessary.
But at least a highly populated and public area makes it slightly less likely I'll get myself killed.
I hope.
Meru.
I'll be damned. You did get the umbrella.

MIND MGMT FIELD GUIDE 29.11. Avoid enemy Eraser agents at all costs.

MIND MGMT FIELD GUIDE 29.12. There is no sure defense against Eraser agents—I'm sure I can. I just need to remember everything I know. Become an Eraser in reverse. Instead of letting my memories get taken away . . .

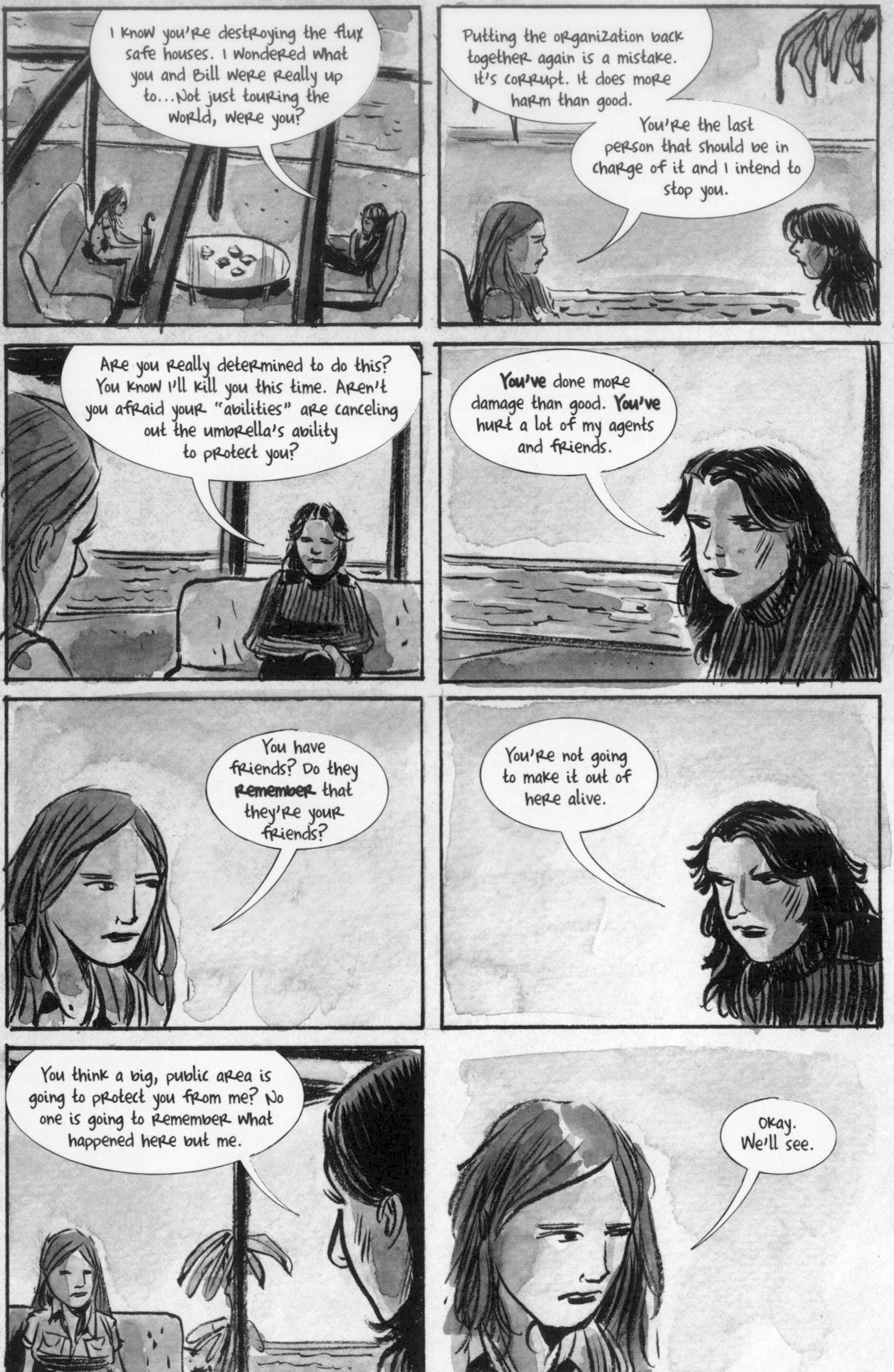
I know you're destroying the flux safe houses. I wondered what you and Bill were really up to...Not just touring the world, were you?
Putting the organization back together again is a mistake. It's corrupt. It does more harm than good.
You're the last person that should be in charge of it and I intend to stop you.
Are you really determined to do this? You know I'll kill you this time. Aren't you afraid your "abilities" are canceling out the umbrella's ability to protect you?
You've done more damage than good. **You've** hurt a lot of my agents and friends.
You have friends? Do they **remember** that they're your friends?
You're not going to make it out of here alive.
You think a big, public area is going to protect you from me? No one is going to remember what happened here but me.
Okay. We'll see.

WHEN FILING REPORT ALL ESSENTIAL DETAILS MUST FALL WITHIN THIS SOLID "LIVE AREA" BOX. THIS IS THE BORDER FOR A STANDARD, NON-BLEED FIELD REPORT

. . . I'll push my memores onto her. Memories of my life . . . and memories of her own. The details she gave me when I interviewed her. Use her own memories against her. The only way . . .

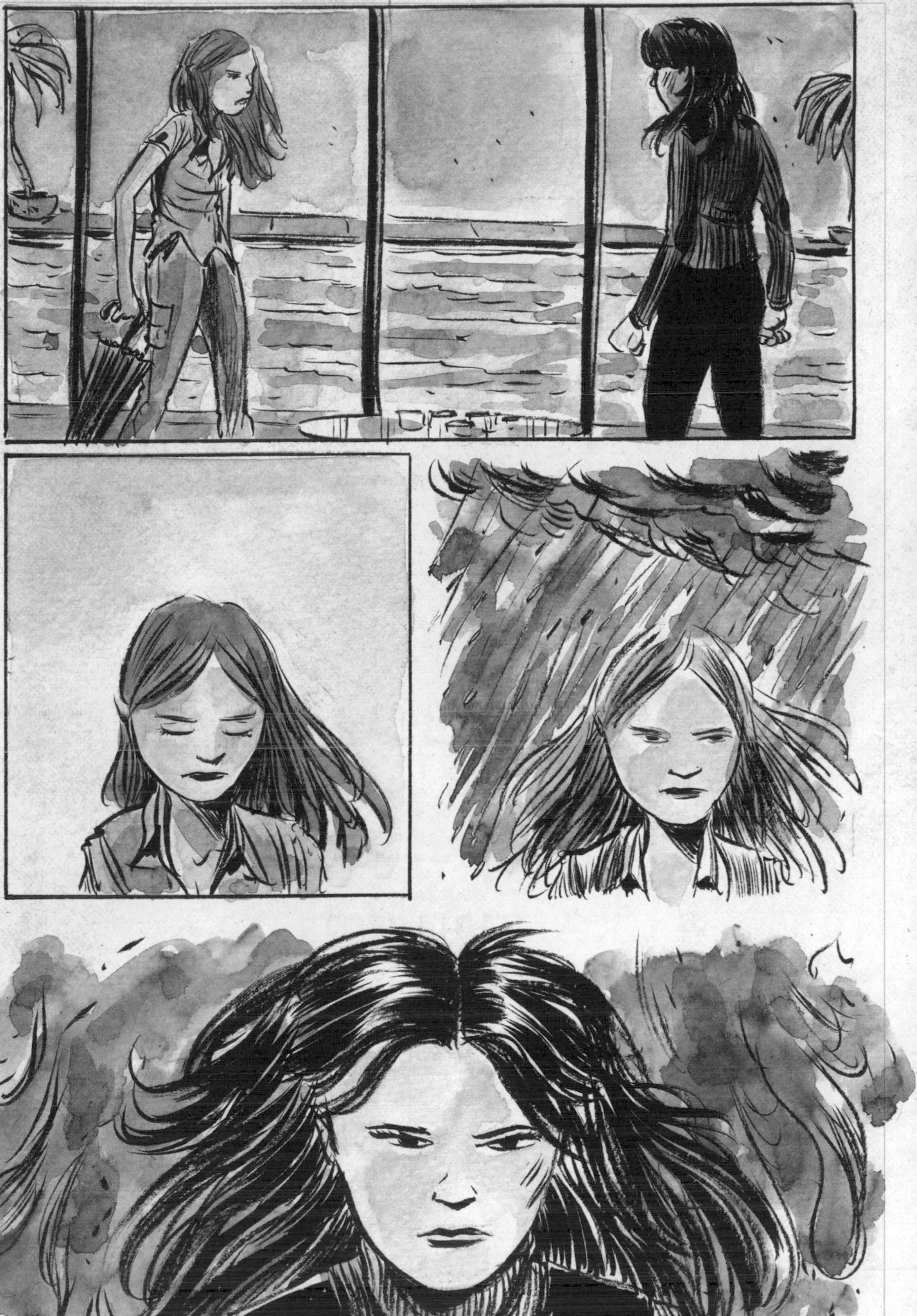

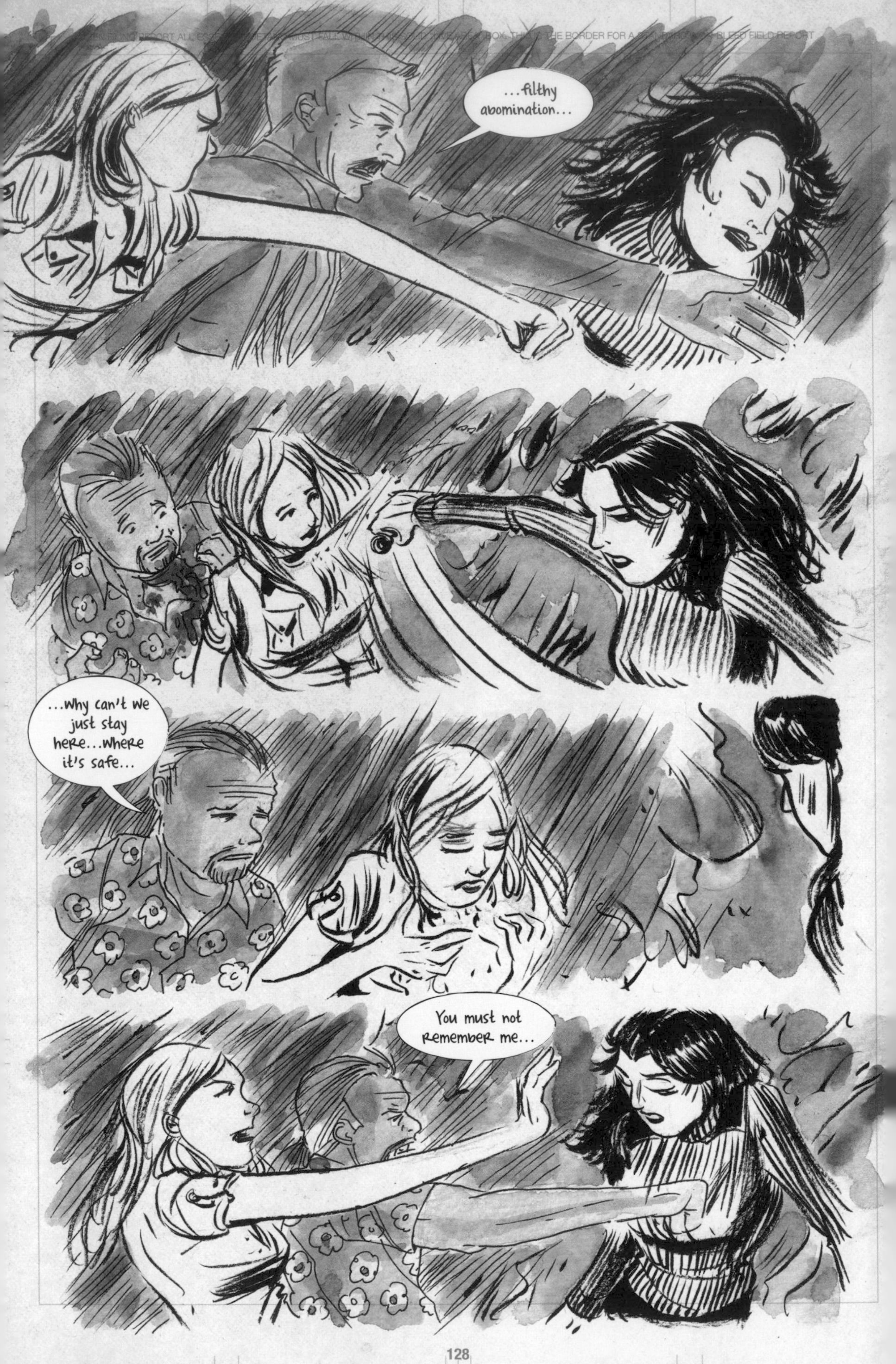
...filthy abomination...
...Why can't we just stay here...where it's safe...
You must not remember me...

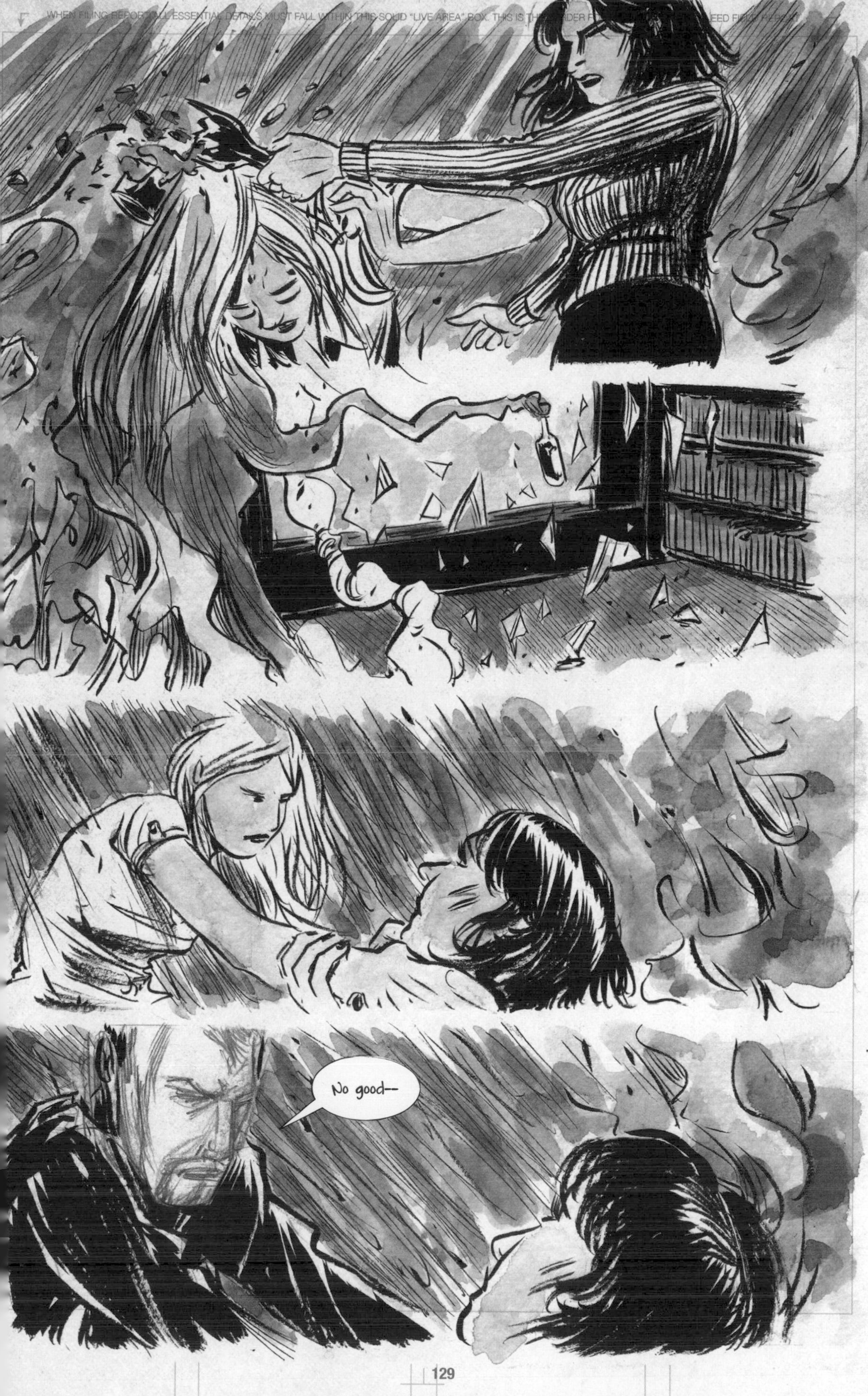
No good--

WHEN FILING REPORT ALL ESSENTIAL DETAILS MUST FALL WITHIN THIS SOLID "LIVE AREA" BOX. THIS IS THE BORDER FOR A STANDARD, NON-BLEED FIELD REPORT.

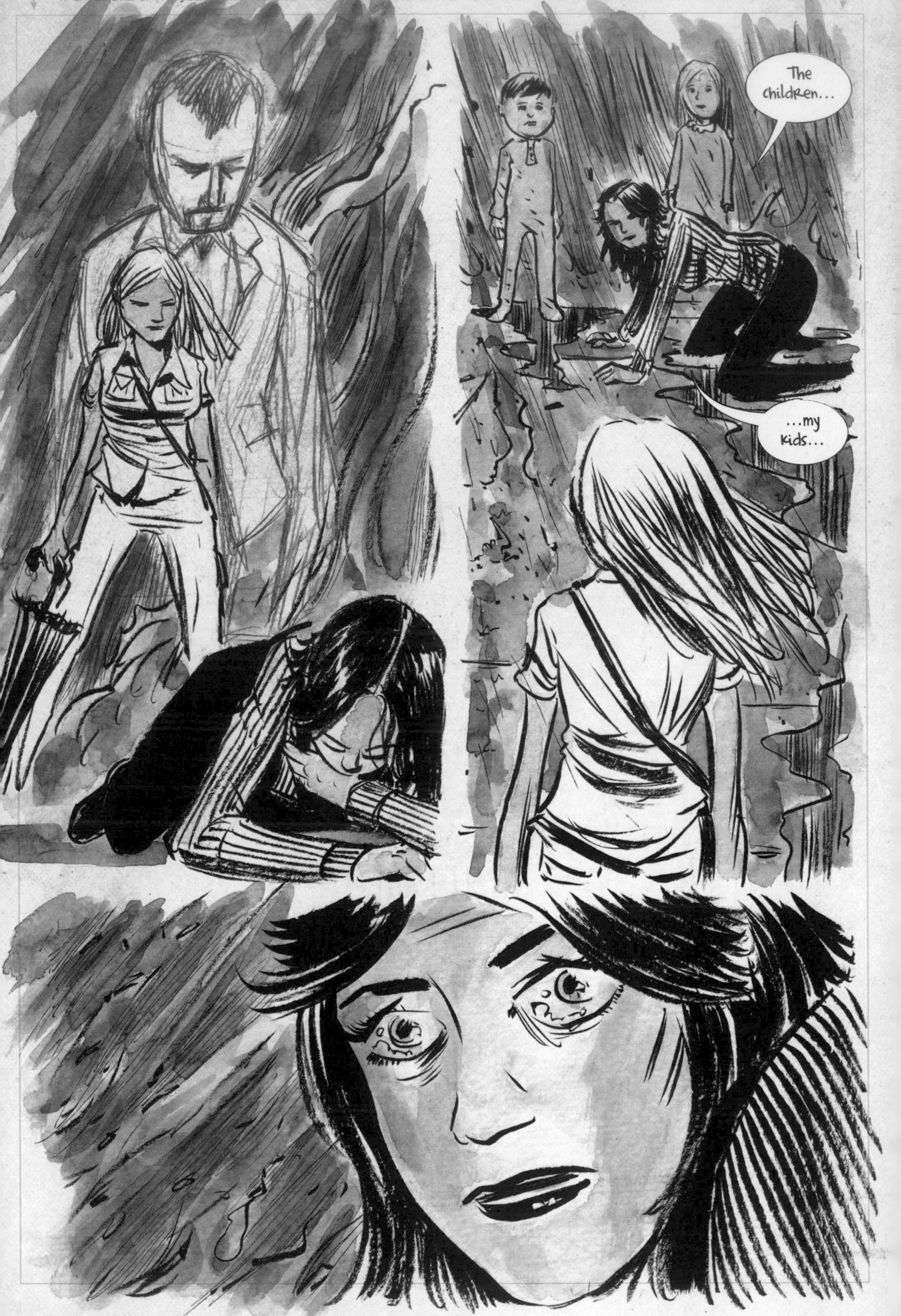

The children...
...my kids...

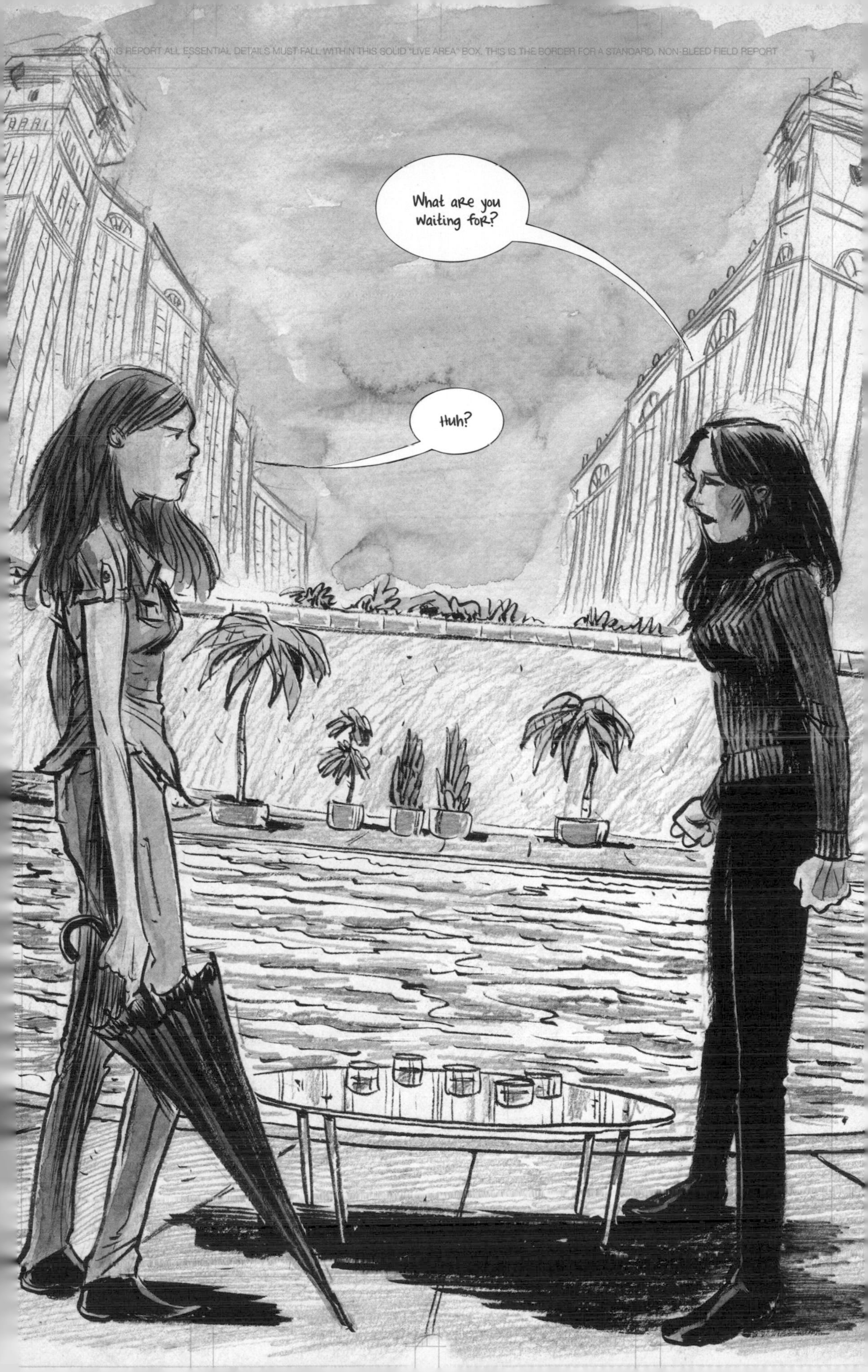
WHEN FILING REPORT ALL ESSENTIAL DETAILS MUST FALL WITHIN THIS SOLID "LIVE AREA" BOX. THIS IS THE BORDER FOR A STANDARD, NON-BLEED FIELD REPORT
What are you waiting for?
Huh?

MIND MGMT FIELD GUIDE 29.18. No . . . not working . . . She's . . . She's twisted it back on me. Distracted me.

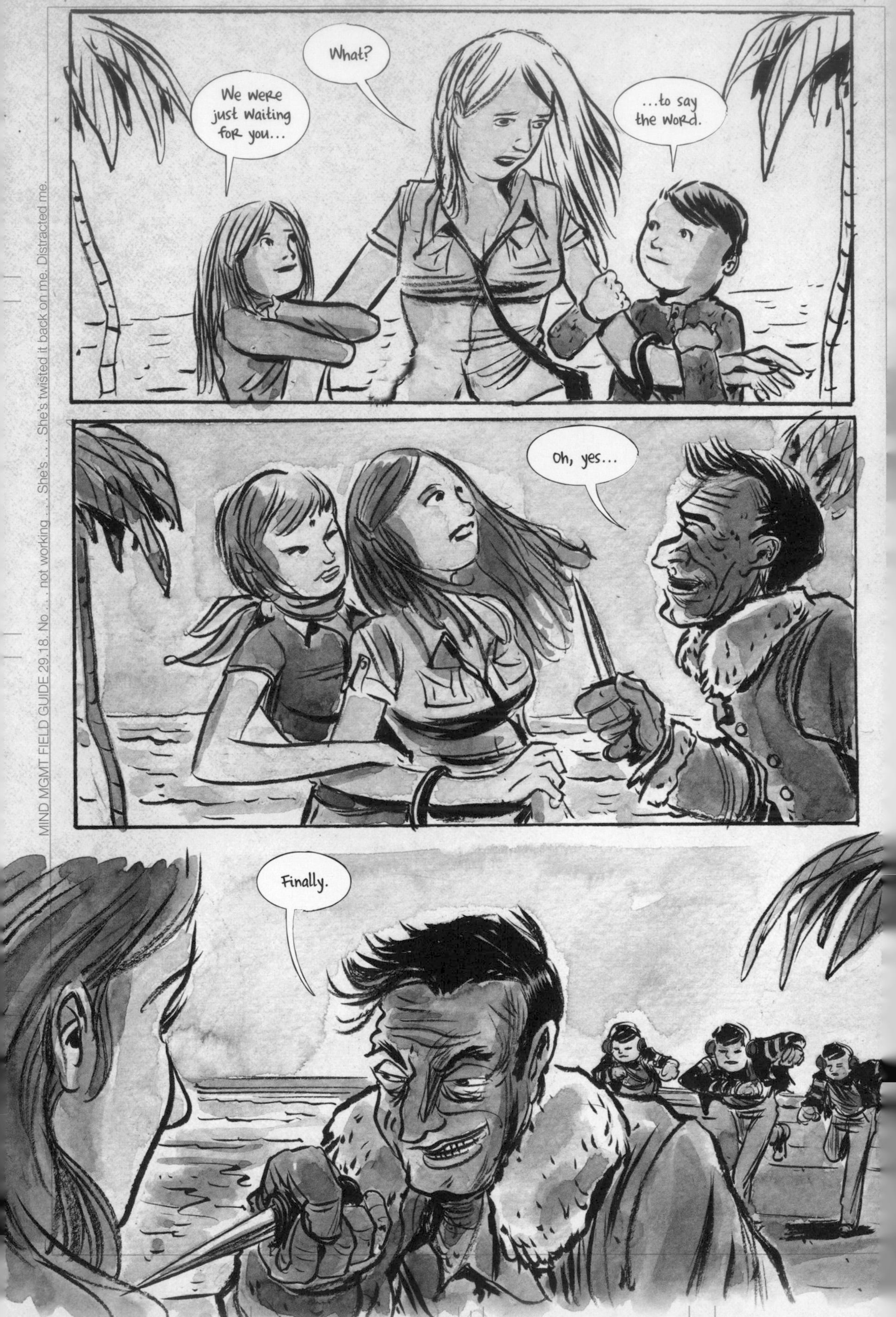
We were just waiting for you...
What?
...to say the word.
Oh, yes...
Finally.

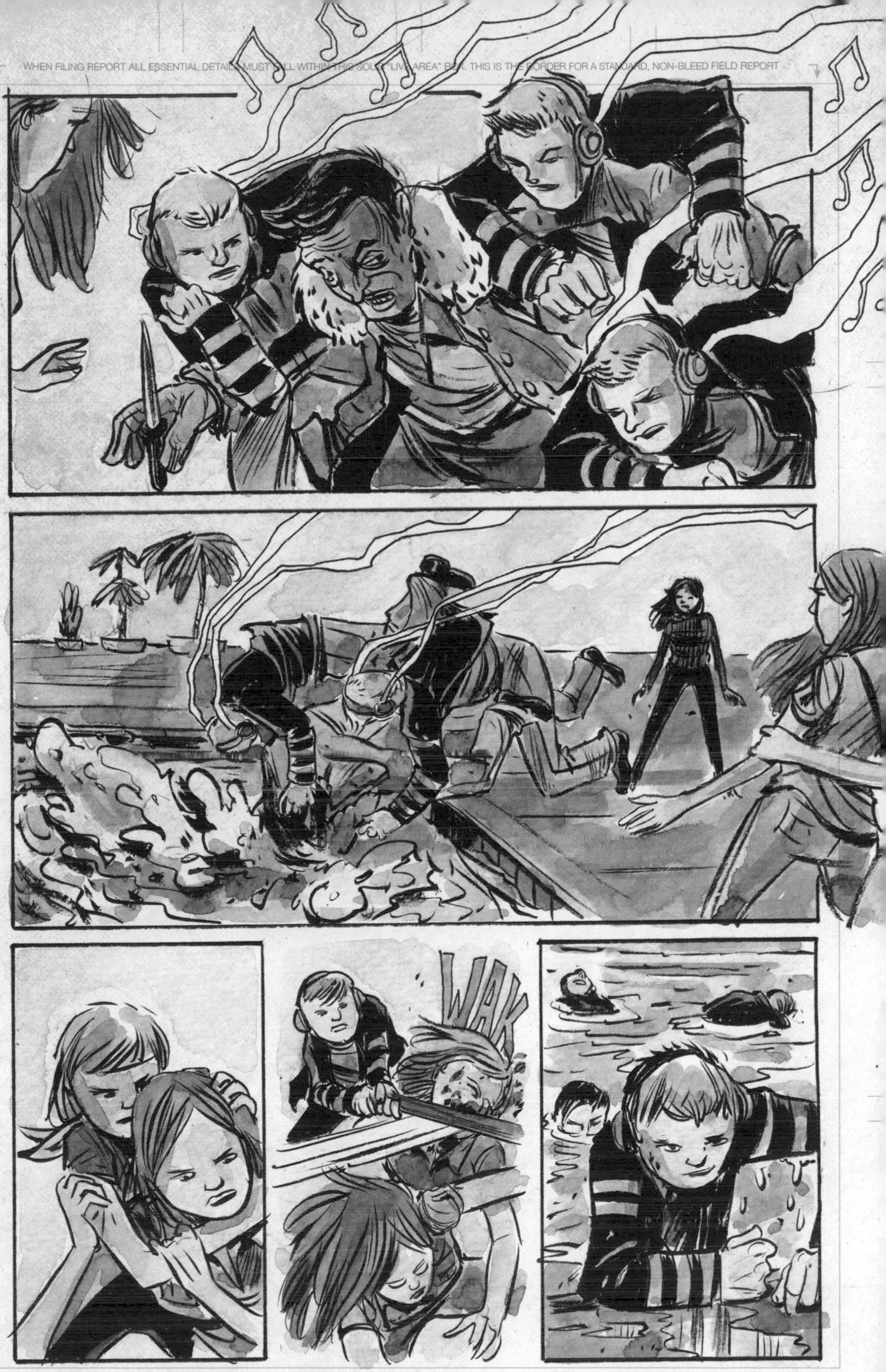
WAK

WHEN FILING REPORT ALL ESSENTIAL DETAILS MUST FALL WITHIN THIS SOLID "LIVE AREA" BOX. THIS IS THE BORDER FOR A STANDARD, NON-BLEED FIELD REPORT

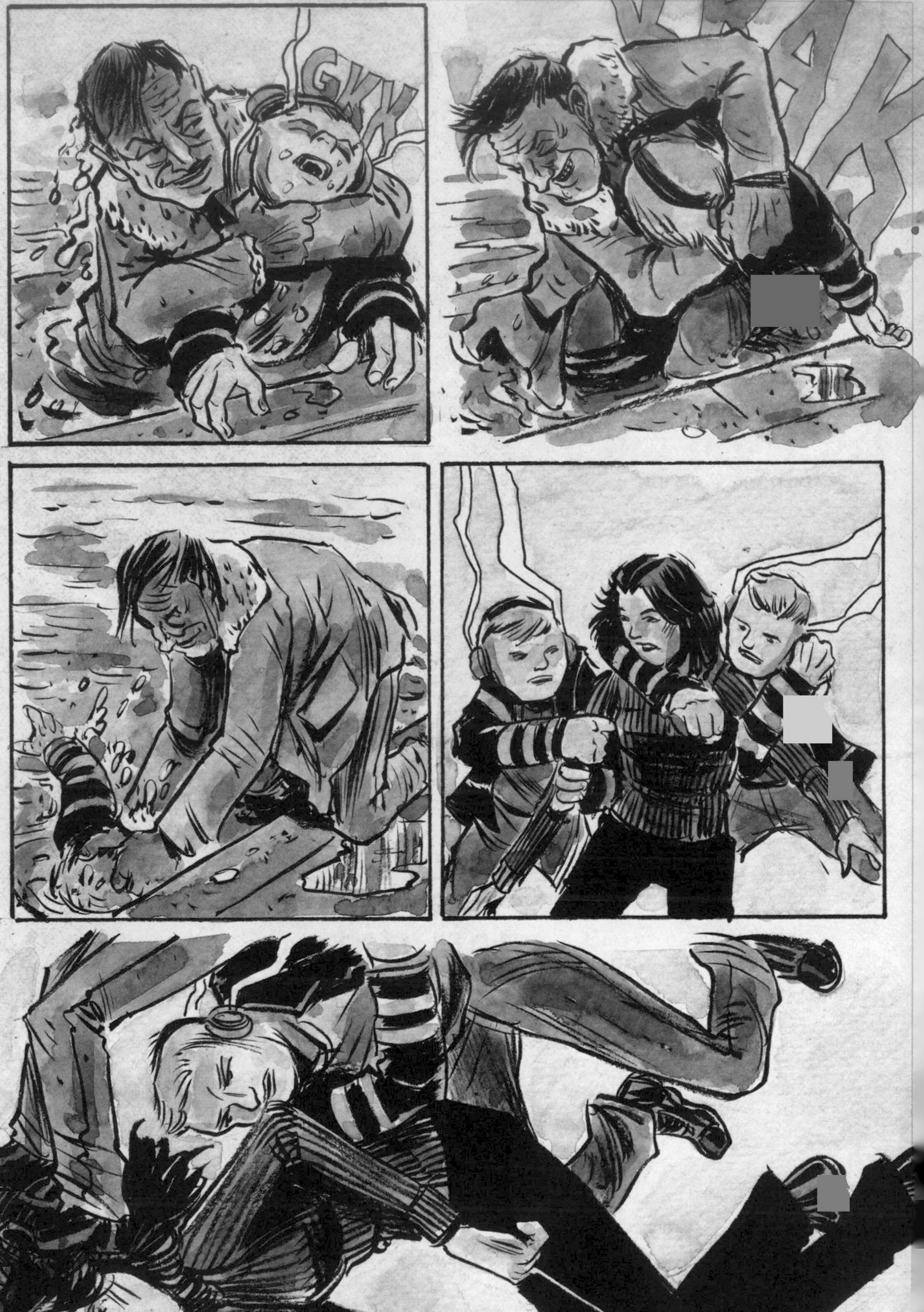
GKK
KRAK

MIND MGMT FIELD GUIDE 29.20. Too many . . . too many variables . . .

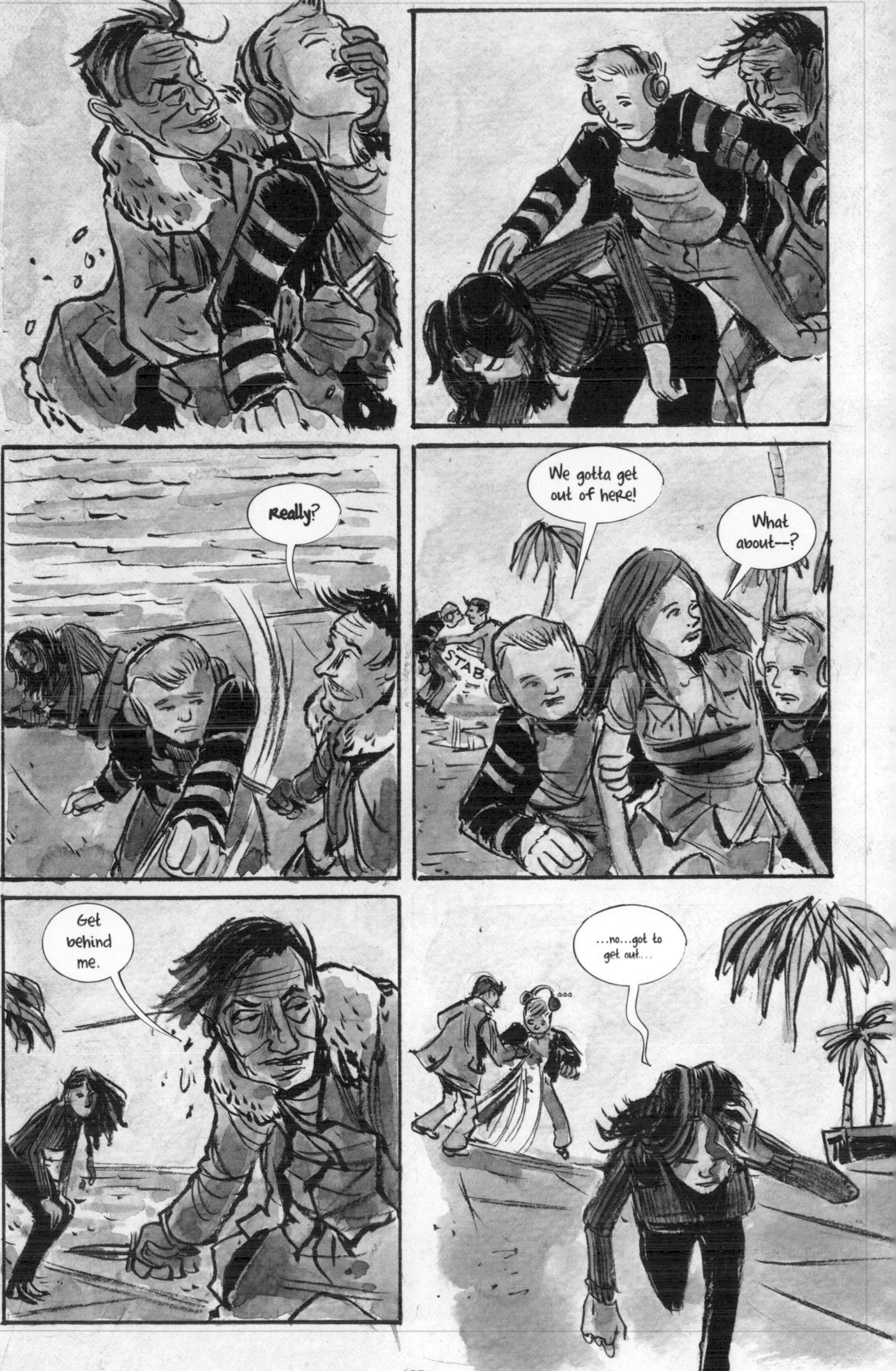
Really?
We gotta get out of here!
STAB
What about--?
Get behind me.
...no...got to get out...

MIND MGMT FIELD GUIDE 29.21. I'm losing . . . losing her . . . where did she go . . .

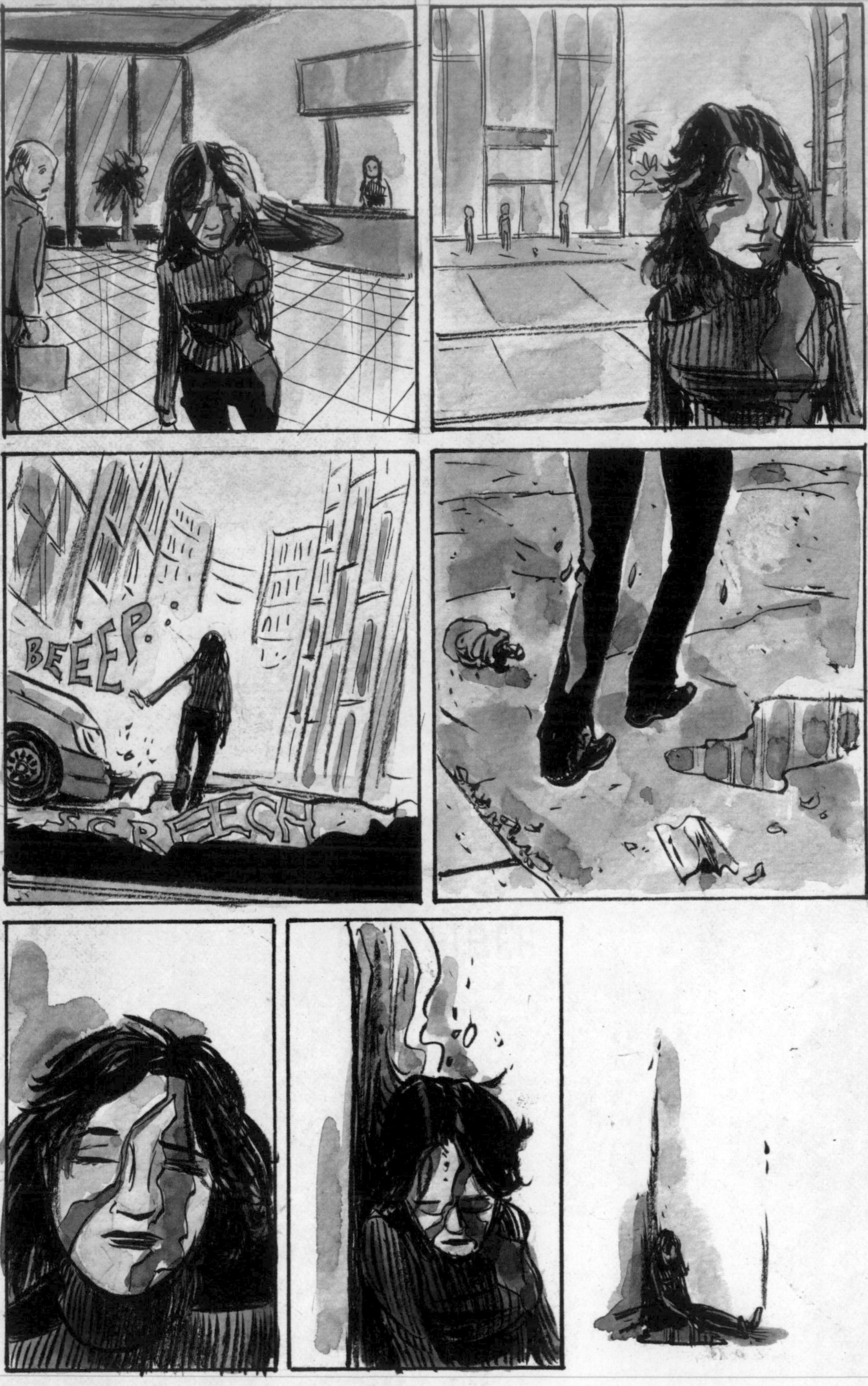
BEEEP
SCREECH

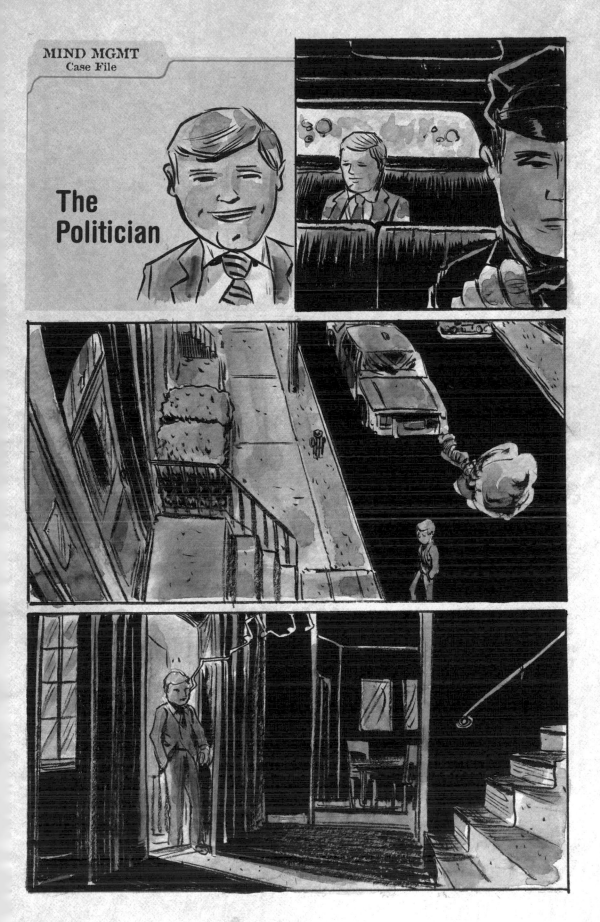

MIND MGMT
Case File

The
Politician

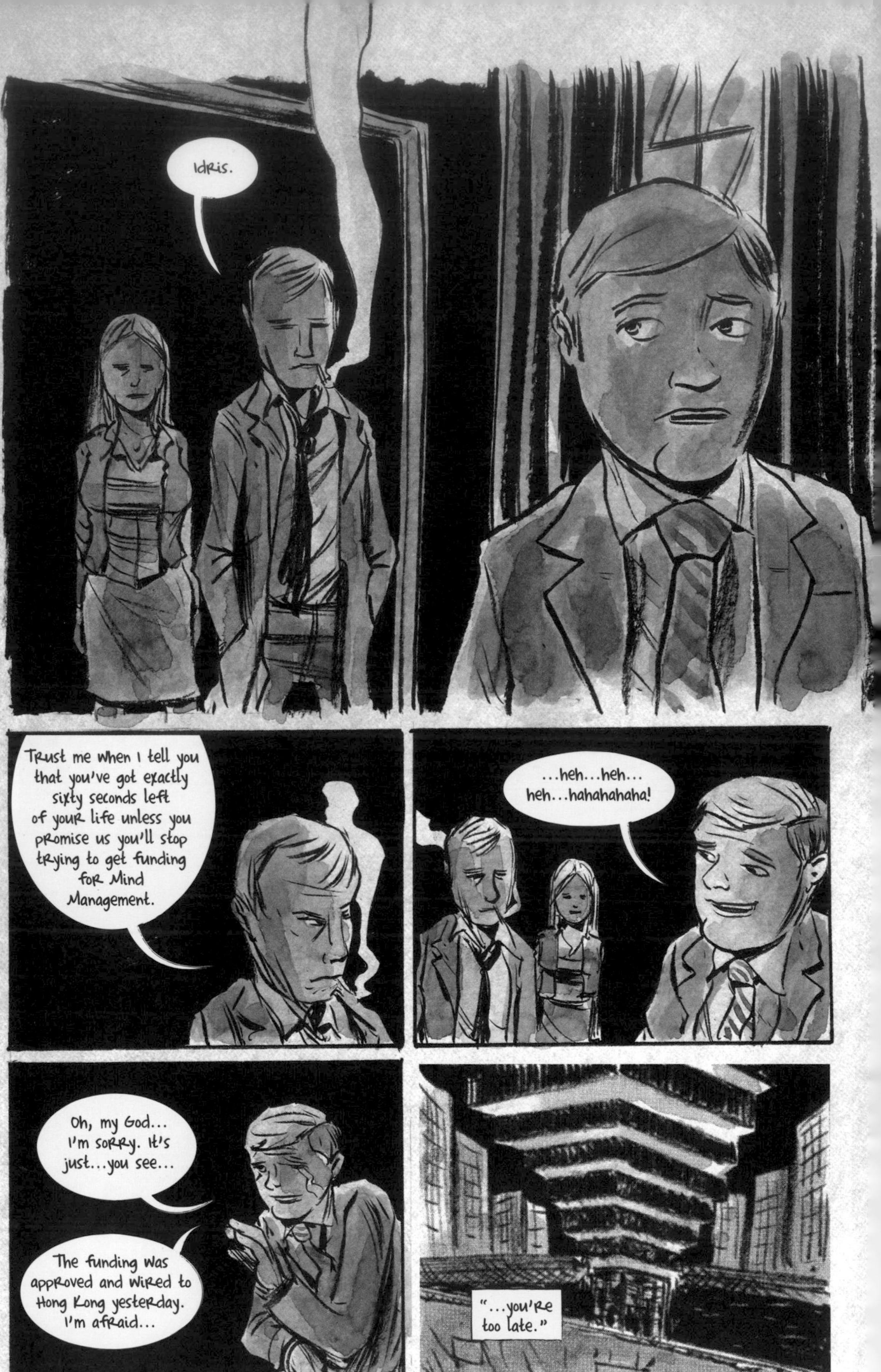
Idris.
Trust me when I tell you that you've got exactly sixty seconds left of your life unless you promise us you'll stop trying to get funding for Mind Management.
...heh...heh... heh...hahahahaha!
Oh, my God... I'm sorry. It's just...you see...
The funding was approved and wired to Hong Kong yesterday. I'm afraid...
"...you're too late."

End Mind Memo.

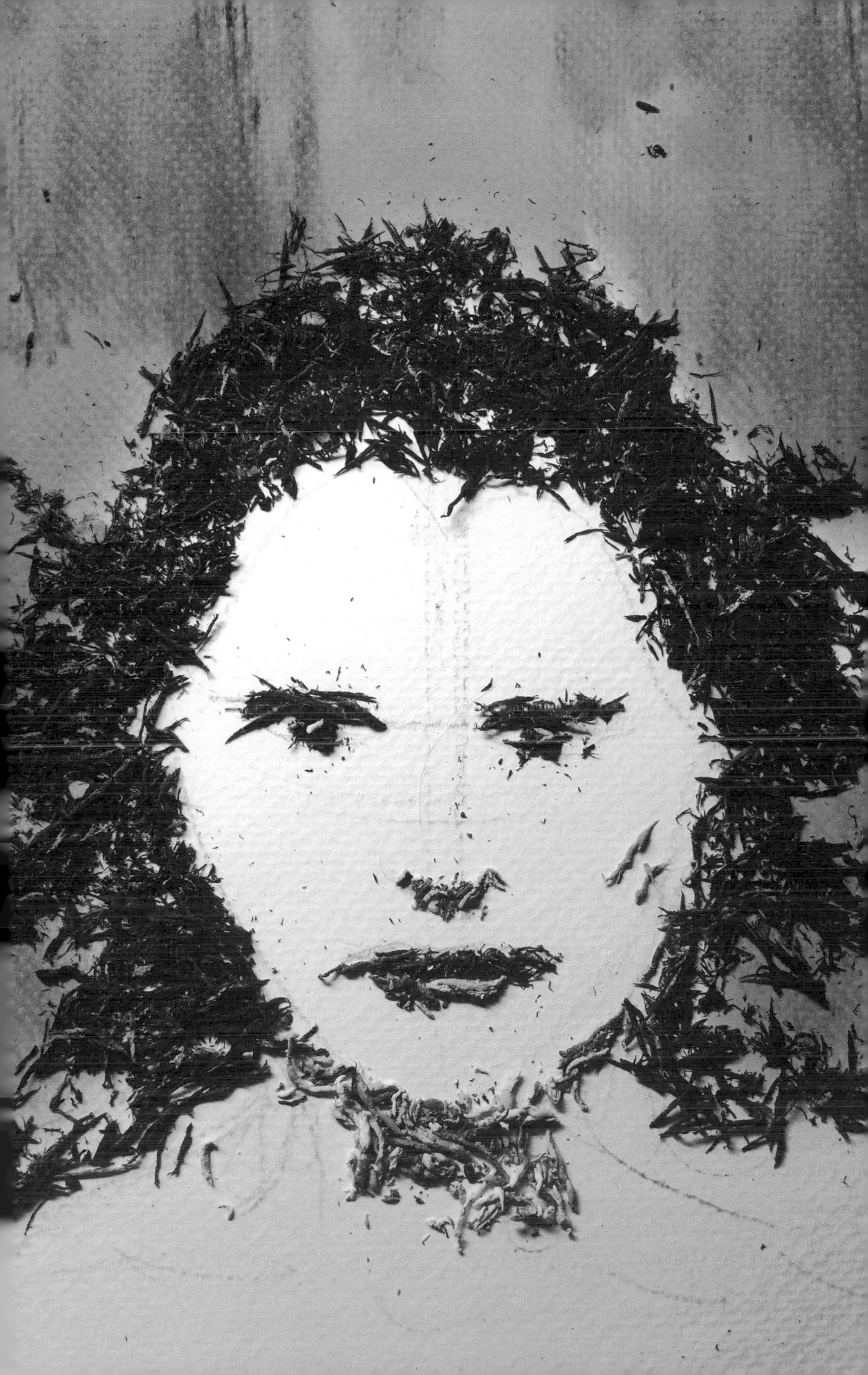

30

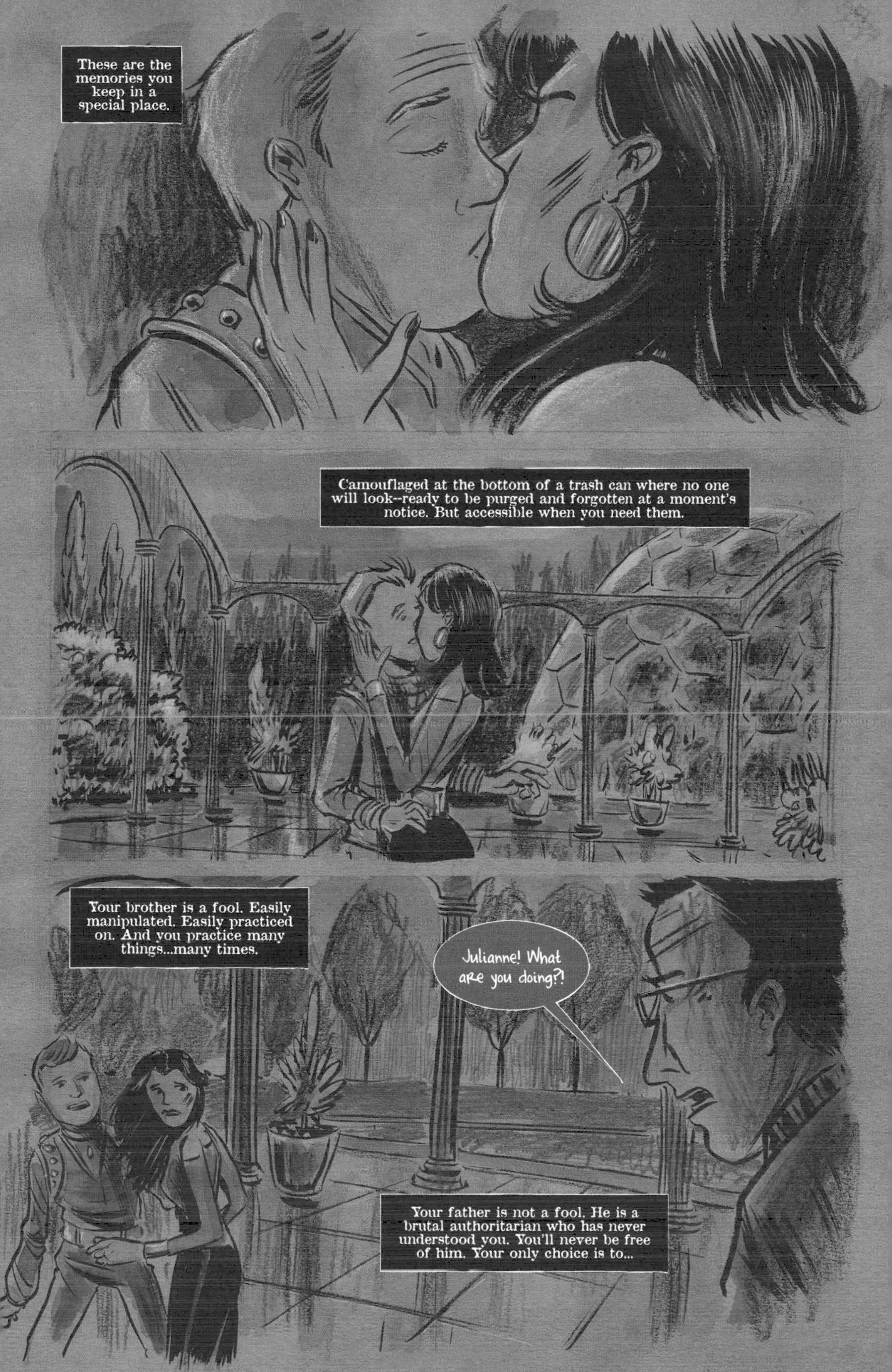
These are the memories you keep in a special place.
Camouflaged at the bottom of a trash can where no one will look--ready to be purged and forgotten at a moment's notice. But accessible when you need them.
Your brother is a fool. Easily manipulated. Easily practiced on. And you practice many things...many times.
Julianne! What are you doing?!
Your father is not a fool. He is a brutal authoritarian who has never understood you. You'll never be free of him. Your only choice is to...

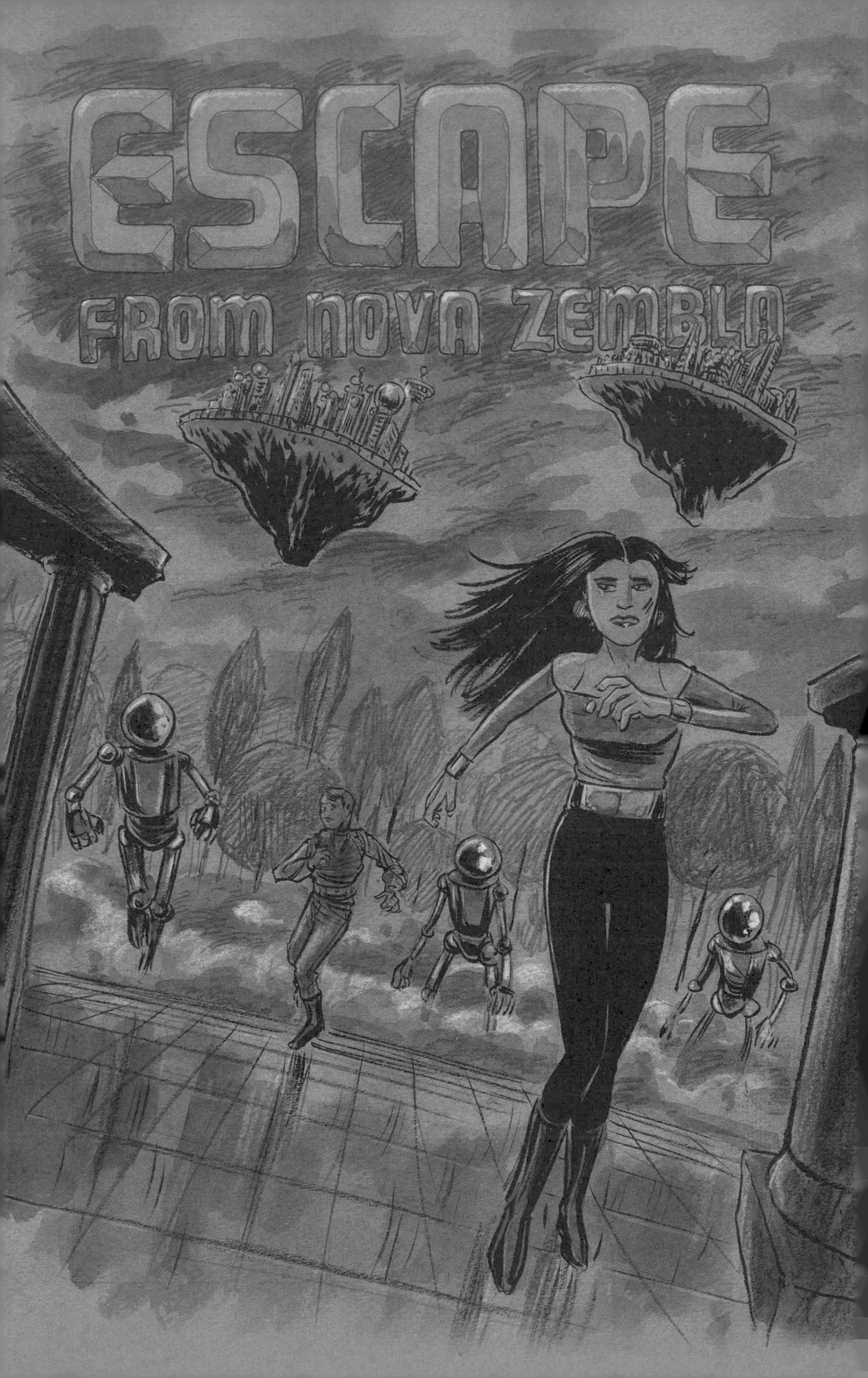
ESCAPE
FROM NOVA ZEMBLA

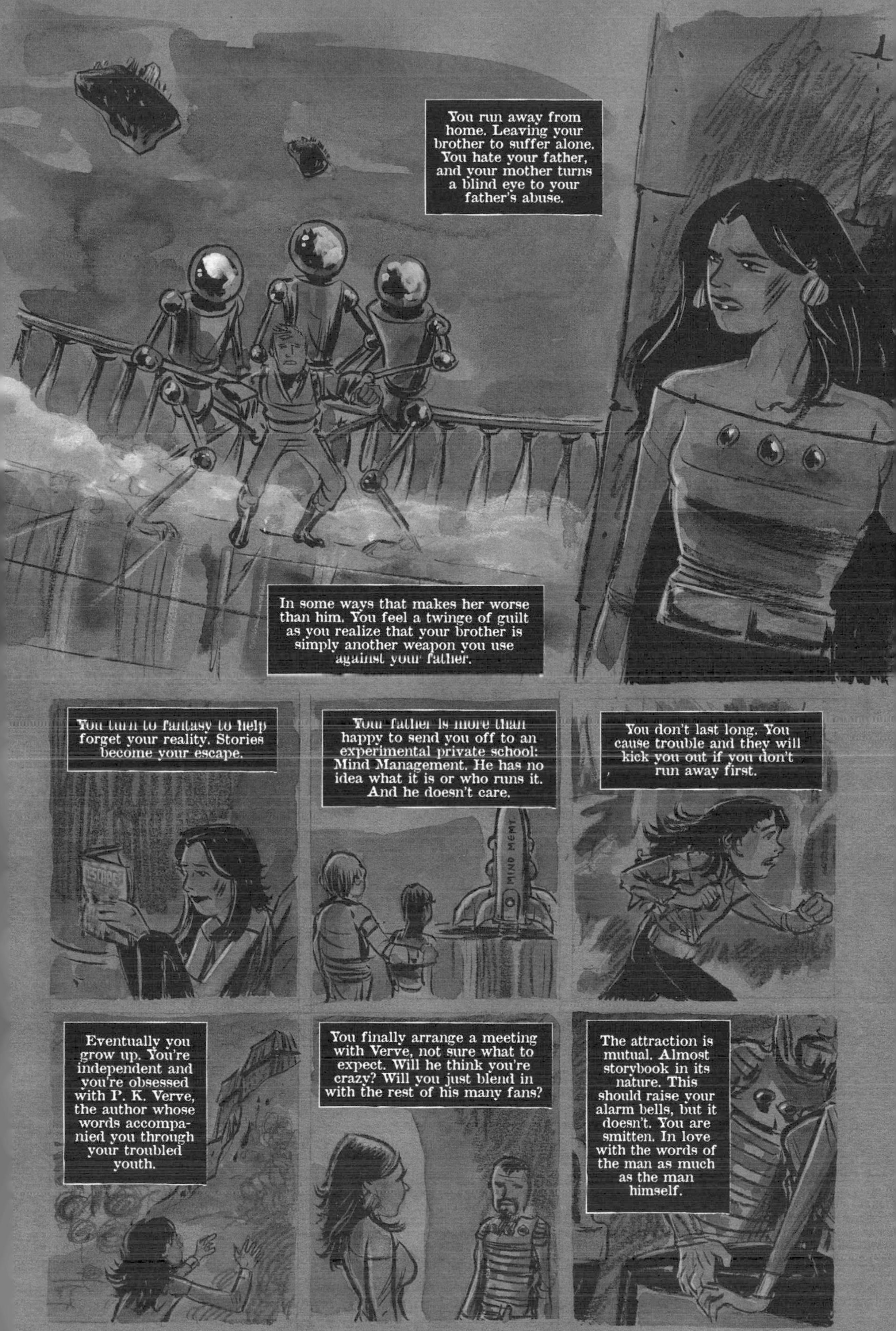
You run away from home. Leaving your brother to suffer alone. You hate your father, and your mother turns a blind eye to your father's abuse.
In some ways that makes her worse than him. You feel a twinge of guilt as you realize that your brother is simply another weapon you use against your father.
You turn to fantasy to help forget your reality. Stories become your escape.
Your father is more than happy to send you off to an experimental private school: Mind Management. He has no idea what it is or who runs it. And he doesn't care.
MIND MGMT
You don't last long. You cause trouble and they will kick you out if you don't run away first.
Eventually you grow up. You're independent and you're obsessed with P. K. Verve, the author whose words accompanied you through your troubled youth.
You finally arrange a meeting with Verve, not sure what to expect. Will he think you're crazy? Will you just blend in with the rest of his many fans?
The attraction is mutual. Almost storybook in its nature. This should raise your alarm bells, but it doesn't. You are smitten. In love with the words of the man as much as the man himself.

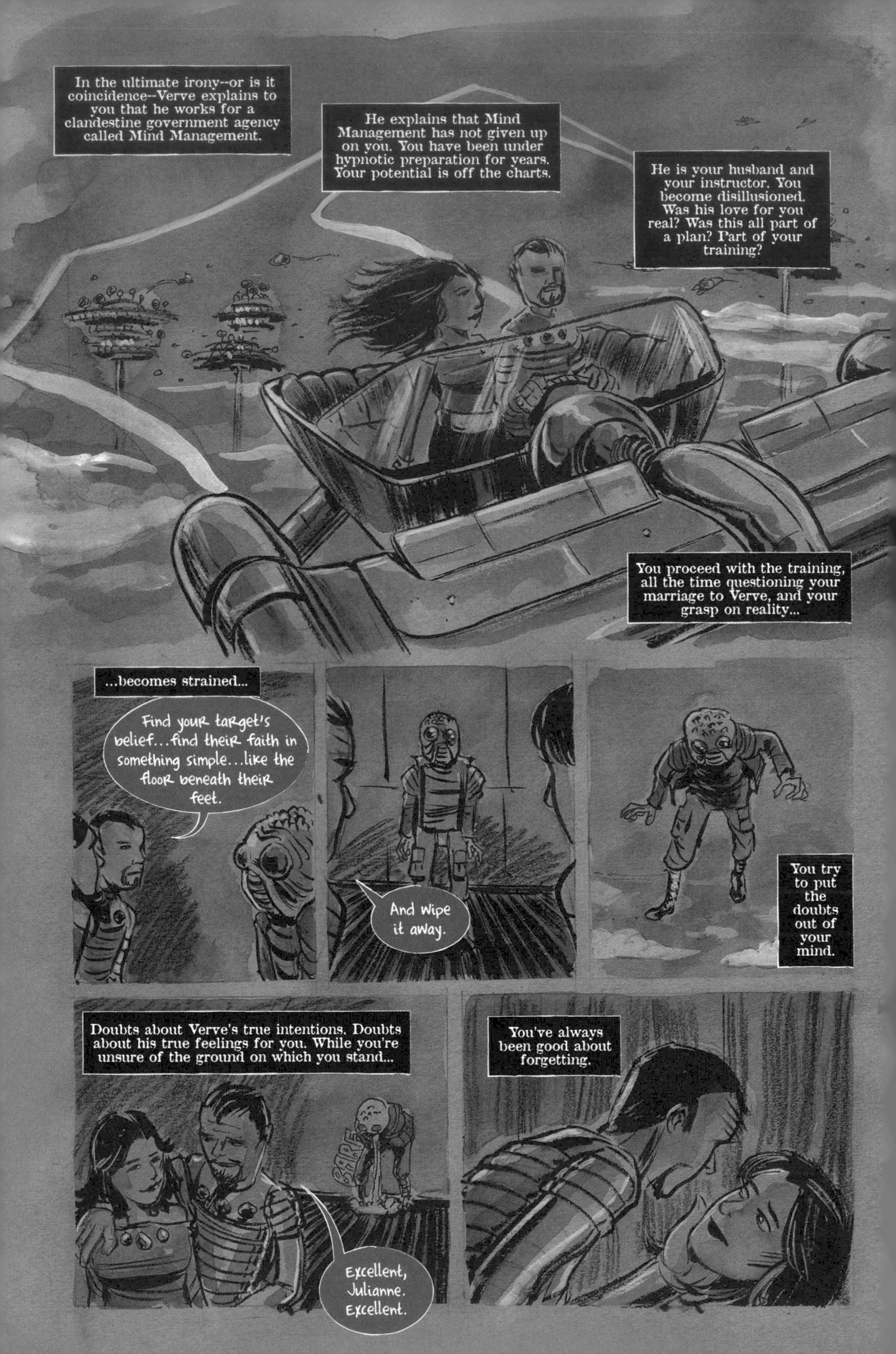
In the ultimate irony--or is it coincidence--Verve explains to you that he works for a clandestine government agency called Mind Management.
He explains that Mind Management has not given up on you. You have been under hypnotic preparation for years. Your potential is off the charts.
He is your husband and your instructor. You become disillusioned. Was his love for you real? Was this all part of a plan? Part of your training?
You proceed with the training, all the time questioning your marriage to Verve, and your grasp on reality...
...becomes strained...
Find your target's belief...find their faith in something simple...like the floor beneath their feet.
And wipe it away.
You try to put the doubts out of your mind.
Doubts about Verve's true intentions. Doubts about his true feelings for you. While you're unsure of the ground on which you stand...
Excellent, Julianne. Excellent.
You've always been good about forgetting.

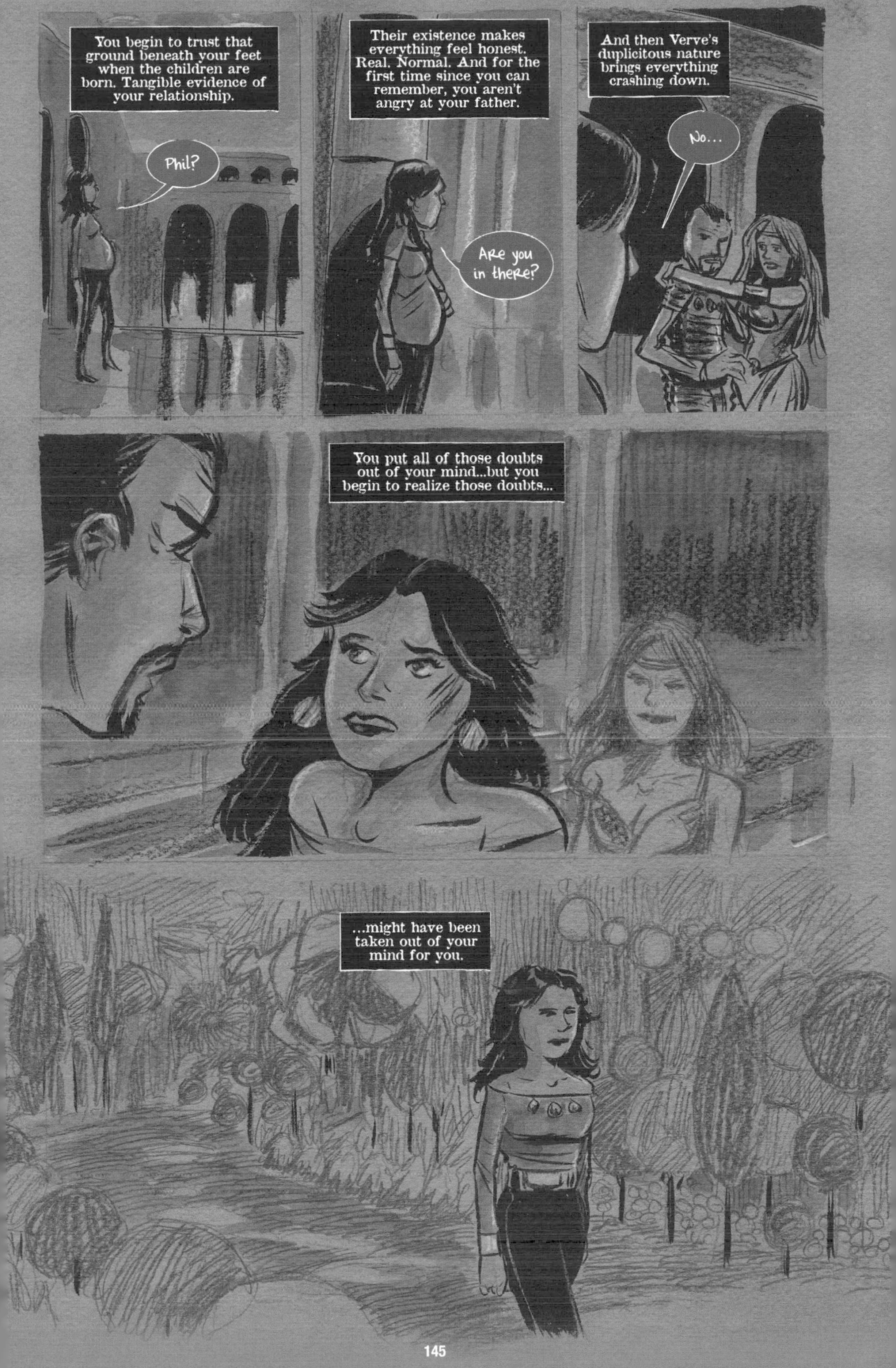

You begin to trust that ground beneath your feet when the children are born. Tangible evidence of your relationship.
Phil?
Their existence makes everything feel honest. Real. Normal. And for the first time since you can remember, you aren't angry at your father.
Are you in there?
And then Verve's duplicitous nature brings everything crashing down.
No...
You put all of those doubts out of your mind...but you begin to realize those doubts...
...might have been taken out of your mind for you.

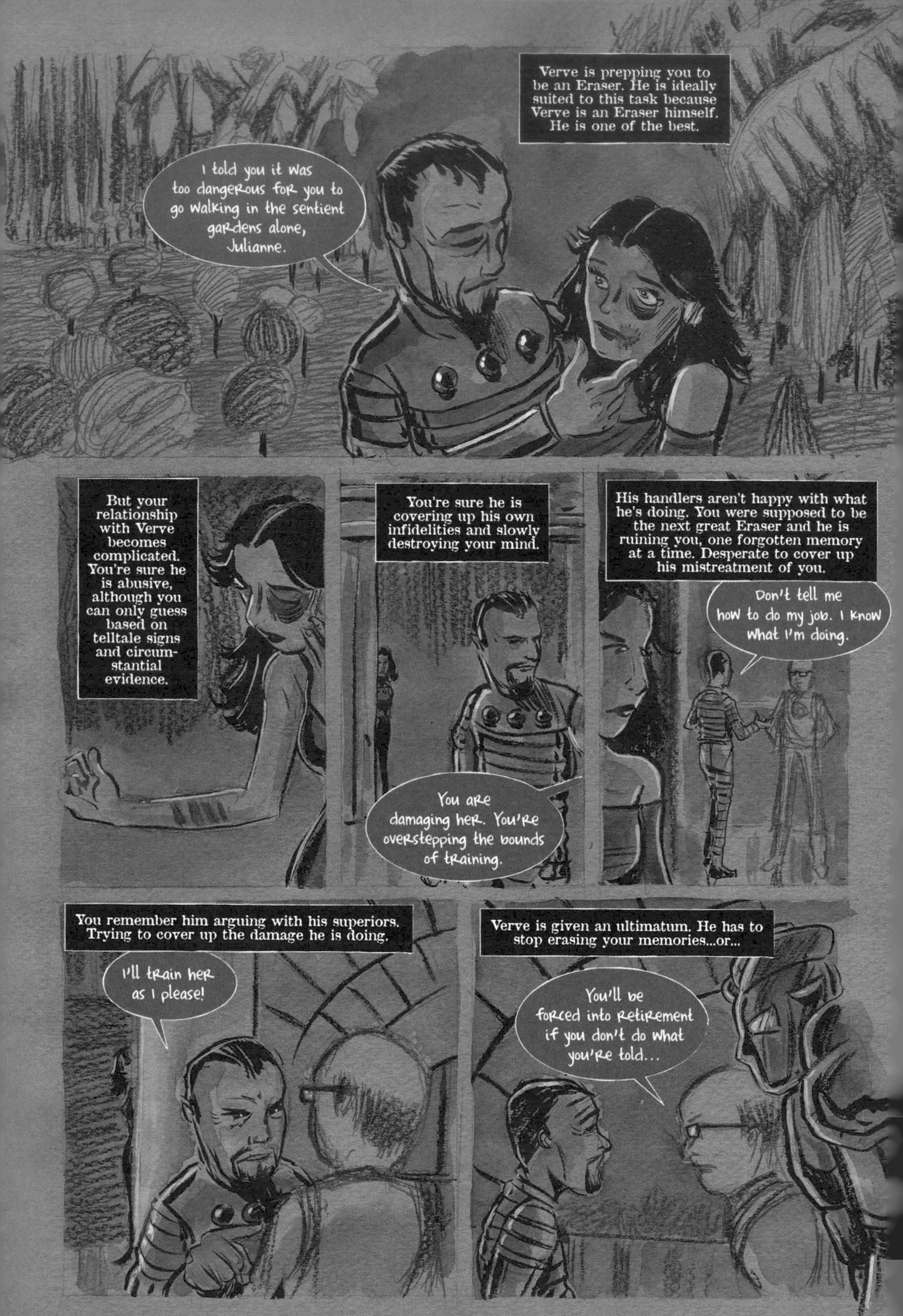
Verve is prepping you to be an Eraser. He is ideally suited to this task because Verve is an Eraser himself. He is one of the best.
I told you it was too dangerous for you to go walking in the sentient gardens alone, Julianne.
But your relationship with Verve becomes complicated. You're sure he is abusive, although you can only guess based on telltale signs and circumstantial evidence.
You're sure he is covering up his own infidelities and slowly destroying your mind.
You are damaging her. You're overstepping the bounds of training.
His handlers aren't happy with what he's doing. You were supposed to be the next great Eraser and he is ruining you, one forgotten memory at a time. Desperate to cover up his mistreatment of you.
Don't tell me how to do my job. I know what I'm doing.
You remember him arguing with his superiors. Trying to cover up the damage he is doing.
I'll train her as I please!
Verve is given an ultimatum. He has to stop erasing your memories...or...
You'll be forced into retirement if you don't do what you're told...

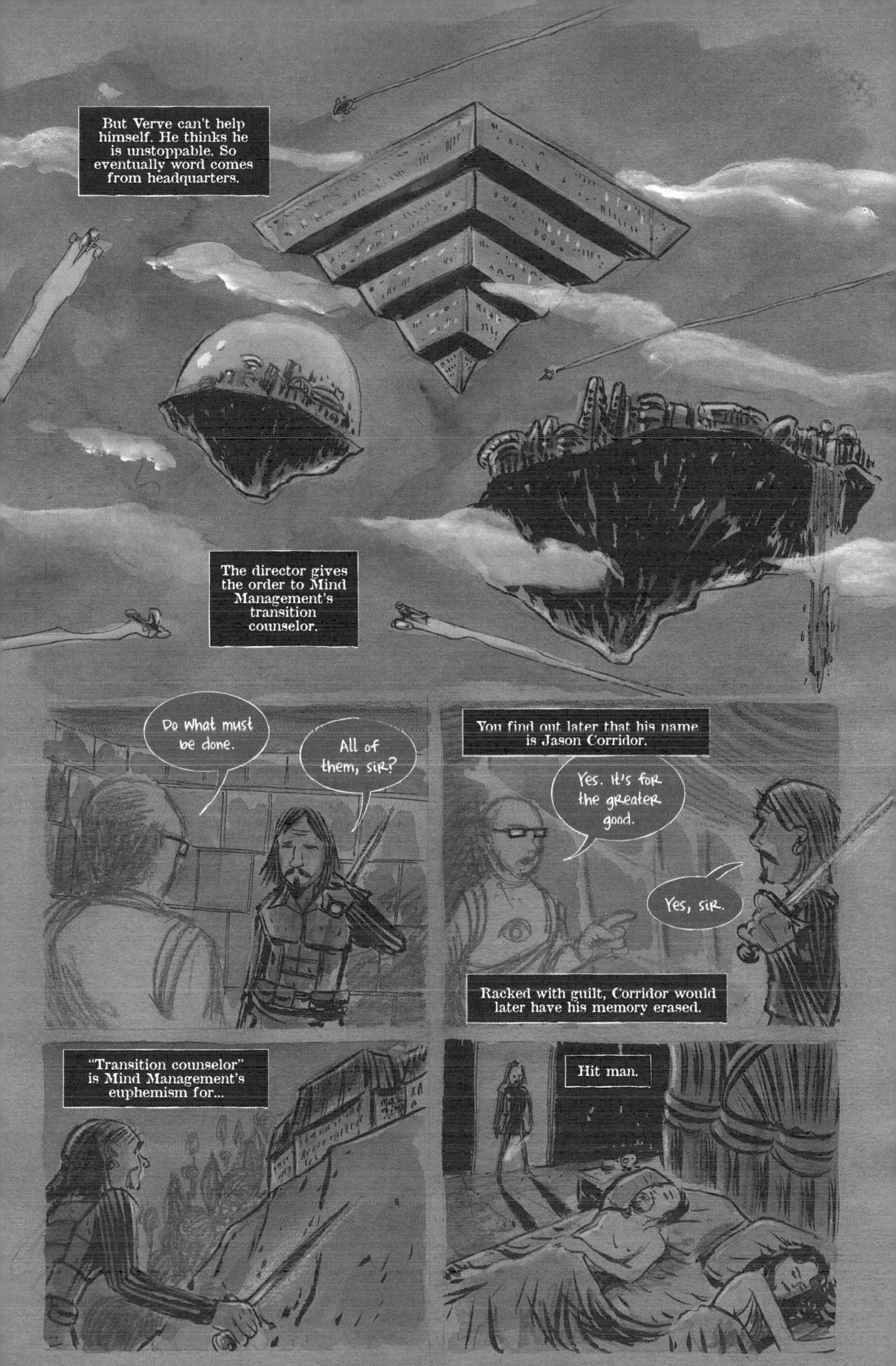
But Verve can't help himself. He thinks he is unstoppable. So eventually word comes from headquarters.
The director gives the order to Mind Management's transition counselor.
Do what must be done.
All of them, sir?
You find out later that his name is Jason Corridor.
Yes. It's for the greater good.
Yes, sir.
Racked with guilt, Corridor would later have his memory erased.
"Transition counselor" is Mind Management's euphemism for...
Hit man.

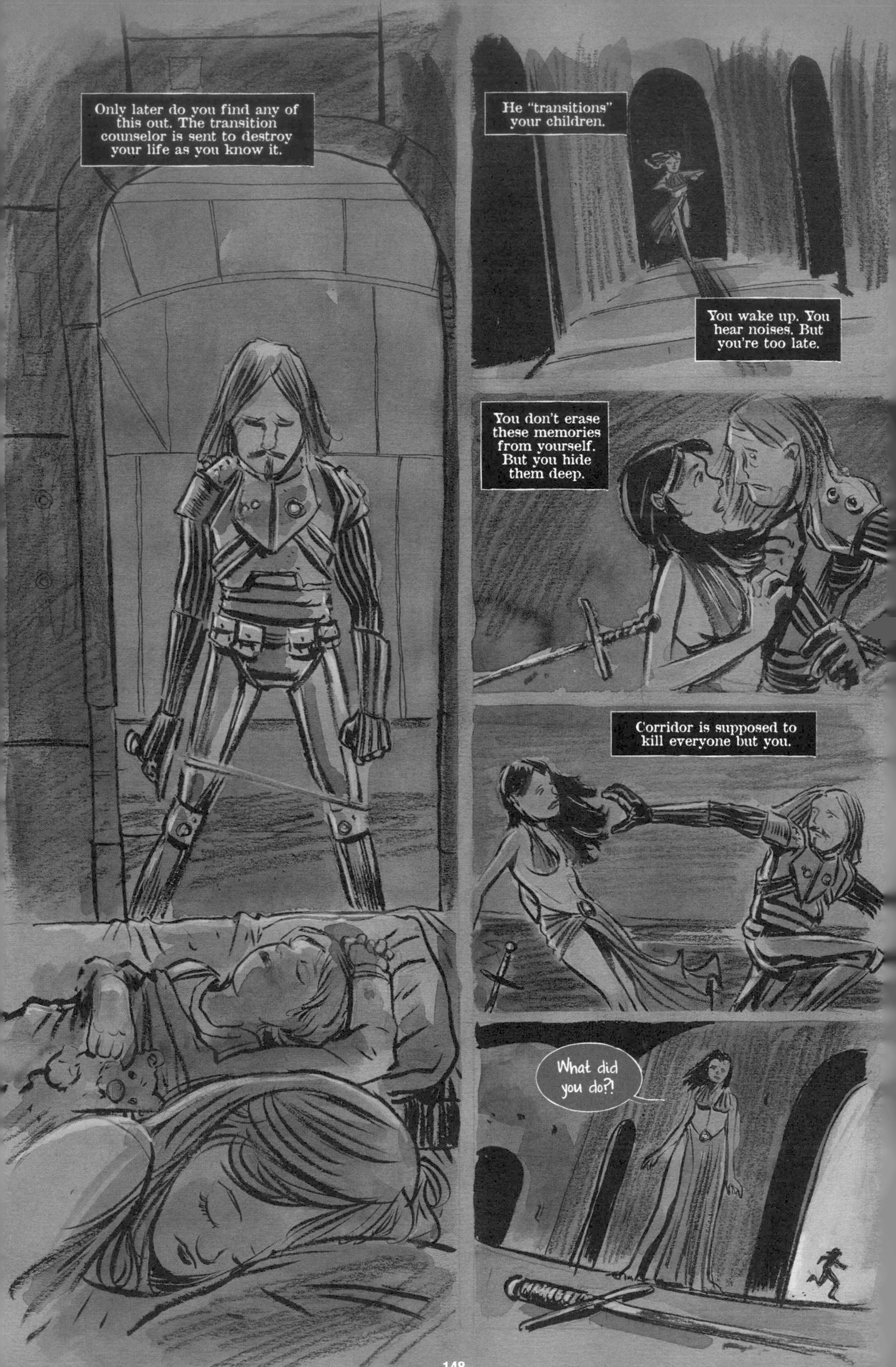
Only later do you find any of this out. The transition counselor is sent to destroy your life as you know it.
He "transitions" your children.
You wake up. You hear noises. But you're too late.
You don't erase these memories from yourself. But you hide them deep.
Corridor is supposed to kill everyone but you.
What did you do?!

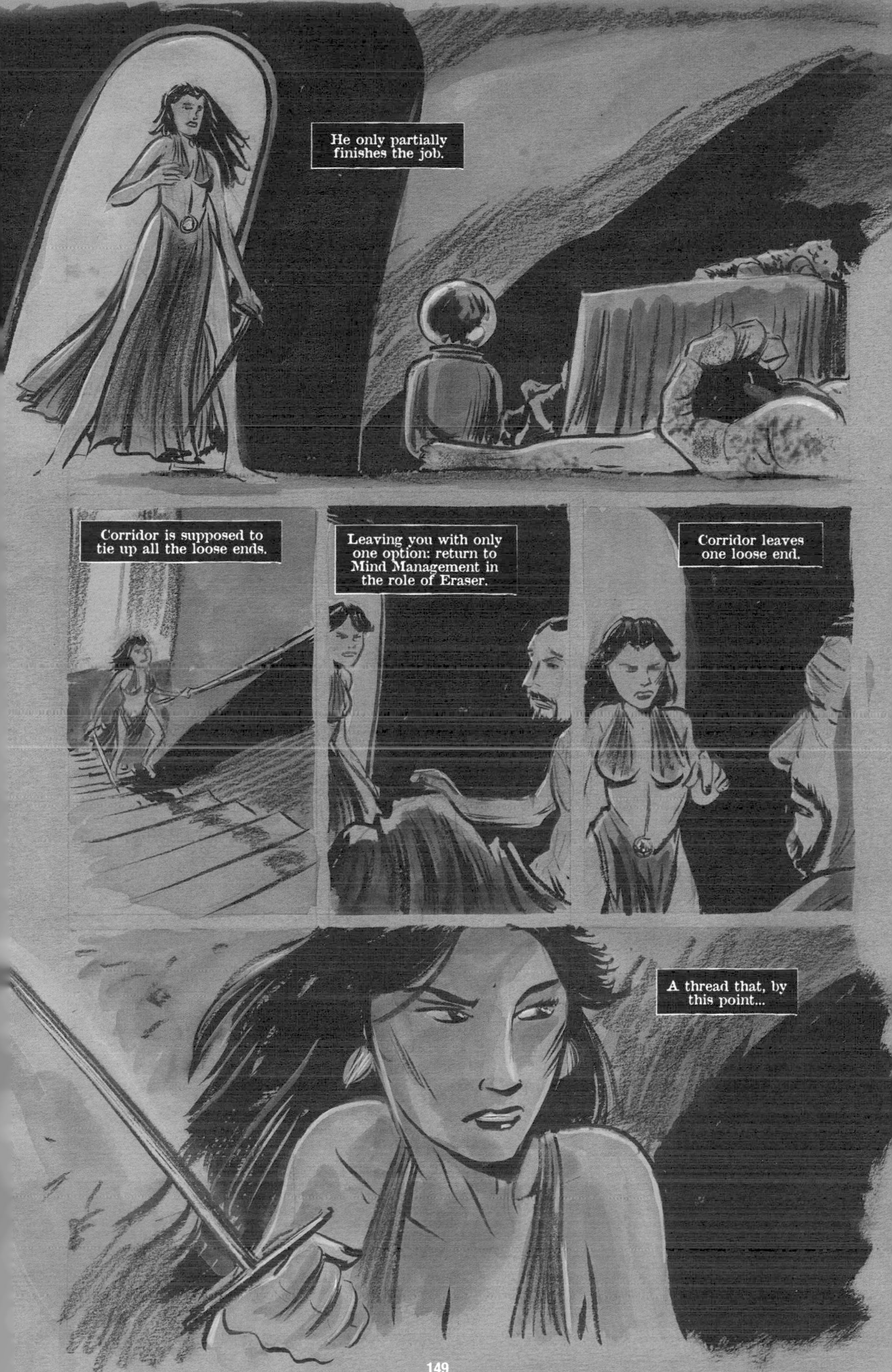
He only partially finishes the job.
Corridor is supposed to tie up all the loose ends.
Leaving you with only one option: return to Mind Management in the role of Eraser.
Corridor leaves one loose end.
A thread that, by this point...

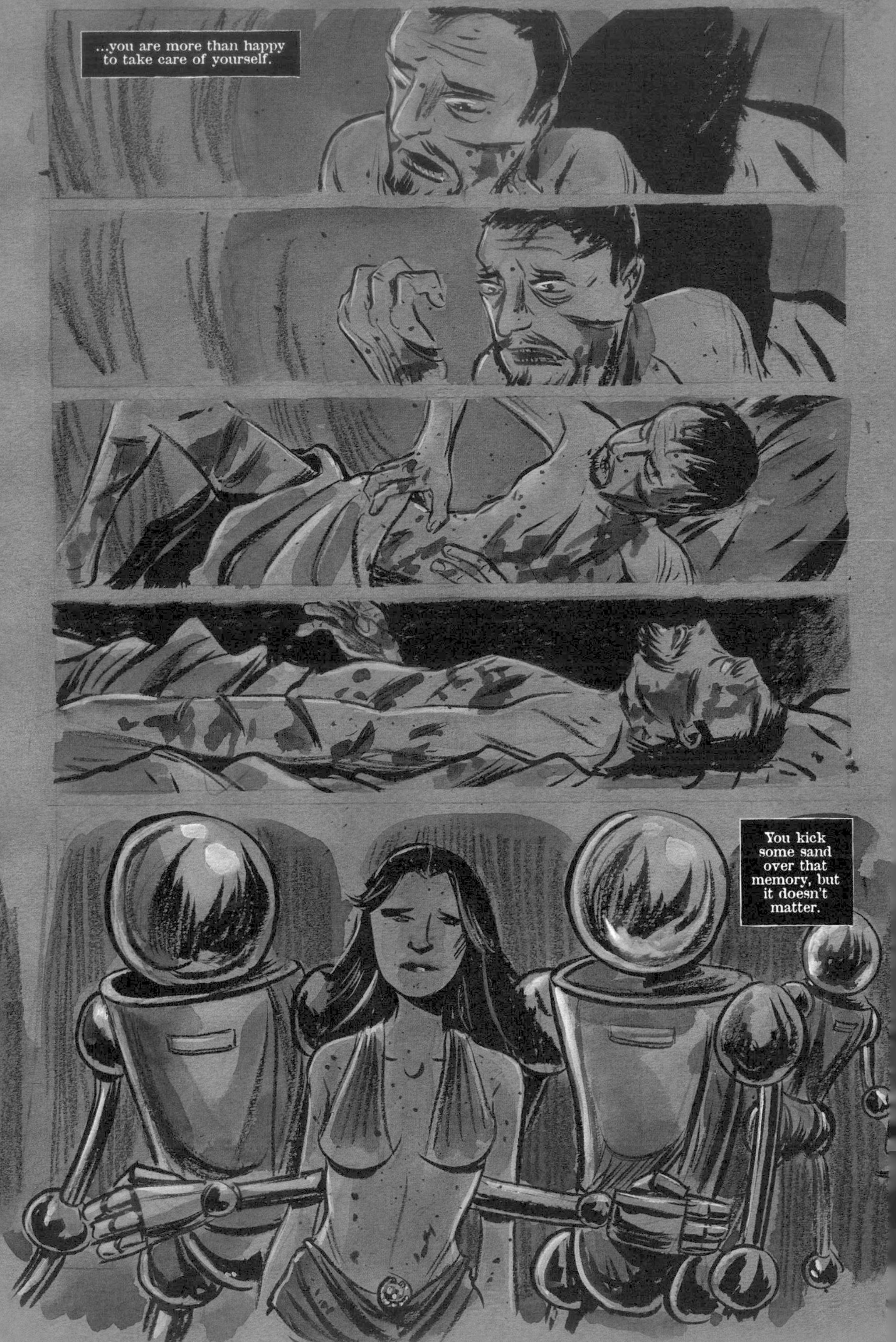
...you are more than happy to take care of yourself.
You kick some sand over that memory, but it doesn't matter.

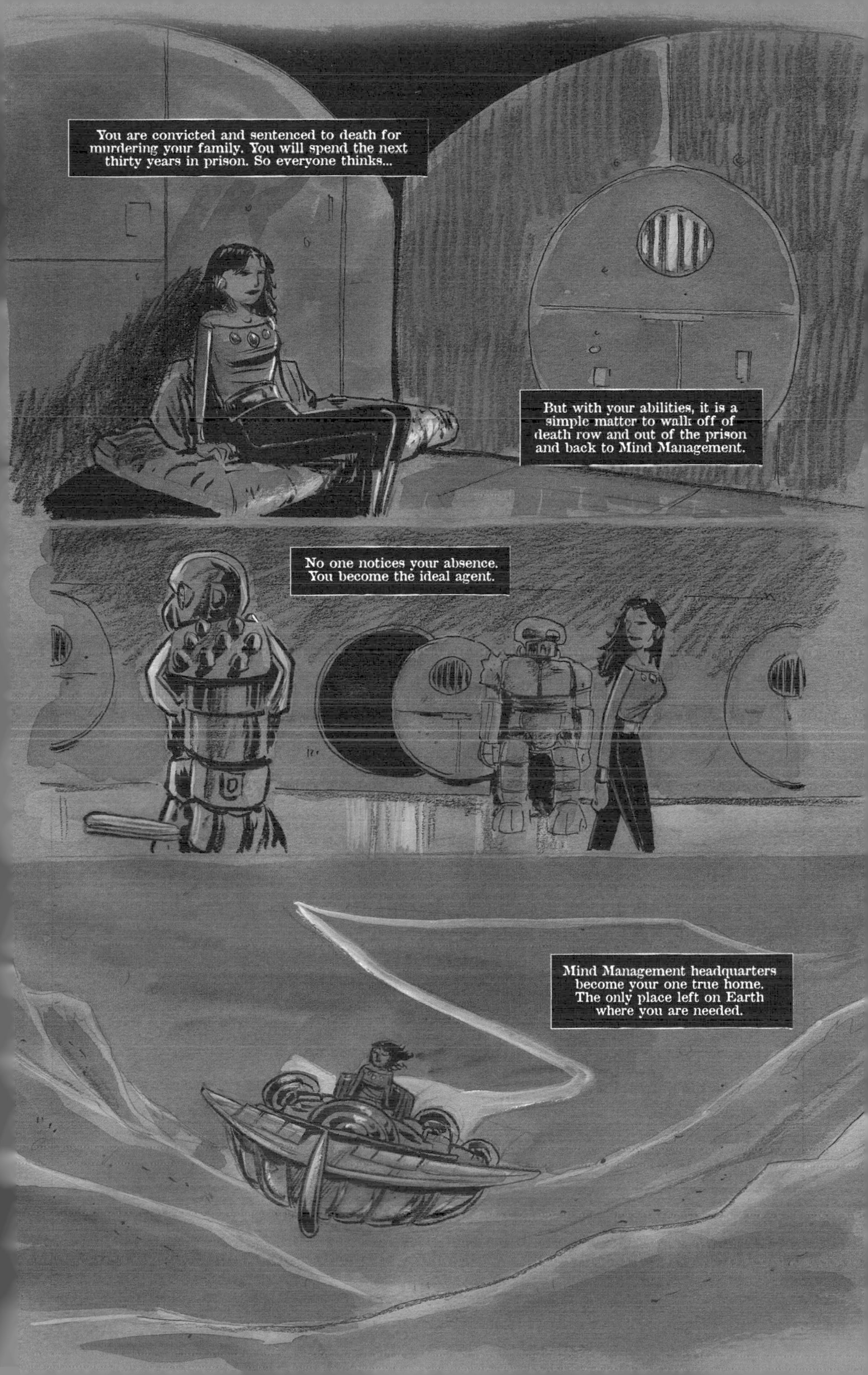
You are convicted and sentenced to death for murdering your family. You will spend the next thirty years in prison. So everyone thinks...
But with your abilities, it is a simple matter to walk off of death row and out of the prison and back to Mind Management.
No one notices your absence. You become the ideal agent.
Mind Management headquarters become your one true home. The only place left on Earth where you are needed.

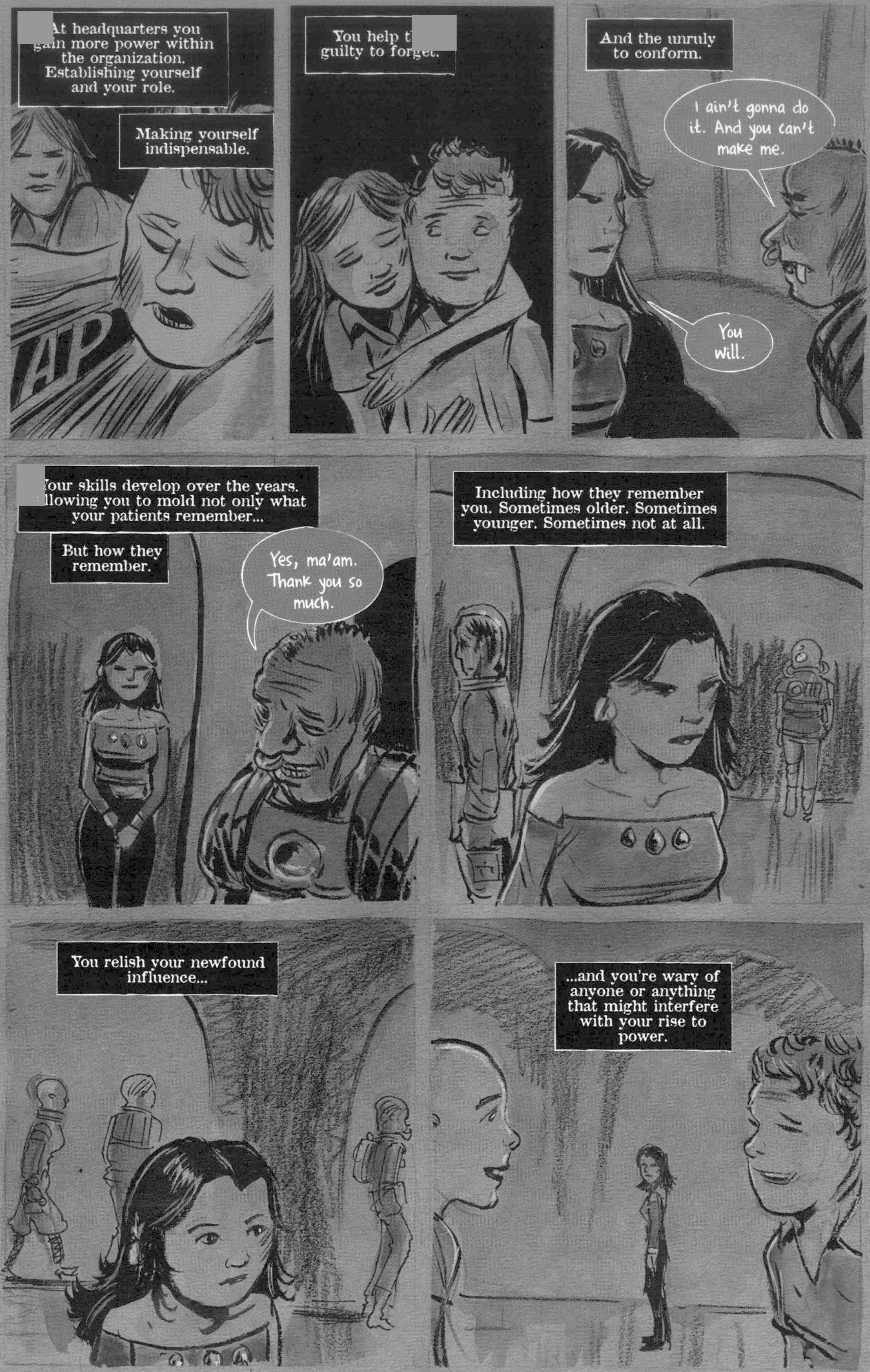
At headquarters you
ain more power within the organization. Establishing yourself and your role.
Making yourself indispensable.
AP
You help t
guilty to forget.
And the unruly to conform.
I ain't gonna do it. And you can't make me.
You will.
our skills develop over the years.
llowing you to mold not only what your patients remember...
But how they remember.
Yes, ma'am. Thank you so much.
Including how they remember you. Sometimes older. Sometimes younger. Sometimes not at all.
You relish your newfound influence...
...and you're wary of anyone or anything that might interfere with your rise to power.

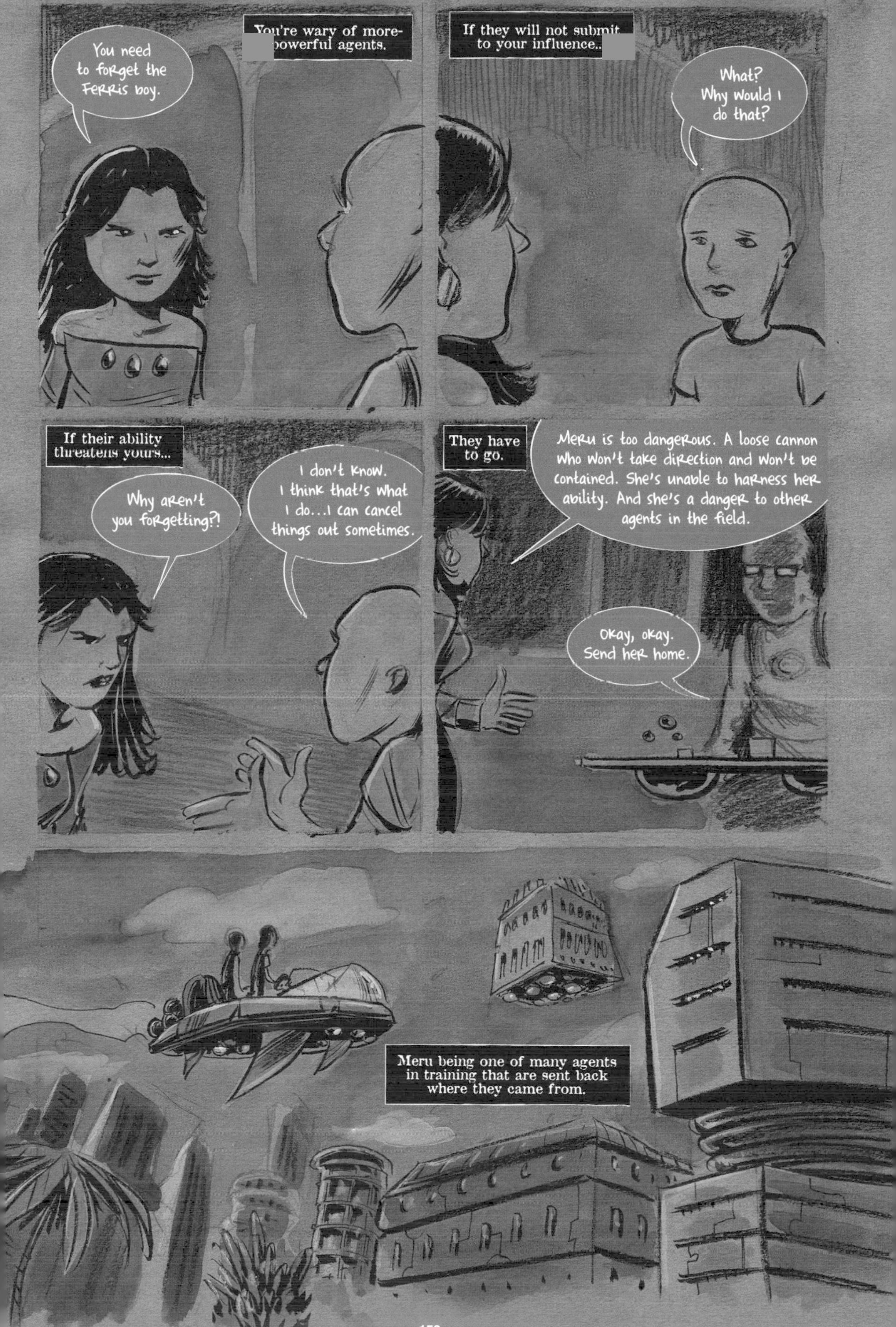
You're wary of more-powerful agents.
You need to forget the Ferris boy.
If they will not submit to your influence..
What? Why would I do that?
If their ability threatens yours...
Why aren't you forgetting?!
I don't know. I think that's what I do...I can cancel things out sometimes.
They have to go.
Meru is too dangerous. A loose cannon who won't take direction and won't be contained. She's unable to harness her ability. And she's a danger to other agents in the field.
Okay, okay. Send her home.
Meru being one of many agents in training that are sent back where they came from.

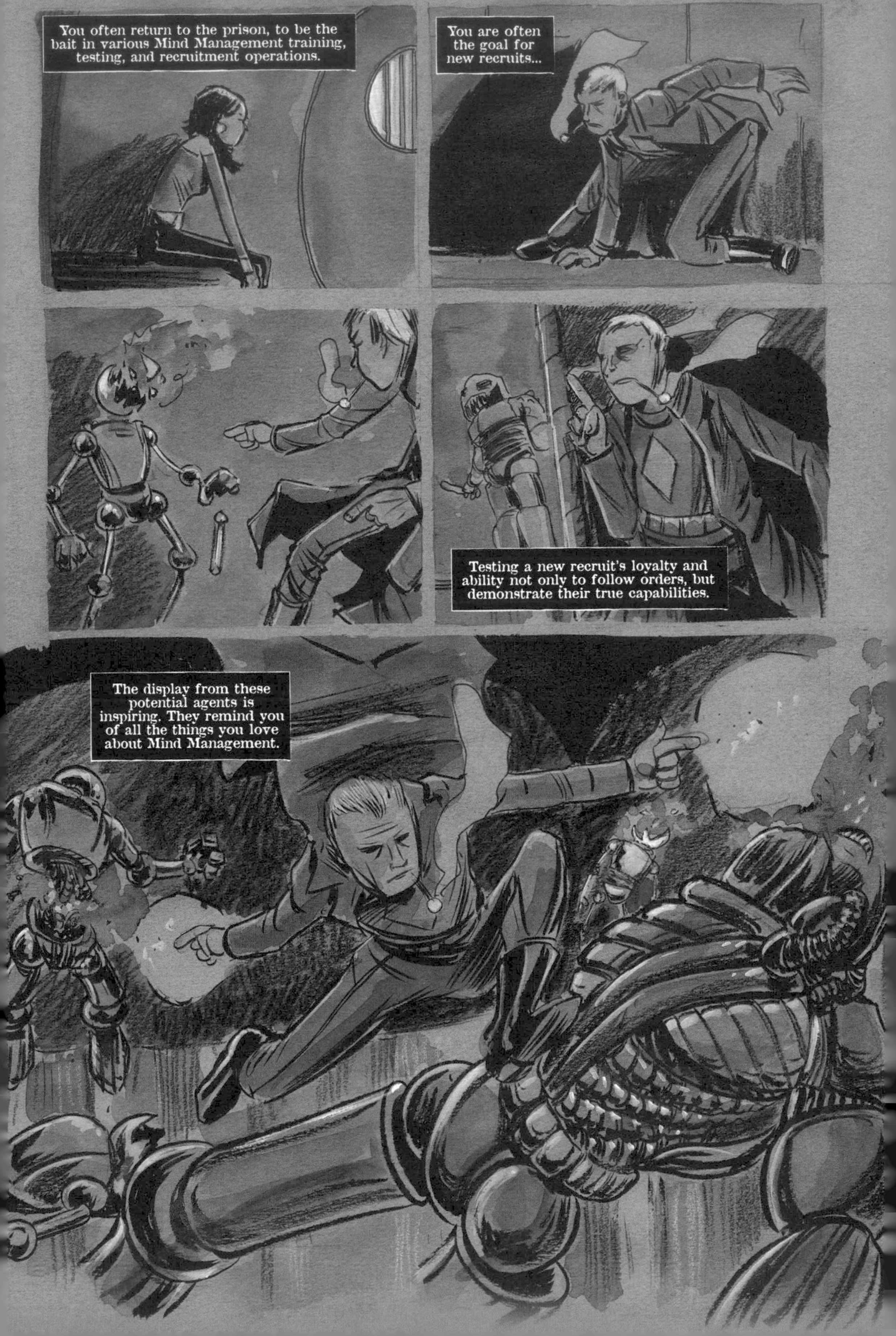
You often return to the prison, to be the bait in various Mind Management training, testing, and recruitment operations.
You are often the goal for new recruits...
Testing a new recruit's loyalty and ability not only to follow orders, but demonstrate their true capabilities.
The display from these potential agents is inspiring. They remind you of all the things you love about Mind Management.

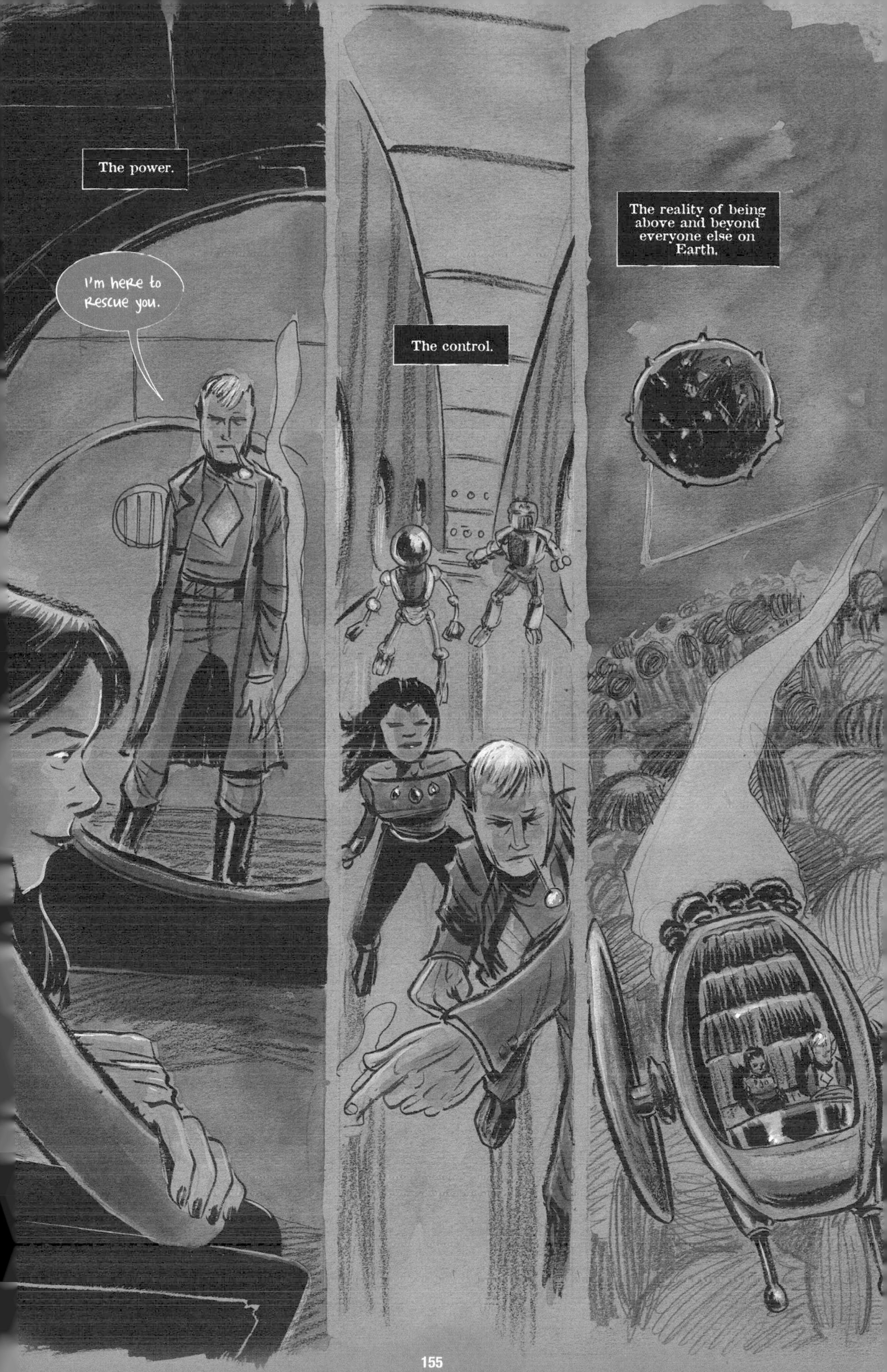
The power.
I'm here to rescue you.
The control.
The reality of being above and beyond everyone else on Earth.

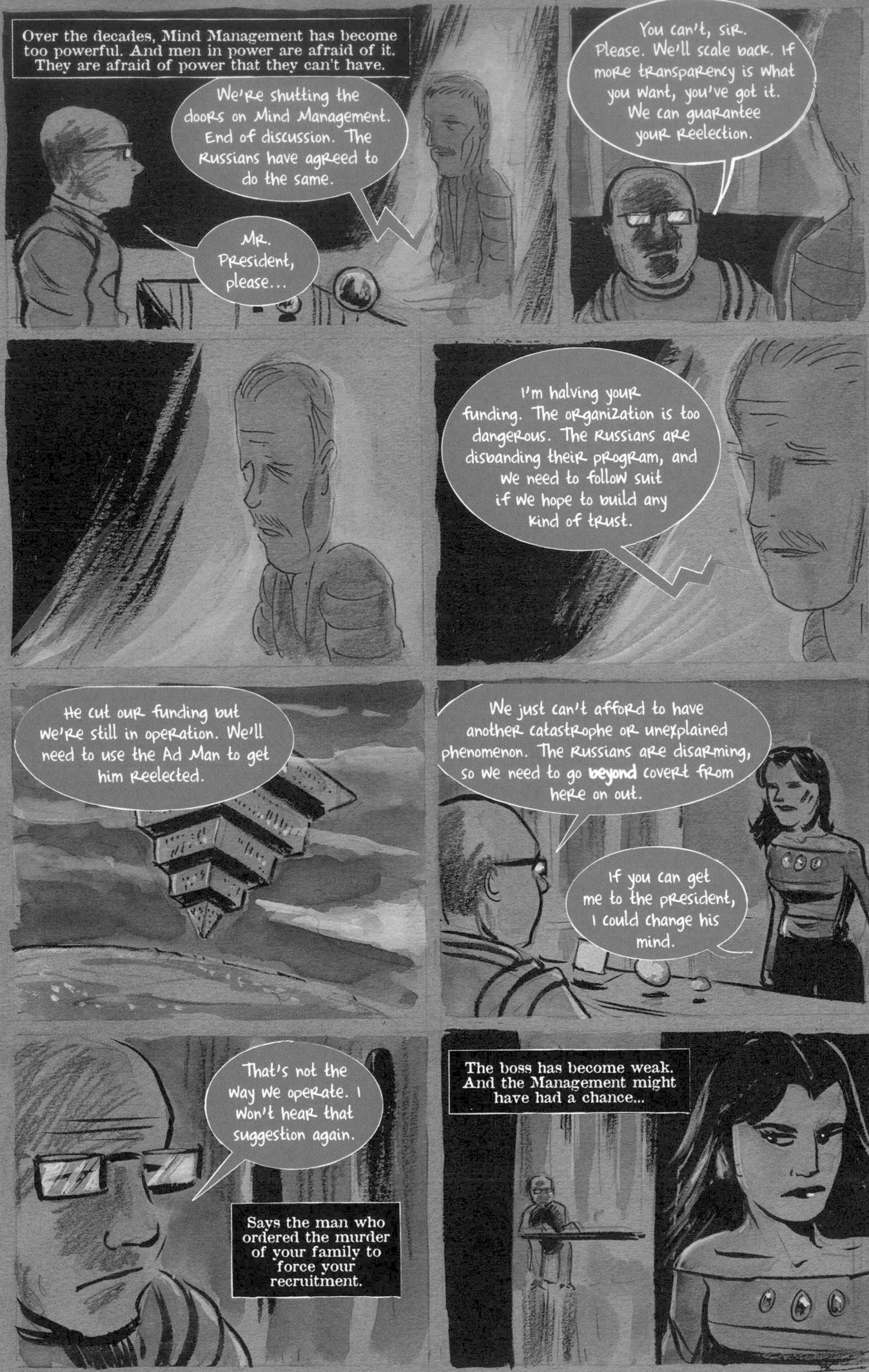
Over the decades, Mind Management has become too powerful. And men in power are afraid of it. They are afraid of power that they can't have.
We're shutting the doors on Mind Management. End of discussion. The Russians have agreed to do the same.
Mr. President, please...
You can't, sir. Please. We'll scale back. If more transparency is what you want, you've got it. We can guarantee your reelection.
I'm halving your funding. The organization is too dangerous. The Russians are disbanding their program, and we need to follow suit if we hope to build any kind of trust.
He cut our funding but we're still in operation. We'll need to use the Ad Man to get him reelected.
We just can't afford to have another catastrophe or unexplained phenomenon. The Russians are disarming, so we need to go **beyond** covert from here on out.
If you can get me to the president, I could change his mind.
That's not the way we operate. I won't hear that suggestion again.
Says the man who ordered the murder of your family to force your recruitment.
The boss has become weak. And the Management might have had a chance...

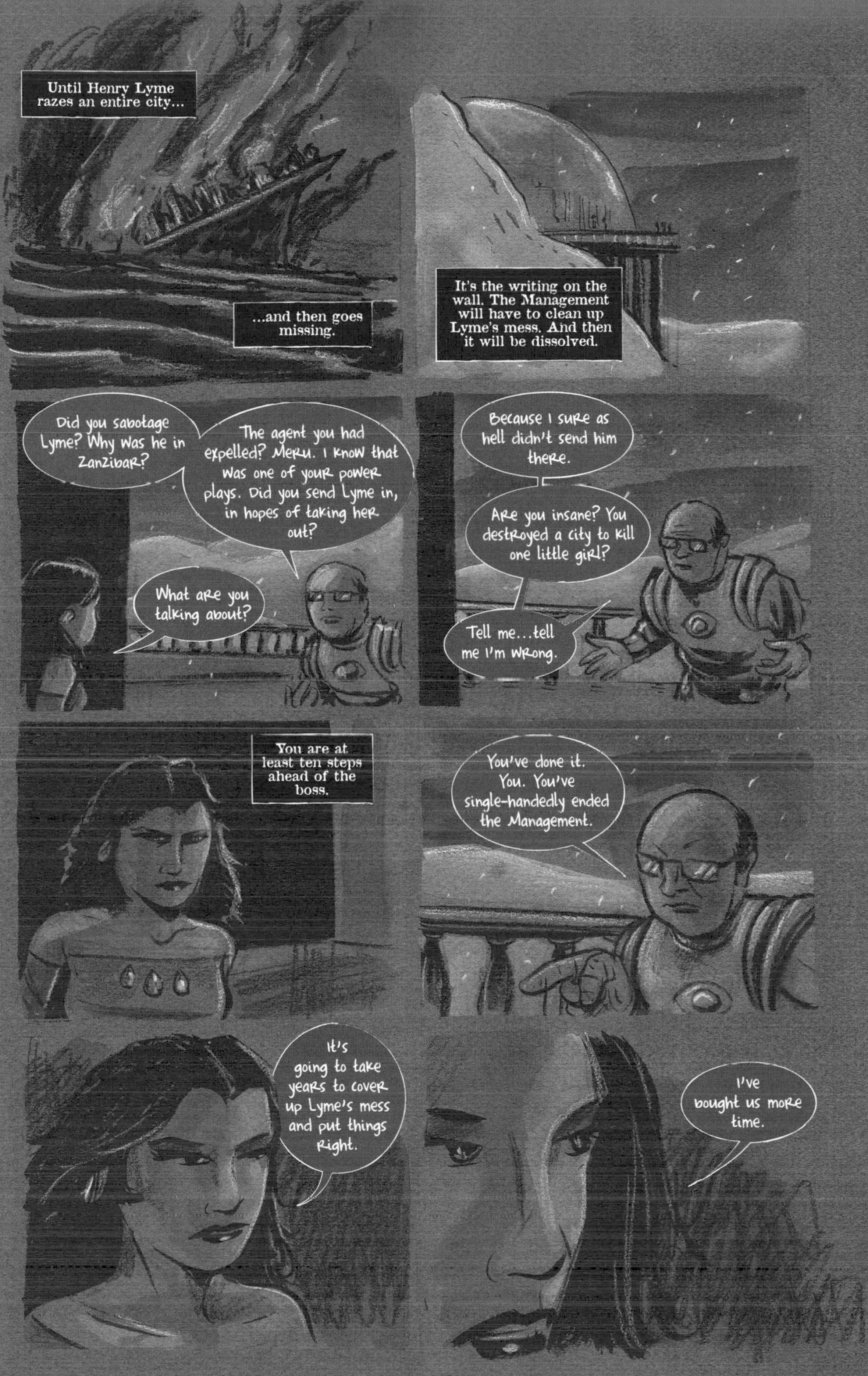

Until Henry Lyme razes an entire city...
...and then goes missing.
It's the writing on the wall. The Management will have to clean up Lyme's mess. And then it will be dissolved.
Did you sabotage Lyme? Why was he in Zanzibar?
The agent you had expelled? Meru. I know that was one of your power plays. Did you send Lyme in, in hopes of taking her out?
What are you talking about?
Because I sure as hell didn't send him there.
Are you insane? You destroyed a city to kill one little girl?
Tell me...tell me I'm wrong.
You are at least ten steps ahead of the boss.
You've done it. You. You've single-handedly ended the Management.
It's going to take years to cover up Lyme's mess and put things right.
I've bought us more time.

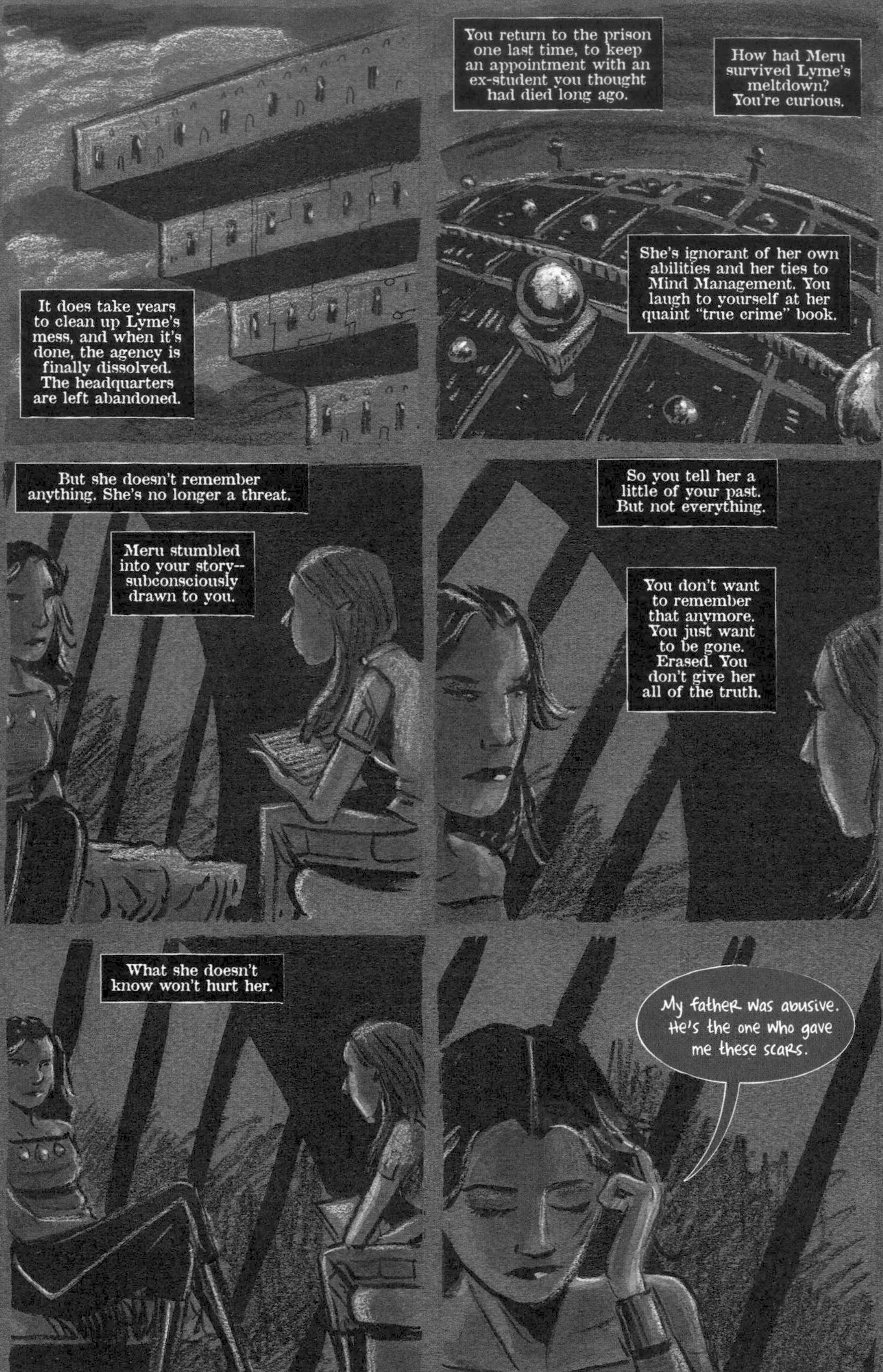
It does take years to clean up Lyme's mess, and when it's done, the agency is finally dissolved. The headquarters are left abandoned.
You return to the prison one last time, to keep an appointment with an ex-student you thought had died long ago.
How had Meru survived Lyme's meltdown? You're curious.
She's ignorant of her own abilities and her ties to Mind Management. You laugh to yourself at her quaint "true crime" book.
But she doesn't remember anything. She's no longer a threat.
Meru stumbled into your story--subconsciously drawn to you.
So you tell her a little of your past. But not everything.
You don't want to remember that anymore. You just want to be gone. Erased. You don't give her all of the truth.
What she doesn't know won't hurt her.
My father was abusive. He's the one who gave me these scars.

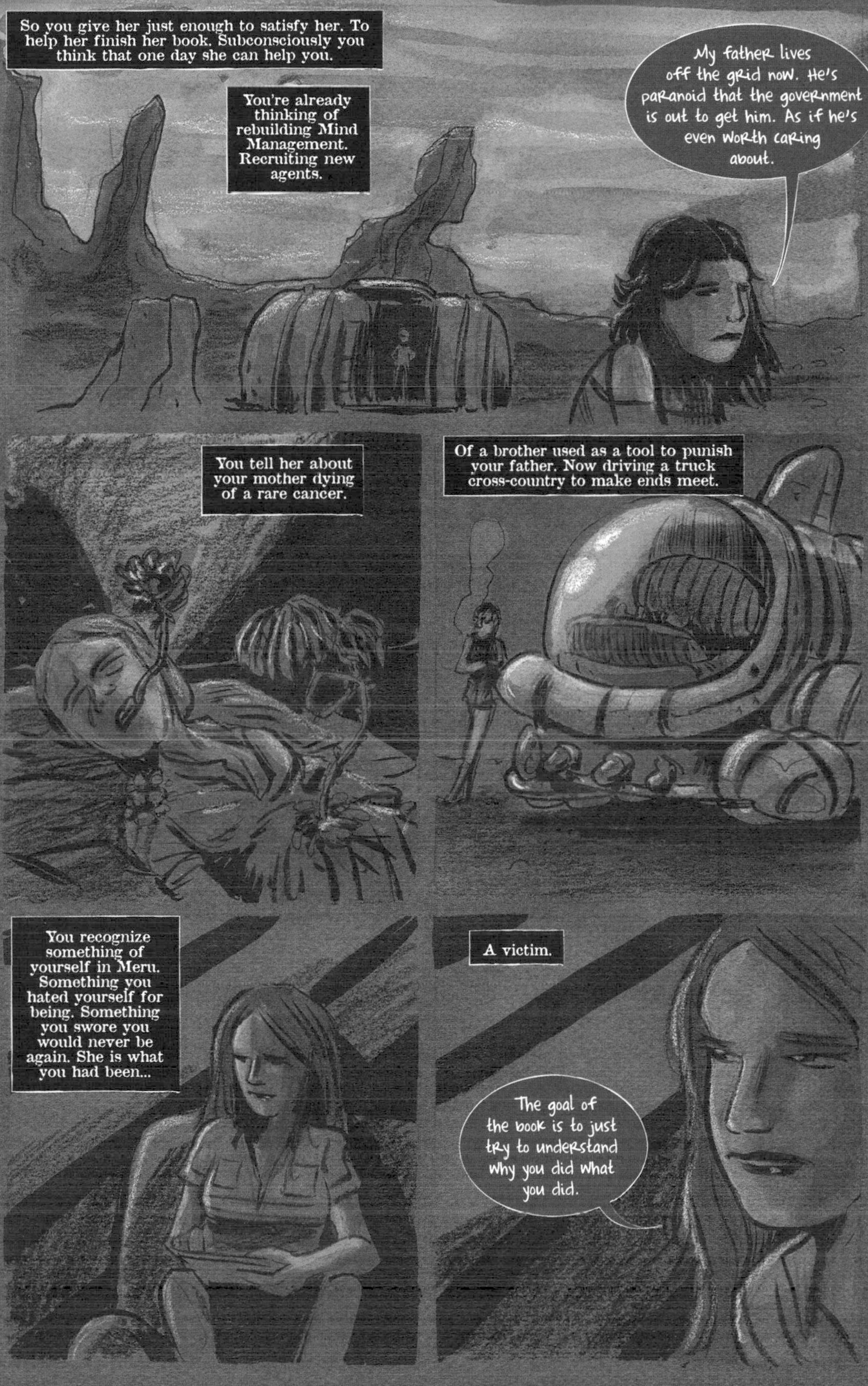
So you give her just enough to satisfy her. To help her finish her book. Subconsciously you think that one day she can help you.
You're already thinking of rebuilding Mind Management. Recruiting new agents.
My father lives off the grid now. He's paranoid that the government is out to get him. As if he's even worth caring about.
You tell her about your mother dying of a rare cancer.
Of a brother used as a tool to punish your father. Now driving a truck cross-country to make ends meet.
You recognize something of yourself in Meru. Something you hated yourself for being. Something you swore you would never be again. She is what you had been...
A victim.
The goal of the book is to just try to understand why you did what you did.

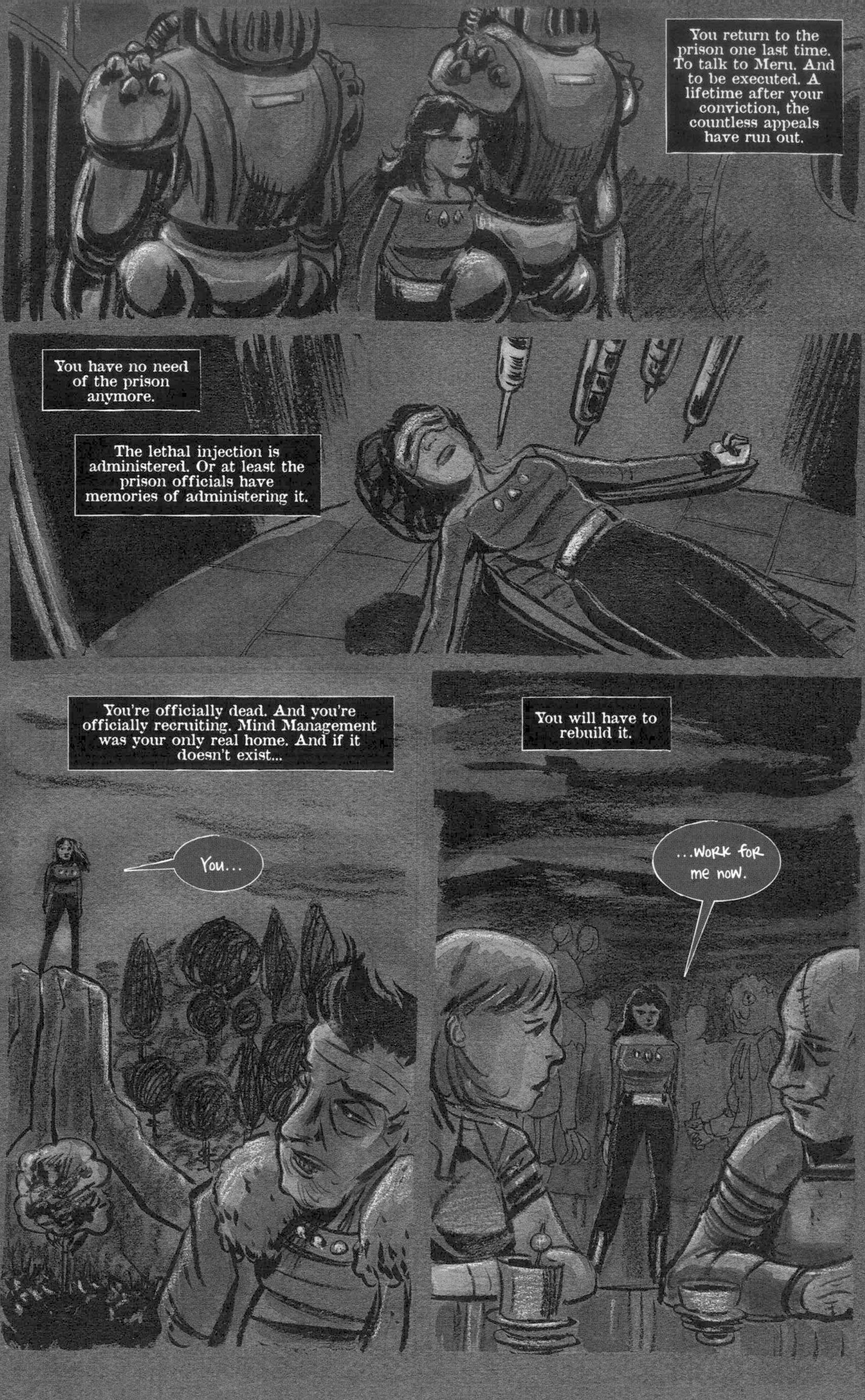
You return to the prison one last time. To talk to Meru. And to be executed. A lifetime after your conviction, the countless appeals have run out.
You have no need of the prison anymore.
The lethal injection is administered. Or at least the prison officials have memories of administering it.
You're officially dead. And you're officially recruiting. Mind Management was your only real home. And if it doesn't exist...
You...
You will have to rebuild it.
...WORK FOR ME NOW.

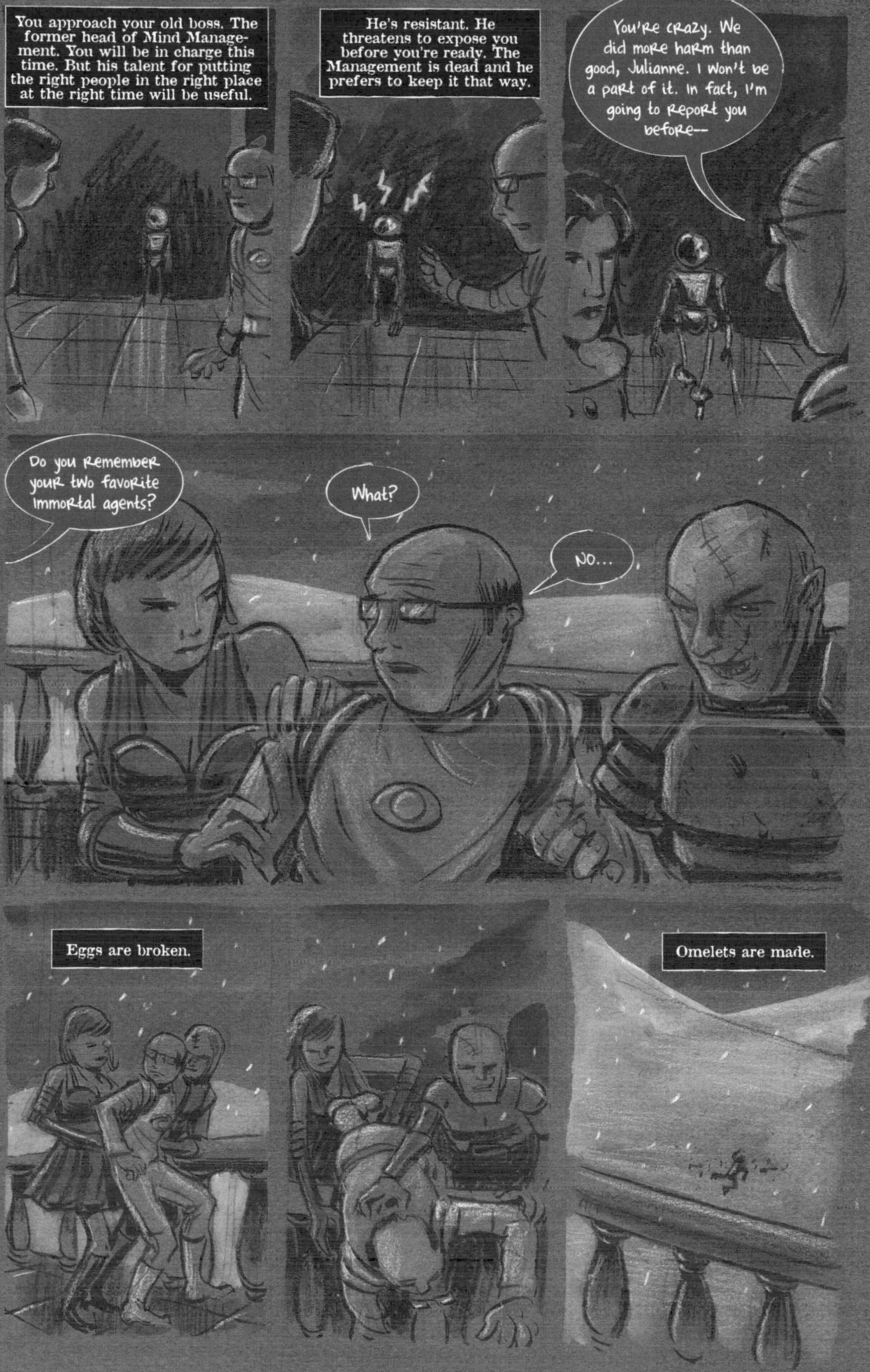
You approach your old boss. The former head of Mind Management. You will be in charge this time. But his talent for putting the right people in the right place at the right time will be useful.
He's resistant. He threatens to expose you before you're ready. The Management is dead and he prefers to keep it that way.
You're crazy. We did more harm than good, Julianne. I won't be a part of it. In fact, I'm going to report you before--
Do you remember your two favorite immortal agents?
What?
No...
Eggs are broken.
Omelets are made.

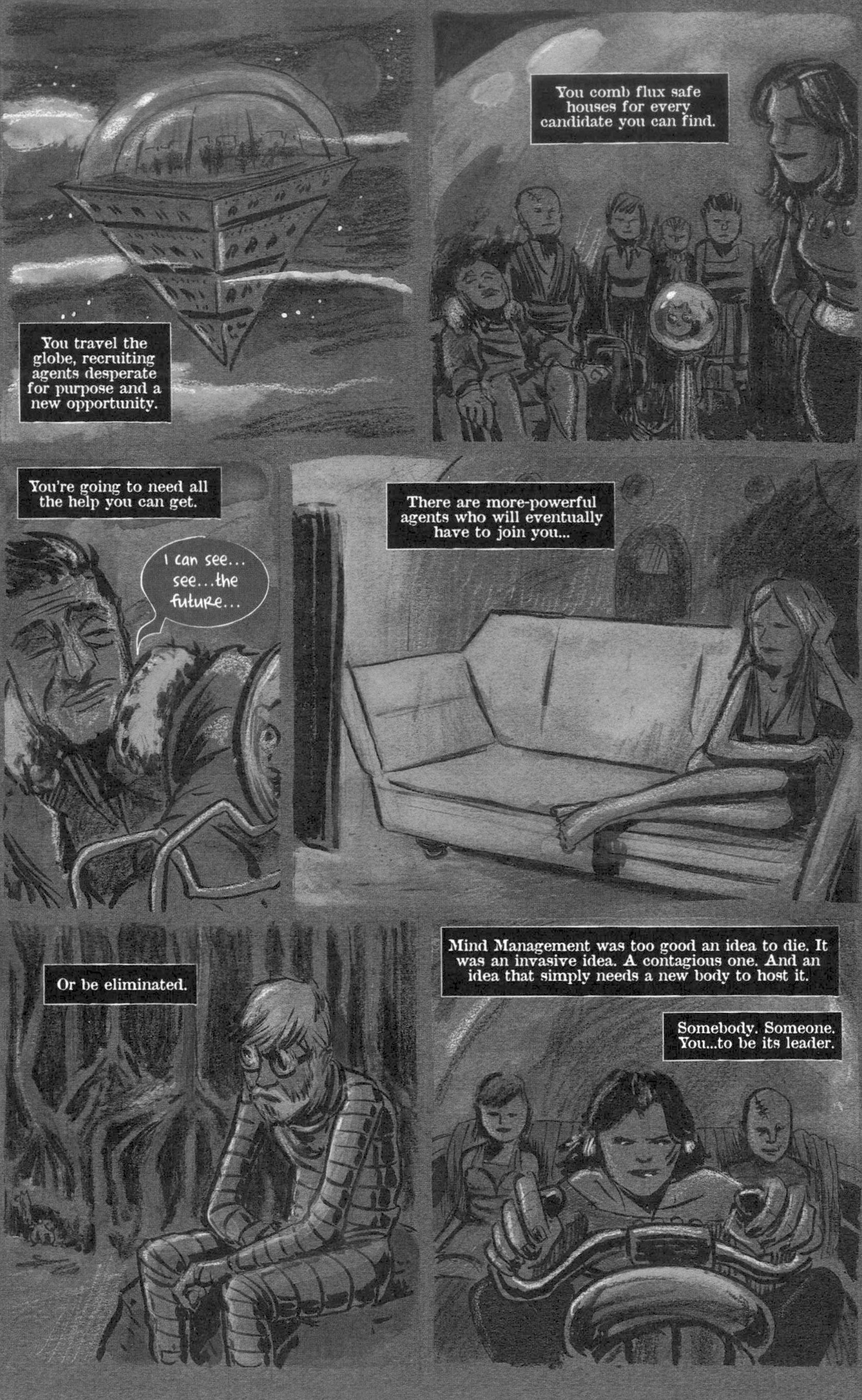
You travel the globe, recruiting agents desperate for purpose and a new opportunity.
You comb flux safe houses for every candidate you can find.
You're going to need all the help you can get.
I can see... see...the future...
There are more-powerful agents who will eventually have to join you...
Or be eliminated.
Mind Management was too good an idea to die. It was an invasive idea. A contagious one. And an idea that simply needs a new body to host it.
Somebody. Someone. You...to be its leader.

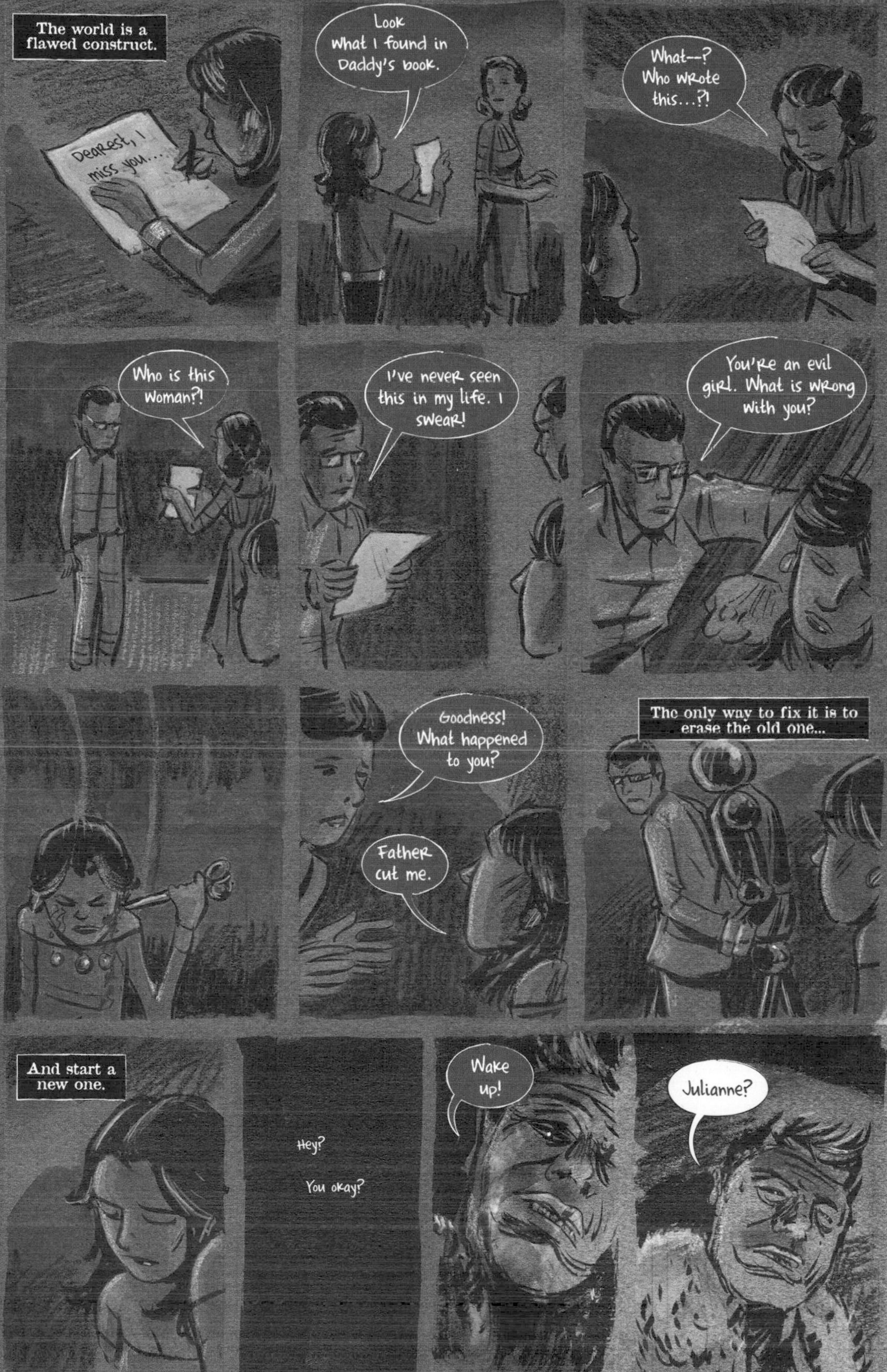
The world is a flawed construct.
Dearest, I miss you...
Look What I found in Daddy's book.
What--? Who wrote this...?!
Who is this woman?!
I've never seen this in my life. I swear!
You're an evil girl. What is wrong with you?
Goodness! What happened to you?
Father cut me.
The only way to fix it is to erase the old one...
And start a new one.
Hey?
You okay?
Wake up!
Julianne?

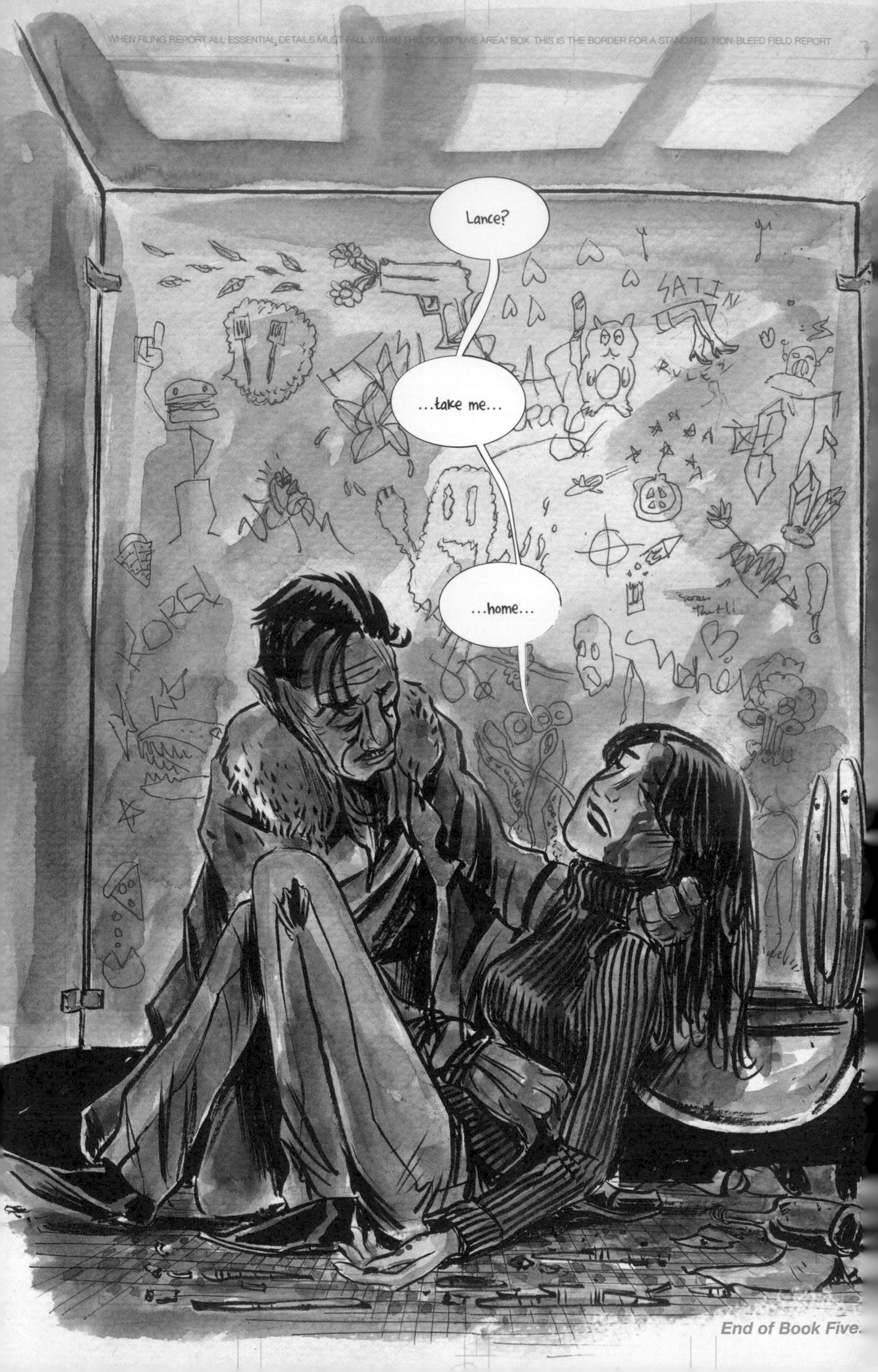
WHEN FILING REPORT ALL ESSENTIAL DETAILS MUST FALL WITHIN THIS SOLID "LIVE AREA" BOX. THIS IS THE BORDER FOR A STANDARD, NON-BLEED FIELD REPORT
Lance?
...take me...
...home...
End of Book Five.

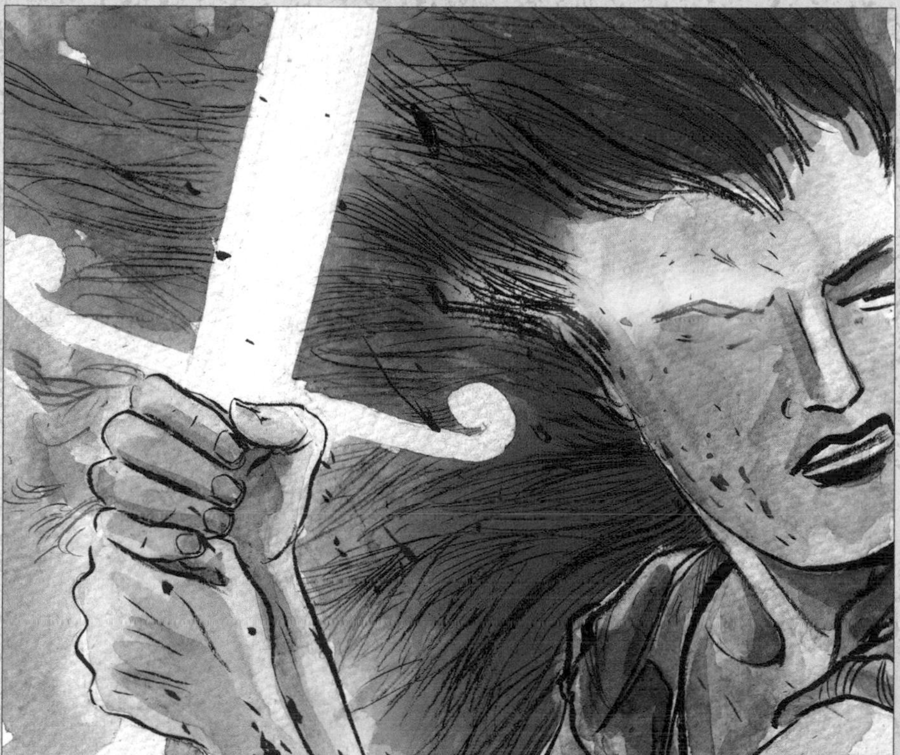

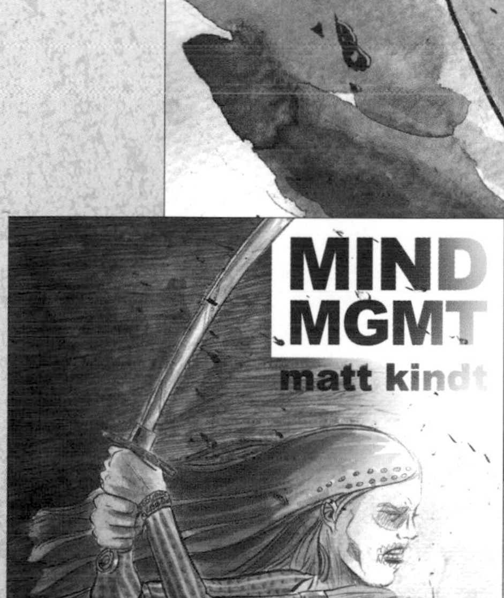
MIND
MGMT
matt kindt

MIND
MGMT

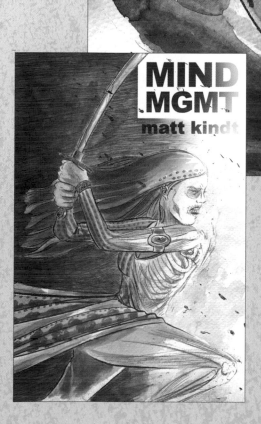

MIND MGMT UNDERCOVER

Unused cover for issue #29.
Following page: *MIND MGMT* commission by Matt.

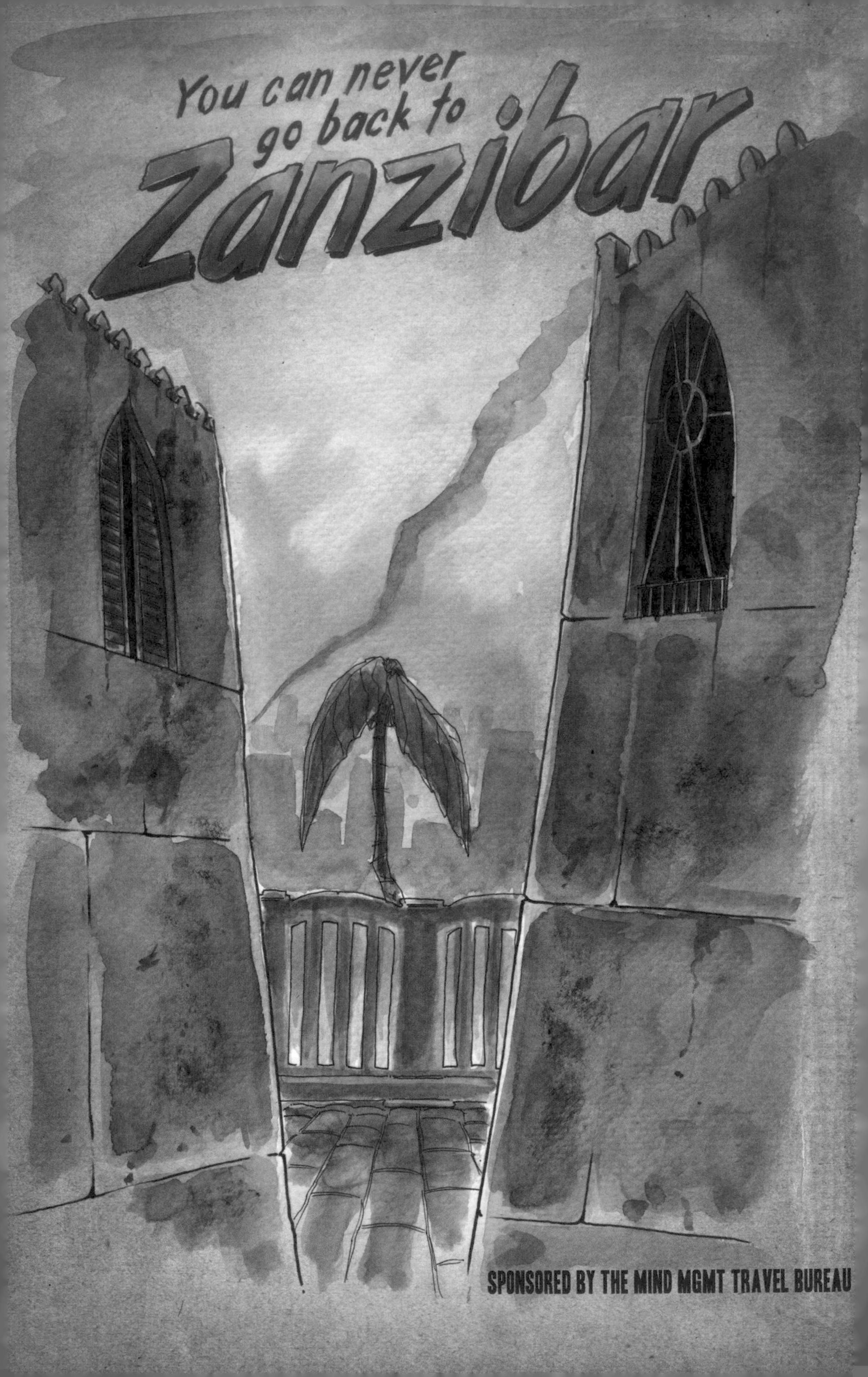
You can never go back to
Zanzibar...
SPONSORED BY THE MIND MGMT TRAVEL BUREAU

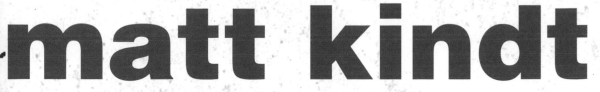

matt kindt

"I'll read anything Kindt does."—Douglas Wolk, author of *Reading Comics*

MIND MGMT
matt kindt
volume one: THE MANAGER

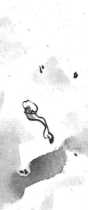

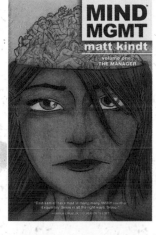

MIND MGMT
VOLUME 1: THE MANAGER
ISBN 978-1-59582-797-5
$19.99

VOLUME 2: THE FUTURIST
ISBN 978-1-61655-198-8
$19.99

VOLUME 3: THE HOME MAKER
ISBN 978-1-61655-390-6
$19.99

VOLUME 4: THE MAGICIAN
ISBN 978-1-61655-391-3
$19.99

VOLUME 5: THE ERASER
ISBN 978-1-61655-696-9
$19.99

PAST AWAYS

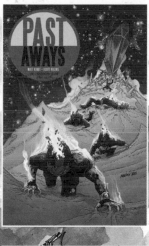

PAST AWAYS
VOLUME 1: FACEDOWN IN THE TIMESTREAM
With Scott Kolins
ISBN 978-1-61655-792-8
$12.99

THE COMPLETE PISTOLWHIP
With Jason Hall
ISBN 978-1-61655-720-1
$27.99

3 STORY
The Secret History of the
Giant Man
Matt Kindt

3 STORY: THE SECRET HISTORY OF THE GIANT MAN
ISBN 978-1-59582-356-4
$19.99

2 SISTERS
ISBN 978-1-61655-721-8
$27.99

AVAILABLE AT YOUR LOCAL COMICS SHOP OR BOOKSTORE!

To find a comics shop in your area, call 1-888-266-4226. For more information or to order direct visit DarkHorse.com or call 1-800-862-0052 Mon.–Fri. 9 AM to 5 PM Pacific Time.

DarkHorse.com

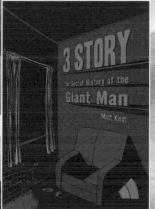

PHOTO BY SHARLENE KINDT

4-09

ABOUT THE AUTHOR

Matt Kindt is the Harvey Award–winning author of the graphic novels *3 Story*, *Red Handed*, *Revolver*, *Super Spy*, and *2 Sisters*, and the artist and cocreator of the *Pistolwhip* series of graphic novels. He has been nominated for four Eisner Awards and three Harveys. Matt lives and works in St. Louis, Missouri, with his wife and daughter. For more information, visit MattKindt.com.